ACCA

PAPER F7

FINANCIAL REPORTING

P
R
A
C
T
I
C
E

&

R
E
V
I
S
I
O
N

K
I
T

BPP Learning Media is an **ACCA Approved Content Provider** for the ACCA qualification. This means we work closely with ACCA to ensure our products fully prepare you for your ACCA exams.

In this Practice & Revision Kit which is has been reviewed by the **ACCA examination team,** we:

- Discuss the **best strategies** for revising and taking your ACCA exams
- Ensure you are well **prepared** for your exam
- Provide you with **lots of great guidance** on tackling questions
- Provide you with **three** mock exams
- Provide **ACCA exam answers** as well as our own for selected questions

FOR EXAMS FROM 1 SEPTEMBER 2015 TO 31 AUGUST 2016

First edition 2008
Ninth edition April 2015

ISBN 9781 4727 2689 6
(previous ISBN 9781 4727 1103 8)

e-ISBN 9781 4727 27411
(previous) e-ISBN 9781 4727 1167 0

British Library Cataloguing-in-Publication Data
A catalogue record for this book
is available from the British Library

Published by

BPP Learning Media Ltd
BPP House, Aldine Place
London W12 8AA

www.bpp.com/learningmedia

Printed in the United Kingdom by Polestar Wheatons

Hennock Road
Marsh Barton
Exeter
EX2 8RP

We are grateful to the Association of Chartered Certified Accountants for permission to reproduce past examination questions. The suggested solutions in the practice answer bank have been prepared by BPP Learning Media Ltd, except where otherwise stated.

Your learning materials, published by BPP Learning Media Ltd, are printed on paper obtained from traceable sustainable sources.

Contents

A note about copyright

Dear Customer

What does the little © mean and why does it matter?

Your market-leading BPP books, course materials and e-learning materials do not write and update themselves. People write them: on their own behalf or as employees of an organisation that invests in this activity. Copyright law protects their livelihoods. It does so by creating rights over the use of the content.

Breach of copyright is a form of theft – as well as being a criminal offence in some jurisdictions, it is potentially a serious breach of professional ethics.

With current technology, things might seem a bit hazy but, basically, without the express permission of BPP Learning Media:

- Photocopying our materials is a breach of copyright
- Scanning, ripcasting or conversion of our digital materials into different file formats, uploading them to Facebook or emailing them to your friends is a breach of copyright

You can, of course, sell your books, in the form in which you have bought them – once you have finished with them. (Is this fair to your fellow students? We update for a reason.) Please note the e-products are sold on a single user licence basis: we do not supply 'unlock' codes to people who have bought them second-hand.

And what about outside the UK? BPP Learning Media strives to make our materials available at prices students can afford by local printing arrangements, pricing policies and partnerships which are clearly listed on our website. A tiny minority ignore this and indulge in criminal activity by illegally photocopying our material or supporting organisations that do. If they act illegally and unethically in one area, can you really trust them?

Question index

The headings in this checklist/index indicate the main topics of questions, but many questions cover several different topics.

Each topic area begins with MCQs on the topic. Your exam will have 20 MCQs.

Examiner's answers: For Mock exam 3 the examiner's answers can be found at the end of this Kit.

BPP
LEARNING MEDIA

BPP
LEARNING MEDIA

Helping you with your revision

As an ACCA **Approved Content Partner**, BPP Learning Media gives you the opportunity to use **exam team–reviewed** revision materials. By incorporating the examination team's comments and suggestions regarding syllabus coverage, the BPP Learning Media Practice & Revision Kit provides excellent, **ACCA-approved** support for your revision.

Tackling revision and the exam

Using feedback obtained from ACCA exam team review:

- We look at the dos and don'ts of revising for, and taking, ACCA exams

- We focus on Paper F7; we discuss revising the syllabus, what to do (and what not to do) in the exam, how to approach different types of question and ways of obtaining easy marks

Selecting questions

We provide a full **question index** to help you plan your revision.

Making the most of question practice

At BPP Learning Media we realise that you need more than just questions and model answers to get the most from your question practice.

- Our **top tips** included for certain questions provide essential advice on tackling questions, presenting answers and the key points that answers need to include.

- We show you how you can pick up **easy marks** on some questions, as we know that picking up all readily available marks often can make the difference between passing and failing.

- We include **marking guides** to show you what the examiner rewards.

- We include **comments from the examiners** to show you where students struggled or performed well in the actual exam.

- We refer to the **2015 BPP Study Text** (for exams up to June 2016) for detailed coverage of the topics covered in questions.

- In a bank at the end of this Kit we include the **official ACCA answers** to the to the June and December 2014 exams. Used in conjunction with our answers they provide an indication of all possible points that could be made, issues that could be covered and approaches to adopt.

Attempting mock exams

There are three mock exams that provide practice at coping with the pressures of the exam day. We strongly recommend that you attempt them under exam conditions. **Mock exams 1 and 2** reflect the question styles and syllabus coverage of the exam; **Mock exam 3** is the December 2014 paper.

Revising F7

From December 2014 the F7 paper has a Section A with twenty MCQs. This gives the examiner greater scope to examine the whole of the syllabus and bring in topics that do not feature in the longer questions. The MCQ section accounts for 40% of the marks on the paper. So it is really not possible to pass this paper by only revising certain topics.

The MCQ section will be followed by three long questions, which are most likely to be consolidations, accounts preparation questions, statements of cash flows or interpretation of accounts, but questions on other areas of the syllabus are also possible.

A consolidation question can be a statement of financial position or statement of profit or loss or both, and it may include an associate, so be prepared for all of this. Therefore you must revise all the consolidation workings, and you must know how to account for an associate. All questions are compulsory.

A single company accounts preparation question allows the examiner to bring in more complex issues that he would not test in the consolidation question. Make sure you can deal with finance leases, deferred tax, calculating finance costs using the effective interest rate, prior period adjustments, discontinued operations and construction contracts.

Other possibilities are statements of cash flow or interpretation of accounts. You have studied both of these at F3/FFA, so make sure you can do them well.

Issues that could appear anywhere are non-current assets and impairment, intangible assets, EPS, provisions and regulatory issues.

There will be a certain amount of discussion in some of the questions, so be prepared to write about financial reporting topics, such as the *Conceptual Framework* or specific accounting standards.

Question practice

This is the most important thing to do if you want to get through. Many of the most up-to-date exam questions are in this Kit, some of them amended to reflect the new exam format. Practise doing them under timed conditions, then go through the answers and go back to the Study Text for any topic you are really having trouble with. Come back to a question week later and try it again – you will be surprised at how much better you are getting. Be very ruthless with yourself at this stage – you have to do the question in the time, without looking at the answer. This will really sharpen your wits and make the exam experience less worrying. Just keep doing this and you will get better at doing questions and you will really find out what you know and what you don't know.

Passing the F7 exam

If you have honestly done your revision then you can pass this exam. What you must do is remain calm and tackle it in a professional manner. The examiner stresses a number of points which you should bear in mind. These apply particularly to the long questions.

- You must read the question properly. Students often fail to read the question properly and miss some of the information. Time spent reading the question a second time would be time well spent. Make yourself do this, don't just rush into it in a panic.

- Workings must be clear and cross-referenced. If the marker can read and understand your workings they can give you credit for using the right method, even if your answer is wrong. If your answer is wrong and there are no workings, or they are illegible and incomprehensible, you will get no marks for that part of the question.

- Stick to the timings and answer all questions. Do not spend too long on one question at the expense of others. The number of extra marks you will gain on that question will be minimal, and you could have at least obtained the easy marks on the next question.

- Do not neglect the short parts of the question. If you get a consolidation with a five-mark discussion topic at the end, leave time for that last part. You can't afford to throw away five marks.

- Make sure you get the easy marks. If an accounts preparation question contains something that you are unable to do, just ignore it and do the rest. You will probably only lose a few marks and if you start trying to puzzle it out you might waste a lot of minutes.

- Answer the question. In a discussion-type question you may be tempted to just write down everything you know about the topic. This will do you no good. The marking parameters for these questions are quite precise. You will only get marks for making points that answer the question exactly as it has been set. So don't waste your time waffling – you could be scoring marks somewhere else.

Note that you have 15 minutes reading time at the start of this exam, during which you are allowed to make notes on the question paper. Use this to read the questions carefully and underline important points. Make note of any points that occur to you which you may otherwise forget. Get really familiar with the paper and focus on what you can do, not the bits you think you can't do.

Gaining the easy marks

The first point to make is that you do not get any marks for just writing down the formats for a financial statement. But, once you have put the formats down, you are then in a position to start filling in the numbers and getting the easy marks. Also, correct formats will give you a guide so that you don't miss things. For instance, it's easy to forget about the non-controlling interest in a group statement of profit or loss. So that's a good place to start.

Having put down the formats, then go through the workings and slot in the figures. Make sure you get in all the ones you can do easily. Complicated parts are well worth doing if you are able to do them – there will be marks for those. Complicated parts which you don't know how to do are best left alone.

If you have an interpretation question, you will not get many marks for just producing lots of ratios or restating information you have already been given in the question. You have to be able to evaluate the information and see what judgements can be made. So go through the information critically and see which ratios are actually relevant. Then calculate them and say something sensible about them.

Multiple choice questions

Some MCQs are easier than others. Answer those that you feel confident about as quickly as you can. Come back later to those you find more difficult. Read the multiple choice questions carefully. If you are really clear about what is being asked then you will be less likely to fall for one of the distractors. If you really cannot do a question, guess the answer and move on. You lose no marks for a wrong answer and you may even be right!

Exam information

Format of the exam

All questions are compulsory.

	Number of marks
Section A – 20 MCQs	40
Section B:	
Question 1	15
Question 2	15
Question 3	30
	100

Time allowed: 3 hours plus 15 minutes reading time

Useful websites

The websites below provide additional sources of information of relevance to your studies for *Financial Reporting.*

- www.accaglobal.com

  ACCA's website. The students' section of the website is invaluable for detailed information about the qualification, past issues of Student Accountant (including technical articles) and a free downloadable Student Planner App.

- www.bpp.com

  Our website provides information about BPP products and services, with a link to the ACCA website.

Questions

1 Multiple choice questions – conceptual framework

1 How does the *Conceptual Framework* define an asset?

    A   A resource owned by an entity as a result of past events and from which future economic benefits are expected to flow to the entity

    B   A resource over which an entity has legal rights as a result of past events and from which economic benefits are expected to flow to the entity

    C   A resource controlled by an entity as a result of past events and from which future economic benefits are expected to flow to the entity

    D   A resource to which an entity has a future commitment as a result of past events and from which future economic benefits are expected to flow from the entity   **(2 marks)**

2 Which one of the following would be classified as a liability?

    A   Dexter's business manufactures a product under licence. In 12 months' time the licence expires and Dexter will have to pay $50,000 for it to be renewed.

    B   Reckless purchased an investment 9 months ago for $120,000. The market for these investments has now fallen and Reckless's investment is valued at $90,000.

    C   Carter has estimated the tax charge on its profits for the year just ended as $165,000.

    D   Expansion is planning to invest in new machinery and has been quoted a price of $570,000.   **(2 marks)**

3 Which one of the following would correctly describe the net <u>realisable</u> value of a two year old asset?

    A   The original cost of the asset less two years' depreciation

    B   The amount that could be obtained from selling the asset, less any costs of disposal

    C   The cost of an equivalent new asset less two years' depreciation

    D   The present value of the future cash flows obtainable from continuing to use the asset   **(2 marks)**

4 The *Conceptual Framework* identifies an **underlying assumption** in preparing financial statements. This is:

    A   Going concern

    B   Materiality

    C   Substance over form

    D   Accruals   **(2 marks)**

5 The *Conceptual Framework* identifies four enhancing qualitative characteristics of financial information. For which of these characteristics is **disclosure of accounting policies** particularly important?

    A   Verifiability

    B   Timeliness

    C   Comparability

    D   Understandability   **(2 marks)**

6 Which of the following is **not** a purpose of the IASB's *Conceptual Framework*?

    A   To assist the IASB in the preparation and review of IFRS

    B   To assist auditors in forming an opinion on whether financial statements comply with IFRS

    C   To assist in determining the treatment of items not covered by an existing IFRS

    D   To be authoritative where a specific IFRS conflicts with the Conceptual Framework   **(2 marks)**

Whenever there is a conflict between an IFRS and the conceptual framework, the IFRS takes precedence.

7   Financial statements represent transactions in words and numbers. To be useful, financial information must represent faithfully these transactions in terms of how they are reported.

Which of the following accounting treatments would be an example of faithful representation?

A   Charging the rental payments for an item of plant to the statement of profit or loss where the rental agreement meets the criteria for a finance lease

B   Including a convertible loan note in equity on the basis that the holders are likely to choose the equity option on conversion

C   Derecognising factored trade receivables sold without recourse

D   Treating redeemable preference shares as part of equity in the statement of financial position

(2 marks)

2 Lisbon (pilot paper amended)   27 mins

(a)   The qualitative characteristics of relevance, faithful representation, comparability and understandability identified in the IASB's *Conceptual Framework for Financial Reporting* are some of the attributes that make financial information useful to the various users of financial statements.

Required

Explain what is meant by relevance, faithful representation, comparability and understandability and how they make financial information useful.   (11 marks)

(b)   During the year ended 31 March 20X6, Lisbon experienced the following transactions or events.

(i)   Sold an asset to a finance company and leased it back for the remainder of its useful life.

(ii)   The company's statement of profit or loss prepared using historical costs showed a loss from operating its shops, but the company is aware that the increase in the value of its properties during the period far outweighed the operating loss.

Required

Explain how you would treat the items above in Lisbon's financial statements and indicate on which of the *Conceptual Framework's* qualitative characteristics your treatment is based.   (4 marks)

(Total = 15 marks)

3 Concepts (6/08 amended)   27 mins

(a)   The IASB's *Conceptual Framework for Financial Reporting* requires financial statements to be prepared on the basis that they comply with certain accounting concepts, underlying assumptions and (qualitative) characteristics. Five of these are:

Matching/accruals
Going concern
Verifiability
Comparability
Materiality

Required

Briefly explain the meaning of each of the above concepts/assumptions.   (5 marks)

(b)   For most entities, applying the appropriate concepts/assumptions in accounting for inventories is an important element in preparing their financial statements.

Required

Illustrate with examples how each of the concepts/assumptions in (a) may be applied to accounting for inventory.   (10 marks)

(Total = 15 marks)

4 Multiple choice questions – regulatory framework

1   The process for developing an International Financial Reporting Standard involves a number of stages. Following receipt and review of comments on a Discussion Paper, what will be the next step undertaken by the IASB?

    Ⓐ   Publication of an Exposure Draft *following review of discussion paper comments*

    B   Establishment of an Advisory Committee

    C   Consultation with the Advisory Committee

    D   Issue of a final IFRS   **(2 marks)**

---

2   Which one of the following would **not** be an advantage of adopting IFRS?

    A   It would be easier for investors to compare the financial statements of companies with those of foreign competitors.

Accountants and auditors may take less defence as in case of a litigation as they will not be able to demonstrate that they

    B   Cross-border listing would be facilitated. *followed some precise rule, but will instead have to defend their application of judgement.*

    Ⓒ   Accountants and auditors would have more defence in case of litigation.

    D   Multinational companies could more easily transfer accounting staff across national borders.   **(2 marks)**

---

3   Which of the following statements regarding systems of regulation of accounting are true?

    (i)   A principles-based system is more prescriptive than a rules-based system.

    (ii)   A rules-based system will require more detailed regulations than a principles-based system.

    (iii)   A principles-based system will tend to give rise to a larger number of accounting standards   than a rules-based system.

    (iv)   A rules-based system seeks to cover every eventuality.

    principle based

    (v)   A rules-based system requires the exercise of more judgement in application than a principles – based system.

    A   (i) and (iii)

    Ⓑ   (ii) and (iv)

    C   (i), (ii) and (v)

    D   (iii), (iv) and (v)   **(2 marks)**

---

5 Baxen (6/12 amended)   27 mins

(a)   The US is currently contemplating the transition to IFRS. US GAAP is regarded by many in the US as the 'gold standard'. It is detailed and rules-based and in many cases industry-specific and there is a perception among some that the adoption of IFRS will compromise the quality of financial reporting.

Required

    (i)   Explain in what ways IFRS differs from US GAAP, as described above.

    (ii)   Discuss the advantages that a country may gain from transitioning to IFRS.   **(9 marks)**

(b)   Baxen is a public listed company that currently uses local Accounting Standards for its financial reporting. The board of directors of Baxen is considering the adoption of International Financial Reporting Standards (IFRS) in the near future. The company has ambitious growth plans which involve extensive trading with many foreign companies and the possibility of acquiring at least one of its trading partners as a subsidiary in the near future.

Required

Identify the advantages that Baxen could gain by adopting IFRS for its financial reporting purposes.

    (6 marks)

    (Total = 15 marks)

6 Regulatory framework (2.5 12/04 amended)

27 mins

Historically financial reporting throughout the world has differed widely. The IFRS Foundation is committed to developing, in the public interest, a single set of high quality, understandable and enforceable global accounting standards that require transparent and comparable information in general purpose financial statements. The various pronouncements of the IFRS Foundation are sometimes collectively referred to as International Financial Reporting Standards (IFRS) GAAP.

Required

(a)   Describe the IFRS Foundation's standard setting process including how standards are produced, enforced and occasionally supplemented.   **(10 marks)**

(b)   Comment on whether you feel the move to date towards global accounting standards has been successful.
                                                                                                    (5 marks)
                                                                                            (Total = 15 marks)

7 Multiple choice questions – tangible non-current assets

1   Kaplow purchased a machine for $30,000 on 1 January 20X5 and assigned it a useful life of 12 years. On 31 March 20X7 it was revalued to $32,000 with no change in useful life.

[handwritten notes in left margin: out of 12 yrs, 3 yrs and 3 months already used, remaining = 11¾ (32000/11¾) = 273.5 × 9 = 2461 = 2461]

What will be depreciation charge in relation to this machine in the financial statements of Kaplow for the year ending 31 December 20X7?

[handwritten working to the right:]
Cost   30000
Depreciation (31.12.05)   (2500)   (30000/12)
Depreci- (31.12.06)   (2500)   (3000/12)
Depreci- (31.03.07)   (625)   (2500 × 3/12)
                                         24375
Revaluation surplus   7625
revaluation amount   32000

A $3,087
B $2,462
C $2,500
D $3,200

(2 marks)

---

2   Foster has built a new factory incurring the following costs:

	$'000
Land	1,200
Materials	2,400
Labour	3,000
Architect's fees	25
Surveyor's fees	15
Site overheads	300
Apportioned administrative overheads	150
Testing of fire alarms	10
Business rates for first year	12
	7,112

What will be the total amount capitalised in respect of the factory?

A $6,112,000
B $6,950,000
C $7,112,000
D $7,100,000

(2 marks)

---

3   Capita had the following bank loans outstanding during the whole of 20X8:

	$m
9% loan repayable 20X9	15
11% loan repayable 20Y2	24

Capita began construction of a qualifying asset on 1 April 20X8 and withdrew funds of $6 million on that date to fund construction. On 1 August 20X8 an additional $2 million was withdrawn for the same purpose.

Calculate the borrowing costs which can be capitalised in respect of this project for the year ended 31 December 20X8.

[handwritten working:]
$(9\% \times 15/39) + (11\% \times 24/39) = 3.5\% + 7\% = 10.5\%$
Borrowing costs = 6m × 10.5% × 9/12 = 472500
                           2m × 10.5% × 5/12 = 87500
                                                       560 000

A $560,000
B $472,500
C $750,000
D $350,000

(2 marks)

4   Carter vacated an office building and let it out to a third party on 30 June 20X8. The building had an original cost of $900,000 on 1 January 20X0 and was being depreciated over 50 years. It was judged to have a fair value on 30 June 20X8 of $950,000. At the year end date of 31 December 20X8 the fair value of the building was estimated at $1.2 million. *(900000 × 8.5/50)*

Cost 1.1.X0   900000
Dep to 30.06.X8   (153000)
Carrying amount 30.6.X8   747000

Carter uses the fair value model for investment property.

Revaluation surplus   203000

What amount will be shown in revaluation surplus at 31 December 20X8 in respect of this building?

Fair value   950000

   A $417,000   *The increase of (1200−950) = 250000 arising*
   B $300,000   *between 30.06.X8 and 31.12.X8 will*
   C $250,000   *be credited to P/L in accordance with*
 (D) $203,000   *IAS 40.*   **(2 marks)**

---

5   Leclerc has borrowed $2.4 million to finance the building of a factory. Construction is expected to take two years. The loan was drawn down and incurred on 1 January 20X9 and work began on 1 March 20X9. $1 million of the loan was not utilised until 1 July 20X9 so Leclerc was able to invest it until needed.

Leclerc is paying 8% on the loan and can invest surplus funds at 6%.

Calculate the borrowing costs to be capitalised for the year ended 31 December 20X9 in respect of this project.

Borrowing cost Mar-Dec ($2.4m × 8% × 10/12)   160 000
Less: investment Income ($1m × 6% × 6/12)   (30000)
                                                  130 000

 (A) $130,000
   B $192,000
   C $100,000
   D $162,000   **(2 marks)**

---

6   Which one of the following would be recognised as an investment property under IAS 40 in the consolidated financial statements of Buildco?

   A   A property intended for sale in the ordinary course of business *] inventory & WIP*
   B   A property being constructed for a customer
 (C) A property held by Buildco under a finance lease and leased out under an operating lease
   D   A property owned by Buildco and leased out to a subsidiary   **(2 marks)**

---

7   Which one of the following is **not true** concerning the treatment of investment properties under IAS 40?

   A   Following initial recognition, investment property can be held at either cost or fair value.
   B   If an investment property is held at fair value, this must be applied to all of the entity's investment property.
   C   An investment property is initially measured at cost, including transaction costs.
 (D) A gain or loss arising from a change in the fair value of an investment property should be recognised in other comprehensive income. *should be credited to P/L*   **(2 marks)**

---

8   A company has the following loans in place throughout the year ended 31 December 20X8.

	$m
10% bank loan	140
8% bank loan	200

On 1 July 20X8 $50 million was drawn down for construction of a qualifying asset which was completed during 20X9.

What amount should be capitalised as borrowing costs at 31 December 20X8 in respect of this asset?

   A $5.6 million   *Weighted capitalisation rate = (10% × 140/340) + (8% × 200/340)*
   B $2.8 million   *= 4.1% + 4.7% = 8.8%*
   C $4.4 million
 (D) $2.2 million   *$50m × 8.8% × 6/12 = $2.2m*   **(2 marks)**

9   Wetherby purchased a machine on 1 July 20X7 for $500,000. It is being depreciated on a straight line basis over its expected life of ten years. Residual value is estimated at $20,000. On 1 January 20X8, following a change in legislation, Wetherby fitted a safety guard to the machine. The safety guard cost $25,000 and has a useful life of five years with no residual value.

What amount will be charged to profit or loss for the year ended 31 March 20X8 in respect of depreciation on this machine?

Machine $((500000 - 20000)/10 \times 9/12)$ 36000
Safety guard $((25000/5) \times 3/12)$ 1250

A $38,750
(B) $37,250
C $41,000
D $39,750

37250

(2 marks)

10   An aircraft requires a planned overhaul each year at a cost of $5,000. This is a condition of being allowed to fly.

How should the cost of the overhaul be treated in the financial statements?

It should not be provided for in advance because there is no obligation arising from a past event - the overhaul could be avoided by selling to operate the aircraft.

A   Accrued for over the year and charged to maintenance expenses
B   Provided for in advance and charged to maintenance expenses
(C)   Capitalised and depreciated over the period to the next overhaul
D   Charged to profit or loss when the expenditure takes place

(2 marks)

11   Which of the following items should be capitalised within the initial carrying amount of an item of plant?

(i)   Cost of transporting the plant to the factory
(ii)   Cost of installing a new power supply required to operate the plant
(iii)   A deduction to reflect the estimated realisable value
(iv)   Cost of a three-year maintenance agreement
(v)   Cost of a three-week training course for staff to operate the plant

(A)   (i) and (ii) only
B   (i), (ii) and (iii)
C   (ii), (iii) and (iv)
D   (i), (iv) and (v)

(2 marks)

8 Preparation question: Plethora plc

The draft financial statements of Plethora plc for the year to 31 December 20X9 are being prepared and the accountant has requested your advice on dealing with the following issues.

(a)   Plethora plc has an administration building which it no longer needs. On 1 July 20X9 Plethora plc entered into an agreement to let the building out to another company. The building cost $600,000 on 1 January 20X0 and is being depreciated over 50 years. Plethora plc applies the fair value model under IAS 40 *Investment property* and the fair value of the building was judged to be $800,000 on 1 July 20X9. This valuation had not changed at 31 December 20X9.

Another building has been let out for a number of years. It had a fair value of $550,000 at 31 December 20X8 and $740,000 at 31 December 20X9.

Required

Explain how these two buildings should be accounted for in the financial statements of Plethora plc for the year to 31 December 20X9 and quantify the amounts involved.

(b)   Plethora plc owns a retail business which has suffered badly during the recession. Plethora plc treats this business as a separate cash generating unit.

The carrying amounts of the assets comprising the retail business are:

	$'000
Building	900
Plant and equipment	300
Inventory	70
Other current assets	130
Goodwill	40

An impairment review has been carried out as at 31 December 20X9 and the recoverable amount of the cash generating unit is estimated at $1.3m.

Required

Restate the carrying amounts of the assets of the retail business after accounting for the result of the impairment review.

9 Dearing (12/08 amended)   27 mins

(a)   On 1 October 20X5 Dearing acquired a machine under the following terms.

	Hours	$
Manufacturer's base price		1,050,000
Trade discount (applying to base price only)		20%
Early settlement discount taken (on the payable amount of the base cost only)		5%
Freight charges		30,000
Electrical installation cost		28,000
Staff training in use of machine		40,000
Pre-production testing		22,000
Purchase of a three-year maintenance contract		60,000
Estimated residual value		20,000
Estimated life in machine hours	6,000	
Hours used – year ended 30 September 20X6	1,200	
– year ended 30 September 20X7	1,800	
– year ended 30 September 20X8 (see below)	850	

On 1 October 20X7 Dearing decided to upgrade the machine by adding new components at a cost of $200,000. This upgrade led to a reduction in the production time per unit of the goods being manufactured using the machine. The upgrade also increased the estimated remaining life of the machine at 1 October 20X7 to 4,500 machine hours and its estimated residual value was revised to $40,000.

Required

Prepare extracts from the statement of profit or loss and statement of financial position for the above machine for each of the three years to 30 September 20X8.   **(10 marks)**

(b)   Dearing is building a new warehouse. The directors are aware that in accordance with IAS 23 *Borrowing Costs* certain borrowing costs have to be capitalised.

Required

Explain the circumstances when, and the amount at which, borrowing costs should be capitalised in accordance with IAS 23.   **(5 marks)**

                    (Total = 15 marks)

10 Flightline (6/09 amended)   27 mins

(a)   Explain what is meant by a 'complex' non-current asset and explain briefly how IAS 16 *Property, plant and equipment* requires expenditure on complex non-current assets to be accounted for.   **(5 marks)**

(b)   Flightline is an airline which treats its aircraft as complex non-current assets. The cost and other details of one of its aircraft are:

	$'000	Estimated life
Exterior structure – purchase date 1 April 20W5*	120,000	20 years
Interior cabin fittings – replaced 1 April 20X5	25,000	5 years
Engines (2 at $9 million each) – replaced 1 April 20X5	18,000	36,000 flying hours

*Ten years before 20X5

No residual values are attributed to any of the component parts.

At 1 April 20X8 the aircraft log showed it had flown 10,800 hours since 1 April 20X5. In the year ended 31 March 20X9, the aircraft flew for 1,200 hours for the six months to 30 September 20X8 and a further 1,000 hours in the six months to 31 March 20X9.

On 1 October 20X8 the aircraft suffered a 'bird strike' accident which damaged one of the engines beyond repair. This was replaced by a new engine with a life of 36,000 hours at cost of $10.8 million. The other engine was also damaged, but was repaired at a cost of $3 million; however, its remaining estimated life was shortened to 15,000 hours. The accident also caused cosmetic damage to the exterior of the aircraft which required repainting at a cost of $2 million. As the aircraft was out of service for some weeks due to the accident, Flightline took the opportunity to upgrade its cabin facilities at a cost of $4.5 million. This did not increase the estimated remaining life of the cabin fittings, but the improved facilities enabled Flightline to substantially increase the air fares on this aircraft

Required

Calculate the charges to profit or loss in respect of the aircraft for the year ended 31 March 20X9 and its carrying amount in the statement of financial position as at that date.

The post-accident changes are deemed effective from 1 October 20X8.　　　**(10 marks)**

(Total = 15 marks)

11 Enca (6/14)　　　　　　　　　　　　　　　　　　27 mins

(a) A director of Enca, a public listed company, has expressed concerns about the accounting treatment of some of the company's items of property, plant and equipment which have increased in value. His main concern is that the statement of financial position does not show the true value of assets which have increased in value and that this 'undervaluation' is compounded by having to charge depreciation on these assets, which also reduces reported profit. He argues that this does not make economic sense.

Required

Respond to the director's concerns by summarising the principal requirements of IAS 16 *Property, Plant and Equipment* in relation to the revaluation of property, plant and equipment, including its subsequent treatment.　　　　　　　　　　　　　　　　　　　　**(5 marks)**

(b) The following details relate to two items of property, plant and equipment (A and B) owned by Delta which are depreciated on a straight-line basis with no estimated residual value:

	Item A	Item B
Estimated useful life at acquisition	8 years	6 years
	$'000	$'000
Cost on 1 April 20X0	240,000	120,000
Accumulated depreciation (two years)	(60,000)	(40,000)
Carrying amount at 31 March 20X2	180,000	80,000
Revaluation on 1 April 20X2:		
Revalued amount	160,000	112,000
Revised estimated remaining useful life	5 years	5 years
Subsequent expenditure capitalised on 1 April 20X3	Nil	14,400

At 31 March 20X4 item A was still in use, but item B was sold (on that date) for $70 million.

Delta makes an annual transfer from its revaluation surplus to retained earnings in respect of excess depreciation.

Required:

Prepare extracts from:

(i)   Delta's statements of profit or loss for the years ended 31 March 20X3 and 20X4 in respect of charges (expenses) related to property, plant and equipment;   **(5 marks)**

(ii)   Delta's statements of financial position as at 31 March 20X3 and 20X4 for the carrying amount of property, plant and equipment and the revaluation surplus.   **(5 marks)**

(Total = 15 marks)

12 Multiple choice questions – intangible assets

1   Geek is developing a new product and expects to be able to capitalise the costs. Which one of the following would preclude capitalisation of the costs?

    A   Development of the product is not yet complete.
    B   No patent has yet been registered in respect of the product.
    C   No sales contracts have yet been signed in relation to the product.
    (D)   It has not been possible to reliably allocate costs to development of the product.   **(2 marks)**

2   A company had $20 million of capitalised development expenditure at cost brought forward at 1 October 20X7 in respect of products currently in production and a new project began on the same date.

    The research stage of the new project lasted until 31 December 20X7 and incurred $1.4 million of costs. From that date the project incurred development costs of $800,000 per month. On 1 April 20X8 the directors became confident that the project would be successful and yield a profit well in excess of costs. The project was still in development at 30 September 20X8. Capitalised development expenditure is amortised at 20% per annum using the straight line method.

    What amount will be charged to profit or loss for the year ended 30 September 20X8 in respect of research and development costs?

                                  research cost   1 400 000   *no depreciation on*
    A $8,280,000 *(Jan-Mar 800×3) expense development 2 400 000*   *new product as*
    B $6,880,000 *Depreciation on capital amount b/f*   *4 000 000*   *it is still being*
    (C) $7,800,000 *20m × 20%*   *7 800 000*   *developed.*
    D $3,800,000   **(2 marks)**

3   Which one of the following internally-generated items may be eligible for capitalisation as intangible assets in accordance with IAS 38 *Intangible Assets?* (Ignore business combinations.)

    A   A customer list
    (B)   A pre-production prototype *is classified as development costs.*
    C   Goodwill
    D   The cost of researching new material   **(2 marks)**

4   At 30 September 20X9 Sandown's trial balance showed a brand at cost of $30 million, less accumulated amortisation brought forward at 1 October 20X8 of $9 million. Amortisation is based on a ten-year useful life. An impairment review on 1 April 20X9 concluded that the brand had a value in use of $12 million and a remaining useful life of three years. However, on the same date Sandown received an offer to purchase the brand for $15 million.

    What should be the carrying amount of the brand in the statement of financial position of Sandown as at 30 September 20X9?   *$m*

                  Recoverable amount – fair value less costs of disposal   *15.0*
    (A) $12,500,000 *Less : Depreciation (1.4.X9 – 30.9.X9 (15m/3 × 6/12)*   *(2.5)*
    B $14,250,000   *12.5*
    C $15,000,000
    D $10,000,000   **(2 marks)**

5   Dempsey's year end is 30 September 20X4. Dempsey commenced the development stage of a project to produce a new pharmaceutical drug on 1 January 20X4. Expenditure of $40,000 per month was incurred until the project was completed on 30 June 20X4 when the drug went into immediate production. The directors became confident of the project's success on 1 March 20X4. The drug has an estimated life span of five years; time apportionment is used by Dempsey where applicable.

    What amount will Dempsey charge to profit or loss for development costs, including any amortisation, for the year ended 30 September 20X4? *Expenses 1 Jan to 1 Mar (40000×2) 80 000*

                                    4 months capitalised & amortised
    A $12,000   *8 000*
    B $98,667   *(40000×4)/5 yrs × 3/12*
    C $48,000   *88 000*
    (D) $88,000   **(2 marks)**

13 Emerald (12/07 amended)   27 mins

(a)   In accordance with IAS 38 *Intangible assets*, briefly discuss whether intangible assets should be recognised, and if so how they should be initially recorded and subsequently amortised in the following circumstances:

    (i)   When they are purchased separately from other assets

    (ii)   When they are obtained as part of acquiring the whole of a business

    (iii)   When they are developed internally

(5 marks)

    Your answer should consider goodwill separately from other intangibles.

(b)   Product development costs are a material cost for many companies. They are either written off as an expense or capitalised as an asset.

    Required

    Discuss the conceptual issues involved and the definition of an asset that may be applied in determining whether development expenditure should be treated as an expense or an asset.   **(4 marks)**

(c)   Emerald has had a policy of writing off development expenditure to profit or loss as it was incurred. In preparing its financial statements for the year ended 30 September 20X7 it has become aware that, under IFRS rules, qualifying development expenditure should be treated as an intangible asset. Below is the qualifying development expenditure for Emerald:

	$'000
Year ended 30 September 20X4	300
Year ended 30 September 20X5	240
Year ended 30 September 20X6	800
Year ended 30 September 20X7	400

    All capitalised development expenditure is deemed to have a four year life. Assume amortisation commences at the beginning of the accounting period following capitalisation. Emerald had no development expenditure before that for the year ended 30 September 20X4.

    Required

    Treating the above as the correction of an error in applying an accounting policy, calculate the amounts which should appear in the statement of profit or loss and statement of financial position (including comparative figures), and statement of changes in equity of Emerald in respect of the development expenditure for the year ended 30 September 20X7.

    Ignore taxation.   **(6 marks)**

(Total = 15 marks)

14 Dexterity (2.5 6/04 amended)   27 mins

Dexterity is a public listed company. It has been considering the accounting treatment of its intangible assets and has asked for your opinion on how the matters below should be treated in its financial statements for the year to 31 March 20X4.

(i)   On 1 October 20X3 Dexterity acquired Temerity, a small company that specialises in pharmaceutical drug research and development. The purchase consideration was by way of a share exchange and valued at $35 million. The fair value of Temerity's net assets was $15 million (excluding any items referred to below). Temerity owns a patent for an established successful drug that has a remaining life of eight years. A firm of specialist advisors, Leadbrand, has estimated the current value of this patent to be $10 million, however the company is awaiting the outcome of clinical trials where the drug has been tested to treat a different illness. If the trials are successful, the value of the drug is then estimated to be $15 million. Also included in the company's statement of financial position is $2 million for medical research that has been conducted on behalf of a client.   **(4 marks)**

(ii)   Dexterity has developed and patented a new drug which has been approved for clinical use. The costs of developing the drug were $12 million. Based on early assessments of its sales success, Leadbrand have estimated its market value at $20 million.   **(3 marks)**

(iii) Dexterity's manufacturing facilities have recently received a favourable inspection by government medical scientists. As a result of this the company has been granted an exclusive five-year licence to manufacture and distribute a new vaccine. Although the licence had no direct cost to Dexterity, its directors feel its granting is a reflection of the company's standing and have asked Leadbrand to value the licence. Accordingly they have placed a value of $10 million on it. **(3 marks)**

(iv) In the current accounting period, Dexterity has spent $3 million sending its staff on specialist training courses. Whilst these courses have been expensive, they have led to a marked improvement in production quality and staff now need less supervision. This in turn has led to an increase in revenue and cost reductions. The directors of Dexterity believe these benefits will continue for at least three years and wish to treat the training costs as an asset. **(2 marks)**

(v) In December 20X3, Dexterity paid $5 million for a television advertising campaign for its products that will run for 6 months from 1 January 20X4 to 30 June 20X4. The directors believe that increased sales as a result of the publicity will continue for two years from the start of the advertisements.

Required

Explain how the directors of Dexterity should treat the above items in the financial statements for the year to 31 March 20X4. **(3 marks)**

(Total = 15 marks)

The values given by Leadbrand can be taken as being reliable measurements. You are not required to consider depreciation aspects.

15 Darby (12/09) 27 mins

(a) An assistant of yours has been criticised over a piece of assessed work that he produced for his study course for giving the definition of a non-current asset as 'a physical asset of substantial cost, owned by the company, which will last longer than one year'.

Required

Provide an explanation to your assistant of the weaknesses in his definition of non-current assets when compared to the International Accounting Standards Board's (IASB) view of assets. **(4 marks)**

(b) The same assistant has encountered the following matters during the preparation of the draft financial statements of Darby for the year ending 30 September 20X9. He has given an explanation of his treatment of them:

(i) Darby spent $200,000 sending its staff on training courses during the year. This has already led to an improvement in the company's efficiency and resulted in cost savings. The organiser of the course has stated that the benefits from the training should last for a minimum of four years. The assistant has therefore treated the cost of the training as an intangible asset and charged six months' amortisation based on the average date during the year on which the training courses were completed. **(3 marks)**

(ii) During the year the company started research work with a view to the eventual development of a new processor chip. By 30 September 20X9 it had spent $1.6 million on this project. Darby has a past history of being particularly successful in bringing similar projects to a profitable conclusion. As a consequence the assistant has treated the expenditure to date on this project as an asset in the statement of financial position.

Darby was also commissioned by a customer to research and, if feasible, produce a computer system to install in motor vehicles that can automatically stop the vehicle if it is about to be involved in a collision. At 30 September 20X9, Darby had spent $2.4 million on this project, but at this date it was uncertain as to whether the project would be successful. As a consequence the assistant has treated the $2.4 million as an expense in the statement of profit or loss. **(4 marks)**

(iii) Darby signed a contract (for an initial three years) in August 20X9 with a company called Media Today to install a satellite dish and cabling system to a newly built group of residential apartments. Media Today will provide telephone and television services to the residents of the apartments via the satellite system and pay Darby $50,000 per annum commencing in December 20X9. Work on the installation commenced on 1 September 20X9 and the expenditure to 30 September 20X9 was $58,000. The installation is expected to be completed by 31 October 20X9. Previous experience with similar contracts indicates that Darby will make a total profit of $40,000 over the three years on this initial contract. The assistant correctly recorded the costs to 30 September 20X9 of $58,000 as a non-current asset, but then wrote this amount down to $40,000 (the expected total profit) because he believed the asset to be impaired.

The contract is not a finance lease. Ignore discounting. **(4 marks)**

Required

For each of the above items (i) to (iii) comment on the assistant's treatment of them in the financial statements for the year ended 30 September 20X9 and advise him how they should be treated under International Financial Reporting Standards.

The mark allocation is shown against each of the three items above. **(Total = 15 marks)**

BPP
LEARNING MEDIA

16 Multiple choice questions – impairment of assets

1 A cash-generating unit comprises the following assets:

	$'000
Building	700
Plant and equipment	200
Goodwill	90
Current assets	20
	1,010

[handwritten: The remaining 130 will be allocated pro rata as follows:-]

[handwritten table:]

	Building	plant
	700	160
Impairment	(106)	(24)
	594	

One of the machines, carried at $40,000, is damaged and will have to be scrapped. The recoverable amount of the cash-generating unit is estimated at $750,000.

What will be the carrying amount of the building when the impairment loss has been recognised? (to the nearest $'000)

[handwritten: Total impairment (1010 − 750)   260 / Goodwill (90) / Damaged plant (40) / 130]

A $597,000
B $577,000
Ⓒ $594,000
D $548,000

(2 marks)

2 What is the **recoverable amount** of an asset?

A Its current market value less costs of disposal
B The lower of carrying amount and value in use
Ⓒ The higher of fair value less costs of disposal and value in use
D The higher of carrying amount and market value

(2 marks)

3 A machine has a carrying amount of $85,000 at the year end of 31 March 20X9. Its market value is $78,000 and costs of disposal are estimated at $2,500. A new machine would cost $150,000. The company which owns the machine expects it to produce net cash flows of $30,000 per annum for the next three years. The company has a cost of capital of 8%. *[handwritten: fair value less cost of disposal (78000) − 2500)]* *[handwritten: 75500]*

What is the impairment loss on the machine to be recognised in the financial statements at 31 March 20X9? *[handwritten: Value in use   30000 × 1/1.08 = 27778]*
[handwritten: 30000 × 1/1.08² = 25720]

Ⓐ $7,687
B $9,500   *[handwritten: 30000 × 1/1.08³ = 23815]*   *[handwritten: 77313]*
C $1,667
D $2,200   *[handwritten: Recoverable amount is 77313, carrying amount is 85000 so impairment is 7687]*

(2 marks)

4 IAS 36 *Impairment of Assets* suggests how indications of impairment might be recognised.

Which one of the following would **not** be an external indicator that one or more of an entity's assets may be impaired?

A An unusually significant fall in the market value of an asset
B Significant change in the technological environment of the business in which the assets are employed
Ⓒ The carrying amount of the entity's net assets being less than its market capitalisation
D An increase in market interest rates used to calculate value in use

(2 marks)

5   The following information relates to an item of plant.

   • Its carrying amount in the statement of the financial position is $3 million.

   • The company has received an offer of $2.7 million from a company in Japan interested in buying the plant.

   • The present value of the estimated cash flows from continued use of the plant is $2.6 million.

   • The estimated cost of shipping the plant to Japan is $50,000.

   What is the amount of the impairment loss that should be recognised on the plant?

   fair value less cost of disposal (2.7m - 50000)   2650000
   (A) $350,000   *value in use*   2600000
   B $300,000
   C $400,000   *Recoverable amount therefore*   2650000
   D $450,000   *Impairment loss*   (350000)
                        carrying amount   3000000   **(2 marks)**

6   A business which comprises a single cash-generating unit has the following assets.

	$m	$m (3)	$m
Goodwill	3	(3)	-
Patent	5	(3)	2
Property	10	(2)	8
Plant and equipment	15	(3)	12
Net current assets	2	-	2
	35	(11)	24

   Following an impairment review it is estimated that the value of the patent is $2 million and the recoverable amount of the business is $24 million.

   At what amount should the property be measured following the impairment review?

   (A) $8 million   *The goodwill is written off, the patent is written*
   B $10 million   *down and the remaining $5m impairment is*
   C $7 million   *allocated pro-rata to the property and the plant.*
   D $5 million   **(2 marks)**

7   Riley acquired a non-current asset on 1 October 20W9 (ie 10 years before 20X9) at a cost of $100,000 which had a useful life of ten years and a nil residual value. The asset had been correctly depreciated up to 30 September 20X4. At that date the asset was damaged and an impairment review was performed. On 30 September 20X4, the fair value of the asset less costs of disposal was $30,000 and the expected future cash flows were $8,500 per annum for the next five years. The current cost of capital is 10% and a five-year annuity of $1 per annum at 10% would have a present value of $3.79.

   What amount would be charged to profit or loss for the impairment of this asset for the year ended 30 September 20X4?

   carrying amount (100000 × 5/10)   50000
   (A) $17,785   *Fair value less cost to sell*   30000   *Recoverable*
   B $20,000   *Value in use (8500 × 3.79)*   32215   *← amount*
   C $30,000
   D $32,215   *impairment loss = 50000 - 32215 = 17785*   **(2 marks)**

17 Telepath (6/12)   27 mins

(a) The objective of IAS 36 *Impairment of assets* is to prescribe the procedures that an entity applies to ensure that its assets are not impaired.

   Required

   Explain what is meant by an impairment review. Your answer should include reference to assets that may form a cash generating unit.

   You are **not** required to describe the indicators of impairment or how impairment losses are allocated against assets.   **(4 marks)**

(b) (i) Telepath acquired an item of plant at a cost of $800,000 on 1 April 20X0 that is used to produce and package pharmaceutical pills. The plant had an estimated residual value of $50,000 and an estimated life of five years, neither of which has changed. Telepath uses straight-line depreciation. On 31 March 20X2, Telepath was informed by a major customer (who buys products produced by the plant) that it would no longer be placing orders with Telepath. Even before this information was known, Telepath had been having difficulty finding work for this plant. It now estimates that net cash inflows earned from the plant for the next three years will be:

		$'000
Year ended:	31 March 20X3	220
	31 March 20X4	180
	31 March 20X5	170

On 31 March 20X5, the plant is still expected to be sold for its estimated realisable value.

Telepath has confirmed that there is no market in which to sell the plant at 31 March 20X2.

Telepath's cost of capital is 10% and the following values should be used:

Value of $1 at:	$
End of year 1	0.91
End of year 2	0.83
End of year 3	0.75

(ii) Telepath owned a 100% subsidiary, Tilda, that is treated as a cash generating unit. On 31 March 20X2, there was an industrial accident (a gas explosion) that caused damage to some of Tilda's plant. The assets of Tilda immediately before the accident were:

	$'000
Goodwill	1,800
Patent	1,200
Factory building	4,000
Plant	3,500
Receivables and cash	1,500
	12,000

As a result of the accident, the recoverable amount of Tilda is $6.7 million.

The explosion destroyed (to the point of no further use) an item of plant that had a carrying amount of $500,000.

Tilda has an open offer from a competitor of $1 million for its patent. The receivables and cash are already stated at their fair values less costs to sell (net realisable values).

Required

Calculate the carrying amounts of the assets in (i) and (ii) above at 31 March 20X2 after applying any impairment losses.

Calculations should be to the nearest $1,000.

The following mark allocation is provided as guidance for this requirement.

(i)   **4 marks**

(ii) **7 marks**

(11 marks)

(Total = 15 marks)

[Handwritten at top:]
Total contract Revenue 2800000
Cost Incurred (740000)
cost to complete (1400000)
expected profit 660000

18 Multiple choice questions – revenue

1   A company entered into a contract on 1 January 20X5 to build a factory. The total contract revenue was $2.8 million. At 31 December 20X5 the contract was certified as 35% complete. Costs incurred during the year were $740,000 and costs to complete are estimated at $1.4 million. $700,000 has been billed to the customer but not yet paid.

[Handwritten: 35% of 660 000 = 231 000]

What amount will be recognised as a contract asset or liability in respect of this contract in the statement of financial position as at 31 December 20X5?

A $271,000 contract asset
B $509,000 contract asset
C $271,000 contract liability
D $509,000 contract liability   **(2 marks)**

[Handwritten:]
Cost incurred   740000
Profit/loss recognition   231000
less: Billing   (700000)
contract asset   271000

2   Which of the following are acceptable methods of accounting for a government grant relating to an asset in accordance with IAS 20 *Accounting for Government Grants and Disclosure of Government Assistance*?

(i)   Set up the grant as deferred income
(ii)   Credit the amount received to profit or loss
(iii)   Deduct the grant from the carrying amount of the asset
(iv)   Add the grant to the carrying amount of the asset

A   (i) and (ii)
B   (ii) and (iv)
C   (i) and (iii)
D   (iii) and (iv)   **(2 marks)**

3   On 1 October 20X2 Pricewell entered into a contract to construct a bridge over a river. The total contract revenue was $50 million and construction is expected to be completed on 30 September 20X4. Costs to date are:

	$m
Materials, labour and overheads	12
Specialist plant acquired 1 October 20X2	8

The sales value of the work done at 31 March 20X3 has been agreed at $22 million and the estimated cost to complete (excluding plant depreciation) is $10 million. The specialist plant will have no residual value at the end of the contract and should be depreciated on a monthly basis. Pricewell recognises satisfaction of performance obligations on the percentage of completion basis as determined by the agreed work to date compared to the total contract price.

What is the profit to date on the contract at 31 March 20X3?

A $8,800,000
B $13,200,000
C $11,440,000
D $10,000,000   **(2 marks)**

[Handwritten:]
Total contract Revenue 50000000
Cost: MLOH   (12000000)
Specialist plant   (8000000)
To complete   (10000000)
                        20000000

Profit to date
20000 000 × 22/50 = $8 800 000

4   The following details apply to a contract where performance obligations are satisfied over time at 31 December 20X5.

	$
Total contract revenue	120,000
Costs to date	48,000
Estimated costs to completion	48,000
Amounts invoiced	50,400

The contract is agreed to be 45% complete at 31 December 20X5.

[Handwritten:]
Cost incurred   48000
Profit recognition   10800
less: Billing   (50400)
Contract asset   8400

Total contract Revenue 120000
Cost to date   (48000)
Cost to completion   (48000)
Total expected Profit   24000 × 45% = 10800

BPP
LEARNING MEDIA

What amount should appear in the statement of financial as at 31 December 20X5 as a contract asset?

A $8,400
B $48,000
C $6,000
D $50,400

(2 marks)

5   Sale and leaseback or sale and repurchase arrangements can be used to disguise the substance of loan transactions by taking them 'off balance sheet'. In this case the legal position is that the asset has been sold but the substance is that the seller still retains the benefits of ownership.

Which one of the following is **not** a feature which suggests that the substance of a transaction differs from its legal form?

A   The seller of an asset retains the ability to use the asset.
B   The seller has no further exposure to the risks of ownership
C   The asset has been transferred at a price substantially above or below its fair value.
D   The 'sold' asset remains on the sellers premises.

(2 marks)

6   Consignment inventory is an arrangement whereby inventory is held by one party but owned by another party. It is common in the motor trade.

Which of the following indicate that the inventory in question is consignment inventory?

(i)   Manufacturer can require dealer to return the inventory
(ii)   Dealer has no right of return of the inventory
(iii)   Manufacturer bears obsolescence risk
(iv)   Dealer bears slow movement risk

A   (i) and (ii)
B   (i) and (iii)
C   (ii) and (iv)
D   (ii), (iii) and (iv)

(2 marks)

7   A company receives a government grant of $500,000 on 1 April 20X7 to facilitate purchase on the same day of an asset which costs $750,000. The asset has a five year useful life and is depreciated on a 30% reducing balance basis. Company policy is to account for all grants received as deferred income.

What amount of income will be recognised in respect of the grant in the year to 31 March 20X9?

A   Nil
B $150,000
C $105,000
D $100,000

Handwritten: Grant 1.4.07   500 / Dep 30%   150 / 1.4.08   350 / Dep 30%   105

(2 marks)

8   Newmarket's revenue as shown in its draft statement of profit or loss for the year ended 31 December 20X9 is $27 million. This includes:

(i) $8 million for a consignment of goods sold on 31 December 20X9 on which Newmarket will incur ongoing service and support costs for two years after the sale. The cost of providing service and support is estimated at $800,000 per annum. Newmarket applies a 30% mark-up to all service costs.

(ii) $4 million collected on behalf of Aintree. Newmarket acts as an agent for Aintree and receives a 10% commission on all sales.

At what amount should revenue be shown in the statement of profit or loss of Newmarket for the year ended 31 December 20X9? (Ignore the time value of money.)

A $22,920,000
B $21,800,000
C $20,520,000
D $21,320,000

Handwritten: Revenue per P/L 27 000 / Servicing cost (800×2×130%) (2080) / Agency collection (4000) / Agency commission (4000×10%) 400

(2 marks)

Handwritten: 21 320

19 Preparation question: Derringdo

Derringdo acquired an item of plant at a gross cost of $800,000 on 1 October 20X2. The plant has an estimated life of ten years with a residual value equal to 15% of its gross cost. Derringdo uses straight-line depreciation on a time apportioned basis. The company received a government grant of 30% of its cost price at the time of its purchase. The terms of the grant are that if the company retains the asset for four years or more, then no repayment liability will be incurred. If the plant is sold within four years a repayment on a sliding scale would be applicable. The repayment is 75% if sold within the first year of purchase and this amount decreases by 25% per annum. Derringdo has no intention to sell the plant within the first four years. Derringdo's accounting policy for capital-based government grants is to treat them as deferred credits and release them to income over the life of the asset to which they relate.

Required

(a)   Discuss whether the company's policy for the treatment of government grants meets the definition of a liability in the IASB's *Conceptual Framework*.

(b)   Prepare extracts of Derringdo's financial statements for the year to 31 March 20X3 in respect of the plant and the related grant:

- Applying the company's policy

- In compliance with the definition of a liability in the *Conceptual Framework*. Your answer should consider whether the sliding scale repayment should be used in determining the deferred credit for the grant.

20 Preparation question: Contract

The following details are as at 31 December 20X5

	Contract 1	Contract 2	Contract 3	Contract 4
Total contract revenue	$120,000	$72,000	$240,000	$500,000
Costs to date	$48,000	$8,000	$103,200	$299,600
Estimated costs to completion	$48,000	$54,000	$160,800	$120,400
Work invoiced to date	$50,400	–	$76,800	$345,200
Cash received to date	$40,000	–	$60,000	$320,000
Date started	1.3.20X5	15.10.20X5	1.7.20X5	1.6.20X4
Estimated completion date	30.6.20X6	15.9.20X6	30.11.20X6	30.7.20X6
% complete	45%	10%	35%	70%

These are all contracts where performance obligations are satisfied over time. You are to assume that profit accrues evenly over each of the contracts.

The statement of profit or loss for the previous year showed revenue of $225,000 and expenses of $189,000 in relation to Contract 4.

The company considers that the outcome of a contract cannot be estimated reliably until a contract is 25% complete. It is, however, probable that the customer will pay for costs incurred so far.

Required

Calculate the amounts to be included in the statement of profit or loss for the year ended 31 December 20X5 and the statement of financial position as at that date.

	Contract 1 $	Contract 2 $	Contract 3 $	Contract 4 $
Statement of profit or loss				
Revenue				
Expenses				
Expected loss				
Recognised profit/(loss)				
Statement of financial position				
Contract assets/liabilities				
Contract costs incurred to date				
Recognised profits less recognised losses				
Less amounts invoiced to date				
Trade receivables				
Amounts invoiced to date				
Less cash received				

Workings

21 Preparation question: Beetie (pilot paper amended)

Beetie is a construction company that prepares its financial statements to 31 March each year. During the year ended 31 March 20X6 the company commenced two contracts. Performance obligations are satisfied over time and the contracts are expected to take more than one year to complete. The position of each contract at 31 March 20X6 is:

	1	2
	$'000	$'000
Total contract revenue	5,500	1,200
Estimated total cost of contract at commencement	4,000	900
Estimated total cost at 31 March 20X6	4,000	1,250
Agreed value of work completed at 31 March 20X6	3,300	840
Invoices issued and cash received at 31 March 20X6	3,000	880
Contract costs incurred to 31 March 20X6	3,900	720

The agreed value of the work completed at 31 March 20X6 is considered to be equal to the revenue earned in the year ended 31 March 20X6. Satisfaction of performance obligations is measured using the percentage of completion method. The percentage of completion is calculated as the agreed value of work completed to the agreed contract price.

Required

Calculate the amounts which should appear in the statement of profit or loss and statement of financial position of Beetie at 31 March 20X6 in respect of the above contracts.

22 Mocca (6/11 amended)   27 mins

IFRS 15 *Revenue from contracts with customers* deals with accounting requirements for contracts in respect of which performance obligations are satisfied over time.

Required

(a)   Describe the issues of revenue and profit recognition relating to contracts where performance obligations are satisfied over time.   **(5 marks)**

(b)   On 1 October 20X0 Mocca entered into a contract where performance obligations were deemed to be satisfied over time. The contract was expected to take 27 months and therefore be completed on 31 December 20X2. Details of the contract are:

	$'000
Total contract revenue	12,500
Estimated total cost of contract (excluding plant)	5,500

Plant for use on the contract was purchased on 1 January 20X1 (three months into the contract as it was not required at the start) at a cost of $8 million. The plant has a four-year life and after two years, when the contract is complete, it will be transferred to another contract at its carrying amount. Annual depreciation is calculated using the straight-line method (assuming a nil residual value) and charged to the contract on a monthly basis at 1/12 of the annual charge.

The correctly reported profit or loss results for the contract for the year ended 31 March 20X1 were:

	$'000
Revenue recognised	3,500
Contract expenses recognised	(2,660)
Profit recognised	840

Details of the progress of the contract at 31 March 20X2 are:

	$'000
Contract costs incurred to date (excluding depreciation)	4,800
Agreed value of work completed and invoiced to date	8,125
Total cash received to date (payments on account)	7,725

The percentage of performance obligation satisfied is calculated as the agreed value of work completed as a percentage of the agreed contract price.

Required

Calculate the amounts which would appear in the statement of profit or loss and statement of financial position of Mocca, including the disclosure note of contract assets/liabilities, for the year ended/as at 31 March 20X2 in respect of the above contract. **(10 marks)**

(Total = 15 marks)

23 Wardle (6/10 amended)   27 mins

(a)   An important aspect of the International Accounting Standards Board's *Conceptual Framework for Financial Reporting* is that transactions should be faithfully represented. Implicit in this is the requirement that they should be recorded on the basis of their substance over their form.

Required

Explain why it is important that financial statements should reflect the substance of the underlying transactions and describe the features that may indicate that the substance of a transaction may be different from its legal form. **(5 marks)**

(b)   Wardle's activities include the production of maturing products which take a long time before they are ready to retail. Details of one such product are that on 1 April 20X0 it had a cost of $5 million and a fair value of $7 million. The product would not be ready for retail sale until 31 March 20X3.

On 1 April 20X0 Wardle entered into an agreement to sell the product to Easyfinance for $6 million. The agreement gave Wardle the right to repurchase the product at any time up to 31 March 20X3 at a fixed price of $7,986,000,at which date Wardle expected the product to retail for $10 million. The compound interest Wardle would have to pay on a three-year loan of $6 million would be:

	$
Year 1	600,000
Year 2	660,000
Year 3	726,000

This interest is equivalent to the return required by Easyfinance.

Required

Assuming the above figures prove to be accurate, prepare extracts from the statement of profit or loss of Wardle for the three years to 31 March 20X3 in respect of the above transaction:

(i)   Reflecting the legal form of the transaction **(2 marks)**
(ii)   Reflecting the substance of the transaction **(3 marks)**

Statement of financial position extracts are not required.

(c)   Comment on the effect the two treatments have on the statements of profit or loss and the statements of financial position and how this may affect an assessment of Wardle's performance. **(5 marks)**

(Total = 15 marks)

24 Multiple choice questions – introduction to groups

1   On what basis may a subsidiary be excluded from consolidation?

    A   The activities of the subsidiary are dissimilar to the activities of the rest of the group.

    B   The subsidiary was acquired with the intention of reselling it after a short period of time.

    C   The subsidiary is based in a country with strict exchange controls which make it difficult for it to transfer funds to the parent.

    (D)   There is no basis on which a subsidiary may be excluded from consolidation.   **(2 marks)**

2   When negative goodwill arises, IFRS 3 *Business combinations* requires that the amounts involved in computing goodwill should first be reassessed. When the amount of the negative goodwill has been confirmed, how should it be accounted for?

    A   Charged as an expense in profit or loss

    B   Capitalised and presented under non-current assets

    (C)   Credited to profit or loss

    D   Shown as a deduction from non-current assets   **(2 marks)**

3   Which of the following is the criterion for treatment of an investment as an associate?

    A   Ownership of a majority of the equity shares   *The other options indicate control*

    B   Ability to exercise control   *over a subsidiary*

    (C)   Existence of significant influence

    D   Exposure to variable returns from involvement with the investee   **(2 marks)**

4   Which of the following statements are correct when preparing consolidated financial statements?

    1   A subsidiary cannot be consolidated unless it prepares financial statements to the same reporting date as the parent.

    (2)   A subsidiary with a different reporting date may prepare additional statements up to the group reporting date for consolidation purposes.

    3   A subsidiary's financial statements can be included in the consolidation if the gap between the parent and subsidiary reporting dates is five months or less.   *3 months not Five*

    (4)   Where a subsidiary's financial statements are drawn up to a different reporting date from those of the parent, adjustments should be made for significant transactions or events occurring between the two reporting dates.

    A   1 only

    B   2 and 3

    (C)   2 and 4

    D   3 and 4   **(2 marks)**

5   IFRS 3 *Business combinations* requires an acquirer to measure the assets and liabilities of the acquiree at the date of consolidation at fair value. IFRS 13 *Fair Value Measurement* provides guidance on how fair value should be established.

    Which of the following is **not** one of the issues to be considered according to IFRS 13 when arriving at the fair value of a non-financial asset?

    A   The characteristics of the asset

    (B)   *not fair value* The present value of the future cash flows that the asset is expected to generate during its remaining life

    C   The principal or most advantageous market for the asset

    D   The highest and best use of the asset   **(2 marks)**

6   Consolidated financial statements are presented on the basis that the companies within the group are treated as if they are a single (economic) entity.

Which of the following are requirements of preparing group accounts?

(i)   All subsidiaries must adopt the accounting policies of the parent.

(ii)   Subsidiaries with activities which are substantially different to the activities of other members of the group should not be consolidated.

(iii) All entity financial statements within a group should (normally) be prepared to the same accounting year end prior to consolidation.

(iv)   Unrealised profits within the group must be eliminated from the consolidated financial statements.

A   All four
B   (i) and (ii) only
C   (i), (iii) and (iv)
D   (iii) and (iv)   (2 marks)

25 Preparation question: Group financial statements

(a)   Set out the exemptions from the requirement to present consolidated financial statements which are available to a parent company.

(b)   Explain why intra-group transactions and balances are eliminated on consolidation.

26 Preparation question with helping hands: Simple consolidation

Boo acquired 80% of Goose's equity for $300,000 on 1 January 20X8. At the date of acquisition Goose had retained earnings of $190,000. On 31 December 20X8 Boo despatched goods which cost $80,000 to Goose, at an invoiced cost of $100,000. Goose received the goods on 2 January 20X9 and recorded the transaction then. The two companies' draft financial statements as at 31 December 20X8 are shown below.

STATEMENTS OF PROFIT OR LOSS AND OTHER COMPREHENSIVE INCOME
FOR THE YEAR ENDED 31 DECEMBER 20X8

	Boo	Goose
	$'000	$'000
Revenue	5,000	1,000
Cost of sales	2,900	600
Gross profit	2,100	400
Other expenses	1,700	320
Profit before tax	400	80
Income tax expense	130	25
Profit for the year	270	55
Other comprehensive income:		
Gain on revaluation of property	20	–
Total comprehensive income for the year	290	55

STATEMENTS OF FINANCIAL POSITION AT 31 DECEMBER 20X8

	$'000	$'000
Assets		
Non-current assets		
Property, plant and equipment	1,940	200
Investment in Goose	300	–
	2,240	200
Current assets		
Inventories	500	120
Trade receivables	650	40
Bank and cash	170	35
	1,320	195
Total assets	3,560	395
Equity and liabilities		
Equity		
Share capital	2,000	100
Retained earnings	500	240
Revaluation surplus	20	–
	2,520	340
Current liabilities		
Trade payables	910	30
Tax	130	25
	1,040	55
Total equity and liabilities	3,560	395

Required

Prepare a draft consolidated statement of profit or loss and other comprehensive income and statement of financial position. It is the group policy to value the non-controlling interest at acquisition at fair value. The fair value of the non-controlling interest in Goose at the date of acquisition was $60,000.

Helping hands

1   This is a very easy example to ease you into the technique of preparing consolidated accounts. There are a number of points to note.

2   Inventory in transit should be included in the statement of financial position and deducted from cost of sales at cost to the group.

3   Similarly, the intra-group receivable and sale should be eliminated as a consolidation adjustment.

4   Boo Co must have included its inter-company account in trade receivables as it is not specifically mentioned elsewhere in the accounts.

5   Remember that only the parent's issued share capital is shown in the group accounts.

6   The non-controlling interest in the statement of profit or loss is easily calculated as 20% of post-tax profit for the year as shown in Goose's accounts. In the statement of financial position, the non-controlling interest will be the amount at acquisition plus 20% of Goose's post-tax profit for the year.

---

27 Multiple choice questions – consolidated statement of financial position

1   Witch acquired 70% of the 200,000 equity shares of Wizard, its only subsidiary, on 1 April 20X8 when the retained earnings of Wizard were $450,000. The carrying amounts of Wizard's net assets at the date of acquisition were equal to their fair values apart from a building which had a carrying amount of $600,000 and a fair value of $850,000. The remaining useful life of the building at the acquisition date was 40 years.

Witch measures non-controlling interest at fair value, based on share price. The market value of Wizard shares at the date of acquisition was $1.75.

At 31 March 20X9 the retained earnings of Wizard were $750,000. At what amount should the non-controlling interest appear in the consolidated statement of financial position of Witch at 31 March 20X9?

A $195,000   Fair value at acquisition (200000 × 30% × 1·75)   105000
(B) $193,125   Share of post acquisition retained earnings ((750-450)×30%)   90000
C $135,000   Depreciation on fair value adjustment((250/40)×20%)   (1875)
D $188,750   193125

(2 marks)

2   Cloud obtained a 60% holding in the 100,000 $1 shares of Mist on 1 January 20X8, when the retained earnings of Mist were $850,000. Consideration comprised $250,000 cash, $400,000 payable on 1 January 20X9 and one share in Cloud for each two shares acquired. Cloud has a cost of capital of 8% and the market value of its shares on 1 January 20X8 was $2.30.

Cloud measures non-controlling interest at fair value. The fair value of the non-controlling interest at 1 January 20X8 was estimated to be $400,000.   consideration transferred !

What was the goodwill arising on acquisition?   cash   250000
                                                                 Deferred consideration (40000/1.08) 370 370
(A) $139,370   shares (30000 × $2·30)   69 000
B $169,000   689 370
C $119,370 fair value of assets   fair value of non-controlling interest   400 000
D $130,370   shares   100 000   1089 370
                   Retained earnings   850000   (950 000)   (2 marks)
                                                                       139 370

3   On 1 June 20X1 Premier acquired 80% of the equity share capital of Sandford. At the date of acquisition the fair values of Sandford's net assets were equal to their carrying amounts with the exception of its property. This had a fair value of $1.2 million **below** its carrying amount. The property had a remaining useful life of eight years.

What effect will any adjustment required in respect of the property have on group retained earnings at 30 September 20X1?   (1·2m /8 × 4/12) × 80% = 40 000

A   Increase $50,000   The adjustment will reduce depreciation over
B   Decrease $50,000   the next 8 yrs, so it will increase retained
(C)   Increase $40,000   earnings
D   Decrease $40,000   **(2 marks)**

4   On 1 August 20X7 Patronic purchased 18 million of the 24 million $1 equity shares of Sardonic. The acquisition was through a share exchange of two shares in Patronic for every three shares in Sardonic. The market price of a share in Patronic at 1 August 20X7 was $5.75. Patronic will also pay in cash on 31 July 20X9 (two years after acquisition) $2.42 per acquired share of Sardonic. Patronic's cost of capital is 10% per annum.

What is the amount of the consideration attributable to Patronic for the acquisition of Sardonic?

(A) $105 million   69000
B $139.5 million   Shares (18m × 2/3 × $5·75)   36000
C $108.2 million   Deferred consideration (18m × $2·42×1 /1·1²)   105 000
D $103.8 million   **(2 marks)**

5   On 1 April 20X0 Picant acquired 75% of Sander's equity shares by means of a share exchange and an additional amount payable on 1 April 20X1 that was contingent upon the post-acquisition performance of Sander. At the date of acquisition Picant assessed the fair value of this contingent consideration at $4.2 million but by 31 March 20X1 it was clear that the amount to be paid would be only $2.7 million.

How should Picant account for this $1.5 million adjustment in its financial statements as at 31 March 20X1?

A   Debit current liabilities/Credit goodwill
B   Debit retained earnings/Credit current liabilities
C   Debit goodwill/Credit current liabilities
D   Debit current liabilities/Credit retained earnings

[handwritten: This adjustment reduces (debits) the liability and the credit is to retained earnings. The remeasurement relates to the post-acquisition period, so goodwill is not affected.]

(2 marks)

6   Crash acquired 70% of Bang's 100,000 $1 ordinary shares for $800,000 when the retained earnings of Bang were $570,000 and the balance in its revaluation surplus was $150,000. Bang also has an internally-developed customer list which has been independently valued at $90,000. The non-controlling interest in Bang was judged to have a fair value of $220,000 at the date of acquisition.

What was the goodwill arising on acquisition?

[handwritten: consideration transferred 800 000 / Fair value of non-controlling interest 220 000 = 1020000]

A $200,000
B $163,000
C $226,000
D $110,000

[handwritten: Fair value of net assets: shares 100 000; Retained earnings 570000; Revaluation surplus 150000; Intangible 90 000 = (910000); 110000]

(2 marks)

28 Preparation question: Goodwill

At 1 January 20X9 Penguin plc paid $1.2m for an 80% share in Platypus Ltd. Platypus Ltd's net assets at the date of acquisition were:

	$'000
Share capital	500
Retained earnings	850
Revaluation surplus	450

It is group policy is to measure non-controlling interests at acquisition at fair value. The fair value of the non-controlling interest at the date of acquisition was $400,000.

Statements of profit or loss for both companies for the year ended 31 December 20X9 were:

	Penguin	Platypus
	$'000	$'000
Revenue	12,500	2,600
Cost of sales	(7,400)	(1,090)
Gross profit	5,100	1,510
Distribution costs	(700)	(220)
Administrative expenses	(1,300)	(550)
Finance costs	(40)	-
Profit before tax	3,060	740
Income tax expense	(900)	(230)
Profit for the year	2,160	510

Required

Calculate the goodwill on acquisition and prepare the consolidated statement of profit or loss of the Penguin Group for the year ended 31 December 20X9.

29 Pedantic (12/08 amended)

mid year acq

54 mins

On 1 April 20X8, Pedantic acquired 60% of the equity share capital of Sophistic in a share exchange of two shares in Pedantic for three shares in Sophistic. The issue of shares has not yet been recorded by Pedantic. At the date of acquisition shares in Pedantic had a market value of $6 each. Below are the summarised draft financial statements of both companies.

STATEMENTS OF PROFIT OR LOSS FOR THE YEAR ENDED 30 SEPTEMBER 20X8

	Pedantic	Sophistic
	$'000	$'000
Revenue	85,000	42,000
Cost of sales	(63,000)	(32,000)
Gross profit	22,000	10,000
Distribution costs	(2,000)	(2,000)
Administrative expenses	(6,000)	(3,200)
Finance costs	(300)	(400)
Profit before tax	13,700	4,400
Income tax expense	(4,700)	(1,400)
Profit for the year	9,000	3,000

STATEMENTS OF FINANCIAL POSITION AS AT 30 SEPTEMBER 20X8

	Pedantic	Sophistic
Assets	$'000	$'000
Non-current assets		
Property, plant and equipment	40,600	12,600
Current assets	16,000	6,600
Total assets	56,600	19,200
Equity and liabilities		
Equity shares of $1 each	10,000	4,000
Retained earnings	35,400	6,500
	45,400	10,500
Non-current liabilities		
10% loan notes	3,000	4,000
Current liabilities	8,200	4,700
Total equity and liabilities	56,600	19,200

The following information is relevant. *adjustment needed*

(i) At the date of acquisition, the fair values of Sophistic's assets were equal to their carrying amounts with the exception of an item of plant, which had a fair value of $2 million in excess of its carrying amount. It had a remaining life of five years at that date (straight-line depreciation is used). Sophistic has not adjusted the carrying amount of its plant as a result of the fair value exercise.

(ii) Sales from Sophistic to Pedantic in the post acquisition period were $8 million. Sophistic made a mark up on cost of 40% on these sales. Pedantic had sold $5.2 million (at cost to Pedantic) of these goods by 30 September 20X8.

(iii) Other than where indicated, profit or loss items are deemed to accrue evenly on a time basis.

(iv) Sophistic's trade receivables at 30 September 20X8 include $600,000 due from Pedantic which did not agree with Pedantic's corresponding trade payable. This was due to cash in transit of $200,000 from Pedantic to Sophistic. Both companies have positive bank balances.

(v) Pedantic has a policy of accounting for any non-controlling interest at full fair value. The fair value of the non-controlling interest in Sophistic at the date of acquisition was estimated to be $5.9 million. Consolidated goodwill was not impaired at 30 September 20X8.

Required

(a) Prepare the consolidated statement of profit or loss for Pedantic for the year ended 30 September 20X8.

(10 marks)

(b) Prepare the consolidated statement of financial position for Pedantic as at 30 September 20X8. **(16 marks)**

A statement of changes in equity is not required.

(c) Pedantic has been approached by a potential new customer, Trilby, to supply it with a substantial quantity of goods on three months credit terms. Pedantic is concerned at the risk that such a large order represents in the current difficult economic climate, especially as Pedantic's normal credit terms are only one month's credit. To support its application for credit, Trilby has sent Pedantic a copy of Tradhat's most recent audited consolidated financial statements. Trilby is a wholly-owned subsidiary within the Tradhat group. Tradhat's consolidated financial statements show a strong statement of financial position including healthy liquidity ratios.

Required

Comment on the importance that Pedantic should attach to Tradhat's consolidated financial statements when deciding on whether to grant credit terms to Trilby.

(4 marks)

(30 marks)

30 Pyramid (specimen paper)   27 mins

On 1 October 20X3, Pyramid acquired 80% of Square's equity shares by means of a share exchange of two shares in Pyramid for every three acquired shares in Square. In addition, Pyramid would make a deferred cash payment of 88 cents per acquired share on 1 October 20X4. Pyramid has not recorded any of the consideration. Pyramid's cost of capital is 10% per annum. The market value of Pyramid's shares at 1 October 20X3 was $6.

The following information is available for the two companies as at 30 September 20X4.

	Pyramid $'000	Square $'000
Assets		
Non-current assets		
Property, plant, and equipment	38,100	28,500
Equity and liabilities		
Equity		
Equity and shares of $1 each	50,000	9,000
Other components of equity	8,000	nil
Retained earnings – at 1 October 20X3	16,200	19,000
– for the year ended 30 September 20X4	14,000	8,000

The following information is relevant:

(i) At the date of acquisition, Square's net assets were equal to their carrying amounts with the following exceptions:

An item of plant which had a fair value of $3 million above its carrying amount. At the date of acquisition it had a remaining life of five years (straight-line depreciation).

Square had an unrecorded deferred tax liability of $1million, which was unchanged as at 30 September 20X4.

(ii) Pyramid's policy is to value the non-controlling interest at fair value at the date of acquisition. For this purpose a share price of $3.50 each is representative of the fair value of the shares in Square held by the non-controlling interest at the acquisition date.

(iii) Consolidated goodwill has not been impaired.

Required

Prepare extracts from Pyramid's consolidated statement of financial position as at 30 September 20X4 for:

(a)	Consolidated goodwill	**(5 marks)**
(b)	Property, plant and equipment	**(2 marks)**
(c)	Equity (share capital and reserves)	**(6 marks)**
(d)	Non-controlling interests	**(2 marks)**

(Total = 15 marks)

31 Multiple choice questions – consolidated statement of profit or loss and other comprehensive income

1   Basil acquired 60% of Parsley on 1 March 20X9. In September 20X9 Basil sold $46,000 worth of goods to Parsley. Basil applies a 30% mark-up to all its sales. 25% of these goods were still held in inventory by Parsley at the end of the year.

An extract from the draft statements of profit or loss of Basil and Parsley at 31 December 20X9 is:

	Basil	Parsley
	$	$
Revenue	955,000	421,500
Cost of sales	(407,300)	(214,600)
Gross profit	547,700	206,900

All revenue and costs arise evenly throughout the year.

What will be shown as gross profit in the consolidated statement of profit or loss of Basil for the year ended 31 December 20X9?

A $717,463
B $751,946
C $716,667
D $751,150

(2 marks)

2   Premier acquired 80% of Sanford on 1 June 20X1. Sales from Sanford to Premier throughout the year ended 30 September 20X1 were consistently $1 million per month. Sanford made a mark-up on cost of 25% on these sales. At 30 September 20X1 Premier was holding $2 million inventory that had been supplied by Sanford in the post-acquisition period.

By how much will the unrealised profit decrease the profit attributable to the non-controlling interest for the year ended 30 September 20X1?

A $1,000,000
B $400,000
C $500,000
D $80,000

(2 marks)

3   Hillusion acquired 80% of Skeptik on 1 July 20X2. In the post-acquisition period Hillusion sold goods to Skeptik at a price of $12 million. These goods had cost Hillusion $9 million. During the year to 31 March 20X3 Skeptik had sold $10 million (at cost to Skeptik) of these goods for $15m million.

How will this affect group cost of sales in the consolidated statement of profit or loss of Hillusion for the year ended 31 March 20X3?

A   Increase by $11.5 million
B   Increase by $9.6 million
C   Decrease by $11.5 million
D   Decrease by $9.6 million

(2 marks)

4   Brigham has owned 70% of Dorset for many years. It also holds a $5 million 8% loan note from Dorset. One of Dorset's non-current assets has suffered an impairment of $50,000 during the year. There is a balance in the revaluation surplus of Dorset of $30,000 in respect of this asset. The impairment loss has not yet been recorded.

The entity financial statements of Dorset show a profit for the year of $1.3 million.

What is the amount attributable to the non-controlling interests in the consolidated statement of profit or loss?

A $264,000
B $255,000
C $300,000
D $348,000

(2 marks)

5   On 1 January 20X4, Viagem acquired 80% of the equity share capital of Greca.

Extracts of their statements of profit or loss for the year ended 30 September 20X4 are: *9/12*

	Viagem	Greca
	$'000	$'000
Revenue	64,600	38,000
Cost of sales	(51,200)	(26,000) *9/12*

×9 ×9/12

Sales from Viagem to Greca throughout the year ended 30 September 20X4 had consistently been $800,000 per month. Viagem made a mark-up on cost of 25% on these sales. Greca had $1.5 million of these goods in inventory as at 30 September 20X4.

What would be the cost of sales in Viagem's consolidated statement of profit or loss for the year ended 30 September 20X4?

Viagem   51200
Greca (26000 × 9/12)   19500
Intercompany Sale (800×9)   (7200)
PUP (1500 × 25/125)   300
*   63800*

- A $59.9 million
- B $61.4 million
- C $63.8 million
- D $67.9 million

(2 marks)

---

6   On 1 July 20X7, Spider acquired 60% of the equity share capital of Fly and on that date made a $10 million loan to Fly at a rate of 8% per annum.

6 months

What will be the effect on group retained earnings at the year end date of 31 December 20X7 when this intragroup transaction is cancelled?

loss of investment Income (10m×8% × 6/12)   (400)
saving of interest payable (40×60%)   240
Net reduction in group retained earnings   160

- A   Group retained earnings will increase by $400,000.
- B   Group retained earnings will be reduced by $240,000.
- C   Group retained earnings will be reduced by $160,000.
- D   There will be no effect on group retained earnings.

(2 marks)

---

7   Wiley acquired 80% of Coyote on 1 January 20X8. At the date of acquisition Coyote had a building which had a fair value $22 million and a carrying amount of $20 million. The remaining useful life was 20 years. At the year end date of 30 June 20X8 the fair value of the building was $23 million.

Coyote's profit for the year to 30 June 20X8 was $1.6 million *×6/12* which accrued evenly throughout the year.

Wiley measures non-controlling interest at fair value. At 30 June 20X8 it estimated that goodwill in Coyote was impaired by $500,000.

6/12

What is the total comprehensive income attributable to the non-controlling interest at 30 June 20X8?

Profit to 30 June 08 (1600 × 6/12)   800000
Additional Depreciation (2/20 × 0.5)   50000
Goodwill Impairment   (500000)
Revaluation Gain   1000000
*   1250000*
NCI 20%   2500 100

- A $250,000
- B $260,000
- C $360,000
- D $400,000

(2 marks)

---

32 Preparation question: Acquisition during the year

Port has many investments, but before 20X4 none of these investments met the criteria for consolidation as a subsidiary. One of these older investments was a $2.3m 12% loan to Alfred which was made 15 years ago and is due to be repaid in 12 years' time.

On 1 November 20X4 Port purchased 75% of the equity of Alfred for $650,000. The consideration was 35,000 $1 equity shares in Port with a fair value of $650,000.

Noted below are the draft statements of profit or loss and other comprehensive income for Port and its subsidiary Alfred for the year ending 31 December 20X4 along with the draft statements of financial position as at 31 December 20X4.

STATEMENTS OF PROFIT OR LOSS AND OTHER COMPREHENSIVE INCOME
FOR THE YEAR ENDING 31 DECEMBER 20X4

	Port $'000	Alfred $'000
Revenue	100	996
Cost of sales	(36)	(258)
Gross profit	64	738
Interest on loan to Alfred	276	–
Other investment income	158	–
Operating expenses	(56)	(330)
Finance costs	–	(276)
Profit before tax	442	132
Income tax expense	(112)	(36)
Profit for the year	330	96
Other comprehensive income:		
Gain on property revaluation	30	–
Total comprehensive income for the year	360	96

STATEMENTS OF FINANCIAL POSITION AS AT 31 DECEMBER 20X4

	Port $'000	Alfred $'000
Non-current assets		
Property, plant and equipment	130	3,000
Loan to Alfred	2,300	–
Other investments	600	–
	3,030	3,000
Current assets	800	139
Total assets	3,830	3,139

	Port $'000	Alfred $'000
Equity and liabilities		
Equity		
$1 Equity shares	200	100
Share premium	500	85
Retained earnings	2,900	331
Revaluation surplus	30	–
	3,630	516
Non-current liabilities		
Loan from Port	–	2,300
Current liabilities		
Sundry	200	323
Total equity and liabilities	3,830	3,139

The following information is relevant.

(i) Port has not accounted for the issue of its own shares or for the acquisition of the investment in Alfred.

(ii) There has been no impairment in the value of the goodwill.

(iii) It is the group policy to value the non-controlling interest at acquisition at fair value. The fair value of the non-controlling interest in Alfred at the date of acquisition was estimated to be $180,000.

Required

Prepare the consolidated statement of profit or loss and other comprehensive income for the Port Group for the year ending 31 December 20X4 and a consolidated statement of financial position as at that date.

Approaching the question

1 Establish the **group structure**, noting for how long Alfred was a subsidiary.

2 Adjust Port's statement of financial position for the issue of its own shares and the cost of the investment in Alfred.

3 Sketch out the **format** of the group statement of profit or loss and other comprehensive income and statement of financial position, and then fill in the amounts for each company directly from the question. (Sub-totals are not normally needed when you do this.)

4 **Time-apportion** the income, expenditure and taxation for the subsidiary acquired.

5 Calculate the **goodwill**.

6 Remember to time-apportion the non-controlling interest in Alfred.

33 Preparation question: Pandar (12/09 amended)

On 1 April 20X9 Pandar purchased 80% of the equity shares in Salva. The acquisition was through a share exchange of three shares in Pandar for every five shares in Salva. The market prices of Pandar's and Salva's shares at 1 April 20X9 were $6 per share and $3.20 respectively. On the same date Pandar acquired 40% of the equity shares in Ambra paying $2 per share. *6/12*

The summarised statements of profit or loss for the three companies for the year ended 30 September 20X9 are:

	Pandar	Salva	Ambra
	$'000	$'000	$'000
Revenue	210,000	150,000 *75000*	50,000
Cost of sales	(126,000)	(100,000) *50000*	(40,000)
Gross profit	84,000	50,000	10,000
Distribution costs	(11,200)	(7,000) *3500*	(5,000)
Administrative expenses	(18,300)	(9,000) *4500*	(11,000)
Investment income (interest and dividends)	9,500		
Finance costs	(1,800)	(3,000) *1500*	nil
Profit (loss) before tax	62,200	31,000	(6,000)
Income tax (expense) relief	(15,000)	(10,000) *5000*	1,000
Profit (loss) for the year	47,200	21,000	(5,000)

The following information for the equity of the companies at 30 September 20X9 is available:

Equity shares of $1 each	200,000	120,000	40,000
Share premium	300,000	nil	nil
Retained earnings 1 October 20X8	40,000	152,000	15,000
Profit (loss) for the year ended 30 September 20X9	47,200	21,000	(5,000)
Dividends paid (26 September 20X9)	nil	(8,000)	nil

The following information is relevant:

17-12 = 5000/5 × 6/12
= 4500

(i) The fair values of the net assets of Salva at the date of acquisition were equal to their carrying amounts with the exception of an item of plant which had a carrying amount of $12 million and a fair value of $17 million. This plant had a remaining life of five years (straight-line depreciation) at the date of acquisition of Salva. All depreciation is charged to cost of sales.

In addition, Salva owns the registration of a popular internet domain name. The registration, which had a negligible cost, has a five year remaining life (at the date of acquisition); however, it is renewable indefinitely at a nominal cost. At the date of acquisition the domain name was valued by a specialist company at $20 million.

The fair values of the plant and the domain name have not been reflected in Salva's financial statements.

No fair value adjustments were required on the acquisition of the investment in Ambra.

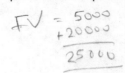

[handwritten top: Intragroup Interest   50 000 × 0·08 = 4000 × 6/12 = 2000   Finance cost = Dr/Cr]

(ii)   Immediately after its acquisition of Salva, Pandar invested $50 million in an 8% loan note from Salva. All interest accruing to 30 September 20X9 had been accounted for by both companies. Salva also has other loans in issue at 30 September 20X9.

(iii)   Pandar has credited the whole of the dividend it received from Salva to investment income.

[handwritten left margin: 15000 Dr Revenue Cr Cos 1000 Dr Cus Cr Inventory]

(iv)   After the acquisition, Pandar sold goods to Salva for $15 million on which Pandar made a gross profit of 20%. Salva had one third of these goods still in its inventory at 30 September 20X9. There are no intra-group current account balances at 30 September 20X9.   *[handwritten: 15000 × 20/100 × 1/3 = 1000 PUP]*

(v)   The non-controlling interest in Salva is to be valued at its (full) fair value at the date of acquisition. For this purpose Salva's share price at that date can be taken to be indicative of the fair value of the shareholding of the non-controlling interest.

(vi)   The goodwill of Salva has not suffered any impairment; however, due to its losses, the value of Pandar's investment in Ambra has been impaired by $3 million at 30 September 20X9.

(vii)   All items in the above statements of profit or loss are deemed to accrue evenly over the year unless otherwise indicated.

Required

(a)   (i)   Calculate the goodwill arising on the acquisition of Salva at 1 April 20X9.

        (ii)   Calculate the carrying amount of the investment in Ambra to be included within the consolidated statement of financial position as at 30 September 20X9.

(b)   Prepare the consolidated statement of profit or loss for the Pandar Group for the year ended 30 September 20X9.

[handwritten: NCI 10000 × 40% × 2/3 × 6.50]

34 Viagem (12/12 amended)   **27 mins**

[handwritten: 250   Cost 10000 × 2/3 × 90% × 476]

On 1 January 20X2, Viagem acquired 90% of the equity share capital of Greca in a share exchange in which Viagem issued two new shares for every three shares it acquired in Greca. Additionally, on 31 December 20X2, Viagem will pay the shareholders of Greca $1.76 per share acquired. Viagem's cost of capital is 10% per annum.

[handwritten: Deferred]

At the date of acquisition, shares in Viagem and Greca had a stock market value of $6.50 and $2.50 each respectively.

[handwritten: 9/12]

STATEMENTS OF PROFIT OR LOSS FOR THE YEAR ENDED 30 SEPTEMBER 20X2

	Viagem	Greca
	$'000	$'000
Revenue	64,600	38,000 *28500*
Cost of sales	(51,200)	(26,000) *19500*
Gross profit	13,400	12,000
Distribution costs	(1,600)	(1,800) *1350*
Administrative expenses	(3,800)	(2,400) *1800*
Investment income	500	–
Finance costs *Share of P/L of associate 2000*	(420)	–
Profit before tax	8,080	7,800 *5850*
Income tax expense	(2,800)	(1,600) *1200*
Profit for the year	5,280	6,200
Equity as at 1 October 20X1		
Equity shares of $1 each	30,000	10,000
Retained earnings	54,000	35,000

The following information is relevant:

(i)   At the date of acquisition the fair values of Greca's assets were equal to their carrying amounts with the exception of two items:

1　An item of plant had a fair value of $1.8 million above its carrying amount. The remaining life of the plant at the date of acquisition was three years. Depreciation is charged to cost of sales.

2　Greca had a contingent liability which Viagem estimated to have a fair value of $450,000. This has not changed as at 30 September 20X2.　*less 450 000*

Greca has not incorporated these fair value changes into its financial statements.

(ii)　Viagem's policy is to value the non-controlling interest at fair value at the date of acquisition. For this purpose, Greca's share price at that date can be deemed to be representative of the fair value of the shares held by the non-controlling interest.

Handwritten: + nfd of year = 6200 × 9/12   Dep @ FVA goodwill = (450) plant = (2000)   = 2200 × 10/ = 220

(iii)　Sales from Viagem to Greca throughout the year ended 30 September 20X2 had consistently been $800,000 per month. Viagem made a mark-up on cost of 25% on these sales. Greca had $1.5 million of these goods in inventory as at 30 September 20X2.

(iv)　Viagem's investment income is a dividend received from its investment in a 40% owned associate which it has held for several years. The underlying earnings for the associate for the year ended 30 September 20X2 were $2 million.

(v)　Although Greca has been profitable since its acquisition by Viagem, the market for Greca's products has been badly hit in recent months and Viagem has calculated that the goodwill has been impaired by $2 million as at 30 September 20X2.

Required

Prepare the consolidated statement of profit or loss for Viagem for the year ended 30 September 20X2. **(15 marks)**

35 Prodigal (6/11 amended)　*160000 ⌄75% × 2/3 ⌄$4*　**54 mins**

On 1 October 20X0 Prodigal purchased 75% of the equity shares in Sentinel. The acquisition was through a share exchange of two shares in Prodigal for every three shares in Sentinel. The stock market price of Prodigal's shares at 1 October 20X0 was $4 per share. The summarised statements of profit or loss and other comprehensive income for the two companies for the year ended 31 March 20X1 are:

Handwritten: 6/12

	Prodigal	Sentinel
	$'000	$'000
Revenue	450,000	240,000
Cost of sales	(260,000)	(110,000)
Gross profit	190,000	130,000
Distribution costs	(23,600)	(12,000)
Administrative expenses	(27,000)	(23,000)
Finance costs	(1,500)	(1,200)
Profit before tax	137,900	93,800
Income tax expense	(48,000)	(27,800)
Profit for the year	89,900	66,000 ✓
Other comprehensive income		
Gain on revaluation of land (note(i))	2,500	1,000
Loss on fair value of equity financial asset investment	(700)	(400)
	1,800	600
Total comprehensive income for the year	91,700	66,600 A/TA

The following information for the equity of the companies at 1 April 20X0 (ie before the share exchange took place) is available:

	$'000	$'000
Equity shares of $1 each	250,000	160,000 A
Share premium	100,000	nil
Revaluation reserve (land)	8,400	nil
Other equity reserve (re equity financial asset investment)	3,200	2,200 A
Retained earnings	90,000	125,000 A

The following information is relevant:

(i)   Prodigal's policy is to revalue the group's land to market value at the end of each accounting period. Prior to its acquisition, Sentinel's land had been valued at historical cost. During the post-acquisition period Sentinel's land had increased in value over its value at the date of acquisition by $1 million. Sentinel has recognised the revaluation within its own financial statements.

(ii) Immediately after the acquisition of Sentinel on 1 October 20X0, Prodigal transferred an item of plant with a carrying amount of $4 million to Sentinel at an agreed value of $5 million. At this date the plant had a remaining life of two and half years. Prodigal had included the profit on this transfer as a reduction in its depreciation costs. All depreciation is charged to cost of sales.

(iii) After the acquisition Sentinel sold goods to Prodigal for $40 million. These goods had cost Sentinel $30 million. $12 million of the goods sold remained in Prodigal's closing inventory.

(iv) Prodigal's policy is to value the non-controlling interest of Sentinel at the date of acquisition at its fair value which the directors determined to be $100 million.   NCI

(v)   The goodwill of Sentinel has not suffered any impairment.

(vi) All items in the above statements of profit or loss and other comprehensive income are deemed to accrue evenly over the year unless otherwise indicated.

Required

(a)   Calculate the goodwill on acquisition of Sentinel.   **(4 marks)**

(b)   (i)   Prepare the consolidated statement of profit or loss and other comprehensive income of Prodigal for the year ended 31 March 20X1.   **(15 marks)**

      (ii) Prepare the equity section (including the non-controlling interest) of the consolidated statement of financial position of Prodigal as at 31 March 20X1.   **(7 marks)**

(c)   IFRS 3 *Business combinations* permits a non-controlling interest at the date of acquisition to be valued by one of two methods:

      (i)   At its proportionate share of the subsidiary's identifiable net assets; or
      (ii) At its fair value (usually determined by the directors of the parent company).

Required

Explain the difference that the accounting treatment of these alternative methods could have on the consolidated financial statements, including where consolidated goodwill may be impaired.   **(4 marks)**
                                                                                            (Total = 30 marks)

36 Penketh (6/14 amended)

90 × 60% × 1/3 × 54

On 1 October 20X3, Penketh acquired 90 million of Sphere's 150 million $1 equity shares. The acquisition was achieved through a share exchange of one share in Penketh for every three shares in Sphere. At that date the stock market prices of Penketh's and Sphere's shares were $4 and $2·50 per share respectively. Additionally, Penketh will pay $1·54 cash on 30 September 20X4 for each share acquired. Penketh's finance cost is 10% per annum.

× 90m ÷ (1·1)

The retained earnings of Sphere brought forward at 1 April 20X3 were $120 million.

The summarised statements of profit or loss and other comprehensive income for the companies for the year ended 31 March 20X4 are: 6/12

	Penketh	Sphere
	$'000	$'000
Revenue	620,000	310,000 155000
Cost of sales	(400,000)	(150,000) 75000
Gross profit	220,000	160,000
Distribution costs	(40,000)	(20,000) 10000
Administrative expenses	(36,000)	(25,000) 12500
Investment income (note (iii))	5,000	1,600 800
Finance costs	(2,000)	(5,600) 2800
Profit before tax	147,000	111,000
Income tax expense	(45,000)	(31,000) 15500
Profit for the year	102,000	80,000 × 6/12
Other comprehensive income		
Gain/(loss) on revaluation of land (notes (i) and (ii))	(2,200)	3,000
	99,800	83,000

The following information is relevant:

(i)   A fair value exercise conducted on 1 October 20X3 concluded that the carrying amounts of Sphere's net assets were equal to their fair values with the following exceptions:

   • The fair value of Sphere's land was $2 million in excess of its carrying amount.

   • An item of plant had a fair value of $6 million in excess of its carrying amount. The plant had a remaining life of two years at the date of acquisition. Plant depreciation is charged to cost of sales.

   • Penketh placed a value of $5 million on Sphere's good trading relationships with its customers. Penketh expected, on average, a customer relationship to last for a further five years. Amortisation of intangible assets is charged to administrative expenses.

(ii)   Penketh's group policy is to revalue land to market value at the end of each accounting period. Prior to its acquisition, Sphere's land had been valued at historical cost, but it has adopted the group policy since its acquisition. In addition to the fair value increase in Sphere's land of $2 million (see note (i)), it had increased by a further $1 million since the acquisition.

(iii)   On 1 October 20X3, Penketh also acquired 30% of Ventor's equity shares. Ventor's profit after tax for the year ended 31 March 20X4 was $10 million and during March 20X4 Ventor paid a dividend of $6 million. Penketh uses equity accounting in its consolidated financial statements for its investment in Ventor.

   Sphere did not pay any dividends in the year ended 31 March 20X4.

(iv)   After the acquisition Penketh sold goods to Sphere for $20 million. Sphere had one fifth of these goods still in inventory at 31 March 20X4. In March 20X4 Penketh sold goods to Ventor for $15 million, all of which were still in inventory at 31 March 20X4. All sales to Sphere and Ventor had a mark-up on cost of 25%.

(v)   Penketh's policy is to value the non-controlling interest at the date of acquisition at its fair value. For this purpose, the share price of Sphere at that date (1 October 20X3) is representative of the fair value of the shares held by the non-controlling interest.

(vi)   All items in the above statements of profit or loss and other comprehensive income are deemed to accrue evenly over the year unless otherwise indicated.

Required

(a)   Calculate the consolidated goodwill as at 1 October 20X3.   **(6 marks)**

(b)   Prepare the consolidated statement of profit or loss and other comprehensive income of Penketh for the year ended 31 March 20X4.   **(19 marks)**

(c)   A financial assistant has observed that the fair value exercise means that a subsidiary's net assets are included at acquisition at their fair (current) values in the consolidated statement of financial position. The assistant believes that it is inconsistent to aggregate the subsidiary's net assets with those of the parent because most of the parent's assets are carried at historical cost.

Comment on the assistant's observation and explain why the net assets of acquired subsidiaries are consolidated at acquisition at their fair values.   **(5 marks)**

(Total = 30 marks)

Cost of Investment   2500
Share of Post acq profit (6400 - 5300) x 30%   330
Purp (700 x 30/130)   (03)
                                                                     ─────
                                                                      2707
                                                                     ─────

37 Multiple choice questions – accounting for associates

1   On 1 October 20X8 Pacemaker acquired 30 million of Vardine's 100 million shares in exchange for 75 million of its own shares. The stock market value of Pacemaker's shares at the date of this share exchange was $1.60 each.

Vardine's profit is subject to seasonal variation. Its profit for the year ended 31 March 20X9 was $100 million. $20 million of this profit was made from 1 April 20X8 to 30 September 20X8.

Pacemaker has one subsidiary and no other investments apart from Vardine.

What amount will be shown as 'investment in associate' in the consolidated statement of financial position of Pacemaker as at 31 March 20X9? 6/12

Handwritten annotations:
Cost (75m x $1.60) → 120
Share of post-acquisition retained Earnings (100-20) x30% → 24
→ 144

A $144 million
B $150 million
C $78 million
D $126 million

(2 marks)

2   How should an associate be accounted for in the consolidated statement of profit or loss?

A   The associate's income and expenses are added to those of the group on a line-by-line basis.

B   The group share of the associate's income and expenses is added to the group figures on a line-by-line basis.

Handwritten annotation: line by line treatment would be correct for a subsidiary, not a associate - The dividends received from the associate are all that is recorded in the individual entity financial statements of the parent, but in the CFS this is replaced by the group share of profit after tax.

C   The group share of the associate's profit after tax is recorded as a one-line entry.

D   Only dividends received from the associate are recorded in the group statement of profit or loss.

2 marks)

3   Wellington owns 30% of Boot, which it purchased on 1 May 20X7 for $2.5 million. At that date Boot had retained earnings of $5.3 million. At the year end date of 31 October 20X7 Boot had retained earnings of $6.4 million after paying out a dividend of $1 million. On 30 September 20X7 Wellington sold $700,000 of goods to Boot, on which it made 30% profit. Boot had resold none of these goods by 31 October.

At what amount will Wellington record its investment in Boot in its consolidated statement of financial position at 31 October 20X7?

Handwritten annotations:
Cost of Investment → 10000
Share of post-acquisition profit (3000 x 4/12)-1000 x3% → 350
Impairment → (500)
→ 9850

A $2,767,000
B $2,900,000
C $2,830,000
D $2,620,000

(2 marks)

4   On 1 February 20X1 Picardy acquired 35% of the equity shares of Avignon, its only associate, for $10 million in cash. The post-tax profit of Avignon for the year to 30 September 20X1 was $3 million. Profits accrued evenly throughout the year. Avignon made a dividend payment of $1 million on 1 September 20X1. At 30 September 20X1 Picardy decided that an impairment loss of $500,000 should be recognised on its investment in Avignon.

What amount will be shown as 'investment in associate' in the statement of financial position of Picardy as at 30 September 20X1?

Handwritten annotations:
Cost of Investment → 10000
Share of post acq profit (3000 x 8/12)-1000 x3% → 350
Impairment → (500)
→ 9850

A $9,967,000
B $9,850,000
C $9,200,000
D $10,200,000

(2 marks)

5   Jarvis owns 30% of McLintock. During the year to 31 December 20X4 McLintock sold $2 million of goods to Jarvis, of which 40% were still held in inventory by Jarvis at the year end. McLintock applies a mark-up of 25% on all goods sold.

What effect would the above transactions have on group inventory at 31 December 20X4?

A   Debit group inventory $48,000 $(2000 \times 25/125) \times 30\% = 48000$
B   Debit group inventory $160,000 $\times 40\%$
Ⓒ   Credit group inventory $48,000
D   No effect on group inventory   **(2 marks)**

6   An associate is an entity in which an investor has significant influence over the investee.

Which of the following indicate(s) the presence of significant influence?   *20 or more 'n sig*

(i)   The investor owns 330,000 of the 1,500,000 equity voting shares of the investee. *22%   not sig*

(ii)   The investor has representation on the board of directors of the investee. ✓

(iii) The investor is able to insist that all of the sales of the investee are made to a subsidiary of the investor.

(iv)   The investor controls the votes of a majority of the board members. *≡*

Ⓐ   (i) and (ii) only
B   (i), (ii) and (iii)
C   (ii) and (iii) only
D   All four   **(2 marks)**

7   The Caddy group acquired 240,000 of August's 800,000 equity shares for $6 per share on 1 April 20X4. August's profit after tax for the year ended 30 September 20X4 was $400,000 and it paid an equity dividend on 20 September 20X4 of $150,000.

On the assumption that August is an associate of Caddy, what would be the carrying amount of the investment in August in the consolidated statement of financial position of Caddy as at 30 September 20X4?

Ⓐ $1,455,000   *Cost of Investment - 240 × 6*   *1440*
B $1,500,000   *Share of post acq ((2400 × 6/12) - 150) × 30%*   *15*
C $1,515,000   *―――*
D $1,395,000   *1455*
                                                                                       (2 marks)

38 Preparation question: Laurel

CONSOLIDATED STATEMENT OF FINANCIAL POSITION   *sub*

Laurel acquired 80% of the ordinary share capital of Hardy for $160m and 40% of the ordinary share capital of Comic for $70m on 1 January 20X7 when the retained earnings balances were $64m in Hardy and $24m in Comic. Laurel, Comic and Hardy are public limited companies.   *associate*

The statements of financial position of the three companies at 31 December 20X9 are set out below:

	Laurel	Hardy	Comic
	$m	$m	$m
Non-current assets			
Property, plant and equipment	220	160	78
Investments	230	-	-
	450	160	78
Current assets			
Inventories	384	234	122
Trade receivables	275	166	67
Cash at bank	42	10	34
	701	410	223
	1,151	570	301

Equity			
Share capital – $1 ordinary shares	400	96	80
Share premium	16	3	-
Retained earnings	278	128	97
	694	227	177
Current liabilities			
Trade payables	457	343	124
	1,151	570	301

You are also given the following information:

1 On 30 November 20X9 Laurel sold some goods to Hardy for cash for $32m. These goods had originally cost $22m and none had been sold by the year end. On the same date Laurel also sold goods to Comic for cash for $22m. These goods originally cost $10m and Comic had sold half by the year end.

2 On 1 January 20X7 Hardy owned some items of equipment with a book value of $45m that had a fair value of $57m. These assets were originally purchased by Hardy on 1 January 20X5 and are being depreciated over 6 years.

3 Group policy is to measure non-controlling interests at acquisition at fair value. The fair value of the non-controlling interests in Hardy on 1 January 20X7 was calculated as $39m.

4 Cumulative impairment losses on recognised goodwill amounted to $15m at 31 December 20X9. No impairment losses have been necessary to date relating to the investment in the associate.

Required

Prepare a consolidated statement of financial position for Laurel and its subsidiary as at 31 December 20X9, incorporating its associate in accordance with IAS 28. Use the following pro-forma.

PROFORMA SOLUTION

LAUREL GROUP – CONSOLIDATED STATEMENT OF FINANCIAL POSITION AS AT 31 DECEMBER 20X9

	$m
Non-current assets	
Property, plant and equipment	
Goodwill	
Investment in associate	_____
	_____
Current assets	
Inventories	
Trade receivables	
Cash	_____
	_____
	_____
Equity attributable to owners of the parent	
Share capital – $1 ordinary shares	
Share premium	
Retained earnings	_____
Non-controlling interests	_____
	_____
Current liabilities	
Trade payables	_____
	_____

Workings

1   *Group structure*

2   *Goodwill*

	$m	$m
Consideration transferred		
Non-controlling interests (at 'full' fair value)		
Fair value of net assets at acq'n:		
Share capital		
Share premium		
Retained earnings		
Fair value adjustment (W7)	____	
		____
Impairment losses		____
		____

3   *Investment in associate*

	$m
Cost of associate	
Share of post acquisition retained reserves (W4)	
Unrealised profit (W6)	
Impairment losses	____
	____

4   *Consolidated retained earnings*

	Laurel $m	Hardy $m	Comic $m
Per question			
Less: provision for unrealised profit re Hardy (W6)			
provision for unrealised profit re Comic (W6)			
Fair value adjustment movement (W7)			
Less: pre-acquisition retained earnings		____	____
Group share of post-acquisition retained earnings:			
Hardy			
Comic			
Less: group share of impairment losses	____		
	____		

5   *Non-controlling interests*

	$m
Non-controlling interests at acquisition (W2)	
NCI share of post-acquisition retained earnings:	
Hardy	
Less: NCI share of impairment losses	____
	____

6   Unrealised profit

     Laurel's sales to Hardy:

         Dr

         Cr

     Laurel's sales to Comic (associate):

         Dr

         Cr

7   Fair value adjustments

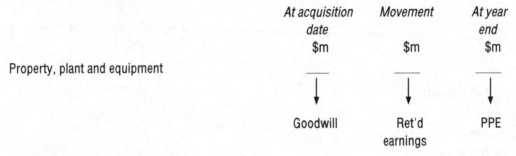

	At acquisition date $m	Movement $m	At year end $m
Property, plant and equipment	↓	↓	↓
	Goodwill	Ret'd earnings	PPE

39 Preparation question: Tyson

CONSOLIDATED STATEMENT OF PROFIT OR LOSS AND OTHER COMPREHENSIVE INCOME

Below are the statements of profit or loss and other comprehensive income of Tyson, its subsidiary Douglas and associate Frank at 31 December 20X8. Tyson, Douglas and Frank are public limited companies.

	Tyson $m	Douglas $m	Frank $m
Revenue ← 66	500	150	70
Cost of sales ← 66 +18	(270)	(80)	(30)
Gross profit	230	70	40
Other expenses +15 (impairment)	(150)	(20)	(15)
Finance income	15	10	–
Finance costs share of associate (10×40%)−2H	(20)	–	(10)
Profit before tax	75	60	15
Income tax expense	(25)	(15)	(5)
PROFIT FOR THE YEAR	50	45	10
Other comprehensive income:			
Gains on property revaluation, net of tax (5×40%)	20	10	5
TOTAL COMPREHENSIVE INCOME FOR THE YEAR	70	55	15

share of CI of associate

You are also given the following information:

1   Tyson acquired 80m shares in Douglas for $188m three years ago when Douglas had a credit balance on its reserves of $40m. Douglas has 100m $1 ordinary shares.

2   Tyson acquired 40m shares in Frank for $60m two years ago when that company had a credit balance on its reserves of $20m. Frank has 100m $1 ordinary shares.

3   During the year Douglas sold some goods to Tyson for $66m (cost $48m). None of the goods had been sold by the year end.   66 − 48 = 18

4   Group policy is to measure non-controlling interests at acquisition at fair value. The fair value of the non-controlling interests in Douglas at acquisition was $40m. An impairment test carried out at the year end

	PFY	TCI
PFY/TCI per q	45	55
PUP	(18)	(18)
impairment	(15)	(15)
	12	22
NCI × 20%	2.4	4.4

resulted in $15m of the recognised goodwill relating to Douglas being written off and recognition of impairment losses of $2.4m relating to the investment in Frank.

Required

Prepare the consolidated statement of profit or loss and other comprehensive income for the year ended 31 December 20X8 for Tyson, incorporating its associate.

PROFORMA SOLUTION

TYSON GROUP - CONSOLIDATED STATEMENT OF PROFIT OR LOSS AND OTHER COMPREHENSIVE INCOME FOR THE YEAR ENDED 31 DECEMBER 20X8

	$m
Revenue	
Cost of sales	
Gross profit	____
Other expenses	
Finance income	
Finance costs	
Share of profit of associate	
Profit before tax	____
Income tax expense	
PROFIT FOR THE YEAR	____
Other comprehensive income:	____
Gains on property revaluation, net of tax	
Share of other comprehensive income of associates	
Other comprehensive income for the year, net of tax	____
TOTAL COMPREHENSIVE INCOME FOR THE YEAR	____
Profit attributable to:	
Owners of the parent	
Non-controlling interests	____
	____
Total comprehensive income attributable to:	
Owners of the parent	
Non-controlling interests	____
	____

Workings

1   *Group structure*

2   *Non-controlling interests*

	PFY $m	TCI $m
PFY/TCI per question		
Unrealised profit (W3)		
Impairment loss		
	____	____
× NCI share	____	____

3   *Unrealised profit*

	$m
Selling price	
Cost	___
Provision for unrealised profit	___

40 Preparation question: Plateau (12/07 amended)

On 1 October 20X6 Plateau acquired the following non-current investments:

- 3 million equity shares in Savannah by an exchange of one share in Plateau for every two shares in Savannah plus $1.25 per acquired Savannah share in cash. The market price of each Plateau share at the date of acquisition was $6 and the market price of each Savannah share at the date of acquisition was $3.25.

- 30% of the equity shares of Axle at a cost of $7.50 per share in cash.

Only the cash consideration of the above investments has been recorded by Plateau. In addition $500,000 of professional costs relating to the acquisition of Savannah are also included in the cost of the investment.

The summarised draft statements of financial position of the three companies at 30 September 20X7 are:

	Plateau $'000	Savannah $'000	Axle $'000
Non-current assets			
Property, plant and equipment	18,400	10,400	18,000
Investments in Savannah and Axle	13,250	nil	nil
Investments in equity instruments	6,500	nil	Nil
	38,150	10,400	18,000
Current assets			
Inventory	6,900	6,200	3,600
Trade receivables	3,200	1,500	2,400
Total assets	48,250	18,100	24,000
Equity and liabilities			
Equity shares of $1 each	10,000	4,000	4,000
Retained earnings			
– at 30 September 20X6	16,000	6,000	11,000
– for year ended 30 September 20X7	9,250	2,900	5,000
	35,250	12,900	20,000
Non-current liabilities			
7% Loan notes	5,000	1,000	1,000
Current liabilities	8,000	4,200	3,000
Total equity and liabilities	48,250	18,100	24,000

The following information is relevant.

(i)   At the date of acquisition Savannah had five years remaining of an agreement to supply goods to one of its major customers. Savannah believes it is highly likely that the agreement will be renewed when it expires. The directors of Plateau estimate that the value of this customer based contract has a fair value of £1 million and an indefinite life and has not suffered any impairment.

(ii)   On 1 October 20X6, Plateau sold an item of plant to Savannah at its agreed fair value of $2.5 million. Its carrying amount prior to the sale was $2 million. The estimated remaining life of the plant at the date of sale was five years (straight-line depreciation).

(iii) During the year ended 30 September 20X7 Savannah sold goods to Plateau for $2.7 million. Savannah had marked up these goods by 50% on cost. Plateau had a third of the goods still in its inventory at 30 September 20X7. There were no intra-group payables/receivables at 30 September 20X7.

(iv)   Impairment tests on 30 September 20X7 concluded that neither consolidated goodwill nor the value of the investment in Axle were impaired.

(v)   The investments in equity instruments are included in Plateau's statement of financial position (above) at their fair value on 1 October 20X6, but they have a fair value of $9 million at 30 September 20X7.

(vi)   No dividends were paid during the year by any of the companies.

(vii)   It is the group policy to value non-controlling interest at acquisition at full (or fair) value. For this purpose the share price of Savannah at this date should be used.

Required

Prepare the consolidated statement of financial position for Plateau as at 30 September 20X7.

41 Paladin (12/11 amended)   54 mins

On 1 October 20X0, Paladin secured a majority equity shareholding in Saracen on the following terms.

An immediate payment of $4 per share on 1 October 20X0; and a further amount deferred until 1 October 20X1 of $5.4 million.

The immediate payment has been recorded in Paladin's financial statements, but the deferred payment has not been recorded. Paladin's cost of capital is 8% per annum.

On 1 February 20X1, Paladin also acquired 25% of the equity shares of Augusta paying $10 million in cash.

The summarised statements of financial position of the three companies at 30 September 20X1 are:

	Paladin $'000	Saracen $'000	Augusta $'000
Assets			
Non-current assets			
Property, plant and equipment	40,000	31,000	30,000
Intangible assets	7,500		
Investments – Saracen (8 million shares at $4 each)	32,000		
– Augusta	10,000	nil	nil
	89,500	31,000	30,000
Current assets			
Inventory	11,200	8,400	10,000
Trade receivables	7,400	5,300	5,000
Bank	3,400	nil	2,000
Total assets	111,500	44,700	47,000
Equity and liabilities			
Equity			
Equity shares of $1 each	50,000	10,000	10,000
Retained earnings – at 1 October 20X0	25,700	12,000	31,800
– for year ended 30 September 20X1	9,200	6,000	1,200
	84,900	28,000	43,000
Non-current liabilities			
Deferred tax	15,000	8,000	1,000
Current liabilities			
Bank	nil	2,500	nil
Trade payables	11,600	6,200	3,000
Total equity and liabilities	111,500	44,700	47,000

The following information is relevant:

(i)   Paladin's policy is to value the non-controlling interest at fair value at the date of acquisition. For this purpose the directors of Paladin considered a share price for Saracen of $3.50 per share to be appropriate.

(ii)   At the date of acquisition, the fair values of Saracen's property, plant and equipment was equal to its carrying amount with the exception of Saracen's plant which had a fair value of $4 million above its carrying amount. At that date the plant had a remaining life of four years. Saracen uses straight-line depreciation for plant assuming a nil residual value.

Also at the date of acquisition, Paladin valued Saracen's customer relationships as a customer base intangible asset at fair value of $3 million. Saracen has not accounted for this asset. Trading relationships with Saracen's customers last on average for six years.

(iii)   At 30 September 20X1, Saracen's inventory included goods bought from Paladin (at cost to Saracen) of $2.6 million. Paladin had marked up these goods by 30% on cost. Paladin's agreed current account balance owed by Saracen at 30 September 20X1 was $1.3 million.

(iv)   Impairment tests were carried out on 30 September 20X1 which concluded that consolidated goodwill was not impaired, but, due to disappointing earnings, the value of the investment in Augusta was impaired by $2.5 million.

(v)   Assume all profits accrue evenly through the year.

Required

(a)   Prepare the consolidated statement of financial position for Paladin as at 30 September 20X1.   **(25 marks)**

(b)   At 30 September 20X1 the other equity shares (75%) in Augusta were owned by many separate investors. Shortly after this date Spekulate (a company unrelated to Paladin) accumulated a 65% interest in Augusta by buying shares from the other shareholders. In May 20X2 a meeting of the board of directors of Augusta was held at which Paladin lost its seat on Augusta's board.

Required

Explain, with reasons, the accounting treatment Paladin should adopt for its investment in Augusta when it prepares its financial statements for the year ending 30 September 20X2.   **(5 marks)**

(Total = 30 marks)

42 Multiple choice questions – financial instruments

1   Which of the following are **not** classified as financial instruments under IAS 32 *Financial Instruments: Presentation*?

A   Share options   *There do not give rise to a present right to receive cash or*
B   Intangible assets   *other financial assets.*
C   Trade receivables   *The other exam options are financial instrument*
D   Redeemable preference shares

(2 marks)

---

2   An 8% $30 million convertible loan note was issued on 1 April 20X5 at par. Interest is payable in arrears on 31 March each year. The loan note is redeemable at par on 31 March 20X8 or convertible into equity shares at the option of the loan note holders on the basis of 30 shares for each $100 of loan. A similar instrument without the conversion option would have an interest rate of 10% per annum.

The present values of $1 receivable at the end of each year based on discount rates of 8% and 10% are:

	8%	10%
End of year 1	0.93	0.91
2	0.86	0.83
3	0.79	0.75
Cumulative	2.58	2.49

Interest years (1-3) (30m × 8/. × 2.49)   5976
Repayment year 3 (30m × 0.75)   22500
Debt component   28476
Equity option (β)   1524
30 000

What amount will be credited to equity on 1 April 20X5 in respect of this financial instrument?

A $5,976,000   *$12500 × 1296/1200*   *13500*
B $1,524,000   *carrying amount*   *(12500)*
C $324,000   *Gain*   *1000*
D $9,000,000

(2 marks)

---

3   Dexon's draft statement of financial position as at 31 March 20X8 shows financial assets at fair value through profit or loss with a carrying amount of $12.5 million as at 1 April 20X7.

These financial assets are held in a fund whose value changes directly in proportion to a specified market index. At 1 April 20X7 the relevant index was 1,200 and at 31 March 20X8 it was 1,296.

What amount of gain or loss should be recognised at 31 March 20X8 in respect of these assets?

A $1,000,000 gain   *$125000 × 1296 /1200*   *13500*
B $96,000 gain   *carrying amount*   *(12500)*
C $1,000,000 loss   *Gain*   *1000*
D $96,000 loss

(2 marks)

---

4   A 5% loan note was issued on 1 April 20X0 at its face value of $20 million. Direct costs of the issue were $500,000. The loan note will be redeemed on 31 March 20X3 at a substantial premium. The effective interest rate applicable is 10% per annum.

At what amount will the loan note appear in the statement of financial position as at 31 March 20X2?

A $21,000,000
B $20,450,000
C $22,100,000
D $21,495,000

(2 marks)

Proceeds (20m – 0.5m)   19500
Interest 10%.   1950
Interest paid (20m × 5%)   (1000)
Balance 30 March 20X1   20450
*   2045*
Interest 10%.
Interest paid (20m × 5%)   (1000)
*   21495*

5 On 1 January 20X8 a company purchased 40,000 $1 listed equity shares at a price of $3 per share. An irrevocable election was made to recognise the shares at fair value through other comprehensive income. Transaction costs were $3,000. At the year end of 31 December 20X8 the shares were trading at $6 per share.

What amount in respect of these shares will be shown under 'investments in equity instruments' in the statement of financial position as at 31 December 20X8?

A $243,000
B $240,000
C $237,000
D $123,000

40000 share @ $6 240000
Transaction cost 3000
243000

(2 marks)

43 Bertrand (12/11 amended)

27 mins

Bertrand issued $10 million convertible loan notes on 1 October 20X0 that carry a nominal interest (coupon) rate of 5% per annum. They are redeemable on 30 September 20X3 at par for cash or can be exchanged for equity shares in Bertrand on the basis of 20 shares for each $100 of loan. A similar loan note, without the conversion option, would have required Bertrand to pay an interest rate of 8%.

When preparing the draft financial statements for the year ended 30 September 20X1, the directors are proposing to show the loan note within equity in the statement of financial position, as they believe all the loan note holders will choose the equity option when the loan note is due for redemption. They further intend to charge a finance cost of $500,000 ($10 million × 5%) in profit or loss for each year up to the date of redemption.

The present value of $1 receivable at the end of each year, based on discount rates of 5% and 8%, can be taken as:

		5%	8%
End of year	1	0.95	0.93
	2	0.91	0.86
	3	0.86	0.79

Required

(a) (i) Explain why the nominal interest rate on the convertible loan notes is 5%, but for non-convertible loan notes it would be 8%. **(2 marks)**

(ii) Briefly comment on the impact of the directors' proposed treatment of the loan notes on the financial statements and the acceptability of this treatment. **(3 marks)**

(b) Prepare extracts to show how the loan notes and the finance charge should be treated by Bertrand in its financial statements for the year ended 30 September 20X1. **(5 marks)**

(c) On 1 January 20X0, Jedders issued $15m of 7% convertible loan notes at par. The loan notes are convertible into equity shares in the company, at the option of the note holders, five years after the date of issue (31 December 20X4) on the basis of 25 shares for each $100 of loan stock. Alternatively, the loan notes will be redeemed at par.

Jedders has been advised by Fab Factors that, had the company issued similar loan notes without the conversion rights, then it would have had to pay interest of 10%; the rate is thus lower because the conversion rights are favourable.

Fab Factors also suggest that, as some of the loan note holders will choose to convert, the loan notes are, in substance, equity and should be treated as such on Jedders' statement of financial position. Thus, as well as a reduced finance cost being achieved to boost profitability, Jedders' gearing has been improved compared to a straight issue of debt.

The present value of $1 receivable at the end of each year, based on discount rates of 7% and 10% can be taken as:

End of year	7%	10%
1	0.93	0.91
2	0.87	0.83
3	0.82	0.75
4	0.76	0.68
5	0.71	0.62

Required

In relation to the 7% convertible loan notes, calculate the finance cost to be shown in the statement of profit or loss and the statement of financial position extracts for the year to 31 December 20X0 for Jedders and comment on the advice from Fab Factors. **(5 marks)**

(Total = 15 marks)

44 Multiple choice questions – leasing

1 On 1 January 20X6 Fellini hired a machine under a finance lease. The cash price of the machine was $3.5 million and the present value of the minimum lease payments was $3.3 million. Instalments of $700,000 are payable annually in advance with the first payment made on 1 January 20X6. The interest rate implicit in the lease is 6%.

What amount will appear under non-current liabilities in respect of this lease in the statement of financial position of Fellini at 31 December 20X7?

- (A) $1,479,000
- B $2,179,000
- C $1,702,000
- D $2,266,000

(handwritten working:)
cum Noncurr
at 1.01.06 PV 3 300
payment (700)
Balance 2600
Int 6% 156
at 1.12.06 Balance 2756
at 1.12.06
Payment 2756
Balance (700)
Interest 2056
123
2179

(2 marks)

2 Which of the following situations does **not** suggest that a leasing arrangement constitutes a finance lease?

- (A) The present value of the minimum lease payments is substantially less than the fair value of the asset. *(handwritten: operating lease)*
- B Ownership in the asset is transferred at the end of the lease term.
- C The lease term is for a major part of the asset's useful life.
- D The lease contains a purchase option at a price below fair value, which is reasonably certain to be exercised.

(2 marks)

3 A company acquired an item of plant under a finance lease on 1 April 20X7. The present value of the minimum lease payments was $15.6 million and the rentals are $6 million per annum paid in arrears for three years on 31 March each year.

The interest rate implicit in the lease is 8% per annum.

What amount will appear under current liabilities in respect of this lease in the statement of financial position at 31 March 20X8?

- (A) $5,132,000
- B $5,716,000
- C $6,000,000
- D $4,752,000

(handwritten working:)
PV 15600
Int 8% 1248
Pay (6000)
Bal 31.3.08 10848
Int 8% 868
Pay (6000)
Bal 31.3.09 5716

10848 – 5716
= 5132

(2 marks)

4 On 1 January 20X6 Platinum entered into a finance lease agreement. The cash price of the asset was $360,000 and the terms of the lease were a deposit of $120,000 payable on 1 January 20X6 and three further instalments of $100,000 payable on 31 December 20X6, 31 December 20X7 and 31 December 20X8. The rate of interest implicit in the lease is 12%.

What will be the amount of the finance charge arising from this lease which will be charged to profit or loss for the year ended 31 December 20X7?

- A $28,800
- (B) $20,256
- C $16,800
- D $14,400

(handwritten working:)
cash price 360 000
Deposit 120 000
240 000
Int 12% 28 800
Payment (100 000)
Bal at 3.12.06 168 800
20256

(2 marks)

5 At what amount does IAS 17 *Leases* require a lessee to capitalise an asset acquired under a finance lease?

- A Cash price of the asset
- B Fair value of the asset
- C Present value of minimum lease payments
- (D) Lower of fair value and present value of minimum lease payments

(2 marks)

6   On 1 October 20X3, Fresco acquired an item of plant under a five-year finance lease agreement. The plant had a cash purchase cost of $25 million. The agreement had an implicit finance cost of 10% per annum and required an immediate deposit of $2 million and annual rentals of $6 million paid on 30 September each year for five years.

What would be the current liability for the leased plant in Fresco's statement of financial position as at 30 September 20X4?

A $19,300,000
B $4,070,000
C $5,000,000
D $3,850,000

(2 marks)

7   The objective of IAS 17 *Leases* is to prescribe the appropriate accounting treatment and required disclosures in relation to leases.

Which **two** of the following situations would normally lead to a lease being classified as a finance lease?

(i)   The lease transfers ownership of the asset to the lessee by the end of the lease term

(ii)   The lease term is for approximately half of the economic life of the asset

(iii)   The lease assets are of a specialised nature such that only the lessee can use them without major modifications being made

(iv)   At the inception of the lease, the present value of the minimum lease payments is 60% of what the leased asset would cost to purchase

A   (i) and (ii)
B   (i) and (iii)
C   (ii) and (iii)
D   (iii) and (iv)

(2 marks)

8   Tourmalet sold an item of plant for $50 million on 1 April 20X4. The plant had a carrying amount of $40 million at the date of sale, which was charged to cost of sales. On the same date, Tourmalet entered into an agreement to lease back the plant for the next five years (being the estimated remaining life of the plant) at a cost of $14 million per annum payable annually in arrears. An arrangement of this type is normally deemed to have a financing cost of 10% per annum.

What amount will be shown as income from this transaction in the statement of profit or loss for the year ended 30 September 20X4?

A $10 million
B $2 million
C $1 million
D   Nil

(2 marks)

45 Preparation question: Branch

Branch acquired an item of plant and equipment on a finance lease on 1 January 20X1. The terms of the agreement were:

Deposit	:	$1,150 (non-refundable)
Instalments	:	$4,000 pa for seven years payable in arrears
Cash price	:	$20,000

The asset has useful life of four years and the interest rate implicit in the lease is 11%.

Required

Prepare extracts from the statement of profit or loss and statement of financial position for the year ending 31 December 20X1, using the following pro-forma.

Workings

STATEMENT OF PROFIT OR LOSS (EXTRACT) $
Depreciation
Finance costs

STATEMENT OF FINANCIAL POSITION (EXTRACT) $
Non-current assets
Property, plant and equipment – assets held under finance leases

Non-current liabilities
Finance lease liabilities

Current liabilities
Finance lease liabilities

46 Fino (12/07 amended)   27 mins

(a)   An important requirement of the IASB's *Conceptual Framework for Financial Reporting* is that an entity's
      financial statements should represent faithfully the transactions and events that it has undertaken.

      Required

      Explain what is meant by faithful representation and how it makes financial information useful.   **(5 marks)**

(b)   On 1 April 20X7, Fino increased the operating capacity of its plant. Due to a lack of liquid funds it was unable
      to buy the required plant which had a cost of $350,000. This was equal to both the fair value of the plant and
      the present value of the minimum lease payments under the lease. On the recommendation of the finance
      director, Fino entered into an agreement to lease the plant from the manufacturer. The lease required four
      annual payments in advance of $100,000 each commencing on 1 April 20X7. The plant would have a useful
      life of four years and would be scrapped at the end of this period. The finance director, believing the lease to
      be an operating lease, commented that the agreement would improve the company's return on capital
      employed (compared to outright purchase of the plant).

      Required

      (i)   Discuss the validity of the finance director's comment and describe how IAS 17 *Leases* ensures that
             leases such as the above are faithfully represented in an entity's financial statements.   **(4 marks)**

      (ii)   Prepare extracts of Fino's statement of profit or loss and statement of financial position for the year
             ended 30 September 20X7 in respect of the rental agreement assuming:

             (1)   It is an operating lease   **(2 marks)**
             (2)   It is a finance lease (use an implicit interest rate of 10% per annum)   **(4 marks)**
                                                                                      (Total = 15 marks)

47 Multiple choice questions – provisions and events after the reporting period

1   Candel is being sued by a customer for $2 million for breach of contract over a cancelled order. Candel has obtained legal opinion that there is a 20% chance that Candel will lose the case. Accordingly Candel has provided $400,000 ($2 million × 20%) in respect of the claim. The unrecoverable legal costs of defending the action are estimated at $100,000. These have not been provided for as the case will not go to court until next year.

What is the amount of the provision that should be made by Candel in accordance with IAS 37 *Provisions, Contingent Liabilities and Contingent Assets* ?

A $2,000,000   *Loss of the case is not 'probable', so no provision is made, but*
B $2,100,000   *the legal costs will have to be paid so should be provided for.*
C $500,000
(D) $100,000   **(2 marks)**

---

2   During the year Peterlee acquired an iron ore mine at a cost of $6 million. In addition, when all the ore has been extracted (estimated ten years' time) the company will face estimated costs for landscaping the area affected by the mining that have a present value of $2 million. These costs would still have to be incurred even if no further ore was extracted.

How should this $2 million future cost be recognised in the financial statements?

(A)   Provision $2 million and $2 million capitalised as part of cost of mine *it will then be depreciated*
B   Provision $2 million and $2 million charged to operating costs *over the useful life.*
C   Accrual $200,000 per annum for next ten years
D   Should not be recognised as no cost has yet arisen   **(2 marks)**

---

3   Hopewell sells a line of goods under a six-month warranty. Any defect arising during that period is repaired free of charge. Hopewell has calculated that if all the goods sold in the last six months of the year required repairs the cost would be $2 million. If all of these goods had more serious faults and had to be replaced the cost would be $6 million.

The normal pattern is that 80% of goods sold will be fault-free, 15% will require repairs and 5% will have to be replaced.

What is the amount of the provision required?

A $2 million   *2m × 15%*   *0.3*
B $1.6 million   *6m × 5%*   *0.3*
C $6 million   *—————*
(D) $0.6 million   *0.6*   **(2 marks)**

---

4   Which one of the following would **not** be valid grounds for a provision?

A   A company has a policy has a policy of cleaning up any environmental contamination caused by its operations, but is not legally obliged to do so.

B   A company is leasing an office building for which it has no further use. However, it is tied into the lease for another year.

C   A company is closing down a division. The Board has prepared detailed closure plans which have been communicated to customers and employees.

(D)   A company has acquired a machine which requires a major overhaul every three years. The cost of the first overhaul is reliably estimated at $120,000.   **(2 marks)**

The cost of the overhaul will be capitalised when it takes place. No obligation exists ~~between~~ before the overhaul is carried out. The other options would all give rise to valid provisions.

5   Which **two** of the following events which occur after the reporting date of a company but before the financial statements are authorised for issue are classified as **adjusting** events in accordance with IAS 10 *Events After the Reporting Period*?

   (i)   A change in tax rate announced after the reporting date, but affecting the current tax liability
   (ii)   The discovery of a fraud which had occurred during the year
   (iii)   The determination of the sale proceeds of an item of plant sold before the year end
   (iv)   The destruction of a factory by fire

   A   (i) and (ii)
   B   (i) and (iii)
   C   (ii) and (iii)
   D   (iii) and (iv)   **(2 marks)**

   i & iv refer to condition after which arose after the reporting period.

6   Which one of the following events taking place after the year end but before the financial statements were authorised for issue would require adjustment in accordance with IAS 10 *Events after the Reporting Period*?

   A   Three lines of inventory held at the year end were destroyed by flooding in the warehouse.
   B   The directors announced a major restructuring.
   C   Two lines of inventory held at the year end were discovered to have faults rendering them unsaleable.
   D   The value of the company's investments fell sharply.   **(2 marks)**

   we can assume that these faults also existed at the end of the year. so this is the only option which would require adjustment - The others have all taken place after the year end.

48 Promoil (12/08)   27 mins

(a)   The definition of a liability forms an important element of the IASB *Conceptual Framework for Financial Reporting* and is the basis for IAS 37 *Provisions, Contingent Liabilities and Contingent Assets*.

   Required

   Define a liability and describe the circumstances under which provisions should be recognised. Give two examples of how the definition of liabilities enhances the reliability of financial statements.   **(5 marks)**

(b)   On 1 October 20X7, Promoil acquired a newly constructed oil platform at a cost of $30 million together with the right to extract oil from an offshore oilfield under a government licence. The terms of the licence are that Promoil will have to remove the platform (which will then have no value) and restore the sea bed to an environmentally satisfactory condition in ten years' time when the oil reserves have been exhausted. The estimated cost of this in ten years' time will be $15 million. The present value of $1 receivable in ten years at the appropriate discount rate for Promoil of 8% is $0.46.

   Required

   (i)   Explain and quantify how the oil platform should be treated in the financial statements of Promoil for the year ended 30 September 20X8.   **(7 marks)**

   (ii)   Describe how your answer to (b)(i) would change if the government licence did not require an environmental cleanup.   **(3 marks)**

                                                                                      (Total = 15 marks)

49 Borough (12/11)   27 mins

(a)   IAS 37 *Provisions, contingent liabilities and contingent assets* prescribes the accounting and disclosure for those items named in its title.

   Required

   Define provisions and contingent liabilities and briefly explain how IAS 37 improves consistency in financial reporting.   **(6 marks)**

(b) The following items have arisen during the preparation of Borough's draft financial statements for the year ended 30 September 20X1.

(i) On 1 October 20X0, Borough commenced the extraction of crude oil from a new well on the seabed. The cost of a ten-year licence to extract the oil was $50 million. At the end of the extraction, although not legally bound to do so, Borough intends to make good the damage the extraction has caused to the seabed environment. This intention has been communicated to parties external to Borough. The cost of this will be in two parts: a fixed amount of $20 million and a variable amount of 2 cents per barrel extracted. Both of these amounts are based on their present values as at 1 October 20X0 (discounted at 8%) of the estimated costs in ten years' time. In the year to 30 September 20X1 Borough extracted 150 million barrels of oil. **(5 marks)**

(ii) Borough owns the whole of the equity share capital of its subsidiary Hamlet. Hamlet's statement of financial position includes a loan of $25 million that is repayable in five years' time. $15 million of this loan is secured on Hamlet's property and the remaining $10 million is guaranteed by Borough in the event of a default by Hamlet. The economy in which Hamlet operates is currently experiencing a deep recession, the effects of which are that the current value of its property is estimated at $12 million and there are concerns over whether Hamlet can survive the recession and therefore repay the loan. **(4 marks)**

Required

Describe, and quantify where possible, how items (i) and (ii) above should be treated in Borough's statement of financial position for the year ended 30 September 20X1.

In the case of item (ii) only, distinguish between Borough's entity and consolidated financial statements and refer to any disclosure notes. Your answer should only refer to the treatment of the loan and should not consider any impairment of Hamlet's property or Borough's investment in Hamlet.

The treatment in profit or loss is **not** required for any of the items. **(Total = 15 marks)**

50 Shawler (12/12 amended) 27 mins

(a) Shawler is a small manufacturing company specialising in making alloy casings. Its main item of plant is a furnace which was purchased on 1 October 20X1. The furnace has two components: the main body (cost $60,000 including the environmental provision – see below) which has a ten-year life, and a replaceable liner (cost $10,000) with a five-year life.

The manufacturing process produces toxic chemicals which pollute the nearby environment. Legislation requires that a clean-up operation must be undertaken by Shawler on 30 September 20Y1 (ten years after 20X1) at the latest.

Shawler received a government grant of $12,000 relating to the cost of the main body of the furnace only.

The following are extracts from Shawler's statement of financial position as at 30 September 20X3 (two years after the acquisition of the furnace).

	Carrying amount	
	$	
Non-current assets		
Furnace: main body	48,000	
replaceable liner	6,000	
Current liabilities		
Government grant	1,200	
Non-current liabilities		
Government grant	8,400	
Environmental provision	18,000	(present value discounted at 8% per annum)

Required

(i) Prepare equivalent extracts from Shawler's statement of financial position as at 30 September 20X4.

(3 marks)

(ii) Prepare extracts from Shawler's statement of profit or loss for the year ended 30 September 20X4 relating to the items in the statement of financial position. **(3 marks)**

(b) On 1 April 20X4, the government introduced further environmental legislation which had the effect of requiring Shawler to fit anti-pollution filters to its furnace within two years. An environmental consultant has calculated that fitting the filters will reduce Shawler's required environmental costs (and therefore its provision) by 33%. At 30 September 20X4 Shawler had not yet fitted the filters.

Required

Advise Shawler as to whether they need to provide for the cost of the filters as at 30 September 20X4 and whether they should reduce the environmental provision at this date. **(4 marks)**

(c) Shawler has recently purchased an item of earth moving plant at a total cost of $24 million. The plant has an estimated life of ten years with no residual value, however its engine will need replacing after every 5,000 hours of use at an estimated cost of $7.5 million. The directors of Shawler intend to depreciate the plant at $2.4 million ($24 million / 10 years) per annum and make a provision of $1,500 ($7.5 million / 5,000 hours) per hour of use for the replacement of the engine.

Required

Explain how the plant should be treated in accordance with International Financial Reporting Standards and comment on the directors' proposed treatment. **(5 marks)**

(Total = 15 marks)

51 Multiple choice questions – inventories and biological assets

32 mins

1   In preparing financial statements for the year ended 31 March 20X6, the inventory count was carried out on 4 April 20X6. The value of inventory counted was $36 million. Between 31 March and 4 April goods with a cost of $2.7 million were received into inventory and sales of $7.8 million were made at a mark-up on cost of 30%.

At what amount should inventory be stated in the statement of financial position as at 31 March 20X6?

A	$32.7 million	per inventory count	36
B	$39.3 million	Received after Y/E	(2.7)
C	$38.76 million	Sold after Y/E (7.8m/1.3)	6
D	$33.24 million		39.3

(2 marks)

2   At 31 March 20X7 Tentacle had 12,000 units of product W32 in inventory, included at cost of $6 per unit. During April and May 20X7 units of W32 were being sold at a price of $5.40 each, with sales staff receiving a 15% commission on the sales price of the product.

At what amount should inventory of product W32 be recognised in the financial statements of Tentacle as at 31 March 20X7?

A $55,080   NRV – (12000 × (5.4 × 85%)) = 55080
B $72,000
C $64,800
D $61,200

(2 marks)

3   Caminas has the following products in inventory at the year end.

Product	Quantity	Cost	Selling price	Selling cost
A	1,000	$40 = 40000	$55	$8
B	2,500	$15 = 37500	$25	$4
C	800	$23 = 17600	$27	$5
		22 95100		

At what amount should total inventory be stated in the statement of financial position?

A $95,900
B $103,100
C $95,100
D $105,100

(2 marks)

4   In which of the following situations is the net realisable value of an item of inventory likely to be lower than cost?

A   The production cost of the item has been falling.
B   The selling price of the item has been rising. we can expect its market value to fall – and eventually
C   The item is becoming obsolete. fall below cost. The other options would all maintain
D   Demand for the item is increasing. or improve the net realisable value of the item

(2 marks)

5   At what amount is a biological asset measured on initial recognition in accordance with IAS 41 *Agriculture*?

A   Production cost
B   Fair value
C   Cost less estimated costs to sell
D   Fair value less estimated costs to sell

(2 marks)

IAS 41 Agriculture requires biological assets to be measured on initial recognition at fair value less estimated cost to sell.

6   Which of the following is **not** the outcome of a biological transformation according to IAS 41?

    A   Growth

    (B) Harvest *is an intervention, not a biological process.*

    C   Procreation   *The rest are biological processes.*

    D   Degeneration   **(2 marks)**

---

7   How is a gain or loss arising on a biological asset recognised in accordance with IAS 41?

    (A) Included in profit or loss for the year

    B   Adjusted in retained earnings

    C   Shown under 'other comprehensive income'

    D   Deferred and recognised over the life of the biological asset   **(2 marks)**

---

8   Which of the following statements about IAS 2 *Inventories* are correct?

    1   Production overheads should be included in cost on the basis of a company's actual level of activity in the period.

    2   In arriving at the net realisable value of inventories, settlement discounts must be deducted from the expected selling price.

    3   In arriving at the cost of inventories, FIFO, LIFO and weighted average cost formulas are acceptable.

    4   It is permitted to value finished goods inventories at materials plus labour cost only, without adding production overheads.

    A   1 only

    B   1 and 2

    C   3 and 4

    (D) None of them   **(2 marks)**

---

9   Isaac is a company which buys agricultural produce from wholesale suppliers for retail to the general public. It is preparing its financial statements for the year ending 30 September 20X4 and is considering its closing inventory.

In addition to IAS 2 *Inventories*, which of the following IFRSs may be relevant to determining the figure to be included in its financial statements for closing inventories?

    (A) IAS 10 *Events After the Reporting Period* *may be relevant as agriculture produce*

    B   IAS 38 *Intangible Assets*   *is perishable and if prices have to be*

    C   IAS 16 *Property, Plant and Equipment* *reduced after the Y/E, this will affect*

    D   IAS 41 *Agriculture*   **(2 marks)**

the Y/E valuation.

52 Multiple choice questions – accounting for taxation

provision b/f

1   A company's trial balance shows a debit balance of $2.1 million brought forward on current tax and a credit balance of $5.4 million on deferred tax. The tax charge for the current year is estimated at $16.2 million and the carrying amounts of net assets are $13 million in excess of their tax base. The income tax rate is 30%

What amount will be shown as income tax in the statement of profit or loss for the year?

A	$15.6 million	*charge of the year*	*16200*
B	$12.6 million	*underprovision*	*2100*
C	$16.8 million	*Adjusted deferred tax(u) (1500)*	
D	$18.3 million	*P or L charge*	*16800*

working
Provision needed (13m × 30%)   3900
Provision b/f   (5400)
Reduced provision   (1500)

(2 marks)

---

2   The statements of financial position of Nedburg include the following extracts:

Statements of financial position as at 30 September

	20X2 $m	20X1 $m
Non-current liabilities		
Deferred tax	310	140
Current liabilities		
Taxation	130	160

The tax charge in the statement of profit or loss for the year ended 30 September 20X2 is $270 million.

What amount of tax was paid during the year to 30 September 20X2?

A	$300 million	*b/f (140+160)*	*300*
B	$140 million	*charge of the year*	*270*
C	$200 million	*c/f (310 + 130)*	*(440)*
D	$130 million	*Tax paid*	*130*

(2 marks)

---

3   A company's trial balance at 31 December 20X3 shows a debit balance of $700,000 on current tax and a credit balance of $8,400,000 on deferred tax. The directors have estimated the provision for income tax for the year at $4.5 million and the required deferred tax provision is $5.6 million, $1.2 million of which relates to a property revaluation.

What is the profit or loss income tax charge for the year ended 31 December 20X3?

A	$1 million	*Prior year underprovision*	*700*
B	$2.4 million	*Current Provision*	*4500*
C	$1.2 million	*Movement of deferred tax (8.4−5.6)*	*(2800)*
D	$3.6 million	*Deferred tax on revaluation surplus*	*(1200)*
		Tax charge of the year	*1200*

(2 marks)

---

4   The trial balance of Highwood at 31 March 20X6 showed credit balances of $800,000 on current tax and $2.6 million on deferred tax. A property was revalued during the year giving rise to deferred tax of $3.75 million. This has been included in the deferred tax provision of $6.75 million at 31 March 20X6.

The income tax charge for the year ended 31 March 20X6 is estimated at $19.4 million.

What will be shown as the income tax charge in the statement of profit or loss of Highwood at 31 March 20X6?

A	$19 million	*current charge*	*19400*
B	$22 million	*Overprovision*	*(800)*
C	$19.8 million	*Deferred tax (w)*	*400*
D	$20.6 million		*19000*

(2 marks)

working
Required provision   6750
less : Revaluation   (3750)
*   3000*
Balance b/f   (2600)
Charge to Income tax   400

5   The statements of financial position of Pinto included the following.

Statements of financial position as at:

	31 March 20X8 $'000	31 March 20X7 $'000
Current assets		
Income tax asset	-	50
Non-current liabilities		
Deferred tax	50	30
Current liabilities		
Income tax payable	150	-

The profit or loss income tax charge for the year ended 31 March 20X8 is estimated at $160,000.

What amount of income tax has been received or paid during the year ended 31 March 20X8?

A $60,000 paid
B $40,000 paid
C $60,000 received
D $40,000 received

(2 marks)

Handwritten margin notes:

B/f current tax   (50)
B/f deferred tax   30
Charge of the year   160
                       ___
                       140

c/f current tax   (150)
c/f deferred tax   (50)
                       ___
Tax received   (60)

53 Preparation question: Julian

Julian recognised a deferred tax liability for the year end 31 December 20X3 which related solely to accelerated tax depreciation on property, plant and equipment at a rate 30%. The net book value of the property, plant and equipment at that date was $310,000 and the tax written down value was $230,000.

The following data relates to the year ended 31 December 20X4:

(i)   At the end of the year the carrying value of property, plant and equipment was $460,000 and their tax written down value was $270,000. During the year some items were revalued by $90,000. No items had previously required revaluation. In the tax jurisdiction in which Julian operates revaluations of assets do not affect the tax base of an asset or taxable profit. Gains due to revaluations are taxable on sale.

(ii)   Julian began development of a new product during the year and capitalised $60,000 in accordance with IAS 38. The expenditure was deducted for tax purposes as it was incurred. None of the expenditure had been amortised by the year end.

(iii)   Julian's statement of profit or loss showed interest income receivable of $55,000, but only $45,000 of this had been received by the year end. Interest income is taxed on a receipts basis.

(iv)   During the year, Julian made a provision of $40,000 to cover an obligation to clean up some damage caused by an environmental accident. None of the provision had been used by the year end. The expenditure will be tax deductible when paid.

The corporate income tax rate recently enacted for the following year is 30% (unchanged from the previous year).

The current tax charge was calculated for the year as $45,000.

Current tax is settled on a net basis with the national tax authority.

Required

(a)   Prepare a table showing the carrying values, tax bases and temporary differences for each for the items above at 31 December 20X4.

(b)   Prepare the statement of profit or loss and statement of financial position notes to the financial statements relating to deferred tax for the year ended 31 December 20X4.

54 Preparation question: Bowtock

(a)   IAS 12 *Income Taxes* details the requirements relating to the accounting treatment of deferred taxes.

Required

Explain why it is considered necessary to provide for deferred tax and briefly outline the principles of accounting for deferred tax contained in IAS 12 *Income taxes*.

(b)   Bowtock purchased an item of plant for $2,000,000 on 1 October 20X0. It had an estimated life of eight years and an estimated residual value of $400,000. The plant is depreciated on a straight-line basis. The tax authorities do not allow depreciation as a deductible expense. Instead a tax expense of 40% of the cost of this type of asset can be claimed against income tax in the year of purchase and 20% per annum (on a reducing balance basis) of its tax base thereafter. The rate of income tax can be taken as 25%.

Required

In respect of the above item of plant, calculate the deferred tax charge/credit in Bowtock's statement of profit or loss for the year to 30 September 20X3 and the deferred tax balance in the statement of financial position at that date.

Work to the nearest $'000.

55 Multiple choice questions – presentation of published financial statements

1   Which one of the following would not **necessarily** lead to a liability being classified as a current liability?

    A   The liability is expected to be settled in the course of the entity's normal operating cycle.
    B   The liability has arisen during the current accounting period.
    C   The liability is held primarily for the purpose of trading.
    D   The liability is due to be settled within 12 months after the end of the reporting period.

        (2 marks)

2   Which one of the following would be shown in the 'other comprehensive income' section of the statement of profit or loss and other comprehensive income?

    A   A revaluation gain on an investment property
    B   Profit on sale of an investment
    C   Receipt of a government grant
    D   Gain on revaluation of a factory building

        (2 marks)

3   Which of the following are **not** items required by IAS 1 *Presentation of Financial Statements* to be shown on the face of the statement of financial position?

    A   Inventories
    B   Provisions
    C   Government grants
    D   Intangible assets

        (2 marks)

4   How does IAS 1 define the 'operating cycle' of an entity?

    A   The time between acquisition of assets for processing and delivery of finished goods to customers
    B   The time between delivery of finished goods and receipt of cash from customers
    C   The time between acquisition of assets for processing and payment of cash to suppliers
    D   The time between acquisition of assets for processing and receipt of cash from customers

        (2 marks)

5   Where are equity dividends paid presented in the financial statements?

    A   As a deduction from retained earnings in the statement of changes in equity
    B   As a liability in the statement of financial position
    C   As an expense in profit or loss
    D   As a loss in 'other comprehensive income'

        (2 marks)

56 Preparation question: Candel (12/08)

The following trial balance relates to Candel at 30 September 20X8.

	$'000	$'000
Leasehold property – at valuation 1 October 20X7	50,000	
Plant and equipment – at cost	76,600	
Plant and equipment – accumulated depreciation at 1 October 20X7		24,600
Capitalised development expenditure – at 1 October 20X7	20,000	
Development expenditure – accumulated amortisation at 1 October 20X7		6,000
Closing inventory at 30 September 20X8	20,000	
Trade receivables	43,100	
Bank		1,300
Trade payables and provisions		23,800
Revenue		300,000
Cost of sales	204,000	
Distribution costs	14,500	
Administrative expenses	22,200	
Preference dividend paid	800	
Interest on bank borrowings	200	
Equity dividend paid	6,000	
Research and development costs	8,600	
Equity shares of 25 cents each		50,000
8% redeemable preference shares of $1 each		20,000
Retained earnings at 1 October 20X7		24,500
Deferred tax		5,800
Property revaluation surplus		10,000
	466,000	466,000

The following notes are relevant.

(i) Non-current assets – tangible:

The property had a remaining life of 20 years at 1 October 20X7. The company's policy is to revalue its property at each year end and at 30 September 20X8 it was valued at $43 million. Ignore deferred tax on the revaluation.

On 1 October 20X7 an item of plant was disposed of for $2.5 million cash. The proceeds have been treated as sales revenue by Candel. The plant is still included in the above trial balance figures at its cost of $8 million and accumulated depreciation of $4 million (to the date of disposal).

All plant is depreciated at 20% per annum using the reducing balance method. Depreciation and amortisation of all non-current assets is charged to cost of sales.

(ii) Non-current assets – intangible:

In addition to the capitalised development expenditure (of $20 million), further research and development costs were incurred on a new project which commenced on 1 October 20X7. The research stage of the new project lasted until 31 December 20X7 and incurred $1·4 million of costs. From that date the project incurred development costs of $800,000 per month. On 1 April 20X8 the directors became confident that the project would be successful and yield a profit well in excess of its costs. The project is still in development at 30 September 20X8.

Capitalised development expenditure is amortised at 20% per annum using the straight-line method. All expensed research and development is charged to cost of sales.

(iii) Candel is being sued by a customer for $2 million for breach of contract over a cancelled order. Candel has obtained legal opinion that there is a 20% chance that Candel will lose the case. Accordingly Candel has provided $400,000 ($2 million × 20%) included in administrative expenses in respect of the claim. The unrecoverable legal costs of defending the action are estimated at $100,000. These have not been provided for as the legal action will not go to court until next year.

(iv) The preference shares were issued on 1 April 20X8 at par. They are redeemable at a large premium which gives them an effective finance cost of 12% per annum.

(v)   The directors have estimated the provision for income tax for the year ended 30 September 20X8 at $11.4 million. The required deferred tax provision at 30 September 20X8 is $6 million.

Required

(a)   Prepare the statement of profit or loss and other comprehensive income for the year ended 30 September 20X8.

(b)   Prepare the statement of changes in equity for the year ended 30 September 20X8.

(c)   Prepare the statement of financial position as at 30 September 20X8.

Notes to the financial statements are not required.

57 Preparation question: Dexon

Below is the summarised draft statement of financial position of Dexon, a publicly listed company, as at 31 March 20X8.

	$'000	$'000	$'000
ASSETS			
Non-current assets			
Property at valuation (land $20m; buildings $165m (note (i))			185,000
Plant (note (i))			180,500
Financial assets at fair value through profit or loss at 1 April 20X7 (note (ii))			12,500
			378,000
Current assets			
Inventory		84,000	
Trade receivables (note (iii))		52,200	
Bank		3,800	140,000
Total assets			518,000
EQUITY AND LIABILITIES			
Equity			
Ordinary shares of $1 each			250,000
Share premium		40,000	
Revaluation surplus		18,000	
Retained earnings – At 1 April 20X7	12,300		
– For the year ended 31 March 20X8	96,700	109,000	167,000
			417,000
Non-current liabilities			
Deferred tax – at 1 April 20X7 (note (iv))			19,200
Current liabilities			81,800
Total equity and liabilities			518,000

The following information is relevant.

(i)   The non-current assets have not been depreciated for the year ended 31 March 20X8.

Dexon has a policy of revaluing its land and buildings at the end of each accounting year. The values in the above statement of financial position are as at 1 April 20X7 when the buildings had a remaining life of 15 years. A qualified surveyor has valued the land and buildings at 31 March 20X8 at $180 million.

Plant is depreciated at 20% on the reducing balance basis.

(ii)   The financial assets at fair value through profit and loss are held in a fund whose value changes directly in proportion to a specified market index. At 1 April 20X7 the relevant index was 1,200 and at 31 March 20X8 it was 1,296.

(iii)   In late March 20X8 the directors of Dexon discovered a material fraud perpetrated by the company's credit controller that had been continuing for some time. Investigations revealed that a total of $4 million of the trade receivables as shown in the statement of financial position at 31 March 20X8 had in fact been paid and the money had been stolen by the credit controller. An analysis revealed that $1.5 million had been stolen in the year to 31 March 20X7 with the rest being stolen in the current year. Dexon is not insured for this loss and it cannot be recovered from the credit controller, nor is it deductible for tax purposes.

(iv) During the year the company's taxable temporary differences increased by $10 million of which $6 million related to the revaluation of the property. The deferred tax relating to the remainder of the increase in the temporary differences should be taken to profit or loss. The applicable income tax rate is 20%.

(v) The above figures do not include the estimated provision for income tax on the profit for the year ended 31 March 20X8. After allowing for any adjustments required in items (i) to (iii), the directors have estimated the provision at $11.4 million (this is in addition to the deferred tax effects of item (iv)).

(vi) On 1 September 20X7 there was a fully subscribed rights issue of one new share for every four held at a price of $1.20 each. The proceeds of the issue have been received and the issue of the shares has been correctly accounted for in the above statement of financial position.

(vii) In May 20X7 a dividend of 4 cents per share was paid. In November 20X7 (after the rights issue in item (vi) above) a further dividend of 3 cents per share was paid. Both dividends have been correctly accounted for in the above statement of financial position.

Required

Taking into account any adjustments required by items (i) to (vii) above:

(a) Prepare a statement showing the recalculation of Dexon's profit for the year ended 31 March 20X8.
(b) Prepare the statement of changes in equity of Dexon for the year ended 31 March 20X8.
(c) Redraft the statement of financial position of Dexon as at 31 March 20X8.

Notes to the financial statements are not required.

58 Highwood (6/11 amended)   54 mins

The following trial balance relates to Highwood at 31 March 20X6:

	$'000	$'000
Equity shares of 50 cents each		56,000
Retained earnings (note (i))		1,400
8% convertible loan note (note (ii))		30,000
Freehold property – at cost 1 April 20X0 (land element $25 million (note (iii))	75,000	
Plant and equipment – at cost	74,500	
Accumulated depreciation – 1 April 20X5 – building		10,000
– plant and equipment		24,500
Current tax (note (iv))		800
Deferred tax (note (iv))		2,600
Inventory – 4 April 20X6 (note (v))	36,000	
Trade receivables	47,100	
Bank		11,500
Trade payables		24,500
Revenue		339,650
Cost of sales	207,750	
Distribution costs	27,500	
Administrative expenses (note (vi))	30,700	
Loan interest paid (note (ii))	2,400	
	500,950	500,950

The following notes are relevant.

(i) An equity dividend of 5 cents per share was paid in November 20X5 and charged to retained earnings.

(ii) The 8% $30 million convertible loan note was issued on 1 April 20X5 at par. Interest is payable annually in arrears on 31 March each year. The loan note is redeemable at par on 31 March 20X8 or convertible into equity shares at the option of the loan note holders on the basis of 30 equity shares for each $100 of loan note. Highwood's finance director has calculated that to issue an equivalent loan note without the conversion rights it would have to pay an interest rate of 10% per annum to attract investors.

The present value of $1 receivable at the end of each year, based on discount rates of 8% and 10% are:

	8%	10%
End of year 1	0.93	0.91
2	0.86	0.83
3	0.79	0.75

(iii) Non-current assets:

On 1 April 20X5 Highwood decided for the first time to value its property at its current value. A qualified property valuer reported that the market value of the property on this date was $80 million, of which $30 million related to the land. At this date the remaining estimated life of the property was 20 years. Highwood does not make a transfer to retained earnings in respect of excess depreciation on the revaluation of its assets.

Plant is depreciated at 20% per annum on the reducing balance method.

All depreciation of non-current assets is charged to cost of sales.

(iv) The balance on current tax represents the under/over provision of the tax liability for the year ended 31 March 20X5. The required provision for income tax for the year ended 31 March 20X6 is $19.4 million. The difference between the carrying amounts of the net assets of Highwood (including the revaluation of the property in note (iii) above) and their (lower) tax base at 31 March 20X6 is $27 million. Highwood's rate of income tax is 25%.

(v) The inventory of Highwood was not counted until 4 April 20X6 due to operational reasons. At this date its value at cost was $36 million and this figure has been used in the cost of sales calculation above. Between the year end of 31 March 20X6 and 4 April 20X6, Highwood received a delivery of goods at a cost of $2.7 million and made sales of $7.8 million at a mark-up on cost of 30%. Neither the goods delivered nor the sales made in this period were included in Highwood's purchases (as part of cost of sales) or revenue in the above trial balance.

(vi) On 31 March 20X6 Highwood factored (sold) trade receivables with a book value of $10 million to Easyfinance. Highwood received an immediate payment of $8.7 million and will pay Easyfinance 2% per month on any uncollected balances. Any of the factored receivables outstanding after six months will be refunded to Easyfinance. Highwood has derecognised the receivables and charged $1.3 million to administrative expenses. If Highwood had not factored these receivables it would have made an allowance of $600,000 against them.

Required

(a) Prepare the statement of profit or loss and other comprehensive income for Highwood for the year ended 31 March 20X6. **(11 marks)**

(b) Prepare the statement of changes in equity for Highwood for the year ended 31 March 20X6. **(4 marks)**

(c) Prepare the statement of financial position of Highwood as at 31 March 20X6. **(10 marks)**

(d) Prepare the basic and diluted EPS of Highwood for the year ended 31 March 20X6. **(5 marks)**

(Total = 30 marks)

Apart from EPS your answers and workings should be presented to the nearest $1,000; notes to the financial statements are not required.

59 Keystone (12/11 amended)

54 mins

The following trial balance relates to Keystone at 30 September 20X1:

	$'000	$'000
Revenue		380,000
Material purchases (note (i))	64,000	
Production labour (note (i))	124,000	
Factory overheads (note (i))	80,000	
Distribution costs	14,200	
Administrative expenses (note (ii))	46,400	
Finance costs	350	
Investment income		800
Leased property – at cost (note (i))	50,000	
Plant and equipment – at cost (note (i))	44,500	
Accumulated amortisation/depreciation at 1 October 20X0		
– leased property		10,000
– plant and equipment		14,500
Financial asset: equity investments (note (iv))	18,000	
Inventory at 1 October 20X0	46,700	
Trade receivables	33,550	
Trade payables		27,800
Bank		2,300
Equity shares of 20 cents each		50,000
Retained earnings at 1 October 20X0		33,600
Deferred tax (note (v))		2,700
	521,700	521,700

The following notes are relevant:

(i)   Non-current assets:

During the year Keystone manufactured an item of plant for its own use. The direct materials and labour were $3 million and $4 million respectively. Production overheads are 75% of direct labour cost and Keystone determines the final selling price for goods by adding a mark-up on total cost of 40%. These manufacturing costs are included in the relevant expense items in the trial balance. The plant was completed and put into immediate use on 1 April 20X1.

All plant and equipment is depreciated at 20% per annum using the reducing balance method with time apportionment in the year of acquisition.

The directors decided to revalue the leased property in line with recent increases in market values. On 1 October 20X0 an independent surveyor valued the leased property at $48 million, which the directors have accepted. The leased property was being amortised over an original life of 20 years which has not changed. Keystone does not make a transfer to retained earnings in respect of excess amortisation. The revaluation gain will create a deferred tax liability (see note (v)).

All depreciation and amortisation is charged to cost of sales. No depreciation or amortisation has yet been charged on any non-current asset for the year ended 30 September 20X1.

(ii)   On 15 August 20X1, Keystone's share price stood at $2.40 per share. On this date Keystone paid a dividend (included in administrative expenses) that was calculated to give a dividend yield of 4%.

(iii)   The inventory on Keystone's premises at 30 September 20X1 was counted and valued at cost of $54.8 million.

(iv)   The equity investments had a fair value of $17.4 million on 30 September 20X1. There were no purchases or disposals of any of these investments during the year. Keystone has not made the election in accordance with IFRS 9 *Financial Instruments*. Keystone adopts this standard when accounting for its financial assets.

(v)   A provision for income tax for the year ended 30 September 20X1 of $24.3 million is required. At
       30 September 20X1, the tax base of Keystone's net assets was $15 million less than their carrying amounts.
       This excludes the effects of the revaluation of the leased property. The income tax rate of Keystone is 30%.

(vi)   On 1 June 20X1 Keystone made a 1 for 4 bonus issue, utilising the share premium account. The issue was
       correctly accounted for.

Required

(a)   Prepare the statement of profit or loss and other comprehensive income for Keystone for the year ended
       30 September 20X1.   **(15 marks)**

(b)   Prepare the statement of changes in equity for Keystone for the year ended 30 September 20X1.   **(6 marks)**

(c)   Prepare the statement of financial position for Keystone as at 30 September 20X1.   **(9 marks)**

Notes to the financial statements are not required.   **(Total = 30 marks)**

60 Fresco (6/12 amended)   54 mins

The following trial balance relates to Fresco at 31 March 20X2:

	$'000	$'000
Equity shares of 50 cents each (note (i))		45,000
Share premium (note (i))		5,000
Retained earnings at 1 April 20X1		5,100
Leased property (12 years) – at cost (note (ii))	48,000	
Plant and equipment – at cost (note (ii))	47,500	
Accumulated amortisation of leased property at 1 April 20X1		16,000
Accumulated depreciation of plant and equipment at 1 April 20X1		33,500
Inventory at 31 March 20X2	25,200	
Trade receivables (note (iii))	28,500	
Bank		1,400
Deferred tax (note (iv))		3,200
Trade payables		27,300
Revenue		350,000
Cost of sales	298,700	
Lease payments (note (ii))	8,000	
Distribution costs	16,100	
Administrative expenses	26,900	
Bank interest	300	
Current tax (note (iv))	800	
Suspense account (note (i))		13,500
	500,000	500,000

The following notes are relevant:

(i)   The suspense account represents the corresponding credit for cash received for a fully subscribed rights
       issue of equity shares made on 1 January 20X2. The terms of the share issue were one new share for every
       five held at a price of 75 cents each. The price of the company's equity shares immediately before the issue
       was $1.20 each.

(ii)   Non-current assets:

       To reflect a marked increase in property prices, Fresco decided to revalue its leased property on 1 April
       20X1. The directors accepted the report of an independent surveyor who valued the leased property at $36
       million on that date. Fresco has not yet recorded the revaluation. The remaining life of the leased property is
       eight years at the date of the revaluation. Fresco makes an annual transfer to retained profits to reflect the
       realisation of the revaluation surplus. In Fresco's tax jurisdiction the revaluation does not give rise to a
       deferred tax liability.

On 1 April 20X1, Fresco acquired an item of plant under a finance lease agreement that had an implicit finance cost of 10% per annum. The lease payments in the trial balance represent an initial deposit of $2 million paid on 1 April 20X1 and the first annual rental of $6 million paid on 31 March 20X2. The lease agreement requires further annual payments of $6 million on 31 March each year for the next four years. Had the plant not been leased it would have cost $25 million to purchase for cash.

Plant and equipment (other than the leased plant) is depreciated at 20% per annum using the reducing balance method.

No depreciation/amortisation has yet been charged on any non-current asset for the year ended 31 March 20X2. Depreciation and amortisation are charged to cost of sales.

(iii)   In March 20X2, Fresco's internal audit department discovered a fraud committed by the company's credit controller who did not return from a foreign business trip. The outcome of the fraud is that $4 million of the company's trade receivables have been stolen by the credit controller and are not recoverable. Of this amount, $1 million relates to the year ended 31 March 20X1 and the remainder to the current year. Fresco is not insured against this fraud.

(iv)   Fresco's income tax calculation for the year ended 31 March 20X2 shows a tax refund of $2.4 million. The balance on current tax in the trial balance represents the under/over provision of the tax liability for the year ended 31 March 20X1. At 31 March 20X2, Fresco had taxable temporary differences of $12 million (requiring a deferred tax liability). The income tax rate of Fresco is 25%.

Required:

(a)   (i)   Prepare the statement of profit or loss and other comprehensive income for Fresco for the year ended 31 March 20X2.   **(9 marks)**

      (ii)   Prepare the statement of changes in equity for Fresco for the year ended 31 March 20X2.   **(5 marks)**

      (iii)   Prepare the statement of financial position of Fresco as at 31 March 20X2.   **(8 marks)**

(b)   Calculate the basic earnings per share for Fresco for the year ended 31 March 20X2.   **(3 marks)**

      Notes to the financial statements are not required.

(c)   Explain why a company such as Fresco may decide to revalue non-current assets and what the requirements are for revaluations as set out in IAS 16 *Property, Plant and Equipment*.   **(5 marks)**
      (Total = 30 marks)

61 Quincy (specimen paper)

The following trial balance relates to Quincy as at 30 September 20X4.

	$'000	$'000
Revenue (note (ii))		213,500
Cost of sales	136,800	
Distribution costs	17,500	
Administrative expenses (note (ii))	19,000	
Loan note interest paid (note (ii))	1,500	
Investment income		400
Equity shares of 25 cents each		60,000
6% loan note (note (ii))		25,000
Retained earnings at 1 October 20X3		4,300
Land and buildings at cost (land element $10 million) (note (iii))	50,000	
Plant and equipment at cost (note (iii))	83,700	
Accumulated depreciation at 1 October 20X3: buildings		8,000
plant and equipment		33,700
Equity financial asset investments (note (iv))	17,000	
Inventory at 30 September 20X4	24,800	
Trade receivables	28,500	
Bank	2,900	
Current tax (note (v))	1,100	
Deferred tax note (note (v))		1,200
Trade payables		36,700
	382,800	382,800

The following notes are relevant.

(i)   On 1 October 20X3, Quincy sold one of its products for $10 million (included in revenue in the trial balance). As part of the sale agreement, Quincy is committed to the ongoing servicing of this product until 30 September 20X6 (ie three years from the date of sale). The value of this service has been included in the selling price of $10 million. The estimated cost to Quincy of the servicing is $600,000 per annum and Quincy's normal gross profit margin on this type of servicing is 25%. Ignore discounting.

(ii)   Quincy issued a $25 million 6% loan on 1 October 20X3. Issue costs were $1 million and these have been charged to administrative expenses. Interest is paid annually on 30 September each year. The loan will be redeemed on 30 September 20X6 at a premium which gives an effective interest rate on the loan of 8%.

(iii)   Non-current assets:

Quincy had been carrying land and buildings at depreciated cost, but due to a recent rise in property prices, it decided to revalue its property on 1 October 20X3 to market value. An independent valuer confirmed the value of the property at $60 million (land element $12 million) as at that date and the directors accepted this valuation. The property had a remaining life of 16 years at the date of its revaluation. Quincy will make a transfer from the revaluation surplus to retained earnings in respect of the realisation of the revaluation. Ignore deferred tax on the revaluation.

On 1 October 20X3, Quincy had a processing plant installed at a cost of $10 million which is included in the trial balance figure of plant and equipment at cost. The process the plant performs will cause immediate contamination of the nearby land. Quincy will have to decontaminate (clean up) this land at the end of the plant's ten-year life (straight-line depreciation). The present value (discounted at a cost of capital of 10% per annum) of the decontamination is $6 million. Quincy has not made any accounting entries in respect of this cost.

All other plant and equipment is depreciated at 12½% per annum using the reducing balance method.

No depreciation has yet been charged on any non-current asset for the year ended 30 September 20X4. All depreciation is charged to cost of sales.

Other than referred to above, there were no acquisitions or disposals of non-current assets.

(iv)   The investments had a fair value of $15.7 million as at 30 September 20X4. There were no acquisitions or disposals of these investments during the year ended 30 September 20X4.

(v)   The balance on current tax represents the under/over provision of the tax liability for the year ended 30 September 20X3. A provision for income tax for the year ended 30 September 20X4 of $7.4 million is required. At 30 September 20X4, Quincy had taxable temporary differences of $5 million requiring a provision for deferred tax. Any deferred tax adjustment should be reported in profit or loss. The income tax rate of Quincy is 20%.

Required

(a)   Prepare the statement of profit or loss and other comprehensive income for Quincy for the year ended 30 September 20X4.   **(12 marks)**

(b)   Prepare the statement of changes in equity for Quincy for the year ended 30 September 20X4.

                                                                                          (3 marks)

(c)   Prepare the statement of financial position of Quincy as at 30 September 20X4.   **(12 marks)**

(d)   Calculate the increase in the carrying amount of property, plant and equipment during the year ended 30 September 20X4 from the perspective of:

(i)   The change between the opening and closing statements of financial position; and
(ii)   The statement of cash flows.

Comment on which perspective may be more useful to users of Quincy's financial statements.   **(3 marks)**

Notes to the financial statements are not required.

                                                                                   (Total = 30 marks)

62 Xtol (6/14 amended)

The following trial balance relates to Xtol at 31 March 20X4:

	$'000	$'000
Revenue		490,000
Cost of sales	290,600	
Distribution costs	33,500	
Administrative expenses	36,800	
Loan note interest and dividends paid (notes(iv) and (v))	13,380	
Bank interest	900	
20-year leased property at cost (note (ii))	100,000	
Plant and equipment at cost (note (ii))	155,500	
Accumulated amortisation/depreciation at 1 April 20X3:		
Leased property		25,000
Plant and equipment		43,500
Inventory at 31 March 20X4	61,000	
Trade receivables	63,000	
Trade payables		32,200
Bank		5,500
Equity shares of 25 cents each (note (ii))		56,000
Share premium		25,000
Retained earnings at 1 April 20X3		26,080
5% convertible loan note (note (iv))		50,000
Current tax (note (vi))	3,200	
Deferred tax (note (vi))		4,600
	757,880	757,880

The following notes are relevant:

(i) Revenue includes an amount of $20 million for cash sales made through Xtol's retail outlets during the year on behalf of Francais. Xtol, acting as agent, is entitled to a commission of 10% of the selling price of these goods. By 31 March 20X4, Xtol had remitted to Francais $15 million (of the $20 million sales) and recorded this amount in cost of sales.

(ii) Plant and equipment is depreciated at 12½% per annum on the reducing balance basis. All amortisation and depreciation of non-current assets is charged to cost of sales.

(iii) On 1 August 20X3, Xtol made a fully subscribed rights issue of equity share capital based on two new shares at 60 cents each for every five shares held. The market price of Xtol's shares before the issue was $1·02 each. The issue has been fully recorded in the trial balance figures.

(iv) On 1 April 20X3, Xtol issued a 5% $50 million convertible loan note at par. Interest is payable annually in arrears on 31 March each year. The loan note is redeemable at par or convertible into equity shares at the option of the loan note holders on 31 March 20X6. The interest on an equivalent loan note without the conversion rights would be 8% per annum.

The present values of $1 receivable at the end of each year, based on discount rates of 5% and 8%, are:

	5%	8%
End of year 1	0·95	0·93
2	0·91	0·86
3	0·86	0·79

(v) An equity dividend of 4 cents per share was paid on 30 May 20X3 and, after the rights issue, a further dividend of 2 cents per share was paid on 30 November 20X3.

(vi) The balance on current tax represents the under/over provision of the tax liability for the year ended 31March 20X3. A provision of $28 million is required for current tax for the year ended 31 March 20X4 and at this date the deferred tax liability was assessed at $8·3 million.

Required

(a) Prepare the statement of profit or loss for Xtol for the year ended 31 March 20X4 **(8 marks)**

(b) Prepare the statement of changes in equity for Xtol for the year ended 31 March 20X4 **(6 marks)**

(c) Prepare the statement of financial position for Xtol for the year ended 31 March 20X4 **(8 marks)**

(d) Calculate basic earnings per share (EPS) for Xtol for the year ended 31 March 20X4 **(3 marks)**

(e) Explain what is meant by diluted EPS (including examples of transactions which may give rise to dilution) and assess the significance of diluted EPS in evaluating the performance of an entity.

(5 marks)

(Total = 30 marks)

Answers and workings (for parts (a) to (c)) should be presented to the nearest $1,000; notes to the financial statements are not required.

63 Multiple choice questions – reporting financial performance

1   Which one of the following would be treated under IAS 8 *Accounting Policies, Changes in Accounting Estimates and Errors* as a change of accounting policy?

   A   A change in valuation of inventory from a weighted average to a FIFO basis
   B   A change of depreciation method from straight line to reducing balance – *accounting estimate*
   C   Adoption of the revaluation model for non-current assets previously held at cost – *IAS 16*
   D   Capitalisation of borrowing costs which have arisen for the first time   **(2 marks)**

2   For an asset to be classified as 'held for sale' under IFRS 5 *Non-current Assets Held for Sale and Discontinued Operations* its sale must be 'highly probable'. Which one of the following is **not** a requirement if the sale is to be regarded as highly probable?

   A   Management must be committed to a plan to sell the asset.
   B   A buyer must have been located for the asset.
   C   The asset must be marketed at a reasonable price.
   D   The sale should be expected to take place within one year from the date of classification.   **(2 marks)**

3   At what amount should an asset classified as 'held for sale' be measured?
   Recoverable value will be
   A   Lower of carrying amount and fair value less costs of disposal
   B   Lower of carrying amount and value in use – *not relevant*
   C   Higher of value in use and fair value less costs of disposal
   D   Higher of carrying amount and recoverable amount   **(2 marks)**

4   Which of the following would be a change in accounting policy in accordance with IAS 8 *Accounting Policies, Changes in Accounting Estimates and Errors*?

   A   Adjusting the financial statements of a subsidiary prior to consolidation as its accounting policies differ from those of its parent
   B   A change in reporting depreciation charges as cost of sales rather than as administrative expenses
   C   Depreciation charged on reducing balance method rather than straight line *change in a/c estimate*
   D   Reducing the value of inventory from cost to net realisable value due to a valid adjusting event after the reporting period

   A + D are simply adjustments   **(2 marks)**

64 Preparation question: Partway (2.5 12/06 amended)

(a)   Partway is in the process of preparing its financial statements for the year ended 31 October 20X6. The company's main activity is in the travel industry mainly selling package holidays (flights and accommodation) to the general public through the Internet and retail travel agencies. During the current year the number of holidays sold by travel agencies declined dramatically and the directors decided at a board meeting on 15 October 20X6 to cease marketing holidays through its chain of travel agents and sell off the related high-street premises. Immediately after the meeting the travel agencies' staff and suppliers were notified of the situation and an announcement was made in the press. The directors wish to show the travel agencies' results as a discontinued operation in the financial statements to 31 October 20X6. Due to the declining business of the travel agents, on 1 August 20X6 (three months before the year end) Partway expanded its Internet operations to offer car hire facilities to purchasers of its Internet holidays.

The following are Partway's summarised profit or loss results – years ended:

| | 31 October 20X6 | | | | 31 October 20X5 |
	Internet	Travel agencies	Car hire	Total	Total
	$'000	$'000	$'000	$'000	$'000
Revenue	23,000	14,000	2,000	39,000	40,000
Cost of sales	(18,000)	(16,500)	(1,500)	(36,000)	(32,000)
Gross profit/(loss)	5,000	(2,500)	500	3,000	8,000
Operating expenses	(1,000)	(1,500)	(100)	(2,600)	(2,000)
Profit/(loss) before tax	4,000	(4,000)	400	400	6,000

The results for the travel agencies for the year ended 31 October 20X5 were: revenue $18 million, cost of sales $15 million and operating expenses of $1.5 million.

Required

(i)   Discuss whether the directors' wish to show the travel agencies' results as a discontinued operation is justifiable.

(ii)   Assuming the closure of the travel agencies is a discontinued operation, prepare the (summarised) statement of profit or loss of Partway for the year ended 31 October 20X6 together with its comparatives.

(b)   (i)   Describe the circumstances in which an entity may change its accounting policies and how a change should be applied.

The terms under which Partway sells its holidays are that a 10% deposit is required on booking and the balance of the holiday must be paid six weeks before the travel date. In previous years Partway has recognised revenue (and profit) from the sale of its holidays at the date the holiday is actually taken. From the beginning of November 20X5, Partway has made it a condition of booking that all customers must have holiday cancellation insurance and as a result it is unlikely that the outstanding balance of any holidays will be unpaid due to cancellation. In preparing its financial statements to 31 October 20X6, the directors are proposing to change to recognising revenue (and related estimated costs) at the date when a booking is made. The directors also feel that this change will help to negate the adverse effect of comparison with last year's results (year ended 31 October 20X5) which were better than the current year's.

Required

(ii)   Comment on whether Partway's proposal to change the timing of its recognition of its revenue is acceptable and whether this would be a change of accounting policy.

65 Preparation question: Skeptic

The following issues have arisen during the preparation of Skeptic's draft financial statements for the year ended 31 March 20X4:

(i)   From 1 April 20X3, the directors have decided to reclassify research and amortised development costs as administrative expenses rather than its previous classification as cost of sales. They believe that the previous treatment unfairly distorted the company's gross profit margin.

(ii)   Skeptic has two potential liabilities to assess. The first is an outstanding court case concerning a customer claiming damages for losses due to faulty components supplied by Skeptic. The second is the provision required for product warranty claims against 200,000 units of retail goods supplied with a one-year warranty.

The estimated outcomes of the two liabilities are:

Court case	*Product warranty claims*
10% chance of no damages awarded	70% of sales will have no claim
65% chance of damages of $4 million	20% of sales will require a $25 repair
25% chance of damages of $6 million	10% of sales will require a $120 repair

(iii) On 1 April 20X3, Skeptic received a government grant of $8 million towards the purchase of new plant with a gross cost of $64 million. The plant has an estimated life of 10 years and is depreciated on a straight-line basis. One of the terms of the grant is that the sale of the plant before 31 March 20X7 would trigger a repayment on a sliding scale as follows:

Sale in the year ended:	Amount of repayment
31 March 20X4	100%
31 March 20X5	75%
31 March 20X6	50%
31 March 20X7	25%

Accordingly, the directors propose to credit to the statement of profit or loss $2 million ($8 million x 25%) being the amount of the grant they believe has been earned in the year to 31 March 20X4. Skeptic accounts for government grants as a separate item of deferred credit in its statement of financial position. Skeptic has no intention of selling the plant before the end of its economic life.

Required

Advise, and quantify where possible, how the above items (i) to (iii) should be treated in Skeptic's financial statements for the year ended 31 March 20X4.

66 Tunshill (12/10) 27 mins

(a) IAS 8 *Accounting Policies, Changes in Accounting Estimates and Errors* contains guidance on the use of accounting policies and accounting estimates.

Required

Explain the basis on which the management of an entity must select its accounting policies and distinguish, with an example, between changes in accounting policies and changes in accounting estimates.   **(5 marks)**

(b) The directors of Tunshill are disappointed by the draft profit for the year ended 30 September 20X3. The company's assistant accountant has suggested two areas where she believes the reported profit may be improved:

(i) A major item of plant that cost $20 million to purchase and install on 1 October 20X0 is being depreciated on a straight-line basis over a five-year period (assuming no residual value). The plant is wearing well and at the beginning of the current year (1 October 20X2) the production manager believed that the plant was likely to last eight years in total (ie from the date of its purchase). The assistant accountant has calculated that, based on an eight-year life (and no residual value) the accumulated depreciation of the plant at 30 September 20X3 would be $7.5 million ($20 million / 8 years × 3). In the financial statements for the year ended 30 September 20X2, the accumulated depreciation was $8 million ($20 million / 5 years × 2). Therefore, by adopting an eight-year life, Tunshill can avoid a depreciation charge in the current year and instead credit $0.5 million ($8 million – $7.5 million) to profit or loss in the current year to improve the reported profit.   **(5 marks)**

(ii) Most of Tunshill's competitors value their inventory using the average cost (AVCO) basis, whereas Tunshill uses the first in first out (FIFO) basis. The value of Tunshill's inventory at 30 September 20X3 (on the FIFO basis) is $20 million, however on the AVCO basis it would be valued at $18 million. By adopting the same method (AVCO) as its competitors, the assistant accountant says the company would improve its profit for the year ended 30 September 20X3 by $2 million. Tunshill's inventory at 30 September 20X2 was reported as $15 million, however on the AVCO basis it would have been reported as $13.4 million.   **(5 marks)**

Required

Comment on the acceptability of the assistant accountant's suggestions and quantify how they would affect the financial statements if they were implemented under IFRS. Ignore taxation.

The mark allocation is shown against each of the two items above.   **(Total = 15 marks)**

67 Manco (12/10 amended) 27 mins

(a) State the definition of both non-current assets held for sale and discontinued operations and explain the usefulness of information for discontinued operations. **(5 marks)**

(b) Manco has been experiencing substantial losses at its furniture making operation which is treated as a separate operating segment. The company's year end is 30 September. At a meeting on 1 July 20X0 the directors decided to close down the furniture making operation on 31 January 20X1 and then dispose of its non-current assets on a piecemeal basis. Affected employees and customers were informed of the decision and a press announcement was made immediately after the meeting. The directors have obtained the following information in relation to the closure of the operation:

(i) On 1 July 20X0, the factory had a carrying amount of $3.6 million and is expected to be sold for net proceeds of $5 million. On the same date the plant had a carrying amount of $2.8 million, but it is anticipated that it will only realise net proceeds of $500,000.

(ii) Of the employees affected by the closure, the majority will be made redundant at cost of $750,000, the remainder will be retrained at a cost of $200,000 and given work in one of the company's other operations.

(iii) Trading losses from 1 July to 30 September 20X0 are expected to be $600,000 and from this date to the closure on 31 January 20X1 a further $1 million of trading losses are expected.

Required

Explain how the decision to close the furniture making operation should be treated in Manco's financial statements for the years ending 30 September 20X0 and 20X1. Your answer should quantify the amounts involved.

(10 marks)
(Total = 15 marks)

68 Multiple choice questions – earnings per share

1   Barwell had 10 million ordinary shares in issue throughout the year ended 30 June 20X3. On 1 July 20X2 it had issued $2 million of 6% convertible loan stock, each $5 of loan stock convertible into 4 ordinary shares on 1 July 20X6 at the option of the holder.

Barwell had profit after tax for the year ended 30 June 20X3 of $1,850,000. It pays tax on profits at 30%.

What was diluted EPS for the year?

Handwritten annotations:

Basic EPS = 1850/10000
= 18.5c

earnings on dilution:-
1850
Basic
Add Back Interest (2000 × 6% × 70%)   84
1934

Diluted EPS = 1934/11600
= 16.7c

shares on dilution:-
Existing   10000
conversion (2m × 4/5)   1600
11600

(A)   16.7c
B   18.5c
C   16.1c
D   17c

(2 marks)

2   At 1 January 20X8 Artichoke had 5 million $1 equity shares in issue. On 1 June 20X8 it made a 1 for 5 rights issue at a price of $1.50. The market price of the shares on the last day of quotation with rights was $1.80.

Total earnings for the year ended 31 December 20X8 was $7.6 million.

What was EPS for the year?

Handwritten annotations:

TERP   5 × 1.8 = 9.00
1 × 1.5 = 1.50
$\frac{10.50}{6}$ /6 = $1.75

shares
5000 × 5/12 × 1.8/1.75 = 2143
6000 × 7/12 = 3500
5643

EPS = $\frac{7600}{5643}$ = $1.35

(A) $1.35
B $1.36
C $1.27
D $1.06

(2 marks)

3   Waffle had share capital of $7.5 million in 50c equity shares at 1 October 20X6. On 1 January 20X7 it made an issue of 4 million shares at full market price immediately followed by a 1 for 3 bonus issue.

The financial statements at 30 September 20X7 showed profit for the year of $12 million.

What was EPS for the year?

Handwritten annotations:

shares
B/f (7500/0.5)   15000
Full market price share (4000×9/12)   3000   issue
Bonus Issue (18000/3)   6000
24000

EPS = $\frac{12}{24}$ = 50c

A   53c
B   73c
C   48c
(D)   50c

(2 marks)

4   Plumstead had 4 million equity shares in issue throughout the year ended 31 March 20X7. On 30 September 20X7 it made a 1 for 4 bonus issue. Profit after tax for the year ended 31 March 20X8 was $3.6 million, out of which an equity dividend of 20c per share was paid. The financial statements for the year ended 31 March 20X7 showed EPS of 70c.

What is the EPS for the year ended 31 March 20X8 and the restated EPS for the year ended 31 March 20X7?

	20X8	20X7
A	72c	87.5c
B	52c	56c
C	80c	87.5c
(D)	72c	56c

Handwritten annotations:

B/f   4000
Bonus Issue   1000
5000

EPS = $\frac{3.6}{5}$ = 72c

(2 marks)

EPS 20X7 = 70c × 4000/5000 = 56c

5   At 30 September 20X2 the trial balance of Cavern includes the following balances:

	$'000
Equity shares of 20c each	50,000
Share premium	15,000

Cavern has accounted for a fully-subscribed rights issue of equity shares made on 1 April 20X2 of one new share for every four in issue at 42 cents each. This was the only share issue made during the year.

What were the balances on the share capital and share premium accounts at 30 September 20X1?

	Share capital	Share premium
	$'000	$'000
A	37,500	11,250
B	40,000	4,000
C	37,500	4,000
D	40,000	11,250

Handwritten annotations:
Shcap   Shpre
Balance 30 Sept 20X2 (250m shares)   50000   15000
Rights Issue:
Share capital (50m x 20c)   (10000)
Share premium (50m x 20c)   —   (11000)
                            4000   4000
Bal at 30 Sept 20X1 (200m shares)

(2 marks)

6   On 1 October 20X3, Hoy had $2·5 million of equity shares of 50 cents each in issue.

No new shares were issued during the year ended 30 September 20X4, but on that date there were outstanding share options to purchase 2 million equity shares at $1.20 each. The average market value of Hoy's equity shares during the year ended 30 September 20X4 was $3 per share.

Hoy's profit after tax for the year ended 30 September 20X4 was $1,550,000.

In accordance with IAS 33 *Earnings per Share*, what is Hoy's diluted earnings per share for the year ended 30 September 20X4?

- A   25.0 cents
- B   22.1 cents
- C   31.0 cents
- D   41.9 cents

Handwritten annotations:
Diluted : 2m shares @ 1.20 is equivalent to 800000 shares at full market price of $3 and the remaining 1.2m shares issued for no consideration.

Diluted EPS = 1550 / ((2500 x 2) + 1200) = 1550 / 6200 = 25c

(2 marks)

69 Preparation question: Fenton

(a)   Fenton had 5,000,000 ordinary shares in issue on 1 January 20X1.

On 31 January 20X1, the company made a rights issue of 1 for 4 at $1.75. The cum rights price was $2 per share.

On 30 June 20X1, the company made an issue at full market price of 125,000 shares.

Finally, on 30 November 20X1, the company made a 1 for 10 bonus issue.

Profit for the year was $2,900,000.

The reported EPS for year ended 31 December 20X0 was 46.4c.

Required

What was the earnings per share figure for year ended 31 December 20X1 and the restated EPS for year ended 31 December 20X0?

(b)   Sinbad had the same 10 million ordinary shares in issue on both 1 January 20X1 and 31 December 20X1. On 1 January 20X1 the company issued 1,200,000 $1 units of 5% convertible loan stock. Each unit of stock is convertible into 4 ordinary shares on 1 January 20X9 at the option of the holder. The following is an extract from Sinbad's statement of profit or loss for the year ended 31 December 20X1.

	$'000
Profit before interest and tax	980
Interest payable on 5% convertible loan stock	(60)
Profit before tax	920
Income tax expense (at 30%)	(276)
Profit for the year	644

Required

What was the basic and diluted earnings per share for the year ended 31 December 20X1?

(c)   Talbot has in issue 5,000,000 50c ordinary shares throughout 20X3.

During 20X1 the company had given certain senior executives options over 400,000 shares exercisable at $1.10 at any time after 31 May 20X4. None were exercised during 20X3. The average market value of one ordinary share during the period was $1.60. Talbot had made a profit after tax of $540,000 in 20X3.

Required

What is the basic and diluted earnings per share for the year ended 31 December 20X3?

70 Barstead (12/09 amended)   27 mins

(a)   The following figures have been calculated from the financial statements (including comparatives) of Barstead for the year ended 30 September 20X1.

Increase in profit after taxation	80%
Increase in (basic) earnings per share	5%
Increase in diluted earnings per share	2%

Required

Explain why the three measures of earnings (profit) growth for the same company over the same period can give apparently differing impressions.   **(4 marks)**

(b)   The profit after tax for Barstead for the year ended 30 September 20X1 was $15 million. At 1 October 20X0 the company had in issue 36 million equity shares and a $10 million 8% convertible loan note. The loan note will mature in 20X2 and will be redeemed at par or converted to equity shares on the basis of 25 shares for each $100 of loan note at the loan-note holders' option. On 1 January 20X1 Barstead made a fully subscribed rights issue of one new share for every four shares held at a price of $2.80 each. The market price of the equity shares of Barstead immediately before the issue was $3.80. The earnings per share (EPS) reported for the year ended 30 September 20X0 was 35 cents.

Barstead's income tax rate is 25%.

Required

Calculate the (basic) EPS figure for Barstead (including comparatives) and the diluted EPS (comparatives not required) that would be disclosed for the year ended 30 September 20X1.   **(6 marks)**

(c)   The issued share capital of Savoir, a publicly listed company, at 31 March 20X5 was $21 million. Its shares are denominated at 25 cents each.

On 1 April 20X5 Savoir issued $20 million 8% convertible loan stock at par. The terms of conversion (on 1 April 20X8) are that for every $100 of loan stock, 50 ordinary shares will be issued at the option of loan stockholders. Alternatively the loan stock will be redeemed at par for cash. Also on 1 April 20X5 the directors of Savoir were awarded share options on 12 million ordinary shares exercisable from 1 April 20X8 at $1.50 per share. The average market value of Savoir's ordinary shares for the year ended 31 March 20X6 was $2.50 each. The income tax rate is 25%. Earnings attributable to ordinary shareholders for the year ended 31 March 20X6 were $25,200,000. The share options have been correctly recorded in the financial statements.

Required

Calculate Savoir's basic and diluted earnings per share for the year ended 31 March 20X6 (comparative figures are not required).

You may assume that both the convertible loan stock and the directors' options are dilutive.   **(5 marks)**

(Total = 15 marks)

71 Rebound (6/11 amended)

27 mins

(a) Your assistant has been reading the IASB's *Conceptual Framework for Financial Reporting* and as part of the qualitative characteristics of financial statements under the heading of 'relevance' he notes that the predictive value of information is considered important. He is aware that financial statements are prepared historically (ie after transactions have occurred) and offers the view that the predictive value of financial statements would be enhanced if forward-looking information (eg forecasts) were published rather than backward-looking historical statements.

Required

By the use of specific examples, provide an explanation to your assistant of how IFRS presentation and disclosure requirements can assist the predictive role of historically prepared financial statements.

(6 marks)

(b) The following summarised information is available in relation to Rebound, a publicly listed company.

Statement of profit or loss extracts years ended 31 March:

	20X2		20X1	
	Continuing	*Discontinued*	*Continuing*	*Discontinued*
	$'000	$'000	$'000	$'000
Profit after tax				
Existing operations	2,000	(750)	1,750	600
Operations acquired on 1 August 20X1	450		nil	

Analysts expect profits from the market sector in which Rebound's existing operations are based to increase by 6% in the year to 31 March 20X3 and by 8% in the sector of its newly acquired operations.

On 1 April 20X0 Rebound had in issue:

- $3 million of 25 cents equity shares

- $5 million 8% convertible loan stock 20X7; the terms of conversion are 40 equity shares in exchange for each $100 of loan stock

Assume an income tax rate of 30%.

On 1 October 20X1 the directors of Rebound were granted options to buy 2 million shares in the company for $1 each. The average market price of Rebound's shares for the year ending 31 March 20X2 was $2.50 each.

Required

(i) Calculate Rebound's estimated profit after tax for the year ending 31 March 20X3 assuming the analysts' expectations prove correct. **(3 marks)**

(ii) Calculate the diluted earnings per share (EPS) on the continuing operations of Rebound for the year ended 31 March 20X2 and the comparatives for 20X1. **(6 marks)**

(Total = 15 marks)

72 Multiple choice questions – analysing and interpreting financial statements

1   An entity has an average operating profit margin of 23% and an average asset turnover of 0.8, which is similar to the averages for the industry.

The entity is likely to be:

The low asset turnover suggests a capital-Intensive industry. This rules out the estate agency or architectural practice. Supermarkets can also be capital-Intensive but tend to operate on low profit margins.

A   An architectural practice
B   A supermarket
C   An estate agent
D   A manufacturer   (2 marks)

2   Extracts from the financial statements of Persimmon are as follows:

Statement of profit or loss	$'000	Statement of financial position	$'000
Operating profit	230	Ordinary shares	2,000
Finance costs	(15)	Revaluation surplus	300
Profit before tax	215	Retained earnings	1,200
Income tax	(15)		3,500
Profit for the year	200	10% loan notes	1,000
		Current liabilities	100
		Total equity and liabilities	4,600

What is the return on capital employed?

A   5.1%
B   4.7%
C   6.6%
D   6%

profit before interest and tax
capital employed (3500 + 1000)

$$\frac{230 \%}{4500} = 5.1 \%$$
                                                                                         (2 marks)

3   Which of the following will increase the length of a company's operating cycle?

A   Reducing the receivables collection period
B   Reducing the inventory holding period
C   Reducing the payables payment period
D   Reducing time taken to produce goods

This will reduce working capital and means that it will take longer to build up working capital needed for production. The other options will all speed up the operating cycle.
                                                                                         (2 marks)

4   In the year to 31 December 20X9 Weston pays an interim equity dividend of 3.4c per share and declares a final equity dividend of 11.1c. It has 5 million $1 shares in issue and the ex div share price is $3.50.

What is the dividend yield?

A   4%
B   24%
C   3.2%
D   4.1%

(Dividends (3.4 + 11.1) / Share price) × 100 =

$$\frac{14.5}{350} \times 100 = 4.1\%$$
                                                                                         (2 marks)

5   Analysis of the financial statements of Capricorn at 31 December 20X8 yields the following information.

Gross profit margin	30%
Current ratio	2.14
ROCE	16.3%
Asset turnover	4.19
Inventory turnover	13.9

What is the net profit margin?

A   3.9%   *Net profit margin is a component of ROCE so 16.3% / 4.19 = 3.9%*
B   7.6%
C   16.1%
D   7.1%   **(2 marks)**

---

6   Camargue is a listed company with four million 50c ordinary shares in issue. The following extract is from its financial statements for the year ended 30 September 20X4.

Statement of profit or loss

	$'000
Profit before tax	900
Income tax expense	(100)
Profit for the year	800

At 30 September 20X4 the market price of Camargue's shares was $1.50. What was the P/E ratio on that date?

A   6.6   *EPS = 800 / 4000 = 20c*
B   7.5
C   3.75   *P/E ratio = 150/20 = 7.5*
D   3.3   **(2 marks)**

---

7   Quartile is in the jewellery retail business which can be assumed to be highly seasonal. For the year ended 30 September 20X4, Quartile assessed its operating performance by comparing selected accounting ratios with those of its business sector average as provided by an agency. You may assume that the business sector used by the agency is an accurate representation of Quartile's business.

Which of the following circumstances may invalidate the comparison of Quartile's ratios with those of the sector average?

(i)   In the current year, Quartile has experienced significant rising costs for its purchases.

(ii)   The sector average figures are compiled from companies whose year end is between 1 July 20X4 and 30 September 20X4.

(iii) Quartile does not revalue its properties, but is aware that other entities in this sector do.

(iv)   During the year, Quartile discovered an error relating to the inventory count at 30 September 20X3. This error was correctly accounted for in the financial statements for the current year ended 30 September 20X4.

A   All four
B   (i), (ii) and (iii)
C   (ii) and (iii) only
D   (ii), (iii) and (iv)   **(2 marks)**

A possible three-month difference in Y/E date can be significant in a seasonal business and Quartile could be expected to show a proportionately higher ROCE than entities that revalue their properties. Rising costs will have been experienced by all companies and the inventory adjustment will have been corrected to make opening inventory for the current year correct –

8   The following information has been taken or calculated from Fowler's financial statements for the year ended 30 September 20X4.

Fowler's cash cycle at 30 September 20X4 is 70 days. Its inventory turnover is six times.

Year-end trade payables are $230,000. Purchases on credit for the year were $2 million. Cost of sales for the year was $1.8 million.

What is Fowler's trade receivables collection period as at 30 September 20X4?

All calculations should be made to the nearest full day. The trading year is 365 days.

A   106 days
B   89 days
C   56 days
D   51 days   (2 marks)

Handwritten annotations:

Inventory days (365/6)   61
Payable days ($230000 /$2m) × 365)   (42)
Receivable days   51
Cash cycle   70

73 Preparation question: Victular (12/08)

Victular is a public company that would like to acquire (100% of) a suitable private company. It has obtained the following draft financial statements for two companies, Grappa and Merlot. They operate in the same industry and their managements have indicated that they would be receptive to a takeover.

STATEMENTS OF PROFIT OR LOSS FOR THE YEAR ENDED 30 SEPTEMBER 20X8

	Grappa	Merlot
	$'000	$'000
Revenue	12,000	20,500
Cost of sales	(10,500)	(18,000)
Gross profit	1,500	2,500
Operating expenses	(240)	(500)
Finance costs – loan	(210)	(300)
– overdraft	nil	(10)
– lease	nil	(290)
Profit before tax	1,050	1,400
Income tax expense	(150)	(400)
Profit for the year	900	1,000
Dividends paid during the year.	250	700

STATEMENTS OF FINANCIAL POSITION AS AT 30 SEPTEMBER 20X8

		Grappa		Merlot
	$'000	$'000	$'000	$'000
Non-current assets				
Factory (note (i))		4,400		nil
Owned plant (note (ii))		5,000		2,200
Leased plant (note (ii))		nil		5,300
		9,400		7,500
Current assets				
Inventory	2,000		3,600	
Trade receivables	2,400		3,700	
Bank	600		nil	
		5,000		7,300
Total assets		14,400		14,800

	Grappa		Merlot
	$'000	$'000	$'000	$'000

Equity and liabilities				
Equity shares of $1 each	2,000		2,000	
Property revaluation reserve	900		nil	
Retained earnings	2,600		800	
		5,500		2,800
Non-current liabilities				
Finance lease obligations (note (iii))	nil		3,200	
7% loan notes	3,000		nil	
10% loan notes	nil		3,000	
Deferred tax	600		100	
Government grants	1,200		nil	
		4,800		6,300
Current liabilities				
Bank overdraft	nil		1,200	
Trade payables	3,100		3,800	
Government grants	400		nil	
Finance lease obligations (note (iii))	nil		500	
Taxation	600		200	
		4,100		5,700
Total equity and liabilities		14,400		14,800

The following information is relevant.

(i)   Both companies operate from similar premises.

(ii)   Additional details of the two companies' plant are:

	Grappa	Merlot
	$'000	$'000
Owned plant – cost	8,000	10,000
Leased plant – original fair value	nil	7,500

There were no disposals of plant during the year by either company.

(iii)   The interest rate implicit within Merlot's finance leases is 7.5% per annum. For the purpose of calculating ROCE and gearing, all finance lease obligations are treated as long-term interest bearing borrowings.

(iv)   The following ratios have been calculated for Grappa and can be taken to be correct.

Return on year end capital employed (ROCE) (capital employed taken as shareholders' funds plus long-term interest bearing borrowings – see Note 3 above)	14.8%
Pre-tax return on equity (ROE)	19.1%
Net asset (total assets less current liabilities) turnover	1.2 times
Gross profit margin	12.5%
Operating profit margin	10.5%
Current ratio	1.2:1
Closing inventory holding period	70 days
Trade receivables' collection period	73 days
Trade payables' payment period (using cost of sales)	108 days
Gearing (see Note 3 above)	35.3%
Interest cover	6 times
Dividend cover	3.6 times

Required

(a)   Calculate for Merlot the ratios equivalent to all those given for Grappa above.

(b) Assess the relative performance and financial position of Grappa and Merlot for the year ended 30 September 20X8 to inform the directors of Victular in their acquisition decision.

(c) Explain the limitations of ratio analysis and any further information that may be useful to the directors of Victular when making an acquisition decision.

74 Bengal (6/11amended)   27 mins

Bengal is a public company. Its most recent financial statements are shown below:

STATEMENTS OF PROFIT OR LOSS FOR THE YEAR ENDED 31 MARCH

	20X1	20X0
	$'000	$'000
Revenue	25,500	17,250
Cost of sales	(14,800)	(10,350)
Gross profit	10,700	6,900
Distribution costs	(2,700)	(1,850)
Administrative expenses	(2,100)	(1,450)
Finance costs	(650)	(100)
Profit before taxation	5,250	3,500
Income tax expense	(2,250)	(1,000)
Profit for the year	3,000	2,500

STATEMENTS OF FINANCIAL POSITION AS AT 31 MARCH

	20X1		20X0	
	$'000	$'000	$'000	$'000
Non-current assets				
Property, plant and equipment		9,500		5,400
Intangibles		6,200		nil
		15,700		5,400
Current assets				
Inventory	3,600		1,800	
Trade receivables	2,400		1,400	
Bank	nil		4,000	
Non-current assets held for sale	2,000	8,000	nil	7,200
Total assets		23,700		12,600
Equity and liabilities				
Equity				
Equity shares of $1 each		5,000		5,000
Retained earnings		4,500		2,250
		9,500		7,250
Non-current liabilities				
5% loan notes		2,000		2,000
8% loan notes		7,000		nil
Current liabilities				
Bank overdraft	200		nil	
Trade payables	2,800		2,150	
Current tax payable	2,200	5,200	1,200	3,350
Total equity and liabilities		23,700		12,600

Additional information:

(i) There were no disposals of non-current assets during the period; however Bengal does have some non-current assets classified as 'held for sale' at 31 March 20X1.

(ii) Depreciation of property, plant and equipment for the year ended 31 March 20X1 was $640,000.

A disappointed shareholder has observed that although revenue during the year has increased by 48% (8,250 / 17,250 × 100), profit for the year has only increased by 20% (500 / 2,500 × 100).

Required

Comment on the performance (including addressing the shareholder's observation) and financial position of Bengal for the year ended 31 March 20X1.   Up to five marks are available for the calculation of appropriate ratios.

(15 marks)

75 Tangier (specimen paper)   27 mins

Tangier's summarised financial statements for the years ended 30 September 20X4 and the comparative figures are shown below.

STATEMENTS OF PROFIT OR LOSS FOR THE YEAR ENDED 30 SEPTEMBER

	20X4	20X3
	$m	$m
Revenue	2,700	1,820
Cost of sales	(1,890)	(1,092)
Gross profit	810	728
Administrative expense	(345)	(200)
Distribution costs	(230)	(130)
Finance costs	(40)	(5)
Profit before taxation	195	393
Income tax expense	(60)	(113)
Profit for the year	135	280

STATEMENTS OF FINANCIAL POSITION AS AT 30 SEPTEMBER

	20X4		20X3	
	$m	$m	$m	$m
Non-current assets				
Property, plant and equipment		680		410
Intangible asset: manufacturing licence		300		200
Investment at cost – Raremetal		230		nil
		1,210		610
Current assets				
Inventory	200		110	
Trade receivables	195		75	
Cash and cash equivalents	nil	395	120	305
Total assets		1,605		915
Equity and liabilities				
Equity shares of $1 each		430		250
Retained earnings		375		295
		805		545
Non-current liabilities				
5% secured loan notes	100		100	
10% secured loan notes	300	400	nil	100
Current liabilities				
Bank overdraft	110		nil	
Trade payables	210		160	
Current tax payable	80	400	110	270
Total equity and liabilities		1,605		915

The following additional information has been obtained in relation to the operations of Tangier for the year ended 30 September 20X4.

(i) On 1 January 20X4, Tangier won a tender for a new contract to supply Jetside with aircraft engines which Tangier manufactures under a recently acquired licence. The bidding process had been very competitive and Tangier had to increase its manufacturing capacity to fulfil the contract.

(ii) The company also decided to invest in Raremetal by buying 8% of its equity shares to secure supplies of specialised materials used in the manufacture of the engines. No dividends were received from Raremetal nor had the value of its shares increased.

On seeing the results for the first time, one of the company's non-executive directors is disappointed by the current year's performance.

Required

Explain how the new contract and its related costs may have affected Tangier's operating performance during the year ended 30 September 20X4, identifying any further information regarding the contract which may be useful to your answer.

Your answer should be supported by appropriate ratios (up to five marks); however, ratios and analysis of working capital are not required. **(15 marks)**

76 Woodbank (6/14 amended)

Shown below are the financial statements of Woodbank for its most recent two years:

STATEMENTS OF PROFIT OR LOSS FOR THE YEAR ENDED 31 MARCH:

	20X4	20X3
	$'000	$'000
Revenue	150,000	110,000
Cost of sales	117,000	(85,800)
Gross profit	33,000	24,200
Distribution costs	(6,000)	(5,000)
Administrative expenses	(9,000)	(9,200)
Finance costs – loan note interest	(1,750)	(500)
Profit before tax	16,250	9,500
Income tax expense	(5,750)	(3,000)
Profit for the year	10,500	6,500

STATEMENTS OF FINANCIAL POSITION AS AT 31 MARCH

	20X4	20X3
	$'000	$'000
ASSETS		
Non-current assets		
Property, plant and equipment	118,000	85,000
Goodwill	30,000	-
	148,000	85,000
Current assets		
Inventory	15,500	12,000
Trade receivables	11,000	8,000
Bank	500	5,000
	27,000	25,000
Total assets	175,000	110,000

	20X4	20X3
	$'000	$'000
EQUITY AND LIABILITIES		
Equity		
Equity shares of $1 each	80,000	80,000
Retained earnings	15,000	10,000
	95,000	90,000
Non-current liabilities		
10% loan notes	55,000	5,000
Current liabilities		
Trade payables	21,000	13,000
Current tax payable	4,000	2,000
	25,000	15,000
Total equity and liabilities	175,000	110,000

The following information is available:

(i) On 1 January 20X4, Woodbank purchased the trading assets and operations of Shaw for $50 million and, on the same date, issued additional 10% loan notes to finance the purchase. Shaw was an unincorporated entity and its results (for three months from 1 January 20X4 to 31 March 20X4) and net assets (including goodwill not subject to any impairment) are included in Woodbank's financial statements for the year ended 31 March 20X4. There were no other purchases or sales of non-current assets during the year ended 31 March 20X4.

(ii) Extracts of the results (for three months) of the previously separate business of Shaw, which are included in Woodbank's statement of profit or loss for the year ended 31 March 20X4, are:

	$'000
Revenue	30,000
Cost of sales	(21,000)
Gross profit	9,000
Distribution costs	(2,000)
Administrative expenses	(2,000)

(iii) The following six ratios have been correctly calculated for Woodbank for the years ended 31 March:

	20X3	20X4
Return on capital employed (ROCE)	10.5%	12%
(profit before interest and tax/year-end total assets less current liabilities)		
Net asset (equal to capital employed) turnover	1.16 times	1.0 times
Gross profit margin	22%	22%
Profit before interest and tax margin	9.1%	12%
Current ratio	1.7:1	1.08:1
Gearing (debt/(debt + equity))	5.3%	36.7%

Required

(a) Calculate for the year ended 31 March 20X4 equivalent ratios to the first FOUR only for Woodbank excluding the effects of the purchase of Shaw. **(4 marks)**

(b) Assess the comparative financial performance and position of Woodbank for the year ended 31 March 20X4. Your answer should refer to the effects of the purchase of Shaw. **(11 marks)**

(Total = 15 marks)

77 Multiple choice questions – limitations of financial statements and interpretation techniques

1   An entity carries its property at revalued amount. Property values have fallen during the current period and an impairment loss has been recognised on the property, however its carrying amount is still higher than its depreciated historical cost.

What is the effect of the impairment on these ratios?

	ROCE	Gearing
A	Decrease	Decrease
B	Decrease	Increase
C	Increase	Decrease
D	Increase	Increase

(2 marks)

2   A company has a current ratio of 1.5, a quick ratio of 0.4 and a positive cash balance. If it purchases inventory on credit, what is the effect on these ratios?

	Current ratio	Quick ratio
A	Decrease	Decrease
B	Decrease	Increase
C	Increase	Decrease
D	Increase	Increase

(2 marks)

3   Fritwell has an asset turnover of 2.0 and an operating profit margin of 10%. It is launching a new product which is expected to generate additional sales of $1.6 million and additional profit of $120,000. It will require additional assets of $500,000.

Assuming there are no other changes to current operations, how will the new product affect these ratios?

	Operating profit margin	ROCE
A	Decrease	Decrease
B	Decrease	Increase
C	Increase	Decrease
D	Increase	Increase

(2 marks)

4   Which of the following is a possible reason why a company's inventory holding period increases from one year to the next?

A   An increase in demand for its products
B   A reduction in selling prices
C   Obsolete inventory lines
D   Seasonal fluctuations in orders

(2 marks)

5   Use of historical cost accounting means asset values can be reliably verified but it has a number of shortcomings which need to be considered when analysing financial statements.

Which one of these is a possible result of the use of historical cost accounting during a period of inflation?

A   Overstatement of non-current asset values
B   Overstatement of profits
C   Understatement of interest costs
D   Understatement of ROCE

(2 marks)

6   Creative accounting measures are often aimed at reducing gearing.

Which one of these is **not** a measure which can be used to reduce (or not increase) gearing?

(A)   Re-negotiating a loan to secure a lower interest rate
B   Treating a finance lease as an operating lease
C   Repaying a loan just before the year end and taking it out again at the beginning of the next year.
D   'Selling' an asset under a sale and leaseback agreement   **(2 marks)**

7   If a company wished to maintain the carrying amount in the financial statements of its non-current assets, which one of the following would it be unlikely to do?

(A)   Enter into a sale and operating leaseback
B   Account for asset –based government grants using the deferral method
C   Revalue its properties
D   Change the depreciation method for new asset acquisitions from 25% reducing balance to ten years straight line   **(2 marks)**

8   Trent uses the formula: (trade receivables at year end/revenue for the year) × 365 to calculate how long on average (in days) its customers take to pay.

Which of the following would **not** affect the correctness of the above calculation of the average number of days a customer takes to pay?

A   Trent experiences considerable seasonal trading
B   Trent makes a number of cash sales through retail outlets
C   Reported revenue does not include a 15% sales tax whereas the receivables do include the tax
(D)   Trent factors with recourse the receivable of its largest customer   **(2 marks)**

78 Waxwork (6/09)   27 mins

(a)   The objective of IAS 10 *Events After the Reporting Period* is to prescribe the treatment of events that occur after an entity's reporting period has ended.

Required

Define the period to which IAS 10 relates and distinguish between adjusting and non-adjusting events.

(5 marks)

(b)   Waxwork's current year end is 31 March 20X9. Its financial statements were authorised for issue by its directors on 6 May 20X9 and the AGM (annual general meeting) will be held on 3 June 20X9. The following matters have been brought to your attention.

(i)   On 12 April 20X9 a fire completely destroyed the company's largest warehouse and the inventory it contained. The carrying amounts of the warehouse and the inventory were $10 million and $6 million respectively. It appears that the company has not updated the value of its insurance cover and only expects to be able to recover a maximum of $9 million from its insurers. Waxwork's trading operations have been severely disrupted since the fire and it expects large trading losses for some time to come.   **(4 marks)**

(ii)   A single class of inventory held at another warehouse was valued at its cost of $460,000 at 31 March 20X9. In April 20X9 70% of this inventory was sold for $280,000 on which Waxworks' sales staff earned a commission of 15% of the selling price.   **(3 marks)**

(iii) On 18 May 20X9 the government announced tax changes which have the effect of increasing Waxwork's deferred tax liability by $650,000 as at 31 March 20X9.   **(3 marks)**

Required

Explain the required treatment of the items (i) to (iii) by Waxwork in its financial statements for the year ended 31 March 20X9.

Assume all items are material and are independent of each other.   **(10 marks as indicated)**

(Total =15 marks)

79 Quartile (12/12 amended)

27 mins

Quartile sells jewellery through stores in retail shopping centres throughout the country. Over the last two years it has experienced declining profitability and is wondering if this is related to the sector as a whole. It has recently subscribed to an agency that produces average ratios across many businesses. Below are the ratios that have been provided by the agency for Quartile's business sector based on a year end of 30 June 20X2 and the equivalent ratios for Quartile.

	Quartile	Sector average
Return on year-end capital employed (ROCE)	12.1%	16.8%
Net asset (total assets less current liabilities) turnover	1.6 times	1.4 times
Gross profit margin	25%	35%
Operating profit margin	7.5%	12%
Current ratio	1.55:1	1.25:1
Average inventory turnover	4.5 times	3 times
Trade payables' payment period	45 days	64 days
Debt to equity	30%	38%

The financial statements of Quartile for the year ended 30 September 20X2 are:

STATEMENT OF PROFIT OR LOSS

	$'000	$'000
Revenue		56,000
Opening inventory	8,300	
Purchases	43,900	
Closing inventory	(10,200)	
Cost of sales		(42,000)
Gross profit		14,000
Operating costs		(9,800)
Finance costs		(800)
Profit before tax		3,400
Income tax expense		(1,000)
Profit for the year		2,400

STATEMENT OF FINANCIAL POSITION

	$'000
ASSETS	
Non-current assets	
Property and shop fittings	25,600
Deferred development expenditure	5,000
	30,600
Current assets	
Inventory	10,200
Bank	1,000
	11,200
Total assets	41,800
EQUITY AND LIABILITIES	
Equity	
Equity shares of $1 each	15,000
Property revaluation reserve	3,000
Retained earnings	8,600
	26,600
Non-current liabilities	
10% loan notes	8,000
Current liabilities	
Trade payables	5,400
Current tax payable	1,800
	7,200
Total equity and liabilities	41,800

The deferred development expenditure relates to an investment in a process to manufacture artificial precious gems for future sale by Quartile in the retail jewellery market.

Required

(a)   Assess the financial and operating performance of Quartile in comparison to its sector averages. **(11 marks)**

(b)   Explain four possible limitations on the usefulness of the above comparison.   **(4 marks)**

(Total = 15 marks)

80 Multiple choice questions – statement of cash flows

1   Extracts from the statements of financial position of Nedburg are as follows.

Statements of financial position as at 30 September:

	20X2	20X1
	$m	$m
Ordinary shares of $1 each	750	500
Share premium	350	100

On 1 October 20X1 a bonus issue of one new share for every 10 held was made, financed from the share premium account. This was followed by a further issue for cash.

What amount will appear under 'cash flows from financing activities' in the statement of cash flows of Nedburg for the year ended 30 September 20X2 in respect of share issues?

A $500 million   B/f (500+100)   600
B $450 million   Cash received (β)   500
C $550 million
D $250 million   c/f (750 + 350)   1100   **(2 marks)**

2   The carrying amount of property, plant and equipment was $410 million at 31 March 20X1 and $680 million at 31 March 20X2. During the year, property with a carrying amount of $210 million was revalued to $290 million. The depreciation charge for the year was $115 million. There were no disposals.

What amount will appear on the statement of cash flows for the year ended 31 March 20X2 in respect of purchases of property, plant and equipment?

A $270 million   B/f   410
B $225 million   Depreciation   (115)
C $235 million   Revaluation   80
D $305 million   Purchases (β)   305
     c/f   680   **(2 marks)**

3   The statement of financial position of Pinto at 31 March 20X7 showed property, plant and equipment with a carrying amount of $1,860,000. At 31 March 20X8 it had increased to $2,880,000.

During the year to 31 March 20X8 plant with a carrying amount of $240,000 was sold at a loss of $90,000, depreciation of $280,000 was charged and $100,000 was added to the revaluation surplus in respect of property, plant and equipment.

What amount should appear under 'investing activities' in the statement of cash flows of Pinto for the year ended 31 March 20X8 as cash paid to acquire property, plant and equipment?

A $1,640,000   Bal b/f   1600 1860
B $1,440,000   Revaluation   100
C $1,260,000   Disposal   (240)
D $1,350,000   Depreciation   (280)
     Additions (β)   1440
     Balance c/f   1440 2880   **(2 marks)**

4   Extracts from Deltoid's statements of financial position are as follows.

Statement of financial position as at 31 March:

	20X1	20X0
	$'000	$'000
Non-current assets		
Property, plant and equipment		
Leased plant	6,500	2,500
Non-current liabilities		
Finance lease obligations	4,800	2,000
Current liabilities		
Finance lease obligations	1,700	800

B/f (2000 + 800)   2800
Additions (6500 – 2500 + 1800)   5800
Payments made (β)   (2100)
c/f (4800 + 1700)   6500

During the year to 31 March 20X1 depreciation charged on leased plant was $1,800,000.

What amount will be shown in the statement of cash flows of Deltoid for the year ended 31 March 20X1 in respect of payments made under finance leases?

A $300,000
B $7,100,000
C $2,100,000
D $5,800,000

(2 marks)

81 Preparation question: Dickson

Below are the statements of financial position of Dickson as at 31 March 20X8 and 31 March 20X7, together with the statement of profit or loss and other comprehensive income for the year ended 31 March 20X8.

	20X8	20X7
	$'000	$'000
Non-current assets		
Property, plant and equipment	925	737
Development expenditure	290	160
	1,215	897
Current assets		
Inventories	360	227
Trade receivables	274	324
Investments	143	46
Cash	29	117
	806	714
Total assets	2,021	1,611
Equity		
Share capital – $1 ordinary shares	500	400
Share premium	350	100
Revaluation surplus	160	60
Retained earnings	229	255
	1,239	815
Non-current liabilities		
6% debentures	150	100
Finance lease liabilities	100	80
Deferred tax	48	45
	298	225
Current liabilities		
Trade payables	274	352
Finance lease liabilities	17	12
Current tax	56	153
Debenture interest	5	–
Bank overdraft	132	54
	484	571
Total equity and liabilities	2,021	1,611

STATEMENT OF PROFIT OR LOSS AND OTHER COMPREHENSIVE INCOME

	$'000
Revenue	1,476
Cost of sales	(962)
Gross profit	514
Other expenses	(157)
Finance costs	(15)
Profit before tax	342
Income tax expense	(162)
Profit for the year	180
Other comprehensive income:	
Gain on revaluation of property, plant and equipment	100
Total comprehensive income for the year	280

Notes

(i)   During 20X8, amortisation of $60,000 was charged on development projects.

(ii)   During 20X8 items of property, plant and equipment with a net book value of $103,000 were sold for $110,000. Profit on sale was netted off against 'other expenses'.

Depreciation charged in the year on property, plant and equipment totalled $57,000. Dickson purchased $56,000 of property, plant and equipment by means of finance leases, payments being made in arrears on the last day of each accounting period.

(iii) The current asset investments are government bonds and management has decided to class them as cash equivalents.

(iv)   The new debentures were issued on 1 April 20X7. Finance cost includes debenture interest and finance lease finance charges only.

(v)   During the year Dickson made a 1 for 8 bonus issue, capitalising its retained earnings, followed by a rights issue.

Required

Using the pro-forma below:

(a)   Prepare a statement of cash flows for Dickson in accordance with IAS 7 using the indirect method.
(b)   Prepare (additionally) net cash from operating activities using the direct method.

(a)   DICKSON
       STATEMENT OF CASH FLOWS FOR THE YEAR ENDED 31 MARCH 20X8

Cash flows from operating activities	$'000	$'000
Profit before taxation		
Adjustments for:		
Depreciation		
Amortisation		
Interest expense		
Profit on disposal of assets	_____	
Movement in inventories		
Movement in trade receivables		
Movement in trade payables	_____	
Cash generated from operations		
Interest paid		
Income taxes paid	_____	
Net cash from operating activities		

Cash flows from investing activities
Development expenditure
Purchase of property, plant & equipment
Proceeds from sale of property, plant & equipment _____
Net cash used in investing activities
Cash flows from financing activities
Proceeds from issue of shares
Proceeds from issue of debentures
Payment of finance lease liabilities
Dividends paid _____
Net cash from financing activities _____
Net decrease in cash and cash equivalents
Cash and cash equivalents at beginning of period _____

Cash and cash equivalents at end of period _____

Workings

(b)   CASH FLOWS FROM OPERATING ACTIVITIES (Direct method)

                                                                    $'000
Cash received from customers
Cash paid to suppliers and employees   _____
Cash generated from operations
Interest paid
Income taxes paid   _____
Net cash from operating activities   _____

Workings

82 Mocha (12/11 amended)

54 mins

(a) The following information relates to the draft financial statements of Mocha.

SUMMARISED STATEMENTS OF FINANCIAL POSITION AS AT 30 SEPTEMBER

	20X1 $'000	20X0 $'000
ASSETS		
Non-current assets		
Property, plant and equipment (note (i))	32,600	24,100
Financial asset: equity investments (note (ii))	4,500	7,000
	37,100	31,100
Current assets		
Inventory	10,200	7,200
Trade receivables	3,500	3,700
Bank	nil	1,400
	13,700	12,300
Total assets	50,800	43,400
EQUITY AND LIABILITIES		
Equity		
Equity shares of $1 each (note (iii))	14,000	8,000
Share premium (note (iii))	nil	2,000
Revaluation reserve (note (iii))	2,000	3,600
Retained earnings	13,000	10,100
	29,000	23,700
Non-current liabilities		
Finance lease obligations	7,000	6,900
Deferred tax	1,300	900
Current liabilities		
Tax	1,000	1,200
Bank overdraft	2,900	nil
Provision for product warranties (note (iv))	1,600	4,000
Finance lease obligations	4,800	2,100
Trade payables	3,200	4,600
Total equity and liabilities	50,800	43,400

SUMMARISED STATEMENTS OF PROFIT OR LOSS FOR THE YEARS ENDED 30 SEPTEMBER:

	20X1 $'000	20X0 $'000
Revenue	58,500	41,000
Cost of sales	(46,500)	(30,000)
Gross profit	12,000	11,000
Operating expenses	(8,700)	(4,500)
Investment income (note (ii))	1,100	700
Finance costs	(500)	(400)
Profit before tax	3,900	6,800
Income tax expense	(1,000)	(1,800)
Profit for the year	2,900	5,000

The following additional information is available.

(i)   Property, plant and equipment

	Cost	Accumulated depreciation	Carrying amount
	$'000	$'000	$'000
At 30 September 20X0	33,600	(9,500)	24,100
New finance lease additions	6,700		6,700
Purchase of new plant	8,300		8,300
Disposal of property	(5,000)	1,000	(4,000)
Depreciation for the year		(2,500)	(2,500)
At 30 September 20X1	43,600	(11,000)	32,600

The property disposed of was sold for $8.1 million.

(ii)   Investments/investment income:

During the year an investment that had a carrying amount of $3 million was sold for $3.4 million. No investments were purchased during the year.

Investment income consists of:

Year to 30 September:	20X1	20X0
	$'000	$'000
Dividends received	200	250
Profit on sale of investment	400	nil
Increases in fair value	500	450
	1,100	700

(iii)   On 1 April 20X1 there was a bonus issue of shares that was funded from the share premium and some of the revaluation reserve. This was followed on 30 April 20X1 by an issue of shares for cash at par.

(iv)   The movement in the product warranty provision has been included in cost of sales.

Required

(a)   Prepare a statement of cash flows for Mocha for the year ended 30 September 20X1, in accordance with IAS 7 *Statement of cash flows*, using the indirect method.   **(19 marks)**

(b)   Comment on the performance and cash flow management of Mocha (ratios are not required).
                                                                                        (5 marks)

(c)   Shareholders can often be confused when trying to evaluate the information provided to them by a company's financial statements, particularly when comparing accruals-based information in the statement of profit or loss and the statement of financial position with that in the statement of cash flows.

Required

In the two areas stated below, illustrate, by reference to the information in the question and your answer to (a), how information in a statement of cash flows may give a different perspective of events than that given by accruals-based financial statements:

(i)   Operating performance   **(3 marks)**
(ii)   Investment in property, plant and equipment   **(3 marks)**

                                                                        (Total = 30 marks)

83 Multiple choice questions – accounting for inflation

1   Historical cost accounting remains in use because of its practical advantages.

Which one of the following is **not** an advantage of historical cost accounting?

A   Amounts of transactions are reliable and can be verified.

B   Amounts in the statement of financial position can be matched to amounts in the statement of cash flows

C   It avoids the overstatement of profit which can arise during periods of inflation.

D   It provides fewer opportunities for creative accounting than systems of current value accounting.   **(2 marks)**

2   The 'physical capital maintenance' concept states that profit is the increase in the physical productive capacity of the business over the period. This concept is applied in:

A   Current cost accounting
B   Historical cost accounting
C   Current value accounting
D   Current purchasing power accounting   **(2 marks)**

3   Which method of accounting adjusts income and capital values to allow for the effects of general price inflation?

A   Historical cost accounting
B   Current purchasing power accounting
C   Current cost accounting
D   Current value accounting   **(2 marks)**

4   Under CCA goods sold are charged to profit or loss at:

A   Historical cost
B   Replacement cost
C   Net realisable value
D   Economic value   **(2 marks)**

5   The use of historical cost accounting during a period of inflation can lead to overstatement of profits. This then leads to a number of other consequences. Which one of the following is **not** a likely consequence of overstatement of profits?

A   Higher wage demands from employees
B   Higher tax bills
C   Reduced dividends to shareholders
D   Overstated EPS   **(2 marks)**

6   Which of the following criticisms does **not** apply to historical cost accounts during a period of rising prices?

A   They contain mixed values; some items are at current values, some at out of date values.
B   They are difficult to verify as transactions could have happened many years ago.
C   They understate assets and overstate profit.
D   They overstate gearing in the statement of financial position.   **(2 marks)**

84 Preparation question: Changing prices

The following information has been extracted from the accounts of Norwich prepared under the historical cost convention for 20X6.

STATEMENT OF PROFIT OR LOSS EXTRACTS 20X6

	$m
Revenue	200
Profit	15
Less finance costs	3
Profit for the year	12

SUMMARISED STATEMENT OF FINANCIAL POSITION AT 31 DECEMBER 20X6

Assets	$m	$m
Property, plant & equipment at cost less depreciation		60
Current assets		
Inventories	20	
Receivables	30	
Bank	2	
		52
Total assets		112
Equity and liabilities		
Equity		62
Non-current liabilities		20
Current liabilities		30
Total equity and liabilities		112

The company's accountant has prepared the following current cost data.

Current cost adjustments for 20X6	$m
Depreciation adjustment	3
Cost of sales adjustment	5
Replacement cost at 31 December 20X6	
Property, plant & equipment, net of depreciation	85
Inventories	21

Required

(a) Calculate the current cost operating profit of Norwich for 20X6 and the summarised current cost statement of financial position of the company at 31 December 20X6, so far as the information permits.

(b) Calculate the following ratios from both the historical cost accounts and current cost accounts:
   (i) Interest cover
   (ii) Rate of return on shareholders' equity
   (iii) Debt/equity ratio

(c) Discuss the significance of the ratios calculated under (b) and of the reasons for differences between them.

Ignore taxation.

Approaching the question

1 To save time in this question, the current cost adjustments are given to you.

2 Part (b) is straightforward. Make sure you allow yourself time to give adequate weight to the discussion in part (c).

85 Update (2.5 6/03 part amended)   27 mins

Most companies prepare their financial statements under the historical cost convention. In times of rising prices it has been said that without modification such financial statements can be misleading.

Required

(a)   Explain the problems that can be encountered when users rely on financial statements prepared under the historical cost convention for their information needs.   **(7 marks)**

Your answer should consider problems with the statement of profit or loss and the statement of financial position.

(b)   Update has been considering the effect of alternative methods of preparing their financial statements. As an example they picked an item of plant that they acquired from Suppliers on 1 April 20X0 at a cost of $250,000.

The following details have been obtained.

- The company policy is to depreciate plant at 20% per annum on the reducing balance basis.

- The movement in the retail price index has been:

1 April 20X0	180
1 April 20X1	202
1 April 20X2	206
31 March 20X3	216

Suppliers' price catalogue at 31 March 20X3 shows an item of similar plant at a cost of $320,000. On reading the specification it appears that the new model can produce 480 units per hour whereas the model owned by Update can only produce 420 units per hour.

Required

Calculate for Update the depreciation charge for the plant for the year to 31 March 20X3 (based on year end values) and its carrying value in the statement of financial position on that date using:

- The historical cost basis
- A current purchasing power basis
- A current cost basis   **(8 marks)**
                                                                                        (Total = 15 marks)

86 Multiple choice questions – specialised, not-for-profit and public sector entities

1   Which of the following are unlikely to be stakeholders in a charity?

     A   Taxpayers
     B   Financial supporters
     C   Shareholders
     D   Government   (2 marks)

2   The International Public Sector Accounting Standards Board regulates public sector entities and is developing a set of accounting standards which closely mirror IFRS.

     Which of these is the main concept which needs to be introduced into public sector accounting?

     A   Materiality
     B   Accruals
     C   Relevance
     D   Faithful representation   (2 marks)

3   Public sector entities have performance measures laid down by government, based on Key Performance Indicators. Which of the following are likely to be financial KPIs for a local council?

     (i)   Rent receipts outstanding
     (ii)   Interest paid
     (iii)   Interest received
     (iv)   Interest cover
     (v)   Dividend cover
     (vi)   Financial actuals against budget
     (vii)   Return on capital employed

     A   (i),(ii),(iii),(iv),(vi)
     B   (i),(ii),(vi),(vii)
     C   (ii),(iii),(iv),(v)
     D   All of them   (2 marks)

4   Which one of the following is **not** true of entities in the charity sector?

     A   Their objective is to provide services to recipients and not to make a profit.
     B   They have to be registered.
     C   Their revenues arise mainly from contributions rather than sales.
     D   They have only a narrow group of stakeholders to consider.   (2 marks)

5   Which one of the following is the main aspect in which public sector bodies differ from charities?

     A   Importance of budgeting
     B   Funded by government
     C   Performance measured by KPIs
     D   No requirement to earn a return on assets   (2 marks)

6   Although the objectives and purposes of not-for-profit entities are different from those of commercial entities, the accounting requirements of not-for-profit entities are moving closer to those entities to which IFRSs apply.

     Which of the following IFRS requirements would **not** be relevant to a not-for-profit entity?

     A   Preparation of a statement of cash flows
     B   Requirement to capitalise a finance lease
     C   Disclosure of earnings per share
     D   Disclosure of non-adjusting events after the reporting date   (2 marks)

87 Preparation question: Appraisal

(a) Explain in what ways your approach to performance appraisal would differ if you were asked to assess the performance of a not-for-profit organisation.

(b) You have been asked to advise on an application for a loan to build an extension to a sports club which is a not-for-profit organisation. You have been provided with the audited financial statements of the sports club for the last four years.

Required

Identify and explain the ratios that you would calculate to assist in determining whether you would advise that the loan should be granted.

Answers

1 Multiple choice answers – conceptual framework

1   C   A resource controlled by an entity as a result of past events and from which future economic benefits are expected to flow to the entity

2   C   This is a valid liability.

           The licence payment could be avoided by ceasing manufacture.

           The fall in value of the investment is a loss chargeable to profit or loss.

           Planned expenditure does not constitute an obligation.

3   B   The amount that could be obtained from selling the asset, less any costs of disposal

4   A   The underlying assumption is going concern.

5   C   Disclosure of accounting policies is particularly important when comparing the results and performance of one entity against another which may be applying different policies.

6   D   Whenever there is a conflict between an IFRS and the *Conceptual Framework*, the IFRS takes precedence.

7   C   Trade receivables factored without recourse should be derecognised. The other accounting treatments are all incorrect.

2 Lisbon

Text reference. Chapter 1.

Top tips. You should have had no trouble explaining the characteristics, but remember to state how they make financial information useful. Working out how the characteristics related to the scenarios took a bit more thought.

Easy marks. Part (a) was 11 easy marks.

Marking scheme

			Marks
(a)	3 marks for each characteristic	12	
	Maximum		11
(b)	2 marks for each transaction or event		4
			15

(a)   **Relevance**

The relevance of information must be considered in terms of the decision-making needs of users. It is relevant when it can influence their economic decisions or allow them to reassess past decisions and evaluations. Economic decisions often have a predictive quality – users may make financial decisions on the basis of what they expect to happen in the future. To some degree past performance gives information on expected future performance and this is enhanced by the provision of comparatives, so that users can see the direction in which the company is moving. The separate presentation of discontinued operations also shows how much profit or loss can be attributed to that part of the operation which will be not be there in the future. One aspect of relevance is materiality. An item is material if its omission or misstatement could influence the economic decisions of users. Relevance would not be enhanced by the inclusion of immaterial items which may serve to obscure the important issues.

Faithful representation

Information can be considered to be a faithful representation when it is complete, neutral and free from bias. The statement of profit or loss must faithfully represent the results of the entity for the period in question and the statement of financial position must faithfully represent its financial position at the end of the period. Financial statements in which provision had not been made for known liabilities or in which asset values had not been correctly stated could not be considered reliable. To be a faithful representation, transactions should be represented in accordance with their economic substance, rather than their legal form. This principle governs the treatment of finance leases, sale and leaseback transactions and consignment inventory. If these types of transactions are not accounted for in accordance with their economic substance, then the financial statements are not a faithful representation.

Comparability

Comparability operates in two ways. Users must be able to compare the financial statements of the entity with its own past performance and they must also be able to compare its results with those of other entities. This means that financial statements must be prepared on the same basis from one year to the next and that, where a change of accounting policy takes place, the results for the previous year must also be restated so that comparability is maintained. Comparability with other entities is made possible by use of appropriate accounting policies, disclosure of accounting policies and compliance with International Financial Reporting Standards. Revisions to standards have to a large degree eliminated alternative treatments, so this has greatly enhanced comparability.

Understandability

The *Conceptual Framework* states that classifying, characterising and presenting information clearly and concisely makes it understandable. Financial statements are produced for a wide range of users, some of whom will have more understanding of financial information than others. The *Conceptual Framework* states that this should not be used as an excuse to omit information from financial statements on the basis that it is difficult to understand. Financial reports are prepared for users who have a 'reasonable knowledge of business and economic activities' and who 'review and analyse the information diligently'. Some phenomena are inherently complex and some users may need the help of an advisor to understand them, but to leave such issues out of the financial statements would make them incomplete and possibly misleading.

(b) (i) As Lisbon is leasing the asset back for the whole of its useful life, it can be assumed that it is being leased back under a finance lease. In effect, Lisbon has obtained a loan with the asset as security. Lisbon should continue to recognise the asset and depreciate it over its useful life (which is the same as the lease term). Any 'profit' on the sale is deferred and amortised over the lease term. A finance lease liability should be set up and will be reduced by the lease payments, less the notional finance charge on the loan, which will be charged to profit or loss. This presents a faithful representation of the transaction.

(ii) This issue has to do with relevance. It could be said that the use of historical cost accounting does not adequately reflect the value of assets in this case. This can be remedied by revaluing the properties. The revaluation surplus will go to 'other comprehensive income', so will not improve the profit for the year. If this is done, all properties in the category will have to be revalued. This will probably give rise to a higher depreciation charge, so it will not improve the operating loss in the statement of profit or loss, but the excess can be credited back to retained earnings in the statement of financial position.

3 Concepts

Marking scheme

		Marks
(a)	Explanations 1 mark each	5
(b)	Examples 2 marks each	10
		15

(a)   **Matching/accruals**

This dictates that the effects of transactions and other events are recognised in the financial statements in the period in which they occur, rather than in the period when cash is received or paid.

Going concern

This is the assumption that the entity has neither the intention nor the necessity to liquidate or curtail major operations. If this assumption did not apply, the financial statements would be prepared on a different basis.

Verifiability

This means that different, knowledgeable and independent observers could agree that a particular depiction of a transaction in the financial statements is a faithful representation.

Comparability

This requires consistent application of accounting policies and adequate disclosure in order that (a) the financial statements of an entity can be compared with its financial statements for previous accounting periods and (b) the financial statements of an entity can be compared with the financial statements of other entities.

Materiality

An item of information is material if omitting it or misstating it could influence the decisions that users make on the basis of the financial statements. An item can be material on account of its nature or on account of its magnitude.

(b)   **Application to inventory**

Matching/accruals

Inventory is charged to profit or loss in the period in which it is used, not the period in which it is received or paid for. This is done by adjusting cost of sales for opening and closing inventory.

Going concern

As long as the going concern assumption applies, inventory valued at lower of cost and NRV will in most cases be valued at cost. If the business is subject to a forced sale, the NRV of inventory is likely to be below cost.

Verifiability

The cost element of inventory is easy to verify as it will be recorded in invoices. The calculation of NRV must also be based on verified information. The annual inventory count provides verifiability on quantities.

Comparability

Inventory should be valued in financial statements using FIFO or weighted average and this should be consistently applied from one period to the next. If a change is made to the method of valuation, it must be disclosed, so that the current and prior periods can still be compared.

Materiality

Inventory is counted at the end of each reporting period and the valuation is based on this physical count, because inventory is generally regarded as a material item. However, it could be decided that a small discrepancy in the count would not be investigated because the amounts involved were too small to affect the decisions of users and so were not material.

4 Multiple choice answers – regulatory framework

1   A   An Exposure Draft will be published following review of Discussion Paper comments.

2   C   Accountants and auditors may have **less** defence in case of litigation as they will not be able to demonstrate that they followed some precise rule, but will instead have to defend their application of judgement.

3   B   A rules-based system has more detailed regulations because it seeks to cover every eventuality. A principles-based system gives rise to fewer accounting standards and requires the exercise of more judgement.

5 Baxen

Text references. Chapters 1 and 2.

Top tips. This is a written question on the *Conceptual Framework* and the advantages of IFRS. In a question like this, make sure that you are answering the question that has been set and that you are addressing the actual situation of Baxen.

Easy marks. This question did not require a lot of technical knowledge. You were bound to know something about principles-based systems such as IFRS and you could work out what the advantages of IFRS would be. Marks here were for valid points. If you made enough valid points you could score full marks.

Examiner's comments. In section (a) some candidates were unable to properly distinguish between rules-based and principles-based systems and seemed not to know whether IFRS is rules-based or principles-based. But there were many good answers to part (b), mentioning issues such as simplifying consolidations, raising finance and improving comparability.

Marking scheme

		Marks
(a)	1 mark per valid point	9
(b)	1 mark per valid point	6
		15

(a)   (i)   IFRS is not a rules-based system. It is a 'principles-based' system. International Financial Reporting Standards are formulated in accordance with the principles set out in the *Conceptual Framework*. For instance, the requirements for recognition of an asset or liability as stated in the *Conceptual Framework* must be complied with when a standard is being formulated.

This differs from a rules-based system where the regulation attempts to cover every eventuality. Obviously new eventualities will arise all the time, so regulation will be constantly expanding to cover them. In a system like this, accountants and auditors expect to be able to find specific rules to cover every situation, and to have rules specific to the industry with which they are involved.

IFRS only provides basic principles, so preparers of IFRS financial statements have to exercise judgement in dealing with transactions and in applying the principles to different industries. This puts more burden on preparers and some accountants and auditors in the US feel that it will afford them less protection from litigation.

(ii)   IFRS is currently mandatory for listed companies in the EU preparing consolidated financial statements, even if their individual company financial statements are prepared under local GAAP. Countries outside the EU which transition to IFRS may find that there are a number of advantages, and these advantages will increase as more countries adopt IFRS.

Multinational companies with subsidiaries which report under IFRS will have a set of group-wide accounting standards to follow. This will make group reporting easier and cheaper and make the

accounting practices of their foreign subsidiaries more transparent, reducing the opportunities for fraud. They will also be able to transfer their accounting staff between group companies in different countries, without the need for them to deal with a new set of standards.

Companies can more easily compare their results with those of their competitors who report under IFRS. Similarly, investors can more easily compare the results of companies in different countries. Companies will be more able to appraise the position and results of foreign companies which are targets for takeovers or mergers and the accounting required to deal with takeovers and mergers will be less complex.

Cross-border listing will be more straightforward, making it easier for companies to raise capital abroad.

(b)   The question does not tell us where Baxen is based but, if it is in the EU, it will be required to prepare its consolidated financial statements in accordance with IFRS when it acquires a subsidiary. It would therefore make sense for it to move to IFRS in anticipation of that.

There are also a number of advantages:

The influence of IFRS around the world continues to grow. IFRS financial statements are now accepted for listings in the EU, Hong Kong and Singapore and more recently in Japan. They will very soon be accepted in the US. Adopting IFRS will enhance Baxen's reputation at home and abroad.

If Baxen prepares its financial statements in accordance with IFRS, its shares will be accepted for listing in London and Tokyo and very few amendments to accord with US GAAP will be required before its shares are accepted for listing in New York. This gives Baxen access to foreign investor capital.

Baxen will be better able to appraise the financial statements of potential foreign trading partners who report under IFRS.

If it acquires a subsidiary that reports under IFRS, the consolidation process will be much easier and Baxen's own accounting staff will be much better able to judge the performance of the subsidiary.

6 Regulatory framework

Text reference. Chapter 2.

Top tips. A basic knowledge of the processes of the IFRS Foundation would probably be enough to earn a pass mark, but parts of this question require a bit of thought. To earn a pass mark, break each question down into its components and write a few lines on each. For example, most people will sketch out the standard setting process, but make sure you also include a sentence or two on enforcing and on supplementing standards.

Easy marks. Part (a) is very straightforward and will earn you a maximum of ten easy marks.

Examiner's comments. Most answers were weak and very short. Enforcement issues were mostly ignored.

Marking scheme

		Marks
(a)	1 mark per relevant point to a maximum	10
(b)	1 mark per relevant point to a maximum	5
		15

(a)   **Setting, enforcing and supplementing standards**

Setting standards

The IFRS Foundation sets the agenda for producing accounting standards, but the IASB produces and issues these standards. The process is:

1   The IFRS Foundation, taking into account advice from the IFRSAC and others, identifies an issue requiring a financial reporting standard.

2   The IASB sets up an Advisory Committee to investigate the issue and report back to the IASB.

3   The IASB issues a Discussion Paper for public comment.

4   The IASB issues an Exposure Draft; comments must be received within ninety days.

5   The IASB issues an International Financial Reporting Standard on the internet. An IFRS must be approved by 8 of the 15 members of the IASB.

Public discussion is encouraged. The basis of conclusions for EDs and IFRSs are published, along with dissenting opinions. Most meetings of the IASB, IFRSIC and IFRSAC are open to the public, and they are exploring ways of using technology to make public access easier globally.

Enforcing standards

The IASB has no legal power to enforce adoption or compliance with standards, but enforcement of a sort is achieved (more or less successfully) in a number of ways:

- Quoted companies within the European Union must comply with IFRSs, but it is up to each member state to police compliance. Some countries have a formal process to review published financial statements and punish non-compliance (for example the FRC Monitoring Committee in the UK), but this is not universal. To a certain extent the onus is on the auditors to police compliance, but auditing standards themselves are not globally consistent.

- Companies using IFRS to obtain cross-border listings are required to have their financial statements audited in accordance with International Auditing Standards. This will help to ensure that these companies are complying with IFRS.

- Many countries are bringing their own standards into line with IFRSs, but again policing of national standards is inconsistent.

Supplementing standards

The IFRSIC issues interpretations when divergent or unacceptable accounting treatments arise, whether through misinterpreting an existing standard or on an important issue not yet covered by a standard. Financial statements must comply with all of these interpretations if they claim to comply with International Financial Reporting Standards.

(b)   **Has the move towards global accounting standards been successful?**

On a practical level the move towards global accounting standards has been one of the accounting successes of the last decade. The standards themselves have improved, with the elimination of contradictory alternatives and the creation of an open and independent standard setting organisation. This in turn has led to greater acceptance of these standards, culminating in 2005 with the adoption of IFRS for consolidated financial statements by all quoted companies in the European Union and in many other countries. The on-going project with the International Organisation of Securities Commissions will encourage the use of IFRS for cross-border listings, paving the way for acceptance of IFRS in the USA.

However, as mentioned earlier, there is no global system of enforcement, and so it is too early to say if IFRS are being adopted properly.

Some countries with their own highly developed accounting standards see the adoption of IFRS as a backward step, whereas other countries see IFRS as unnecessarily complicated.

There is also the assumption that the globalisation of accounting standards is a good thing. Recent developments in IFRS have focussed on quoted companies in the western world; they may not be suitable for all types and sizes of business organisation, or for all stages of economic development.

7 Multiple choice answers – tangible non-current assets

1   A

	$
Cost 1.1.X5	30,000
Depreciation to 31.12.X5 (30,000 / 12)	(2,500)
Depreciation to 31.12.X6	(2,500)
Depreciation to 31.3.X7 (2,500 × 3/12)	(625)
	24,375
Revaluation surplus	7,625
Revalued amount	32,000

The machine will now be depreciated over the remaining 9 years 9 months = 117 months. So the charge for the remaining 9 months of 20X7 is $2,462 ((32,000 / 117) × 9).

So total depreciation for the year ended 31.12.X7 is (625 + 2,462) = $3,087

2   B

	$'000
Land	1,200
Materials	2,400
Labour	3,000
Architects fees	25
Surveyors fees	15
Site overheads	300
Testing fire alarms	10
	6,950

3   A   Weighted average capitalisation rate =

(9% × 15 / 39) + (11% × 24 / 39) = 3.5% + 7% = 10.5%

		$
Borrowing costs =	$6m × 10.5% × 9/12	472,500
+	$2m × 10.5% × 5/12	87,500
		560,000

4   D

	$
Cost 1.1.X0	900,000
Depreciation to 30.6.X8 (900,000 × 8.5 / 50)	(153,000)
Carrying amount 30.6.X8	747,000
Revaluation surplus	203,000
Fair value 30.6.X8	950,000

The increase of (1,200 – 950) = $250,000 arising between 30.6.X8 and 31.12.X8 will be credited to profit or loss in accordance with IAS 40.

5   A

	$
Borrowing costs March – December ($2.4m × 8% × 10/ 12)	160,000
Less investment income ($1m × 6% × 6/12)	(30,000)
	130,000

6   C   A and B would be classified as inventory and WIP. The property leased out to a subsidiary would be regarded as an investment property in the single entity financial statements of Buildco but is treated as owner-occupied in the **consolidated** financial statements.

7   D   A gain or loss arising from a change in the fair value of an investment property is recognised in profit or loss. The other options are all correct.

8   D   Weighted capitalisation rate =

(10% × 140 / 340) + (8% × 200 / 340) = 4.1% + 4.7% = 8.8%

$50 million × 8.8% × 6/12 = $2.2 million

9   B
	$'000
Machine ((500,000 – 20,000) / 10 × 9/12)	36,000
Safety guard ((25,000/5) × 3/12)	1,250
	37,250

10   C   The expenditure should be capitalised when it takes place and depreciated over the period to the next overhaul. It should not be provided for in advance because there is no obligation arising from a past event – the overhaul could be avoided by ceasing to operate the aircraft.

11   A   Only the transportation and the power supply can be included. The maintenance agreement and the training course are profit or loss items. Non-current assets are capitalised at cost, not realisable value.

8 Preparation question: Plethora plc

(a)   *Building transferred to investment property*

	$'000
Original cost	600
Depreciation 1.1.X0 to 1.7.X9 ((600 / 50) × 9.5)	(114)
Carrying amount at 1.7.X9	486
Revaluation surplus	314
Fair value	800

The amount of $314,000 will go to the revaluation surplus as per IAS 16 and the carrying amount of the building will be restated at $800,000. After this point the building will be accounted for under IAS 40 *Investment property*. If there had been any increase in value after 1.7.X9, this would have been credited to profit or loss.

Existing investment property

The increase in value in this case of $190,000 (740,000 – 550,000) will be credited to profit or loss in accordance with IAS 40.

(b)
	Prior to review $'000	After review $'000
Building	900	825
Plant and equipment	300	275
Inventory	70	70
Other current assets	130	130
Goodwill	40	–
	1,440	1,300
Recoverable amount	(1,300)	
Impairment loss	140	

The impairment loss is allocated first against goodwill and then pro-rata against the tangible non-current assets. This means writing $75,000 off the carrying amount of the building and $25,000 off plant and equipment.

9 Dearing

Marking scheme

			Marks
(a)	Initial capitalised cost	2	
	Upgrade improves efficiency and life therefore capitalise	1	
	Revised carrying amount at 1 October 20X8	1	
	Annual depreciation (1 mark each year)	3	
	Maintenance costs charged at $20,000 each year	1	
	Discount received (profit or loss)	1	
	Staff training (not capitalised and charged to income)	1	10
(b)	1 mark per valid point		5
			15

(a)

Year ended	30 Sept 20X6	30 Sept 20X7	30 Sept 20X8
Statement of profit or loss:	$	$	$
Depreciation (W3)	180,000	270,000	119,000
Maintenance (60,000/3)	20,000	20,000	20,000
Discount received (840,000 × 5%)	(42,000)	–	–
Staff training	40,000	–	–
	198,000	290,000	139,000

As at:	30 Sept 20X6	30 Sept 20X7	30 Sept 20X8
Statement of financial position	$	$	$
Property, plant and equipment:			
Cost/valuation (W1), (W2)	920,000	920,000	670,000
Accumulated depreciation	(180,000)	(450,000)	(119,000)
Carrying amount	740,000	470,000	551,000

Workings

1   *Cost price*

	$
Base price	1,050,000
Trade discount (1,050,000 × 20%)	(210,000)
	840,000
Freight charges	30,000
Electrical installation cost	28,000
Pre-production testing	22,000
	920,000

2   *Valuation after upgrade*

	$
Original cost	920,000
Depreciation to 30 September 20X7 (W3)	(450,000)
Carrying amount	470,000
Upgrade	200,000
Valuation	670,000

3   Depreciation

	$
30 September 20X6:	
$(920,000 - 20,000) \times 1,200 / 6,000$	180,000
30 September 20X7:	
$(920,000 - 20,000) \times 1,800 / 6,000$	270,000
	450,000
30 September 20X8:	
$(670,000 - 40,000) \times 850 / 4,500$	119,000

(b)   'Qualifying' borrowing costs are borrowing costs incurred in the acquisition, construction or production of qualifying assets. These are assets that necessarily take a substantial period of time to get ready for intended use or sale. Since the revision of IAS 23, qualifying borrowing costs now **must** be capitalised.

Where funds are borrowed specifically to finance the construction of a qualifying asset, the amount eligible for capitalisation will be the borrowing costs incurred at the effective rate of interest, less any investment income earned on the temporary investment of those borrowings.

Where funds are borrowed generally and the borrowings attributable to a particular asset cannot be readily identified, the amount eligible for capitalisation will have to be estimated by applying a weighted capitalisation rate to the funds used in constructing the asset.

Capitalisation commences when expenditure and necessary activities begin on the asset and borrowing costs are incurred. Capitalisation is suspended during any period in which activities on the asset are suspended and it ceases when substantially all activities necessary to prepare the asset for its intended use or sale are complete.

10 Flightline

Text reference. Chapter 3

Top tips. This was a very time pressured question with a lot of work to do. It is important in a question like this to provide really clear workings so that you get the marks for all the parts you do correctly.

Easy marks. The amounts for the exterior structure and the cabin fittings were relatively easy to calculate, so you should have done those before embarking on the engines.

Examiner's comments. A significant number of candidates did not start this question and many more appeared to run out of time. Many answers lacked a methodical approach and then got hopelessly lost in the detail, with the engines causing the most problems.

Marking scheme

		Marks
(a)	1 mark per valid point – to maximum	5
(b)	Financial statement extracts:	
	Statement of profit or loss	
	Depreciation – Exterior	1
	– Cabin fittings	2
	– Engines	2
	Loss on write off of engine	1
	Repairs	1
	Statement of financial position	
	Carrying amount at 31 March 20X9	3
		15

(a) A complex asset has a number of separate components, each with a separate useful life. An obvious example would be a ship or an aircraft. A ship can have internal fittings which require replacement several times during the life of the hull. The landing gear of an aircraft will require replacement after a specified number of landings. IAS 16 requires each separate component to be separately depreciated over its useful life. When a component has to be replaced, the existing component is derecognised and the new component is recognised and depreciated over its useful life. IAS 16 gives the example of a furnace which may require relining after a specified number of hours of use. When relining takes place, the old lining will be derecognised and the new lining depreciated over the number of hours of use before next replacement.

This should not be confused with the replacement of small parts, which would be described as 'repairs and maintenance' and charged to profit or loss.

(b) STATEMENT OF PROFIT OR LOSS (EXTRACT) FOR THE YEAR ENDED 31 MARCH 20X9

	$'000
Depreciation:	
Exterior structure (W1)	6,000
Cabin fittings (W2)	6,500
Engines (W3)	1,300
	13,800
Loss on disposal of engine (W3)	6,000
Engine repairs	3,000
Exterior painting	2,000

STATEMENT OF FINANCIAL POSITION (EXTRACT) AT 31 MARCH 20X9

		$'000
Property, plant and equipment		
Aircraft	– Exterior (W1)	36,000
	– Cabin (W2)	8,000
	– Engines (W3)	16,100
		60,100

Workings

1 *Exterior structure*

	$'000
Cost	120,000
Accumulated depreciation to 31.3.X8 (120,000 × 13 / 20)	(78,000)
	42,000
Depreciation to 31.3.X9 (120,000 / 20)	(6,000)
Carrying amount	36,000

2 *Cabin fittings*

	$'000
Cost	25,000
Accumulated depreciation to 31.3.X8 (25,000 × 3 / 5)	(15,000)
	10,000
Depreciation to 1.10.X8 (25,000 / 5 × 6/12)	(2,500)
Upgrade	4,500
	12,000
Depreciation to 31.3.X9 (12,000 × 6 / 18)	(4,000)
Carrying amount	8,000
Total depreciation for current year (2,500 + 4,000)	6,500

3   *Engines*

		$'000
Replaced engine:		
Cost		9,000
Depreciation to 31.3.X8 (9,000 × 10.8 / 36)		(2,700)
Carrying amount at 1.4.X8		6,300
Depreciation to 1.10.X8 (9,000 × 1.2 / 36)		(300)
Written off at 1.10.X8		6,000
Replacement:		
Cost		10,800
Depreciation to 31.3.X9 (10,800 / 36)		(300)
Carrying amount		10,500
Damaged engine:		
Carrying amount at 1.4.X8		6,300
Depreciation to 1.10.X8		(300)
Carrying amount at 1.10.X8		6,000
Depreciation to 31.3.X9 (6,000 / 15)		(400)
Carrying amount at 31.3.X9		5,600
Total carrying amount (10,500 + 5,600)		16,100
Total current year depreciation		
(300 + 300 + 300 + 400)		1,300

11 Enca

Text reference. Chapter 3

Top tips. This question requires the standard PPE working, so that you can line up all the information. Make it clear and easy for the marker to read.

Easy marks. Part (a) is five easy marks.

Examiner's comments Some candidates did not answer the question in (a) and wasted time discussing issues such as impairment and depreciation methods. In part (b) many candidates produced working schedules for each asset without actually preparing the extracts.

			Marks
(a)	1 mark per valid point – to maximum		5
(b)	Financial statement extracts:		
	Statement of profit or loss		
	Year ended 31 March 20X3	3	
	Year ended 31 March 20X4	2	
			5
	Statement of financial position		
	As at 31 March 20X3	3	
	As at 31 March 20X4	2	
			5
			15

(a) IAS 16 *Property, Plant and Equipment* allows two models – a cost model and a fair value model. If it adopted the fair value model, Enca could revalue its property, plant and equipment to fair value. This would reflect the increase in market value.

If the fair value model is adopted, it would be necessary to revalue all assets in a class. An entity is not allowed to revalue just those assets which have increased in value (this is known as 'cherry picking'). Furthermore, revaluations must be kept up to date. A revaluation gain is credited to the revaluation surplus. Any subsequent fall in value can be debited to the revaluation surplus to the extent of any existing surplus on the asset in question. Below that, revaluation losses are charged to profit or loss.

The director may be less pleased to realise that a higher asset value will lead to a higher depreciation charge and hence lower profits. Entities are allowed to make a transfer each year of 'excess' depreciation – that is, the difference between current depreciation and the depreciation which would have been charged had the assets not been revalued. The transfer is from the revaluation surplus to retained earnings, so does not remove the charge from current year profits.

When a revalued asset is disposed of, any surplus held in respect of the asset is realised and transferred to profit or loss.

(b) (i) Statements of profit or loss (extracts)

	Year to 31.3.20X3 $'000	Year to 31.3.20X4 $'000
Impairment loss Item A	(20,000)	
Depreciation: (32,000 + 22,400)	(54,400)	
(32,000 + 26,000)		(58,000)
Loss on disposal		(8,000)

(ii) Statements of financial position (extracts)

	31.3.20X3 $'000	31.3.20X4 $'000
Property, plant and equipment (128,000 + 89,600)	217,600	96,000
Revaluation surplus	25,600 *	- **

*Gain on Item B (32,000) less transfer to retained earnings (32,000/5)

** Asset has been disposed of and balance transferred to retained earnings

Working

	Item A $'000	Item B $'000
Cost	240,000	120,000
Carrying amount 31.2.X2	180,000	80,000
Loss – to P/L	(20,000)	
Gain – to other comprehensive income		32,000
Revalued amount	160,000	112,000
Depreciation to 31.3.X3:		
160,000/5	(32,000)	
112,000/5		(22,400)
Carrying amount 31.3.X3	128,000	89,600
Addition 1.4.X3		14,400
	128,000	104,000
Depreciation to 31.3.X4	(32,000)	(26,000)
	96,000	78,000
Disposal proceeds		(70,000)
Loss on disposal		8,000

12 Multiple choice answers – intangible assets

1   D   In order for capitalisation to be allowed it is not necessary for development to be completed, patents to be registered or sales contracts signed. However, an intangible asset can only be recognised if its cost can be reliably measured.

2   C

	$
Research costs	1,400,000
Expensed development Jan-Mar (800 × 3)	2,400,000
Depreciation on capitalised amount b/f (20m × 20%)	4,000,000
	7,800,000

Note that no depreciation is charged on the new project as it is still in development.

3   B   A pre-production prototype is classified as a development cost, so it is eligible to be capitalised. Internally-generated customer lists and goodwill cannot be capitalised. IAS 38 does not allow capitalisation of research costs.

4   A

	$m
Recoverable amount – fair value less costs of disposal	15.0
Less depreciation 1.4.X9 – 30.9.X9 (15m / 3 × 6/12)	(2.5)
	12.5

5   D

	$
Expenses 1 January to 1 March (40,000 × 2)	80,000
4 months capitalised and amortised	
((40,000 × 4) / 5 years × 3/12)	8,000
	88,000

13 Emerald

Text reference. Chapter 4

Top tips. There were two aspects to this question – the treatment of intangible assets and development costs and accounting for prior period adjustments. It was important to set out a proper working for the calculation part of the question so that you could see what you were doing.

Examiner's comments. Answers to this question were generally quite poor. Many candidates did not apply the definition of an asset to the development expenditure. In part (b) some candidates assumed that amortisation commenced in the year of capitalisation, rather than the following year. The prior period adjustment was rarely mentioned.

Marking scheme

			Marks
(a)	1 mark per valid point to maximum		5
(b)	1 mark per valid point to maximum		4
(c)	Amortisation in profit or loss	1½	
	Cost in statements of financial position	1	
	Accumulated amortisation	1½	
	Prior year adjustment in changes in equity	2	
			6
			15

(a) **Recognition and amortisation**

Goodwill

Only goodwill arising from a business combination is recognised. Under IFRS 3 goodwill is the excess of the cost of a business combination over the acquirer's interest in the net fair value of the assets, liabilities and contingent liabilities of the business acquired. Once recognised goodwill is held indefinitely, without amortisation but is subject to impairment reviews.

One of the key aspects of goodwill is that it cannot be separated from the business that it belongs to. Therefore goodwill cannot be purchased separately from other assets. In addition, IAS 38 states that internally generated goodwill must not be capitalised.

Other intangible assets

Other intangibles can be recognised if they can be distinguished from goodwill; typically this means that they can be separated from the rest of the business, or that they arise from a legal or contractual right.

Intangibles acquired as part of a business combination are recognised at fair value provided that they can be valued separately from goodwill. The acquirer will recognise an intangible even if the asset had not been recognised previously. If an intangible cannot be valued, then it will be subsumed into goodwill.

Internally generated intangibles can be recognised if they are acquired as part of a business combination. For example, a brand name acquired in a business combination is capitalised whereas an internally generated brand isn't. Expenditure on research cannot be capitalised. Development expenditure is capitalised if it meets the IAS 38 criteria. It is then amortised over the life-cycle of the product.

Goodwill and intangibles with an indefinite useful life are not amortised but tested annually for impairment.

(b) The IASB *Conceptual Framework* defines an asset as a resource controlled by the entity as a result of past events and from which future economic benefits are expected to flow to the entity. The recognition criteria also require that the asset has a cost or value that can be measured reliably.

In the case of development expenditure it is not always possible to determine whether or not economic benefits will result. IAS 38 deals with this issue by laying down the criteria for recognition of an intangible asset arising from development expenditure. An entity must be able to demonstrate that it is able to complete and use or sell the asset and has the intention to do so, that the asset will generate probable future economic benefits and that the expenditure attributable to the asset can be reliably measured. If these criteria are met, the asset is recognised and will be amortised from the date when it is available for use.

(c)

	20X7 $'000	20X6 $'000
Statement of profit or loss		
Amortisation of development expenditure (W)	335	135
Statement of financial position		
Intangible asset: development expenditure (W)	1,195	1,130
Statement of changes in equity		
Prior period adjustment		
Added to retained earnings balance at 1.10.X5 (W)		465

Working

	Expenditure $'000	Amortisation $'000	Carrying amount $'000
20X4	300		300
20X5	240	(75)*	165
Balance 20X5	540	(75)	465
20X6	800	(135)**	665
Balance 20X6	1,340	(210)	1,130
20X7	400	(335)***	65
	1,740	(545)	1,195

*300 × 25% **540 × 25% ***1,340 × 25%

14 Dexterity

Marking scheme

		Marks
(i)	One mark for each item in statement of financial position	4
(ii)	Does it qualify as development expenditure	1
	The need for an active market	1
	Drugs are unique, not homogeneous	1
(iii)	Neither an acquired asset nor internally generated	1
	Really recognition of goodwill	1
	Can recognise both the asset and the grant at fair value	1
	Or at cost – granted asset has zero cost	1
(iv)	In reality a valuable asset, in accounting a pseudo-asset	1
	Cannot control workforce	1
	Does not meet recognition criteria	1
(v)	Effective advertising really part of goodwill	1
	Cannot be recognised as a non-current asset	1
	Prepayment of $2.5 million	1
	Cannot spread over two years	1
	Available	18
	Maximum	15

(i) *Temerity*

The following assets will be recognised on acquisition:

	$m
Fair value of sundry net assets	15
Patent at fair value	10
Research carried out for customer	2
Goodwill (balancing figure)	8
Total consideration	35

The patent is recognised at its fair value at the date of acquisition, even if it hadn't previously been recognised by Temerity. It will be amortised over the remaining eight years of its useful life with an assumed nil residual value.

The higher value of $15m can't be used because it depends on the successful outcome of the clinical trials. The extra $5m is a contingent asset, and contingent assets are not recognised in a business combination. (Only assets, liabilities and contingent liabilities are recognised.)

Although research is not capitalised, this research has been carried out for a customer and should be recognised as work-in-progress in current assets. It will be valued at the lower of cost and net realisable value unless it meets the definition of a construction contract.

The goodwill is capitalised at cost. It is not amortised but it will be tested for impairment annually.

(ii) *New drug*

Under IAS 38 the $12m costs of **developing** this new drug are capitalised and then amortised over its commercial life. (The costs of **researching** a new drug are never capitalised.)

Although IAS 38 permits some intangibles to be held at valuation it specifically forbids revaluing patents, therefore the $20m valuation is irrelevant.

(iii) *Government licence*

IAS 38 states that assets acquired as a result of a government grant may be capitalised at fair value, along with a corresponding credit for the value of the grant. Therefore Dexterity may recognise an asset and grant of $10m which are then amortised/released over the five year life of the license. The net effect on profits and on shareholders' funds will be nil.

(iv) *Training costs*

Although well trained staff adds value to a business IAS 38 prohibits the capitalisation of training costs. This is because an entity has 'insufficient control over the expected future economic benefits' arising from staff training; in other words trained staff are free to leave and work for someone else. Training is part of the general cost of developing a business as a whole.

(v) *Advertising costs*

IAS 38 Para 69 states that advertising and promotional costs should be recognised as an expense when incurred. This is because the expected future economic benefits are uncertain and they are beyond the control of the entity.

However, because the year end is half way through the campaign there is a $2.5m prepayment to be recognised as a current asset.

15 Darby

Text references. Chapters 3, 4 and 5.

Top tips. It was important for this question to know the IASB definition. This made it possible to do a good answer to part (a) and know where you were going with part (b). It was important to spend time on all four parts of the question and read the scenarios carefully.

Easy marks. This was all quite easy until you got to (b)(iii), which was a slightly confusing scenario. The clue was in 'the assistant *correctly* recorded the costs..', which would have told you that the point at issue was the impairment write-down.

Marking scheme

		Marks
(a)	1 mark per valid point	4
(b)	(i) to (iii) – 1 mark per valid point as indicated	11
		15

(a) The IASB *Conceptual Framework* defines an asset as 'a resource controlled by the entity as a result of past events and from which future economic benefits are expected to flow to the entity'. IAS 1 sets out the defining features of a current asset (intended to be realised during the normal operating cycle or within 12 months of the year end, held for trading or classified as cash or a cash equivalent). All other assets are classified as non-current.

The assistant's definition diverges from this in a number of ways:

(i) A non-current asset does not have to be physical. The definition can include intangible assets such as investments or capitalised development costs.

(ii)   A non-current asset does not have to be of substantial cost. An item of immaterial value is unlikely to be capitalised, but this is not part of the definition.

(iii)   A non-current asset does not have to be legally owned. The accounting principle is based on 'substance over form' and relies on the ability of the entity to **control** the asset. This means for instance that an asset held under a finance lease is treated as an asset by the lessee, not the lessor.

(iv)   It is generally the case that non-current assets will last longer than one year. IAS 16 specifies that property, plant and equipment 'are expected to be used during more than one period'. However, if a non-current asset failed to last longer than one year, it would **still be classified as a non-current asset during its life**.

(b) (i)   IAS 38 makes the point that 'an entity usually has **insufficient control** over the expected future economic benefits arising from a team of skilled staff'. This is the case in this situation. Darby's trained staff may stay with the company for the next four years or they may decide to leave and take their skills with them. Darby has no control over that. For this reason, the expenditure on training **can not be treated as an asset** and must be charged to profit or loss.

(ii)   The work on the new processor chip is research with the aim of eventually moving into development work. IAS 38 requires all research expenditure to be expensed as incurred. Even at the development stage, it **will not be possible to capitalise the development costs unless they satisfy the IAS 38 criteria**. When the criteria are satisfied and development costs can be capitalised, it will still not be possible to go back and capitalise the research costs. The company's past successful history makes no difference to this.

The research work on the braking system is a different case, because here the work has been commissioned by a customer and the customer will be paying, regardless of the outcome of the research. In this situation, as long as Darby has no reason to believe that the customer will not meet the costs in full, the costs should be treated as **work in progress**, rather than being charged to profit or loss.

(iii)   If we agree that the assistant was correct to record $58,000 as a non-current asset, the only question is whether it should be regarded as impaired.

An impairment has occurred when the recoverable amount of an asset falls below its carrying amount.

The projected results for this contract are:

	$
Revenue (50,000 × 3)	150,000
Costs (bal)	(110,000)
Profit	40,000

If we ignore discounting, the future cash flows are $150,000, less remaining costs of $52,000 ($110,000 – $58,000), which amounts to $98,000. This is well in excess of the $58,000 carrying amount, so **no impairment has taken place** and the non-current asset should remain at $58,000.

16 Multiple choice answers – impairment of assets

1   C

	$'000
Total impairment (1,010 – 750)	260
Goodwill	(90)
Damaged plant	(40)
Balance to allocate	130

The remaining $130,000 will be allocated pro rata as follows.

	Building $'000	Plant $'000
	700	160
Impairment	(106)	(24)
	594	

2   C   Recoverable amount is the higher of fair value less costs of disposal and value in use.

3   A

Fair value less costs of disposal (78,000 – 2,500)		$75,500
Value in use:	$30,000 \times 1 / 1.08 = 27,778$	
	$30,000 \times 1 / 1.08^2 = 25,720$	
	$30,000 \times 1 / 1.08^3 = 23,815$	$77,313$

Recoverable amount is $77,313 and carrying amount is $85,000, so impairment is $7,687.

4   C   A market capitalisation greater than the amount of net assets is a favourable indicator rather than an indicator of impairment. The other options are indications of impairment.

5   A

	$
Fair value less costs of disposal (2.7m – 50,000)	2,650,000
Value in use	2,600,000
Recoverable amount is therefore:	2,650,000
Impairment loss (β)	350,000
Carrying amount	3,000,000

6   A

	$m	$m	$m
Goodwill	3	(3)	–
Patent	5	(3)	2
Property	10	(2)	8
Plant and equipment	15	(3)	12
Current assets	2	-	2
	35	(11)	24

The goodwill is written off, the patent is written down and the remaining $5m impairment is allocated pro-rata to the property and the plant.

7   A

	$
Carrying amount (100,000 × 5/10)	50,000
Fair value less costs to sell	30,000
Value in use (8,500 × 3.79)	32,215

Recoverable amount is $32,215 and impairment loss = 50,000 – 32,215 = $17,785

17 Telepath

Marking scheme

			Marks
(a)	1 mark per valid point		4
(b)(i)	Carrying amount before impairment test	1	
	Value in use	2	
	Not impaired – leave at carrying amount	1	4
(b)(ii)	Damaged plant written off	1	
	Goodwill written off	1	
	Patent at $1m	1	
	Cash and receivables – no impairment	1	
	Pro rata of remaining loss	1	
	Apply to building and plant only	2	7
			15

(a) An impairment review as laid out in IAS 36 *Impairment of Assets* is carried out to determine whether the value of an asset may have fallen below its carrying amount in the statement of financial position. It is a requirement for goodwill carried in the statement of financial position that it should be tested annually for impairment.

An asset is considered to be impaired if its carrying amount exceeds its recoverable amount, defined as the higher of fair value less costs to sell and value in use. Value in use is the present value of the future cash flows which will be generated by the asset. It is often not possible to attribute cash flows to an individual asset, so in this case the impairment review is carried out at the level of the cash generating unit to which the asset belongs. A cash generating unit is a group of assets which together generate cash flows. For instance, a production unit in a factory could be treated as a cash generating unit and any impairment identified will be apportioned between the assets of the CGU.

(b) (i) Carrying amount of the plant at 31.3.X2

		$'000
1.4.X0	Cost	800,000
	Depreciation ((800,000 – 50,000) / 5)	(150,000)
31.3.X1	Balance	650,000
	Depreciation	(150,000)
31.3.X2	Balance	500,000

As there is currently no market in which to sell the plant, its recoverable amount will be its value in use, calculated as:

Year ended	Cash flow $'000	Discount factor 10%	Present value $'000
31 March 20X3	220	0.91	200
31 March 20X4	180	0.83	149
31 March 20X5	170 + 50	0.75	165
			514

As this is greater than the carrying amount, the plant is not impaired and will be left at its carrying amount of $500,000.

(ii)   The impairment loss will be allocated as follows.

	$'000		$'000	$'000
Goodwill	1,800	Written off	(1,800)	–
Patent	1,200	W/D to realisable amount	(200)	1,000
Factory building	4,000	Working	(1,600)	2,400
Plant	3,500	Working	(1,700)	1,800
Receivables and cash	1,500	No impairment	–	1,500
	12,000		(5,300)	6,700

Working

The total amount of the impairment loss to be allocated is $5.3m.

		$'000
The initial write-offs are:	Damaged plant	500
	Goodwill	1,800
	Patent	200
		2,500

This leaves $2.8m impairment loss to be allocated between the factory building (4,000) and the remaining plant (3,000). The allocation will be:

Factory (2,800 × 4,000 / 7,000)	1,600
Plant (2,800 × 3,000 / 7,000)	1,200
	2,800

18 Multiple choice answers – revenue

1 A

	$
Costs incurred to date	740,000
Recognised profits (W)	231,000
Amounts invoiced	(700,000)
Contract asset	271,000

Working

Total contract revenue	2,800,000
Costs to date	(740,000)
Costs to complete	(1,400,000)
Total expected profit	660,000
Profit to date (660,000 × 35%)	231,000

2 C The grant can be treated as deferred income or deducted from the carrying amount of the asset. It cannot be credited directly to profit or loss.

3 A

	$'000
Total contract revenue	50,000
Costs to date	(12,000)
Specialist plant	(8,000)
Costs to complete	(10,000)
Total profit on contract	20,000

Profit to date = $20m × 22 / 50 = $8,800,000

4 A

	$
Costs incurred to date	48,000
Recognised profits (W)	10,800
Amounts invoiced	(50,400)
Contract asset	8,400

Working

Total contract revenue	120,000
Costs to date	(48,000)
Costs to complete	(48,000)
Total expected profit	24,000
Profit to date (24,000 × 45%)	10,800

5 B This feature suggests that the transaction is a genuine sale.

If the seller retains the right to use the asset or it remains on his premises, then the risks and rewards have not been transferred. If the sale price does not equal market value, then the transaction is likely to be a secured loan.

6 B These both indicate that the manufacturer retains ownership of the inventory. (i) and (iii) would indicate that the risks and rewards have been transferred to the dealer.

7 C

	$
Grant received 1.4.X7	500,000
Recognised year to 31.3.X8 (500,000 × 30%)	(150,000)
Balance 31.3.X8	350,000
Recognised year to 31.3.X9 (350,000 × 30%)	105,000

		$'000
8	D	
	Revenue per draft profit or loss	27,000
	Servicing costs (800 × 2 × 130%)	(2,080)
	Agency collections	(4,000)
	Agency commission (4,000 × 10%)	400
		21,320

19 Preparation question: Derringdo

(a) *Liability*

There are two issues here:

(i) Should a capital grant be treated as deferred income in the financial statements?

(ii) Should a liability be recognised for the potential repayment of the grant?

Derringdo has credited the $240,000 grant to a deferred income account which is shown as a liability in the statement of financial position. It is then released to profit or loss over the ten year life of the related asset. However, the *Conceptual Framework* states that a liability should only be recognised if there is a probable outflow of economic benefits. This is not true for a grant; under normal circumstances the grant will not have to be repaid and so a liability does not exist.

This example is complicated by the possibility of having to repay the grant if the asset is sold. At the end of the reporting period the asset has not been sold, and so there is no past event to give rise to a liability. Derringdo intends to keep the asset for its ten year useful life. Nor can it be classified as a contingent liability. Under IAS 37 the 'uncertain future event' that creates a contingent liability must be 'not wholly within the control of the entity'. In this case Derringdo will make the decision to keep or sell the asset.

Following on from the above, the *Conceptual Framework* would not permit the grant to be shown as a liability. Instead the grant would be claimed as income in the year that it was received (provided that there was no intention to sell the asset within the four year claw-back period). However, the treatment of the grant as deferred income is in accordance with IAS 20 *Accounting for government grants.*

(b) *Extracts* (Company policy complies with one of the two alternatives in IAS 20)

STATEMENT OF PROFIT OR LOSS

	$
Operating expenses	
Depreciation charge (W1)	34,000
Release of grant (W2)	(12,000)
	22,000

STATEMENT OF FINANCIAL POSITION

	$
Non-current assets	
Property, plant and equipment (W1)	766,000
Non-current liabilities	
Deferred income (W2)	204,000
Current liabilities	
Deferred income (W2)	24,000
	228,000

Workings

1	Property, plant, equipment	$
	Cost (gross, excluding grant)	800,000
	Depreciation (10 years straight line, 15% residual value for 6 months	
	800,000 × 85% × 10% × $^6/_{12}$)	(34,000)
	Carrying amount	766,000

2   *Deferred income*

	$
Grant received ($800,000 × 30%)	240,000
Release for this year ($240,000 × 10% × $^6/_{12}$)	(12,000)
Total balance at year-end	228,000

Presentation

Current liability ($240,000 × 10%)	24,000
Non-current liability (balance)	204,000
	228,000

Theoretical approach under the Conceptual Framework

Because the 'deferred' element of the grant cannot be recognised as a liability, the grant will be claimed in full in the year that it is received. The repayment clause will not affect this policy because, at the end of the reporting period, Derringdo has not sold the asset and so no liability exists.

STATEMENT OF PROFIT OR LOSS

	$
Operating expenses	
Depreciation charge (as before)	34,000
Grant received and claimed	(240,000)
	(206,000)

STATEMENT OF FINANCIAL POSITION

	$
Non-current assets	
Property, plant and equipment	766,000

20 Preparation question: Contract

	Contract 1 $	Contract 2 $	Contract 3 $	Contract 4 $
STATEMENT OF PROFIT OR LOSS				
	(W1)	(W2)	(W3)	(W4)
Revenue	54,000	8,000	84,000	125,000
Expenses	(43,200)	(8,000)	(92,400)	(105,000)
Expected loss	–	–	(15,600)	–
Recognised profit/(loss)	10,800	–	(24,000)	20,000
Contract asset				
Contract costs incurred	48,000	8,000	103,200	299,600
Recognised profits less recognised losses	10,800	–	(24,000)	56,000
	58,800	8,000	79,200	355,600
Less amounts invoiced to date	(50,400)	–	(76,800)	(345,200)
	8,400	8,000	2,400	10,400
Trade receivables				
Amounts invoiced to date	50,400	–	76,800	345,200
Less cash received	(40,000)	–	(60,000)	(320,000)
	10,400	–	16,800	25,200

Workings

1   *Contract 1* $

    Revenue   45% × 120,000 =   54,000
    Expenses   45% × (48,000 + 48,000) =   43,200

2   *Contract 2*

    Expenses   All costs to date charged as expense ∴ 8,000
    Revenue   Probable that all costs incurred will be recovered ∴ 8,000

3   *Contract 3* $

    Revenue   35% × 240,000 =   84,000
    Expenses   35% × (103,200 + 160,800) =   (92,400)
    Loss   (8,400)
     ∴ Expected loss   (15,600)
    Total loss 240,000 − (103,200 + 160,800) =   (24,000)

4   *Contract 4* $

    Revenue   (70% × 500,000) − 225,000 =   125,000
    Expenses   (70% × 420,000) − 189,000 =   105,000

21 Preparation question: Beetie

STATEMENT OF PROFIT OR LOSS

	Contract 1	Contract 2	Total
	$'000	$'000	$'000
Contract revenue	3,300	840	4,140
Contract expenses: (Contract 1: 4,000 × 60%)	(2,400)	(720)	(3,120)
Expected loss recognised (Contract 2)	–	(170)	(170)
Attributable profit/(loss)	900	(50)	850

STATEMENT OF FINANCIAL POSITION

	$'000
Current assets	
Contract asset	1,800
Current liabilities	
Contract liability	210

Workings

Contract 1

	$'000
Total contract revenue	5,500
Costs to date	(3,900)
Costs to complete (4,000 − 3,900)	(100)
Estimated total profit	1,500
Profit to date: 1,500 × 3,300 / 5,500 =	900
Contract asset	
Costs to date	3,900
Profit to date	900
Less amounts invoiced	(3,000)
	1,800

Contract 2

	$'000
Revenue to date (1,200 × 70%)	840
Costs to date (1,250 × 70%)	(875)
Loss to date	(35)
Expected loss	(15)
Recognised loss	(50)
Contract liability	
Costs to date	720
Recognised loss	(50)
Less amounts invoiced	(880)
	(210)

22 Mocca

Text reference. Chapter 6

Top tips. Start by working out the total profit on the contract and you can then deduct the amounts that were accounted for in the previous year. Note that the contract should only be charged with half of the useful life of the plant as it will be kept in use after the contract.

Easy marks. This is quite an easy question and should have been no problem for those who had revised IFRS 15. Part (a) is straightforward and a careful reading of the question and the application of general accounting principles would have secured some marks on the profit or loss extracts.

Examiner's comments. Candidates that gave this question serious attention scored quite well. Most calculated the profit and percentage of completion correctly but failed to deduct the results of the previous year. In amounts due from customers (contract assets) candidates often deducted progress payments received rather progress billings.

Marking scheme

		Marks
(a)	1 mark per valid point	5
(b)	Revenue	3
	Profit	1½
	Plant in statement of financial position	1½
	Amounts due from customers	1
	Trade receivables	1
	Disclosure note	2
		15

(a) Revenue recognition is an important issue in financial reporting and it is generally accepted that revenue is earned when goods have been accepted by the customer or services have been delivered. At that stage the performance obligation has been satisfied and revenue is said to have been realised. However, if this were applied to contracts where performance obligations are satisfied over time, the effect would not necessarily be to give a faithful representation.

As a contract where performance obligations are satisfied over time can span several accounting periods, if no revenue were recognised until the end of the contract, this would certainly be prudent but would not be in accordance with the accruals concept. The financial statements would show all of the profit in the final period, when in fact some of it had been earned in prior periods. This is remedied by recognising attributable profit as the performance obligations are satisfied, as long as ultimate profitability is expected. Any foreseeable loss is recognised immediately.

(b)   *Profit or loss amounts*

	$'000
Revenue (8,125 – 3,500)	4,625
Cost of sales ((9,500 (W1) × 65%) – 2,660)	(3,515)
Profit (1,950 (W2) – 840)	1,110

Statement of financial position amounts

	$'000
Non-current assets	
Plant (8,000 – 2,500 (W1))	5,500
Current assets	
Trade receivables (8,125 – 7,725)	400
Contract asset (see below)	1,125

Contract asset

	$'000
Costs to date (4,800 + 2,500)	7,300
Profit to date (W2)	1,950
Less amounts invoiced	(8,125)
Contract asset	1,125

Workings

1   *Total contract profit*

	$'000	$'000
Total contract revenue		12,500
Costs to date	4,800	
Further costs to complete (5,500 – 4,800)	700	
Plant depreciation to date (8,000 × 15/48)	2,500	
Remaining depreciation (8,000 × 9/48)	1,500	
Total expected costs		(9,500)
Total expected profit on contract		3,000

2   *Profit to date*

% work completed = 8,125 / 12,500 = 65%

Profit to date = 3,000 × 65% = 1,950

23 Wardle

Text references. Chapter 6.

Top tips. Part (a) was straightforward as long as you remembered to answer the question. It asked why the principle of substance over form is important and required features that indicate that substance is different from legal form. If you stick to those two issues you are far more likely to get the marks than if you just put down everything you know and hope there's something relevant in there. Part (b) required an understanding of what a sale and repurchase transaction is. It's important to remember that all the information you are given has a purpose. In this case, the interest information told you that the substance of the transaction was a secured loan. Setting out a sensible format for the statement of profit or loss extract was vital for this part, and it gave you the information you needed to answer part (c).

Easy marks. It was not hard to pick up at least a few marks in part (a). Part (b) was easy once you knew what you were doing and part (c) was simple if you had managed to deal with part (b).

Marking scheme

		Marks
(a)	1 mark per valid point	5
(b)	(i) and (ii) 1 mark per reported profit figure	5
(c)	1 mark per valid point	5
		15

(a) It is important that financial statements should reflect the economic substance of a transaction, where this differs from legal form, because this provides users with a 'faithful representation' of the transaction.

For instance, if an asset held under a finance lease were treated according to its legal form it would not appear under non-current assets and the related lease liability would not be shown. This would make the entity's gearing look lower than it actually was and probably inflate its ROCE. This treatment is not allowed under IFRS.

Sale and leaseback or sale and repurchase arrangements can be used to disguise the substance of loan transactions by taking them 'off balance sheet'. In this case the legal position is that the asset has been sold, but the substance of the transaction is that the seller still retains the benefits of ownership.

Features which suggest that the substance of a transaction may differ from its legal form are:

- The seller of an asset retains the ability to use the asset
- The seller remains exposed to the risks of ownership eg maintenance
- An asset which has been sold is one that can reasonably only be used by the seller
- A 'sold' asset remains on the sellers premises
- An asset has been transferred at a price substantially above or below its fair value
- An asset has been 'sold' under terms which make it very unlikely that it will not be repurchased
- A number of linked transactions have taken place

All of these features suggest that 'control' has been separated from legal ownership and that the substance of the transaction may not have been correctly represented.

(b) Wardle has entered into a repurchase agreement involving a call option at a price greater than the original selling price. This means that Easyfinance does not obtain control of the asset and IFRS 15 requires this transaction to be treated as a financing arrangement.

(i)	Legal form 31 March:	20X1	20X2	20X3	Total
		$'000	$'000	$'000	$'000
	Revenue	6,000	–	10,000	16,000
	Cost of sales	(5,000)	–	(7,986)	(12,986)
	Gross profit	1,000	–	2,014	3,014
	Finance costs	–	–	–	–
	Net profit	1,000	–	2,014	3,014

(ii) Substance 31 March:	20X1 $'000	20X2 $'000	20X3 $'000	Total $'000
Revenue	–	–	10,000	10,000
Cost of sales	–	–	(5,000)	(5,000)
Gross profit	–	–	5,000	5,000
Finance costs	(600)	(660)	(726)	(1,986)
Net profit	(600)	(660)	4,274	3,014

(c) While net profit at the end of the three-year period is the same under both treatments, we can see that under the legal form revenue is much greater, because of the assumption that Wardle has 'sold' the asset twice. This leads to profit being split between two of the three years rather than shown wholly in year 3, so there is some 'smoothing' effect. Reporting under the legal form of the transaction removes the finance cost, which will have a favourable effect on interest cover, and will also have removed the loan from the statement of financial position, thus making gearing appear lower. Similarly, under the legal form, the asset will not appear in the statement of financial position, which will make ROCE appear higher than it would otherwise have been.

24 Multiple choice answers – introduction to groups

1 D There is now no basis on which a subsidiary may be excluded from consolidation.

2 C IFRS 3 requires negative goodwill to be credited to profit or loss.

3 C Existence of significant influence. The other options indicate control over a subsidiary.

4 C A subsidiary may prepare additional statements up to the group reporting date and, where statements for a different date are used, adjustments should be made for significant transactions. The allowable gap between reporting dates is three months, not five.

5 B The present value of the future cash flows that the asset is expected to generate measures present value, not fair value. The other items would be considered in determining fair value.

6 D Consolidated financial statements should be prepared using uniform accounting policies, making whatever adjustments are needed if a group company has applied different policies. This does not mean that all subsidiaries must adopt the accounting policies of the parent. Subsidiaries with substantially different activities are still consolidated,

   Unrealised profit must be eliminated because consolidated financial statements are only concerned with profits earned by transactions with parties outside the group.

25 Preparation question: Group financial statements

(a) A parent need not present consolidated financial statements if one of the following exemptions applies.

   - It is itself a wholly or partly-owned subsidiary of another entity and its other owners do not object to it not preparing consolidated financial statements.

   - Its shares or debt instruments are not traded on any stock exchange.

   - Its financial statements are not being filed with any regulatory organisation for the purpose of issuing any debt or equity instruments on any stock exchange.

   - Its own or ultimate parent produces publicly-available financial statements that comply with IFRS.

(b) IFRS 10 *Consolidated financial statements* requires intragroup balances, transactions, income and expenses to be eliminated in full. The purpose of consolidated financial statements is to present the financial position of the parent and subsidiaries as that of a **single entity**, the group. This means that, in the consolidated statement of profit or loss, the only profits recognised should be those earned by the group in trading with entities outside the group. Similarly, inventory should be valued at cost to the group.

   When a company sells goods to another company in the same group it will recognise revenue and profit in its individual financial statements. However, from the point of view of the group, no sale has taken place, because the goods are still held by the group. The sale must therefore be eliminated from revenue and the unrealised profit must be eliminated from group inventory.

   Where one group company owes money to another group company or one company holds loan stock of another company, the asset and liability balances will be eliminated on consolidation. As far as the group is concerned, they do not represent amounts due to or from third parties.

26 Preparation question: Simple consolidation

BOO GROUP – CONSOLIDATED STATEMENT OF PROFIT OR LOSS AND OTHER COMPREHENSIVE INCOME
FOR THE YEAR ENDED 31 DECEMBER 20X8

	$'000
Revenue (5,000 + 1,000 – 100 (W5))	5,900
Cost of sales (2,900 + 600 – 100 + 20 (W5))	(3,420)
Gross profit	2,480
Other expenses (1,700 + 320)	(2,020)
Profit before tax	460
Tax (130 + 25)	(155)
Profit for the year	305
Other comprehensive income	
Gain on property revaluation	20
Total comprehensive income for the year	325
Profit attributable to	
Owners of the parent	294
Non-controlling interest (20% × 55)	11
	305
Total comprehensive income attributable to	
Owners of the parent (ß)	314
Non-controlling interest	11
	325

CONSOLIDATED STATEMENT OF FINANCIAL POSITION AS AT 31 DECEMBER 20X8

	$'000	$'000
Assets		
Non-current assets (1,940 + 200)		2,140
Goodwill (W2)		70
Current assets		
Inventory (500 + 120 + 80)	700	
Trade receivables (650 – 100 (W5) + 40)	590	
Bank and cash (170 + 35)	205	
		1,495
Total assets		3,705
Equity and liabilities		
Equity attributable to owners of the parent		
Share capital (Boo only)		2,000
Retained earnings (W3)		520
Revaluation surplus		20
		2,540
Non-controlling interest (W4)		70
Total equity		2,610
Current liabilities		
Trade payables (910 + 30)	940	
Tax (130 + 25)	155	
		1,095
Total equity and liabilities		3,705

Workings

1   *Group structure*

    Boo

       ↓ 80%

    Goose

2   *Goodwill*

	$'000	$'000
Consideration transferred		300
Fair value of non-controlling interest		60
		360
Fair value of net assets:		
Share capital	100	
Retained earnings	190	(290)
Goodwill		70

3   *Retained earnings*

	Boo	*Goose*
	$'000	$'000
Per question	500	240
Unrealised profit (W5)	(20)	
	480	
Less pre acquisition		(190)
		50
Goose: 80% × 50	40	
Group total	520	

4   *Non-controlling interest*

	$'000
NCI at acquisition	60
NCI share of post - acquisition retained earnings (50 × 20%)	10
	70

5   *Intragroup issues*

Step 1: Record Goose's purchase

DEBIT Cost of sales	$100,000	
CREDIT Payables		$100,000
DEBIT Closing inventory (SFP)	$100,000	
CREDIT Cost of sales		$100,000

These transactions can be simplified to:

DEBIT Inventory	$100,000	
CREDIT Payables		$100,000

Step 2: Cancel unrealised profit

DEBIT COS (and retained earnings) in Boo	$20,000	
CREDIT Inventory (SFP)		$20,000

Step 3: Cancel intragroup transaction

DEBIT Revenue	$100,000	
CREDIT Cost of sales		$100,000

Step 4: Cancel intragroup balances

DEBIT Payables	$100,000	
CREDIT Receivables		$100,000

27 Multiple choice answers – consolidated statement of financial position

			$
1	B		
		Fair value at acquisition (200,000 × 30% × $1.75)	105,000
		Share of post-acquisition retained earnings ((750 – 450) × 30%)	90,000
		Depreciation on fair value adjustment ((250 / 40) × 30%)	(1,875)
			193,125

			$	$
2	A			
		Consideration transferred:		
		Cash		250,000
		Deferred consideration (400,000 / 1.08)		370,370
		Shares (30,000 × $2.30)		69,000
				689,370
		Fair value of non-controlling interest		400,000
				1,089,370
		Fair value of net assets:		
		Shares	100,000	
		Retained earnings	850,000	
				(950,000)
				139,370

3   C   ($1.2 million / 8 × 4/12) × 80% = $40,000

The adjustment will reduce depreciation over the next 8 years, so it will *increase* retained earnings.

			$'000
4	A		
		Shares (18m × 2/3 × $5.75)	69,000
		Deferred consideration (18m × $2.42 × 1 / 1.1^2)	36,000
			105,000

5   D   This adjustment reduces (debits) the liability and the credit is to retained earnings. The remeasurement relates to the post-acquisition period, so goodwill is not affected.

			$	$
6	D			
		Consideration transferred		800,000
		Fair value of non-controlling interest		220,000
				1,020,000
		Fair value of net assets:		
		Shares	100,000	
		Retained earnings	570,000	
		Revaluation surplus	150,000	
		Intangible	90,000	
				(910,000)
				110,000

28 Preparation question: Goodwill

Goodwill on acquisition

	$'000	$'000
Consideration transferred		1,200
Fair value of non-controlling interest		400
Net assets at acquisition:		
Share capital	500	
Retained earnings	850	
Revaluation surplus	450	
		(1,800)
Negative goodwill*		(200)

* Negative goodwill is known as 'gain on a bargain purchase' (IFRS 3 *Business combinations*).

CONSOLIDATED STATEMENT OF PROFIT OR LOSS FOR THE YEAR ENDED 31 DECEMBER 20X9

	$'000
Revenue (12,500 + 2,600)	15,100
Cost of sales (7,400 + 1,090)	(8,490)
Gross profit	6,610
Distribution costs (700 + 220)	(920)
Administrative expenses (1,300 + 550 − 200*)	(1,650)
Finance costs	(40)
Profit before tax	4,000
Income tax expense (900 + 230)	(1,130)
Profit for the year	2,870
Profit attributable to:	
Owners of Penguin (ß)	2,768
Non-controlling interest (510 × 20%)	102
	2,870

* Penguin plc should double-check the valuation of Platypus Ltd's assets and liabilities and reassess the valuation of the consideration paid. If it is satisfied that it has indeed secured a 'bargain purchase' then $200,000 should be credited to profit or loss. Note that IFRS 3 requires this gain to be attributed to the acquirer; none of it is attributed to the non-controlling interest.

29 Pedantic

Text references. Chapters 8 and 9

Top tips. The first point to note here is that the subsidiary was acquired mid-year. Remember this when it comes to preparing the statement of profit or loss and working out the depreciation on the fair value adjustment. This question had lots to do but no real problems. Get the formats down, note the adjustments on the question paper and then start working through.

Easy marks. There were lots of easy marks here. The statement of profit or loss needed no real working out apart from cost of sales and non-controlling interest. There were lots of marks available in the statement of financial position even if you did not get the goodwill quite right. Correctly calculating the figures from the share exchange would have gained you marks on goodwill, share capital and share premium.

Examiner's comments. This question was generally well answered by most candidates. The two areas of serious errors were:

- Failure to time apportion the results of the subsidiary
- Proportional consolidation of 60% of the subsidiary's figures

			Marks
(a)	Statement of profit or loss:		
	Revenue	1½	
	Cost of sales	3½	
	Distribution costs	½	
	Administrative expenses	1	
	Finance costs	1	
	Income tax	½	
	Non-controlling interest	2	10
(b)	Statement of financial position:		
	Property, plant and equipment	2	
	Goodwill	5	
	Current assets	1½	
	Equity shares	1	
	Share premium	1	
	Retained earnings	2	
	Non-controlling interest	2	
	10% loan notes	½	
	Current liabilities	1	16
(c)	1 mark per valid point to maximum		4
			30

(a) PEDANTIC – CONSOLIDATED STATEMENT OF PROFIT OR LOSS FOR THE YEAR ENDED 30 SEPTEMBER 20X8

	$'000
Revenue (85,000 + (42,000 × 6/12) − 8,000 (W8))	98,000
Cost of sales (63,000 + 16,000 + 200 − 8,000 + 800) (or see (W9))	(72,000)
Gross profit	26,000
Distribution costs (2,000 + (2,000 × 6/12))	(3,000)
Administrative expenses (6,000 + (3,200 × 6/12))	(7,600)
Finance costs (300 + (400 × 6/12))	(500)
Profit before tax	14,900
Income tax expense (4,700 + (1,400 × 6/12)	(5,400)
Profit for the year	9,500
Profit attributable to:	
Owners of the parent	9,300
Non-controlling interests (W2)	200
	9,500

(b) PEDANTIC – CONSOLIDATED STATEMENT OF FINANCIAL POSITION AT 30 SEPTEMBER 20X8

	$'000
Non-current assets	
Property, plant and equipment (40,600 + 12,600 + 1,800 (W7))	55,000
Goodwill (W3)	4,500
	59,500
Current assets (16,000 + 6,600 − 800 − 600 + 200) (or see (W10))	21,400
Total assets	80,900

Equity attributable to owners of the parent	
Share capital (10,000 +1,600 (W6))	11,600
Share premium (W6)	8,000
Retained earnings (W4)	35,700
	55,300
Non-controlling interests (W5)	6,100
	61,400
Non-current liabilities	
10% loan notes (3,000 + 4,000)	7,000
Current liabilities (8,200 + 4,700 – 400 (W11))	12,500
	80,900

(c)   Pedantic cannot take assurance from the Tradhat group financial statements that Trilby would be able to meet its liability in respect of the goods. The group financial statements will have aggregated the assets and liabilities of all the group companies and it will not be possible to use them to calculate liquidity ratios for any one company.

This is important, because Pedantic's contract would not be with the Tradhat group, it would be with Trilby. If Trilby defaulted on its obligations, the Tradhat group would be under no legal obligation to step in, so that the fact that the group has a strong financial position is not really relevant. It would only become relevant if Tradhat were willing to offer a parent company guarantee.

In the absence of a parent company guarantee, Pedantic must base its decision on the financial position of Trilby as shown in its individual company financial statements. It should also obtain references from other suppliers of Trilby, specifically those who supply it with large orders on 90-day credit terms.

Workings

1   *Group structure*

Pedantic

1.4.X8   60%   Mid-year acquisition, six months before year end

Sophistic

2   *Non-controlling interests*

Statement of profit or loss

	$'000
Post-acquisition profit of Sophistic (3,000 × 6/12)	1,500
PUP (W8)	(800)
Movement on FVA (W7)	(200)
	500
× 40%	200

3   *Goodwill*

	$'000	$'000
Consideration transferred (W6)		9,600
Fair value of non-controlling interests		5,900
Less: Fair value of net assets at acquisition:		
Share capital	4,000	
Retained earnings (6,500 – (3,000 × 6/12))	5,000	
Fair value adjustment (W7)	2,000	
		(11,000)
Goodwill		4,500

4 Retained earnings

	Pedantic $'000	Sophistic $'000
Per question	35,400	6,500
Movement on FV adjustment (W6)		(200)
PUP (W8)		(800)
Pre- acquisition (W3)		(5,000)
		500
Group share (500 × 60%)	300	
	35,700	

5 Non-controlling interests

Statement of financial position

	$'000
NCI at acquisition (W3)	5,900
NCI share of post-acquisition retained earnings ((W4) 500 × 40%)	200
	6,100

6 Share exchange

	Dr $'000	Cr $'000
Consideration transferred (4,000 × 60% × 2/3 = 1,600 × $6)	9,600	
Share capital of Pedantic (1,600 × $1)		1,600
Share premium of Pedantic (1,600 × $5)		8,000

7 Fair value adjustments

	$,000 Acq'n 1.4.X8	$'000 Mov't 6/12	$'000 Year end 30.9.X8
Plant (*$2m / 5 × 6/12)	2,000	(200)*	1,800

8 Intragroup trading

	Dr $'000	Cr $'000
Cancel intragroup sales/purchases:		
Sales	8,000	
Purchases		8,000
Eliminate unrealised profit:		
Cost of sales/retained earnings ((8,000 – 5,200) × 40 / 140)	800	
Inventories (SOFP)		800

9 Cost of sales (supplementary working)

	$,000
Pedantic	63,000
Sophistic (32,000 × 6/12)	16,000
Movement on FV adjustment (W7)	200
Intragroup purchases (W8)	(8,000)
Unrealised profit (W8)	800
	72,000

10 Current assets (supplementary working)

	$'000
Pedantic	16,000
Sophistic	6,600
Unrealised profit in inventory (W8)	(800)
Intercompany receivables (per question)	(600)
Cash in transit (W11)	200
	21,400

11   *Cash in transit*

	Dr	Cr
Receivables		600
Payables	400	
Cash	200	

30 Pyramid (specimen paper)

Text reference. Chapter 8

Top tips. This is a consolidated statement of financial position extracts question. Students should be very familiar with these elements.

Easy marks. The only complex bits in this question were the share exchange and the deferred consideration. Other than that, there were plenty of easy marks.

Marking scheme

			Marks
(a)	Goodwill		5
(b)	Property, plant and equipment		2
(c)	Equity:		
	Equity shares	1½	
	Other equity reserves	1½	
	Retained earnings	3	
			6
(d)	Non-controlling interest		2
			15

(a)   *Goodwill*

	$'000	$'000
Consideration transferred		
Share exchange ($6 × (9,000 × 80%) × 2/3)	28,800	
Deferred consideration (((9,000 × 80%) × 0.88) × 1/1.1)	5,760	
		34,560
Non-controlling interest at fair value ((9,000 × 20%) × 3.5)		6,300
		40,860
Fair value of net assets:		
Shares	9,000	
Retained earnings	19,000	
Fair value adjustment on plant	3,000	
Deferred tax liability	(1,000)	
		(30,000)
Goodwill		10,860

(b)   *Property, plant and equipment*

	$'000
Pyramid	38,100
Square	28,500
Fair value adjustment	3,000
Depreciation on fair value adjustment (3,000 / 5)	(600)
	69,000

(c)   *Equity*
Attributable to owners of parent:

			$'000
Share capital (50,000 + (9,000 × 80%) × 2/3))			54,800
Share premium (4,800 × $5)			24,000
Other components of equity			8,000
Retained earnings (W)			35,544
			122,344

Working
Retained earnings

	Pyramid	Square
	$'000	$'000
Per question	30,200	27,000
Less pre-acquisition		(19,000)
		8,000
Depreciation on fair value adjustment		(600)
Unwinding of discount on deferred consideration (5,760 × 10%)	(576)	
	29,624	7,400
Square (7,400 × 80%)	5,920	
	35,544	

(d)   *Non-controlling interests*

	$'000
FV of NCI at acquisition (a)	6,300
Share of post-acquisition retained earnings ((8,000 – 600) × 20%)	1,480
	7,780

31 Multiple choice answers – consolidated statement of profit or loss and other comprehensive income

1   A

	$
Basil	547,700
Parsley (206,900 × 10/12)	172,417
PURP ((46,000 × 30 / 130) × 25%)	(2,654)
	717,463

2   D $2 million × 25 / 125 × 20% = $80,000

3   C

	$m
Decrease	12.0
Increase ($2m × 25% (profit margin))	0.5
Net decrease	11.5

4   A

	$'000
Profit for the year	1,300
Intra-group interest (5m × 8%)	(400)
Impairment (50,000 – 30,000)	(20)*
	880
× 30%	264

* The revaluation surplus is eliminated first and the remainder charged to profit or loss.

5   C

	$'000
Viagem	51,200
Greca (26,000 × 9/12)	19,500
Intercompany sales (800 × 9)	(7,200)
PURP (1,500 × 25/125)	300
	63,800

6   C

	$'000
Loss of investment income(10m × 8% × 6/12)	(400)
Saving of interest payable (400 × 60%)	240
Net reduction in group retained earnings	(160)

7   A

	$
Profit to 30 June 20X8 (1.6m × 6/12)	800,000
Additional depreciation on FVA ((2m/20) × 6/12)	(50,000)
Goodwill impairment	(500,000)
Other comprehensive income – revaluation gain	1,000,000
	1,250,000
NCI share 20%	250,000

32 Preparation question: Acquisition during the year

CONSOLIDATED STATEMENTOF PROFIT OR LOSS AND OTHER COMPREHENSIVE INCOME
FOR THE YEAR ENDING 31 DECEMBER 20X4

	Port	Alfred 2/12	Adjustment	Group
	$'000	$'000		$'000
Revenue	100	166		266
Cost of sales	(36)	(43)		(79)
Gross profit				187
Interest on loan to Alfred	276	–	(46)	230
Other investment income	158	–		158
Operating expenses	(56)	(55)		(111)
Finance costs	–	(46)	46	–
Profit before tax				464
Taxation	(112)	(6)		(118)
Profit for the year				346
Other comprehensive income:				
Gain on property revaluation	30			30
Total comprehensive income for the year				376
Profit attributable to:				
Owners of the parent				342
Non-controlling interest (W5)				4
				346
Total comprehensive income attributable to:				
Owners of the parent				372
Non-controlling interest				4
				376

PORT GROUP STATEMENT OF FINANCIAL POSITION AS AT 31 DECEMBER 20X4

		Adjustments	Group $'000
Assets			
Non-current assets			
Goodwill		(W2)	330
Property, plant and equipment	130 + 3,000		3,130
Investments			
Loan to Alfred	2,300 + 0	(2,300)	–
Other investments	600 + 0		600
			4,060
Current assets	800 + 139		939
Total assets			4,999
Equity and liabilities			
Equity attributable to owners of the parent			
$1 equity shares		(W3)	235
Share premium		(W3)	1,115
Retained earnings		(W4)	2,912
Revaluation surplus			30
			4,292
Non-controlling interest		(W5)	184
Total equity			4,476
Non-current liabilities			
Loan from Port	0 + 2,300	(2,300)	–
Current liabilities	200 + 323		523
Total equity and liabilities			4,999

Workings

1   *Group structure*

Port	
	75% Subsidiary
	Two months only
Alfred	

2   *Goodwill*

	$'000	$'000	$'000
Consideration transferred (shares)			650
Non-controlling interests at acquisition			180
Net assets at date of acquisition (Note)			
Share capital		100	
Share premium		85	
Retained earnings:			
Opening (331 – 96)	235		
Add accrued profit for the year: $96,000 × 10/12	80		
Pre-acquisition retained earnings		315	
			(500)
Goodwill			330

The net assets at the date of acquisition are also calculated by time-apportioning profits. The share capital and retained earnings brought forward obviously all arose before acquisition. The profit for the year is assumed to have arisen evenly over time.

3   *Issue of shares*

	Draft	New issue	Revised
	$'000	$'000	$'000
Share capital	200	35	235
Share premium	500	615	1,115
Fair value of proceeds		650	

4   *Group retained earnings*

	Port	Alfred
	$'000	$'000
Per question	2,900	331
Less pre acquisition (W2)		(315)
		16
Share of Alfred: (16 × 75%)	12	
	2,912	

5   *Non-controlling interests*
Statement of profit or loss

The rule here is to time apportion the non-controlling interest in the subsidiary acquired during the year. After all, you can only take out in respect of the non-controlling interest what was put in the first place. So, if two months were consolidated then two months of non-controlling interest will be deducted.

$96,000 × 2/12 × 25% = $4,000.

Statement of financial position

	$'000
NCI at acquisition	180
NCI share of post-acquisition retained earnings ((W4) 16 × 25%)	4
	184

33 Preparation question: Pandar

(a) (i) *Goodwill*

	$'000	$'000
Consideration transferred (120m × 80% × 3/5 × $6)		345,600
Non-controlling interest (120m × 20% × $3.20)		76,800
FV of identifiable net assets acquired:		
Share capital	120,000	
Reserves (152,000 + ((21,000 + (W4) 2,000*) × 6/12))	163,500	
FV adjustments (W3)	25,000	
		(308,500)
		113,900

* The interest on the loan note is a post-acquisition cost for Salva, so it is added back for the purpose of calculating pre-acquisition reserves.

(ii) *Investment in Ambra*

	$'000
Cost (40m × 40% × $2)	32,000
Share of post-acquisition loss (5,000 × 40% × 6/12)	(1,000)
Impairment loss	(3,000)
	28,000

(b) PANDAR GROUP – CONSOLIDATED STATEMENT OF PROFIT OR LOSS
FOR THE YEAR ENDED 30 SEPTEMBER 20X9

	$'000
Revenue (210,000 + (150,000 × 6/12) – (W5) 15,000)	270,000
Cost of sales (126,000+(100,000 × 6/12) + (W3) 500 - (W5)15,000 + (W5) 1,000)	(162,500)
Gross profit	107,500
Distribution costs (11,200 + (7,000 × 6/12)	(14,700)
Administrative expenses (18,300 + (9,000 × 6/12)	(22,800)
Investment income (9,500 – (W4) 2,000 – (8,000 × 80%))	1,100
Finance costs (1,800 + (3,000 x 6/12) – ((W4) 2,000 × 6/12) + (W4) 2,000 – (W4) 2,000)	(2,300)
Share of loss of associate ((5,000 × 40% × 6/12)+(3,000) impairment)	(4,000)
Profit before tax	64,800
Income tax expense (15,000 + (10,000 × 6/12))	(20,000)
Profit for the year	44,800
Profit attributable to:	
Owners of the parent	43,000
Non-controlling interest (W2)	1,800
	44,800

Workings

1 Timeline

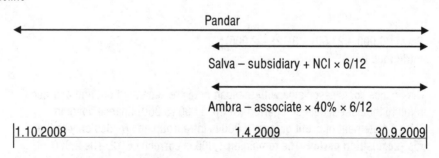

2   Non-controlling interest

	$'000
Salva's post acquisition profit ((21,000 × 6/12) + ((W4)2,000 × 6/12) − (W4)2,000)*	9,500
Depreciation on FVA (W3)	(500)
	9,000
× 20%	1,800

3   Fair value adjustments

	Acquisition 1.4.X9 $'000		Movement $'000	Year end 30.9.X9 $'000
Plant (17,000 − 12,000)	5,000	5000 / 5 × 6/12	(500)	4,500
Domain name	20,000		–	20,000
	25,000			24,500

4   Intragroup interest

Interest 50,000 × 8% × 6/12 = $2,000
Dr Finance income/Cr Finance costs

5   Intragroup trading

Cancel intragroup sales/purchases:
Dr Revenue 15,000/Cr Cost of sales 15,000

Unrealised profit 15,000 × 1/3 × 20%:
Dr Cost of sales 1,000/Cr Inventories (SOFP) 1,000

[The following supplementary workings are included for additional explanation. Note that in the exam you will not have time to prepare these workings and you should do them as shown above, on the face of the statement of profit or loss.]

Cost of sales

	$'000
Pandar	126,000
Salva (100,000 × 6/12)	50,000
Intragroup (W5)	(15,000)
Depreciation on FVA (W3)	500
Unrealised profit (W5)	1,000
	162,500

Investment income

	$'000
Pandar	9,500
Intragroup interest (W4)	(2,000)
Intragroup dividend (8,000 × 80%)	(6,400)
	1,100

Finance costs

	$'000
Pandar	1,800
Salva ((3,000 − 2,000) × 6/12) + 2,000)*	2,500
Intragroup (W4)	(2,000)
	2,300

*The finance costs associated with the loan note are separated out and charged in full to the post-acquisition period. Of the 3,000 ($'000) finance costs in Salva's statement of profit or loss, 2,000 is intragroup and relates only to the **post-acquisition period**. The remaining 1,000 is correctly 6/12. The 2,000 intragroup is then cancelled on consolidation, leaving a balance in group finance costs of 1,800 + (1,000 × 6/12) = 2,300.

34 Viagem

Marking scheme

	Marks
Consolidated statement of profit or loss:	
Revenue	2
Cost of sales	3
Distribution costs	1
Administrative expenses	2
Share of profit of associate	1½
Finance costs	2
Income tax	1
Profit for year – attributable to parent	½
– attributable to NCI	2
	15

VIAGEM GROUP – CONSOLIDATED STATEMENT OF PROFIT OR LOSS FOR THE YEAR ENDED 30 SEPTEMBER 20X2

	$'000
Revenue (64,600 + (38,000 × 9/12) – 7,200 (W2))	85,900
Cost of sales (51,200 + (26,000 × 9/12) – 7,200 + 300 (W2) + 450 (W3))	(64,250)
Gross profit	21,650
Distribution costs (1,600 + (1,800 × 9/12))	(2,950)
Administrative expenses (3,800 + (2,400 × 9/12) + 2,000 (goodwill impairment))	(7,600)
Finance costs (W4)	(1,500)
Share of profit of associate (2,000 × 40%)	800
Profit before tax	10,400
Income tax expense (2,800 + (1,600 × 9/12))	(4,000)
Profit for the year	6,400
Profit attributable to	
Owners of the parent (ß)	6,180
Non-controlling interest (W5)	220
	6,400

Workings

1   *Group structure*

Viagem

1 Jan 20X2   ↓   90%   Mid-year acquisition, nine months before year end

Greca

2   Intragroup trading

	$'000	$'000
Intragroup trading (800 × 9 months)		
DEBIT Revenue	7,200	
CREDIT Cost of sales		7,200
PURP (1,500 × 25/125)		
DEBIT Cost of sales	300	
CREDIT Group inventory (SFP)		300

3   Fair value adjustment

	Acquisition $'000	Movement $'000	Year end $'000
Plant	1,800	(450)*	1,350

*(1,800 / 3) × 9/12

4   Finance costs

	$'000
Viagem per statement of profit or loss	420
Unwinding of discount on deferred consideration:	
((14,400 × 10%) × 9/12)	1,080
	1,500

5   Non-controlling interest

	$'000
Profit for the year (6,200 × 9/12)	4,650
Depreciation on fair value adjustment (W3)	(450)
Goodwill impairment	(2,000)
	2,200
Non-controlling share 10%	220

35 Prodigal

Text reference. Chapter 9.

Top tips. The first point to note is that Sentinel was acquired mid-year. Always pay close attention to dates.

Easy marks. Revenue is relatively straightforward for two marks and for all of the expense categories apart from cost of sales it was only necessary to take Prodigal's balance plus 6/12 Sentinel. The other comprehensive income was also easy, and you should have been able to score well on part (b) and part (c).

Examiner's comments. There were many good scores here. Two problem areas were dealing with the elimination of intra-group sales and the additional depreciation on the asset transfer. Some candidates failed to calculate NCI in the total comprehensive income. Very few candidates correctly calculated 'other equity reserve' and many calculated goodwill, which was not required. The written section of part (b) was often ignored and a lot of answers did not answer the question ie did not explain the **effect** of the two treatments.

Marking scheme

			Marks	
(a)		Goodwill on acquisition		
		Consideration transferred	2	
		Fair value of NCI	½	
		Fair value of net assets	1½	4
(b)	(i)	Statement of profit or loss and other comprehensive income		
		Revenue	2	
		Cost of sales	4	
		Distribution costs and administrative expenses	2	

			Marks
	Finance costs	1	
	Income tax expense	1	
	Non-controlling interest in profit for the year	1½	
	Other comprehensive income	2	
	Non-controlling interest in other comprehensive income	1½	15
(ii)	Consolidated equity		
	Share capital	1	
	Share premium	1	
	Revaluation surplus (land)	1	
	Other equity reserve	1	
	Retained earnings	1½	
	Non-controlling interest	1½	
			7
(c)	1 mark per valid point		4
			30

(a) Goodwill on acquisition of Sentinel

	$'000	$'000
Consideration (((160,000 × 75%) × 2/3) × $4)		320,000
Fair value of non-controlling interest		100,000
		420,000
Fair value of net assets:		
Shares	160,000	
Other equity reserve	2,200	
Retained earnings (125,000 + (66,000 × 6/12))	158,000	
		(320,200)
Goodwill		99,800

(b) (i) CONSOLIDATED STATEMENT OF PROFIT OR LOSS AND OTHER COMPREHENSIVE INCOME FOR THE YEAR ENDED 31 MARCH 20X1

	$'000
Revenue (450,00 + (240,000 × 6/12) – (W4) 40,000)	530,000
Cost of sales (260,000 + (110,000 × 6/12) + (W3) 800 – (W4) 40,000 + 3,000)	(278,800)
Gross profit	251,200
Distribution costs (23,600 + (12,000 × 6/12))	(29,600)
Administrative expenses (27,000 + (23,000 × 6/12))	(38,500)
Finance costs (1,500 + (1,200 × 6/12))	(2,100)
Profit before tax	181,000
Income tax expense (48,000 + (27,800 × 6/12))	(61,900)
Profit for the year	119,100
Other comprehensive income:	
Gain on land revaluation (2,500 + 1,000)*	3,500
Investments in equity instruments** (700 + (400 × 6/12))	(900)
Other comprehensive income, net of tax	2,600
Total comprehensive income for the year	121,700
Profit attributable to:	
Owners of the parent (bal)	111,600
Non-controlling interests (W2)	7,500
	119,100
Total comprehensive income attributable to:	
Owners of the parent (bal)	114,000
Non-controlling interests (W2)	7,700
	121,700

*All post - acquisition

**Could also be described as equity financial asset investments

(ii)

	$'000
Equity attributable to owners of the parent:	
Share capital (250,000 + (W7) 80,000)	330,000
Share premium (100,000 + (W7) 240,000)	340,000
Retained earnings (W5)	201,600
Revaluation surplus (8,400 + 2,500 + (1,000 × 75%))	11,650
Other equity reserve (3,200 – 700 – (400 × 6/12 × 75%))	2,350
	885,600
Non-controlling interests (W6)	107,700
	993,300

(c) The argument behind allowing the non-controlling interest to be valued at fair value is that the traditional method (valued at proportionate share of subsidiary's net assets) does not take account of goodwill attributable to the non-controlling interest. Goodwill is based upon the amount the parent paid for shares in the subsidiary. The non-controlling interest also holds shares which would have had the same market value at the acquisition date, so their holding also includes an element of goodwill. The fair value option takes account of this.

The fair value of the non-controlling interest can be based on share price or on a valuation by the parent company. Use of the fair value option means that the goodwill amount in the consolidated statement of financial position will normally be higher than where share of net assets is used, and the non-controlling interest will also be higher. Also, when goodwill is impaired, the impairment will be allocated between the group and the non-controlling interest, based on their relative shareholdings.

Workings

1   *Group structure and timeline*
    Prodigal

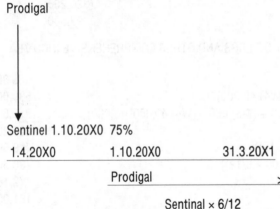

Sentinel 1.10.20X0 75%

1.4.20X0	1.10.20X0	31.3.20X1

        Prodigal   >

            Sentinal × 6/12

2   *Non-controlling interests*

	Profit for year	*Total comprehensive income*
	$'000	$'000
Per question (66,000 × 6/12) ((66,000–400) × 6/12 + 1,000))	33,000	33,800
PUP (W4)	(3,000)	(3,000)
	30,000	30,800
×	25%	25%
	7,500	7,700

3   *Transfer of plant*

	$'000
1.10.20X0 Profit on transfer (5,000 – 4,000)	1,000
Proportion depreciated (½ / 2½)	(200)
Unrealised profit	800
Required adjustment:	
Dr Cost of sales (and retained earnings)	800
Cr Plant	800

4   *Intragroup trading*
     Cancel intragroup sales/purchases:

	$'000	$'000
Dr Group revenue	40,000	
Cr Group cost of sales		40,000
((40,000 – 30,000) × 12,000 / 40,000) = 3,000		
DR Cost of sales (Sentinel) (NCI)	3,000	
CR Group inventories		3,000

5   *Retained earnings*

	Prodigal $'000	*Sentinel* $'000
Per question: (90,000 + 89,900) (125,000 + 66,000)	179,900	191,000
PUP on transfer of plant (W3)	(800)	
PUP on transfer of inventories (W4)		(3,000)
Pre-acq retained earnings (125,000 + (66,000 × 6/12))		(158,000)
		30,000
Group share (30,000 × 75%)	22,500	
	201,600	

6   *Non-controlling interests*

	$'000
NCI at acquisition	100,000
NCI share of post-acquisition:	
– Retained earnings ((W5) 30,000 × 25%)	7,500
– Revaluation surplus (1,000 × 25%)	250
– Investment in equity instruments ((400 × 6/12) × 25%)	(50)
	107,700

7   *Share for share exchange*

	$'000	$'000
Dr Cost of investment in S	320,000	
Cr Share capital (160,000 × 75% × 2/3 × $1)		80,000
Cr Share premium (160,000 × 75% × 2/3 × $3)		240,000

36 Penketh (6/14 amended)

Text references. Chapter 9

Top tips. Note that, as is usual when you have a consolidated statement of profit or loss to prepare, this is a mid-year acquisition. Do not forget to adjust for additional depreciation and amortisation arising from the acquisition.
Easy marks. The goodwill working and part (c) are both easy marks.

Examiner's comments. Most candidates made a reasonable attempt at this. The most common errors arose in dealing with the deferred consideration, the fair value of the non-controlling interests, the time apportionment, the unrealised profit and the other comprehensive income.

		Marks
(a)	Consolidated goodwill	6

(b) Consolidated statement of profit or loss and other comprehensive income:

Revenue	2	
Cost of sales	4	
Distribution costs	½	
Administrative expenses	1½	
Share of profit of associate	2	
Investment income	2	
Finance costs	1½	
Income tax	1	
Other comprehensive income	1½	
Profit for year attributable to NCI	2	
Total comprehensive income attributable to NCI	1	
		19

(c) 1 mark per valid point   5
                                30

(a) Goodwill

	$'000	$'000
Consideration transferred:		
Share exchange (90m/3 × $4)		120,000
Deferred consideration (90m × $1.54 ×1/1.1)		126,000
		246,000
Fair value of non-controlling interest (60m × $2.50)		150,000
		396,000
Fair value of net assets:		
Share capital	150,000	
Retained earnings (120m + (80m × 6/12))	160,000	
Fair value adjustments:		
Land	2,000	
Plant	6,000	
Customer relationships	5,000	
		323,000
Goodwill		73,000

(b) CONSOLIDATED STATEMENT OF PROFIT OR LOSS AND OTHER COMPREHENSIVE INCOME FOR THE YEAR ENDED 31 MARCH 20X4

	$,000
Revenue (620,000 + (310,000 × 6/12) – 20,000 (W5))	755,000
Cost of sales (400,000 + (15,000 × 6/12) – 20,000 + 1,500 (W4) + 800 + 900 (W5))	(458,200)
Gross profit	296,800
Distribution costs (40,000 + (20,000 × 6/12))	(50,000)
Administrative expenses (36,000 + (25,000 × 6/12) + 500 (W4))	(49,000)
Investment income ((1,600 × 6/12) + (5,000 – 1,800 (dividend from associate)))	4,000
Finance costs (2,000 + (5,600 × 6/12) + 6,300 (W3))	(11,100)
Share of profit of associate (10,000 × 30% × 6/12)	1,500
Profit before tax	192,200
Income tax expense (45,000 + (31,000 × 6/12))	(60,500)
Profit for the year	131,700

	$,000
Other comprehensive income:	
Loss on revaluation of land (2,200 – 1,000 (W4))	(1,200)
Total comprehensive income for the year	130,500
Profit attributable to:	
Owners of Penketh	116,500
Non-controlling interest (W2)	15,200
	131,700
Total comprehensive income attributable to:	
Owners of Penketh	114,900
Non-controlling interest (W2)	15,600
	130,500

Workings

1   *Group structure and timeline*

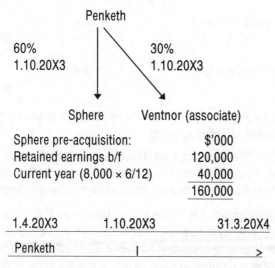

Sphere pre-acquisition:	$'000
Retained earnings b/f	120,000
Current year (8,000 × 6/12)	40,000
	160,000

1.4.20X3	1.10.20X3	31.3.20X4
Penketh	>

Sphere x 6/12

2   *Non-controlling interests (SPLOCI)*

	$'000
Per question: (80,000 × 6/12)	40,000
Fair value movement (W4)	(2,000)
	38,000
× 40%	15,200
Other comprehensive income (1,000 (W4) × 40%)	400
	15,600

3   *Consideration transferred*

	$'000
Share for share exchange (90,000 × 1/3 ×$4)	120,000
Deferred consideration (90,000 ×$1.54 × 1/1.10)	126,000
	246,000
Deferred consideration liability at 1.10.20X3	126,000
Interest to 31.3.20X4 (126,000 × 10% × 6/12)	6,300
	132,300

4 *Fair value adjustments / Accounting policy alignments*

	Acquisition 1.10.20X3 $'000	Movement $'000		Year end 31.3.20X4 $'000
Land	2,000	1,000	(to OCI)	3,000
Plant	6,000	(1,500)	(6,000/2 × 6/12)	4,500
Customer relationships	5,000	(500)	(5,000/2 × 6/12)	4,500
	13,000	(1,000)		12,000

	P&L	TCI
	(2,000)	1,000

5 *Intragroup trading*

	$'000	$'000
(1) Cancel intragroup sales/purchases		
DR Revenue	20,000	
CR Cost of sales		20,000
(2) Cancel unrealised profit		
P sales to S:		
DR Cost of sales (20,000 ×1/5 × 25%/125%)	800	
CR Inventories		800
P sales to V (associate):		
DR Cost of sales (15,000 ×25%/125% × 30%)	900	
CR Investment in associate		900

(c) IFRS 3 *Business Combinations* requires the consideration for a business combination to be allocated to the fair values of the assets, liabilities and contingent liabilities acquired.

Although this is usually not the same as the original cost of the asset when acquired by the subsidiary, it is taken to be the cost of the asset to the group. If assets are not valued at fair value, this leads to an incorrect goodwill valuation and incorrect depreciation and goodwill impairment charges in subsequent years.

The financial assistant is confusing two different issues. The assets of the subsidiary are assumed to be acquired at their fair value at the date of acquisition by the parent. After acquisition they will be carried at depreciated amount, rather than subjected to regular revaluations. So they will be treated in the same way as other assets owned by the parent. The parent may decide to revalue all the assets of a class, including those acquired as part of a business combination, in which case they would all be carried at revalued amount.

37 Multiple choice answers – accounting for associates

1	A		$m
		Cost (75m × $1.60)	120
		Share of post-acquisition retained earnings (100 – 20) × 30%	24
			144

2   C   The group's share of the associate's profit after tax is recorded as a one-line entry. Line by line treatment would be correct for a subsidiary, not an associate. The dividends received from the associate are all that is recorded in the individual entity financial statements of the parent, but in the consolidated financial statements this is replaced by the group share of profit after tax.

3	A		$'000
		Cost of investment	2,500
		Share of post-acquisition profit (6,400 – 5,300) × 30%)	330
		PURP (700 × 30% ×30%)	(63)
			2,767

4	B		$'000
		Cost of investment	10,000
		Share of post-acquisition profit (3,000 × 8/12) – 1,000) × 35%	350
		Impairment	(500)
			9,850

5   C   (($2m × 40%) × 25 / 125) × 30% = $48,000

This adjustment is removing profit from inventory so it is a credit entry.

6   A   The present of significant influence is indicated by a shareholding of 20% or more (i) or representation on the board (ii). Regarding (iii), material transactions would need to be between the investor itself and the investee. (iv) denotes control, not significant influence.

7	A		$'000
		Cost of investment (240 × 6)	1,440
		Share of post-acquisition retained earnings	
		((400 × 6/12) – 150) × 30%	15
			1,455

38 Preparation question: Laurel

LAUREL GROUP - STATEMENT OF FINANCIAL POSITION AS AT 31 DECEMBER 20X9

	$m
Non-current assets	
Property, plant and equipment (220 + 160 + (W7) 3)	383
Goodwill (W2)	9
Investment in associate (W3)	96.8
	488.8
Current assets	
Inventories (384 + 234 – (W6) 10)	608
Trade receivables (275 + 166)	441
Cash (42 + 10)	52
	1,101
	1,589.8

Equity attributable to owners of the parent

Share capital – $1 ordinary shares	400
Share premium	16
Retained earnings (W4)	326.8
	742.8
Non-controlling interests (W5)	47
	789.8

Current liabilities

Trade payables (457 + 343)	800.0
	1,589.8

Workings

1   *Group structure*

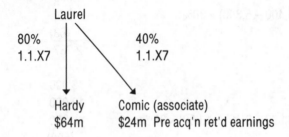

Laurel

80% 1.1.X7 → Hardy $64m

40% 1.1.X7 → Comic (associate) $24m Pre acq'n ret'd earnings

2   *Goodwill*

	$'m	$'m
Consideration transferred		160
Non-controlling interests (at fair value)		39
Fair value of net assets at acq'n:		
Share capital	96	
Share premium	3	
Retained earnings	64	
Fair value adjustment (W7)	12	
		(175)
		24
Impairment losses		(15)
		9

3   *Investment in associate*

	$'m
Cost of associate	70
Share of post acquisition retained reserves (W4)	29.2
Unrealised profit (W6)	(2.4)
Impairment losses	(0)
	96.8

4   *Consolidated retained earnings*

	Laurel $'m	Hardy $'m	Comic $'m
Per question	278	128	97
Less: PUP re Hardy (W6)	(10)		
PUP re Comic (W6)	(2.4)		
Fair value adjustment movement (W7)		(9)	
Less pre-acquisition retained earnings		(64)	(24)
		55	73

	Laurel	Hardy	Comic
Group share of post-acquisition retained earnings:			
Hardy (55 × 80%)	44		
Comic (73 × 40%)	29.2		
Less group share of impairment losses (15 × 80%)	(12.0)		
	326.8		

5 *Non-controlling interests*

	$'m
Non-controlling interests at acquisition (W2)	39
NCI share of post-acquisition retained earnings:	
Hardy (55 × 20%)	11
Less NCI share of impairment losses (15 × 20%)	(3)
	47

6 *Unrealised profit*

Laurel's sales to Hardy: $32m – $22m = $10m

DR Retained earnings (Laurel)	$10m
CR Group inventories	$10m

Laurel's sales to Comic (associate) ($22m – $10m) × ½ × 40% share = $2.4m.

DR Retained earnings (Laurel)	$2.4m
CR Investment in associate	$2.4m

7 *Fair value adjustments*

	At acquisition date	Movement	At year end
	$'m	$'m	$'m
PPE (57 – 45)	+12	(9)*	+3

*Extra depreciation $12m × ¾

At acquisition date	Movement	At year end
↓	↓	↓
Goodwill	Ret'd earnings	PPE

39 Preparation question: Tyson

STATEMENT OF PROFIT OR LOSS AND OTHER COMPREHENSIVE INCOME FOR THE YEAR ENDED 31 DECEMBER 20X8

	$'m
Revenue (500 + 150 – 66)	584
Cost of sales (270 + 80 – 66 + (W3) 18)	(302)
Gross profit	282
Other expenses (150 + 20 + 15)	(185)
Finance income (15 + 10)	25
Finance costs	(20)
Share of profit of associate [(10 × 40%) – 2.4*]	1.6
Profit before tax	103.6
Income tax expense (25 + 15)	(40)
Profit for the year	63.6
Other comprehensive income:	
Gains on property revaluation, net of tax (20 + 10)	30
Share of other comprehensive income of associate (5 × 40%)	2
Other comprehensive income for the year, net of tax	32.0
Total comprehensive income for the year	95.6

Profit attributable to:
Owners of the parent (63.6 – 2.4)   61.2
Non-controlling interests (W2)   2.4
                                     63.6

Total comprehensive income attributable to:
Owners of the parent (95.6 – 4.4)   91.2
Non-controlling interests (W2)   4.4
                                     95.6

*Impairment losses could either be included in expenses or deducted from the share of profit of associates figure. IAS 28 is not prescriptive.

Workings

1   *Group structure*

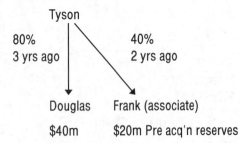

Tyson

80%   40%
3 yrs ago   2 yrs ago

Douglas   Frank (associate)
$40m $20m Pre acq'n reserves

2   *Non-controlling interests*

	PFY $'m	TCI $'m
PFY/TCI per question	45	55
Unrealised profit (W3)	(18)	(18)
Impairment loss	(15)	(15)
	12	22
× NCI share (20%)	2.4	4.4

3   *Unrealised profit*

	$'m
Selling price	66
Cost	(48)
PUP	18

40 Preparation question: Plateau

PLATEAU – CONSOLIDATED STATEMENT OF FINANCIAL POSITION AS AT 30 SEPTEMBER 20X7

	$'000
Non-current assets	
Property, plant and equipment (18,400 + 10,400 – (W7) 400)	28,400
Goodwill (W3)	5,000
Intangible asset – customer contract	1,000
Investment in associate (W4)	10,500
Investment in equity instruments (note v to question)	9,000
	53,900
Current assets	
Inventories (6,900 + 6,200 – (W7) 300)	12,800
Trade receivables (3,200 + 1,500)	4,700
	17,500
Total assets	71,400
	$,000

Equity attributable to owners of the parent

Share capital (10,000 + (W2) 1,500)	11,500
Share premium (W2)	7,500
Retained earnings (W5)	30,300
	49,300
Non-controlling interest (W6)	3,900
	53,200

Non-current liabilities

7% loan notes (5,000 + 1,000)	6,000
Current liabilities (8,000 + 4,200)	12,200
Total equity and liabilities	71,400

Workings

1   *Group structure*

Plateau

1.10.X6   1.10.X6

75%   30%

Savannah   Axle

2   *Purchase of Savannah*

DEBIT Cost of Savannah (3m / 2 × $6) + (3m × $1.25)	12.75m	
CREDIT Share capital (3m / 2 × $1)		1.5m
CREDIT Share premium (3m / 2 × $5)		7.5m
CREDIT Cash		3.75m

3   *Goodwill– Savannah*

	$'000	$'000
Consideration transferred		12,750
Non-controlling interests at acquisition (1,000 shares @ $3,25)		3,250
Less: Net fair value of assets and liabilities at acquisition:		
Share capital	4,000	
Retained earnings	6,000	
Fair value adjustment (W8)	1,000	
		(11,000)
		5,000

4   *Investment in Axle*

	$'000
Cost (4,000 × 30% × $7.50)	9,000
Share of post-acquisition retained earnings (W5)	1,500
	10,500

5   *Group retained earnings*

	Plateau	Savannah	Axle
	$'000	$'000	$'000
Per statement of financial position	25,250	2,900	5,000
Unrealised profit (W7)	(400)	(300)	–
	24,850	2,600	5,000
Group share: 2,600 × 75%	1,950		
5,000 × 30%	1,500		
Gain on investment			
(9,000 – 6,500)	2,500		
Professional costs of acquisition	(500)		
Group retained earnings	30,300		

6   *Non-controlling interests – Savannah*

	$'000
NCI at acquisition (W3)	3,250
NCI share of post-acquisition retained earnings ((W5) 2,600 × 25%)	650
	3,900

7   *Intragroup trading*

Unrealised profit on sale of inventories:

$2.7m × 50/150 × 1/3 $0.3m

Dr Cost of sales/Cr Inventories in books of Savannah (affects NCI)

Unrealised profit on transfer of plant:

Unrealised profit ($2.5m – $2m)	0.5m
Less realised by use (depreciation) 1/5	(0.1m)
	0.4m

DEBIT Retained earnings/CREDIT Property, plant and equipment in books of Plateau

8   *Fair value adjustment – customer contract*

Acquisition date		*End of reporting period*
1.10.X6	*Movement*	30.9.X7
1,000	–	1,000

9   *Investments in equity instruments*

	$'000
Fair value at 1 October 20X6	6,500
Fair value at 30 September 20X7	9,000
Increase in fair value	2,500

DEBIT Investments in equity instruments/CREDIT Retained earnings

41 Paladin

Marking scheme

		Marks
(a)	Consolidated statement of financial position	
	Property, plant and equipment	2½
	Goodwill	5
	Other intangibles	2½
	Investment in associate	2
	Inventory	1
	Receivables	1
	Bank	½
	Equity shares	½
	Retained earnings	5
	Non-controlling interest	2
	Deferred tax	½
	Bank overdraft	½
	Deferred consideration	1
	Trade payables	1
		25
(b)	1 mark per valid point to maximum	5
		30

(a)   CONSOLIDATED STATEMENT OF FINANCIAL POSITION AS AT 30 SEPTEMBER 20X1

	$'000
ASSETS	
Non-current assets	
Property, plant and equipment (40,000 + 31,000 + 3,000 (W6))	74,000
Goodwill (W2)	15,000
Intangible assets (7,500 + 2,500 (W6))	10,000
Investment in associate (W3)	7,700
	106,700

Current assets

Inventories (11,200 + 8,400 − 600 (W7))	19,000
Trade receivables (7,400 + 5,300 − 1,300 (W7))	11,400
Bank	3,400
	33,800
Total assets	140,500

EQUITY AND LIABILITIES
Equity attributable to owners of Paladin

Share capital	50,000
Retained earnings (W4)	35,200
	85,200
Non-controlling interests (W5)	7,900
	93,100

Non-current liabilities

Deferred tax (15,000 + 8,000)	23,000

Current liabilities

Overdraft	2,500
Payables (11,600 + 6,200 − 1,300 (W7))	16,500
Deferred consideration (5,000 + 400 (W2))	5,400
	24,400
Total equity and liabilities	140,500

Workings

1   *Group structure*

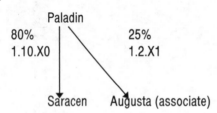

Paladin

80%   25%
1.10.X0   1.2.X1

Saracen   Augusta (associate)

2   *Goodwill*

	$'000	$'000
Consideration transferred:		
Cash		32,000
Deferred consideration (5,400 × 1 / 1.08)		5,000
		37,000
Non-controlling interest (2,000 × $3.50)		7,000
		44,000
Fair value of net assets:		
Share capital	10,000	
Retained earnings	12,000	
Fair value adjustment on plant	4,000	
Intangible asset	3,000	
		(29,000)
Goodwill		15,000

3   *Investment in associate*

	$'000
Cost of investment	10,000
Share of post-acquisition retained earnings (800 (W4) × 25%)	200
Impairment	(2,500)
	7,700

4   Retained earnings

	Paladin	Saracen	Augusta
	$'000	$'000	$'000
Per question – 1.10.20X0	25,700	12,000	31,800
– year to 30.9.20X1	9,200	6,000	1,200
		18,000	33,000
PURP (W7)	(600)		
Depreciation on fair value adjustments (W6)		(1,500)	
Unwinding of discount (5,400 – 5,000 (W2))	(400)		
Less pre-acquisition retained earnings to 1.10.20X0		(12,000)	(31,800)
Less pre-acquisition to 1.2.X1 (1,200 × 4/12)		–	(400)
		4,500	800
Saracen (4,500 × 80%)	3,600		
Augusta (800 × 25%)	200		
Impairment of investment in associate (W3)	(2,500)		
	35,200		

5   Non-controlling interests

	$'000
NCI at acquisition (W2)	7,000
Share of post-acquisition retained earnings (4,500 (W4) × 20%)	900
	7,900

6   Fair value adjustments

	Acquisition		Movement	Year end
	$'000		$'000	$'000
Plant	4,000	1/4	(1,000)	3,000
Intangible asset (customer relationships)	3,000	1/6	(500)	2,500
	7,000		(1,500)	5,500

7   Intragroup trading

Unrealised profit:

	$'000	$'000
Dr Cost of sales/retained earnings (2,600 × 30/130)	600	
Cr Inventories		600
Current account:		
Dr Group trade payables	1,300	
Cr Group trade receivables		1,300

(b)   At 30 September 20X1 Paladin could be presumed to have 'significant influence' over Augusta arising from its 25% shareholding.   Augusta was therefore treated as an associate and its results were brought into Paladin's financial statements using the equity method.

Spekulate's purchase of 65% changes Paladin's position. Spekulate now has control, so Paladin can no longer be presumed to have significant influence. That significant influence has been lost is then confirmed by the fact that Paladin has lost its seat on the board.   Paladin's investment in Augusta should be treated in the financial statements for the year ended 30 September 20X2 under IFRS 9 *Financial Instruments*, carried at fair value, with any gains or losses taken to profit or loss.

42 Multiple choice answers – financial instruments

1 B Intangible assets. These do not give rise to a present right to receive cash or other financial assets. The other options are financial instruments.

2 B

	$'000
Interest years 1–3 (30m × 8% × 2.49)	5,976
Repayment year 3 (30m × 0.75)	22,500
Debt component	28,476
Equity option (β)	1,524
	30,000

3 A

	$'000
$12,500 × 1,296 / 1,200	13,500
Carrying amount	(12,500)
Gain	1,000

4 D

	$'000
Proceeds (20m – 0.5m)	19,500
Interest 10%	1,950
Interest paid (20m × 5%)	(1,000)
Balance 30 March 20X1	20,450
Interest 10%	2,045
Interest paid (20m × 5%)	(1,000)
	21,495

5 A

	$
40,000 shares @ $6	240,000
Transaction costs	3,000
	243,000

43 Bertrand

Text reference. Chapter 11

Top tips. This was a quite easy question on convertible loan notes – easy if you had revised this and knew what to do with them. Remember that the interest charge must use the effective interest rate, not the nominal rate.

Easy marks. Even if you got mixed up with the calculations, you should have been able to do part (a), which was worth half the marks.

Examiner's comments. Some candidates were able to explain how the convertible loan should be treated in part (a) but were then unable to apply it in practice in part (b). Candidates who had studied this topic were able to score full marks, those who had not scored very few.

Marking scheme

			Marks
(a)	(i)	1 mark per valid point	2
	(ii)	1 mark per valid point	3
(b)		Finance cost	2
		Value of equity option	1
		Value of debt at 30 September 20X1	2
(c)		Comment on advice	2
		Financial statement extracts	3
			15

(a) (i) The convertible loan notes carry a lower rate of interest because holders are considered to have foregone 3% interest in order to have the conversion option. Without the conversion option, Bertrand would have to offer 8% in order to attract investors.

     (ii) The directors' proposed treatment will classify an amount that should be shown as a non-current liability as equity, which will make the financial statements misleading. A finance cost of 5% on the whole amount is not correct and will understate the cost of the loan to the company.

(b)

	$'000
STATEMENT OF PROFIT OR LOSS	
Finance costs (9,190 (W) × 8%)	735
STATEMENT OF FINANCIAL POSITION	
Equity	
Equity option (W)	810
Non-current liabilities	
5% convertible loan notes (W)	9,425

Working

	$'000
Interest payable ($10m × 5% × 2.58*)	1,290
Capital repayable ($10m × 0.79)	7,900
Debt element	9,190
Equity element (β)	810
	10,000

*(0.93 + 0.86 + 0.79 = 2.58)

The debt element of $9,190,000 will appear under non-current liabilities, the equity element should appear under equity.

The debt element at 30 September 20X1 will be as follows:

	$'000
1 October 20X0	9,190
Finance charge 8%	735
Interest paid (10,000 × 5%)	(500)
Balance 30 September 20X1	9,425

(c) IAS 32 *Financial instruments: presentation* requires the issuer of a **hybrid or compound instrument** of this nature – containing elements that are characteristic of both debt and equity – to separate out the components of the instrument and classify them separately. Fab Factors are thus wrong in their advice that such instruments should be recorded and shown as debt.

The proceeds of issue should be split between the amounts attributable to the conversion rights, which are classed as **equity**, and the remainder which must be classed as a **liability**. Although there are several methods that might be used, the question only gives sufficient information to allow the amounts of debt liability to be calculated, leaving the equity element as the residual.

Year	Cash flows $'000	Factor at 10%	Present value $'000
1 Interest ($15m × 7%)	1,050	0.91	955.5
2	1,050	0.83	871.5
3	1,050	0.75	787.5
4	1,050	0.68	714.0
5 Interest + capital	16,050	0.62	9,951.0
Total debt component			13,279.5
Proceeds of issue			15,000.0
Equity component (residual)			1,720.5

STATEMENTOF PROFIT OR LOSS (EXTRACTS)

	$'000
Interest paid ((7% × $15m) + 278 (W1))	1,328

Working

((10% × $13.2795m) – $1.05m) (rounded)	278

STATEMENT OF FINANCIAL POSITION (EXTRACTS)

	$'000
Non-current liabilities	
7% convertible loan notes (13,279.5 + 278)	13,557.5
Equity	
Option to convert to equity	1,720.5

44 Multiple choice answers – leasing

1	A		$,000
		PVMLPs	3,300
		Payment	(700)
			2,600
		Interest 6%	156
		Balance 31.12.X6	2,756
		Payment	(700)
			2,056
		Interest 6%	123
		Balance 31.12.X7	2,179
		Current	700
		Non-current	1,479
			2,179

2   A   This would suggest that the lease is an operating lease. The other options all point to a finance lease.

3	A		$'000
		PVMLPs	15,600
		Interest 8%	1,248
		Payment	(6,000)
		Balance 31.3.X8	10,848
		Interest 8%	868
		Payment	(6,000)
		Balance 31.3.X9	5,716

Current liability = 10,848 – 5,716 = 5,132

4	B		$
		Cash price	360,000
		Deposit	(120,000)
			240,000
		Interest 12%	28,800
		Payment	(100,000)
		Balance 3.12.X6	168,800
		Interest to 31.12.X7 12%	20,256

5   D   An asset acquired under a finance lease should be capitalised at the lower of fair value and the present value of minimum lease payments. These amounts will often be the same.

6	B		$'000
		Liability 1 October 20X3 (25m – 2m)	23,000
		Interest 10%	2,300
		Rental	(6,000)
		Balance 30 September 20X4	19,300
		Interest 10%	1,930
		Rental	(6,000)
		Balance 30 September 20X5	15,230

So current liability = (19,300,000 – 15,230,000) = $4,070,000

7	B	A lease which transfers ownership at the end of the lease term would normally be classified as a finance lease as would lease of an asset of a specialised nature, such that it can only be used by the lessee unless modifications are made. The lease term would need to be for 'the major part' (not approximately half) of the economic life of the asset if the criterion in (ii) were being used. Regarding (iv), the present value of the minimum lease payments would have to amount to 'substantially all' of the fair value of the asset.
8	C	This is in substance a secured loan, so the asset will be recognised at its new carrying amount of $50m and a lease liability will be set up for the same amount.

The $10m increase in carrying amount will be treated as other income deferred over the life of the asset. The amount which can be recognised for the year to 30 September 20X4 is:

($10m / 5) × 6/12 = $1m

45 Preparation question: Branch

STATEMENT OF PROFIT OR LOSS (EXTRACT)

	$
Depreciation (W1)	5,000
Finance costs (W2)	2,074

STATEMENT OF FINANCIAL POSITION (EXTRACT)	$
Non-current assets	
Property, plant and equipment	
Assets held under finance leases (20,000 – (20,000 / 4))	15,000
Non-current liabilities	
Finance lease liabilities (W2)	14,786
Current liabilities	
Finance lease liabilities (W2) (16,924 – 14,786)	2,138

Workings

1   *Depreciation*

$$\frac{20,000}{4} = \$5,000 \text{ pa}$$

2   *Finance leases liabilities*

		$
Year ended 31 December 20X1		
1.1.X1	Liability b/d	20,000
1.1.X1	Deposit	(1,150)
		18,850
1.1.X1 – 31.12.X1	Interest at 11%	2,074
31.12.X1	Instalment	(4,000)
31.12.X1	Liability c/d	16,924
Year ended 31 December 20X2		
1.1.X2 – 31.12.X2	Interest at 11%	1,862
31.12.X2	Instalment	(4,000)
31.12.X2	Liability c/d	14,786

46 Fino

Marking scheme

				Marks
(a)	1 mark per valid point to			
				5
(b)	(i)	1 mark per valid point to		4
	(ii)	(1)	Operating lease – Charge to profit or loss	1
			– Prepayment	1
		(2)	Finance lease – Depreciation and finance costs	1
			Asset, current and non-current liability	3
				15

(a) The concept of faithful representation requires that the financial statements give a true picture of the nature and effect of financial transactions. If users can be confident that this is the case, then the financial statements can be relied upon.

This means that assets and liabilities as shown in the statement of financial position exist, are assets or liabilities of the entity and are shown at the correct amount, in accordance with the stated accounting policies of the entity. For instance, it may seem that a property shown at original cost when its market value is twice that amount is not faithfully represented, but if the disclosed accounting policy of the entity is not to revalue its properties, users will know what they are looking at and can adjust accordingly.

The most obvious examples of lack of faithful representation involve off-balance-sheet finance transactions, such as sale and leaseback, where secured loans are disguised as the sale of assets. This keeps borrowing out of the statement of financial position and avoids any consequent impact on gearing. The accounting scandals of the past decade revealed numerous off-balance-sheet schemes and underlined the importance of faithful representation.

(b) (i) The finance director is correct in that, if the plant is regarded as being held under an operating lease, it will not be capitalised. In this case the cost of the plant will not be included in capital employed and so will not have an adverse effect on ROCE.

However, the finance director's comments betray an ignorance of IAS 17 *Leases*. Under IAS 17 leases are classified according to the **substance** of the transaction, on the basis of whether or not the risks and rewards of ownership have been transferred. The standard gives examples of situations where a lease would normally be classified as a finance lease, including:

- Where the lease transfers ownership to the lessee at the end of the lease term

- Where an option to purchase exists on terms which make it reasonably certain that the option will be exercised

- Where the lease term is for the major part of the asset's economic life

- Where the present value of the minimum lease payments amounts to at least substantially all of the fair value of the asset

In this case the lease term is for the whole of the asset's economic life and the present value of the minimum lease payments (four payments of $100,000 over three years) amounts to substantially all of the fair value of the plant. This must therefore be regarded as a finance lease and consequently will impact the ROCE.

(ii) 1 *Operating lease*

		$
Statement of profit or loss		
Payment under operating lease (100,000 × 6/12)		50,000
Statement of financial position		
Current assets		
Prepayment (100,000 × 6/12)		50,000

2 *Finance lease*

	$
Statement of profit or loss	
Depreciation (350,000/4 × 6/12)	43,750
Finance costs (W)	12,500
Non-current assets	
Leased plant (350,000 – 43,750)	306,250
Non-current liabilities	
Amount due under finance lease (W)	175,000
Current liabilities	
Amount due under finance lease	
(262,500 – 175,000)	87,500

Working

	$
Cost 1.4.X7	350,000
1.4.X7 deposit	(100,000)
Balance 1.4.X7	250,000
Interest to 30.9.X7 (250,000 × 10% × 6/12)	12,500
Balance 30.9.X7	262,500
Interest to 1.4.X8 (250,000 × 10% × 6/12)	12,500
1.4.X8 payment	(100,000)
Capital balance due 30.9.X8	175,000

47 Multiple choice answers – provisions and events after the reporting period

1	D	Loss of the case is not 'probable', so no provision is made, but the legal costs will have to be paid so should be provided for.
2	A	$2 million should be provided for and capitalised as part of the cost of the mine. It will then be depreciated over the useful life.

3   D

	$m
$2 million × 15%	0.3
$6 million × 5%	0.3
	0.6

4	D	The cost of the overhaul will be capitalised when it takes place. No obligation exists before the overhaul is carried out. The other options would all give rise to valid provisions.
5	C	(ii) and (iii) both provide evidence of conditions that existed at the end of the reporting period. (i) and (iv) refer to conditions which arose after the reporting period.
6	C	We can assume that these faults also existed at the year end, so this is the only option which would require adjustment. The others have all taken place after the year end.

48 Promoil

				Marks
(a)		1 mark per relevant point		5
(b)	(i)	Explanation of treatment	2	
		Depreciation	1	
		Finance cost	1	
		Non-current asset	2	
		Provision	1	
				7
	(ii)	Figures for asset and depreciation if not a constructive obligation	1	
		What may cause a constructive obligation	1	
		Subsequent treatment if it is a constructive obligation	1	
				3
				15

(a) The *Conceptual Framework* defines a liability as a present obligation of an entity arising from past events, the settlement of which is expected to result in an outflow from the entity of resources embodying economic benefits. The obligation can be legal or constructive.

A provision is a liability of uncertain timing or amount. It can be recognised when the outflow of resources is probable and when the amount concerned can be reliably estimated. Because it is regarded as a liability, a provision must meet the definition of a liability. This regulates when a provision should, or should not, be made. For instance, entities are not allowed to provide for future operating losses, which used to be a means of 'profit smoothing', because the losses are in the future, rather than arising from past events. At the same time, an entity which has a future environmental liability because of past polluting activities, is required to make a provision as soon as the liability becomes apparent.

(b) (i) Promoil must provide for dismantling and restoration costs at 30 September 20X8, as the liability came into existence with the granting of the licence and the cost has been reliably estimated.

The provision at 30 September 20X8 will be for the future cost discounted over ten years. This will be added to the carrying amount of the oil platform and depreciated over ten years. The discount will be 'unwound' each year and charged to finance costs. The credit entry will increase the provision until at the end of ten years it will stand at $15m.

At 30 September 20X8:

STATEMENT OF PROFIT OR LOSS

	$'000
Depreciation (see SFP)	3,690
Finance costs (6,900 (see SFP) × 8%)	552

STATEMENT OF FINANCIAL POSITION

		$'000
Non-current assets:		
Oil platform	30,000	
Dismantling (15m × 0.46)	6,900	
		36,900
Depreciation (36,900 / 10)		(3,690)
Carrying amount		33,210
Non-current liabilities:		
Environmental provision at 1 October 20X7		6,900
Discount unwound (6,900 × 8%)		552
		7,452

(ii) If the government licence did not require an environmental clean-up, Promoil would have no legal obligation. It would then be necessary to determine whether or not Promoil had a constructive obligation. This would apply if on past performance it had established a practice of carrying out an environmental clean-up where required, which would give rise to the expectation that it would do so in this case. If a constructive obligation existed, the accounting would be as per the above.

If no obligation were established, there would be no liability. No provision would be made for the clean-up. The platform would be capitalised at $30m and depreciated over ten years. There would be no finance costs.

49 Borough

Text references. Chapter 13.

Top tips. Six marks are available for part (a), so a proper answer to this part of the question is required, not just a couple of sentences. (b)(ii) looks more complex than it is, looking at the entity and consolidated financial statements will help you sort it out.

Easy marks. Part (a) was easy and (b)(i) was straightforward, although you may have wondered about the variable amount.

Examiner's comments. Most candidates had learned the definitions from IAS 37 but had more trouble explaining the consistency aspects. Part (b) tested application to environmental costs and a contingent liability. Many candidates did not know how to deal with the variable element of the environmental costs and few were able to deal with the loan guarantee or determine in which financial statements it should be disclosed.

			Marks
(a)		Definition of provisions	2
		Definition of contingent liabilities	2
		How IAS 37 improves comparability	2
			6
(b)	(i)	Constructive obligation	1
		Explanation of treatment	1
		Non-current asset and amortisation	1½
		Environmental provision and unwinding of discount	1½
	(ii)	Entity financial statements – contingent liability	1
		No obligation for secured $15m	1
		Consolidated statements – $25m liability	1
		If not going concern – current liability in entity statements	1
			9
			15

(a) A provision is a liability of uncertain timing or amount. A provision should be recognised when an entity has a present obligation, it is probable that it will result in an outflow of economic benefits and a reliable estimate can be made of the amount.

A contingent liability is a possible obligation relying on the occurrence or non-occurrence of a future event which the entity cannot control, or an obligation regarding which the outflow of economic resources is not probable or cannot be reliably estimated.

IAS 37 *Provisions, contingent liabilities and contingent assets* was introduced to regulate the use of provisions. A provision cannot be made unless it satisfies the criteria above. This prevents companies from making excessive provisions in profitable years and the writing these amounts back to boost profits in less profitable years. Companies cannot make provisions for expected future losses or for restructuring to which they are not irrevocably committed. This makes financial statements more transparent and improves consistency from year to year and between entities.

IAS 37 also requires companies to provide for a liability if it meets the criteria. For instance, deferred environmental obligations must be provided for in full at the outset rather than being accrued for over the period of the obligation.

(b) (i) Borough has a constructive obligation to deal with these environmental costs, so a provision must be set up.

The fixed cost of making good the damage must be added to the cost of the licence and set up as a provision. The provision will be increased each year according to the number of barrels extracted.

At 30 September 20X1 the statement of financial position will show:

	$'000
Non-current assets	
Intangible asset – extraction licence ((50m + 20m) × 9 / 10)	63,000
Non-current liabilities	
Environmental provision (20m + (150m × 0.02)) × 1.08	24,840

(ii) Legally, Borough and Hamlet are separate companies and in its individual financial statements Borough will simply show its investment in Hamlet as an asset. The guarantee of $10m will be disclosed as a contingent liability. Borough will not need to reflect the $15m which is secured on Hamlet's property. If at some point it is decided that Hamlet is not a going concern, then Borough's loan guarantee will need to be provided for.

In its group financial statements Borough will consolidate the whole of the $25m loan.

50 Shawler

27 mins

Text references Chapters 3 and 13

Top tips The issues here are the complex asset, the government grant and the environmental provision and it is important not to get them mixed up. Read the question carefully and make a note of the dates.

Easy marks Part (a) was very straightforward, up to six marks for very simple calculations. Parts (b) and (c) were a bit more challenging, but you should have been able to make enough points for half marks.

Marking scheme

				Marks
(a)	(i)	Furnace	1	
		Government grant (½ for split)	1	
		Environmental provision	1	
				3
	(ii)	Depreciation	1	
		Government grant (credit)	1	
		Finance costs	1	
				3
(b)		Not an obligating event as legislation not yet in force	1	
		Need not provide for filters even when it is in force	1	
		May need separate provision for a fine	1	
		Cannot reduce the environmental provision	1	
				4
(c)		No provision required	1	
		Treat as complex asset	1	
		Depreciation calculation	3	
				5
				15

(a) (i)   STATEMENT OF FINANCIAL POSITION EXTRACTS 30 SEPTEMBER 20X4

	Carrying amount
	$
Non-current assets	
Furnace: main body (48,000 × 7 / 8)	42,000
liner (6,000 – 2,000)	4,000
Non-current liabilities	
Government grant (8,400 – 1,200)	7,200
Environmental provision (18,000 × 1.08)	19,440
Current liabilities	
Government grant	1,200

(ii)   STATEMENT OF PROFIT OR LOSS EXTRACTS

	$	$
Income: government grant		1,200
Depreciation: furnace/ main body	6,000	
furnace/ liner	2,000	
		(8,000)
Unwinding of discount on provision (19,440 – 18,000)		(1,440)

(b) **No provision** should be made for the filters at this point in time because the **legislation does not come into force for two years**. When Shawler fits the anti-pollution filters, they should be capitalised and depreciated over their useful life. At that point the existing environmental provision should be reviewed, but not before.

It may be expected that a provision will be required in two years' time to cover the fitting of the filters. However IAS 37 states that where an entity needs to carry out expenditure in order to operate in a particular way in the future, that expenditure could be avoided by **changing its method of operation**, so **no provision is recognised**. In the case of Shawler, it could be said that it could find some other way of reducing its pollution. If the legislation comes into force without Shawler having fitted the filters, it may recognise a provision for any fines payable.

(c) No obligation exists to replace the engine and so it is wrong to create a provision for its replacement. Shawler may decide to trade in the earthmover rather than replace the engine. Also, the $2.4m depreciation charge includes an element in respect of the engine, so to make a provision as well is double-counting.

Instead IAS 16 states that the earth-mover should be treated as an asset with two separate components (the engine and the rest) with different useful lives. The engine (cost $7.5m) will be depreciated on a machine hours basis over 5,000 hours, while the rest of the machine (cost $16.5m) will be depreciated over ten years.

	Cost	Depreciation charge
	$'000	
Engine	7,500	Depreciated on a machine hour basis over 5,000 hours. The charge is $1,500 per Hour.
The rest	16,500	Depreciated on a straight line basis over its ten year useful life. The charge is $1,650,000 per annum.
Total	24,000	

When the engine is replaced the cost and accumulated depreciation on the existing engine will be retired and the cost of the new engine will be capitalised and depreciated over its working life.

51 Multiple choice answers – inventories and biological assets

1   B
		$m
Per inventory count		36.0
Received after year end		(2.7)
Sold after year end (7.8m / 1.3)		6.0
		39.3

2   A   NRV – (12,000 × (5.4 × 85%)) = $55,080

3   C
Product		$
A 1,000 × 40		40,000
B 2,500 × 15		37,500
C 800 × 22		17,600
		95,100

4   C   As the item becomes obsolete we can expect its market price to fall – and eventually fall below cost. The other options would all maintain or improve the net realisable value of the item.

5   D   IAS 41 *Agriculture* requires biological assets to be measured on initial recognition at fair value less estimated costs to sell.

6   B   Harvest is an intervention, not a biological process. Growth, procreation and degeneration are natural biological processes.

7   A   A gain or loss on a biological asset is included in profit or loss for the year.

8   D   None of these statements is correct. Production overheads are allocated on the basis of a company's *normal* level of activity. Settlement discounts are not deducted to arrive at NRV. The LIFO formula is not allowed under IAS 2 *Inventories*.   Valuation of finished goods should include production overheads.

9   A   IAS 10 *Events after the reporting period* may be relevant as agricultural produce is perishable and if prices have to be reduced after the year end, this will affect the year end valuation.

52 Multiple choice answers – taxation

1	C		$'000
		Charge for year	16,200
		Underprovision	2,100
		Adjust deferred tax (W)	(1,500)
		Profit or loss charge	16,800
		Working	
		Provision needed (13m × 30%)	3,900
		Provision b/f	(5,400)
		Reduce provision	(1,500)

2	D		$m
		B/f (140 + 160)	300
		Charge for year	270
		C/f (310 + 130)	(440)
		Tax paid	130

3	C		$'000
		Prior year underprovision	700
		Current provision	4,500
		Movement of deferred tax (8.4 – 5.6)	(2,800)
		Deferred tax on revaluation surplus	(1,200)
		Tax charge for the year	1,200

4	A		$'000
		Current charge	19,400
		Overprovision	(800)
		Deferred tax (W)	400
			19,000
		Working	
		Required provision	6,750
		Less revaluation	(3,750)
			3,000
		Balance b/f	(2,600)
		Charge to income tax	400

5	C		$'000
		B/f current tax	(50)
		B/f deferred tax	30
		Charge for year	160
			140
		C/f current tax	(150)
		C/f deferred tax	(50)
		Tax received	(60)

53 Preparation question: Julian

(a)

	Carrying amount $'000	Tax base $'000	Temporary difference $'000
Property, plant and equipment	460	270	190
Development expenditure	60		60
Interest receivable (55 – 45)	10		10
Provision	(40)		(40)
			220

(b) **Note to the statement of financial position**

Deferred tax liability

	$'000
At 1 January 20X4 [(310 – 230) × 30%]	24
Amount charged to profit or loss (balancing figure)	15
Amount charged to equity (90 × 30%)	27
At 31 December 20X4 (220 × 30%)	66

Note to the statement of profit or loss

Income tax expense

	$'000
Current tax	45
Deferred tax	15
	60

54 Preparation question: Bowtock

(a) **Principles of deferred tax**

In many countries different rules are used for calculating accounting profit (as used by investors) and taxable profit. This can give rise to **temporary differences**.

Temporary differences arise when income or expenditure is recognised in the financial statements in one year, but is charged or allowed for tax in another. Deferred tax needs to be provided for on these items.

The most important temporary difference is that between depreciation charged in the financial statements and capital allowances in the tax computation. In practice capital allowances tend to be higher than depreciation charges, resulting in accounting profits being higher than taxable profits. This means that the actual tax charge (known as **current tax**) is too low in comparison with accounting profits. However, these differences even out over the life of an asset, and so at some point in the future the accounting profits will be lower than the taxable profits, resulting in a relatively high current tax charge.

These differences are misleading for investors who value companies on the basis of their post tax profits (by using EPS for example). Deferred tax adjusts the reported tax expense for these differences. As a result the reported tax expense (the current tax for the period plus the deferred tax) will be comparable to the reported profits, and in the statement of financial position a provision is built up for the expected increase in the tax charge in the future.

There are many ways that deferred tax could be calculated. IAS 12 states that the **liability method** should be used. This provides for the tax on the difference between the carrying value of an asset (or liability) and its tax base. The tax base is the value given to an asset (or liability) for tax purposes. The deferred tax charge (or credit) in profit or loss is the increase (or decrease) in the provision reported in the statement of financial position.

(b)

The provision for deferred tax in Bowtock's statement of financial position at 30 September 20X3 will be the potential tax on the difference between the accounting carrying value of $1,400,000 and the tax base of $768,000. The difference is $632,000 and the tax on the difference is $158,000.

The charge (or credit) for deferred tax in profit or loss represents the increase (or decrease) in the provision during the year. The closing provision of $158,000 is less than the opening provision of $160,000, so there is a credit for $2,000 in respect of this year.

Movement in the provision for deferred tax for the year-ending 30 September 20X3

	$
Opening provision	160,000
Credit released to profit or loss	(2,000)
Closing provision	158,000

Workings

		Accounting carrying amount		Tax base	Difference	Tax @ 25%
Y/E 09/X1		$		$	$	$
Purchase		2,000,000		2,000,000	–	–
Depreciation	W1	(200,000)	W2	(800,000)		
Balance		1,800,000		1,200,000	600,000	150,000
Y/E 09/X2						
Depreciation		(200,000)	W3	(240,000)		
Balance		1,600,000		960,000	640,000	160,000
Y/E 09/X3						
Depreciation		(200,000)	W4	(192,000)		
Balance		1,400,000		768,000	632,000	158,000

(W1) $2,000,000 cost – $400,000 residual value over eight years
(W2) $2,000,000 × 40%
(W3) $1,200,000 × 20%
(W3) $960,000 × 20%

55 Multiple choice answers – presentation of published financial statements

1   B   The fact that a liability has arisen during the current accounting period does not make it a current liability. The other options would all lead to classification as a current liability.

2   D   The revaluation gain on the factory will be presented under 'other comprehensive income'. The other items will be recognised in profit or loss. Note that gains on investment properties go through profit or loss.

3   C   Inventories, provisions and intangible assets are shown separately. There is no such requirement for government grants.

4   D   The time between acquisition of assets for processing and receipt of cash from customers

5   A   Equity dividends are presented in the statement of changes in equity.

56 Preparation question: Candel

(a)   STATEMENT OF PROFIT OR LOSS AND OTHER COMPREHENSIVE INCOME FOR THE YEAR ENDED 30 SEPTEMBER 20X8

	$'000
Revenue (300,000 – 2,500 (plant disposal))	297,500
Cost of sales (W1)	(225,400)
Gross profit	72,100
Distribution costs	(14,500)
Administrative expenses (W1)	(21,900)
Finance costs (1,200 (W5) + 200)	(1,400)
Profit before tax	34,300
Income tax expense (W6)	(11,600)
Profit for the year	22,700
Other comprehensive income:	
Loss on property revaluation (W2)	(4,500)
Total comprehensive income for the year	18,200

(b)   STATEMENT OF CHANGES IN EQUITY FOR THE YEAR ENDED 30 SEPTEMBER 20X8

	Share capital $'000	Retained earnings $'000	Revaluation Surplus $'000	Total $'000
Balance at 1 October 20X7	50,000	24,500	10,000	84,500
Dividends paid	–	(6,000)	–	(6,000)
Total comprehensive income (W2)	–	22,700	(4,500)	18,200
Balance at 30 September 20X8	50,000	41,200	5,500	96,700

(c)   STATEMENT OF FINANCIAL POSITION AT 30 SEPTEMBER 20X8

	$'000	$'000
ASSETS		
Non-current assets		
Property, plant and equipment (W2)		81,400
Development expenditure (W3)		14,800
		96,200
Current assets		
Inventory	20,000	
Trade receivables	43,100	
		63,100
Total assets		159,300

	$'000	$'000
EQUITY AND LIABILITIES		
Equity		
Share capital		50,000
Retained earnings		41,200
Revaluation surplus		5,500
		96,700
Non-current liabilities		
Redeemable preference shares (W5)		20,400
Deferred tax (5,800 + 200 (W6))		6,000
Current liabilities		
Trade payables	23,400	
Provision (W4)	100	
Tax payable	11,400	
Overdraft	1,300	
		36,200
Total equity and liabilities		159,300

Workings

1 *Expenses*

	Cost of sales $'000	Distribution $'000	Admin $'000
Per question	204,000	14,500	22,200
Depreciation: Property	2,500	–	–
Plant and equipment	9,600	–	–
Loss on plant (4,000 – 2,500)	1,500	–	–
Research and development (W3)	3,800	–	–
Amortisation (W3)	4,000	–	–
Legal claim (W4)	–	–	(300)
	225,400	14,500	21,900

2 *Property, plant and equipment*

	Property $'000	P & E $'000	Total $'000
Cost/valuation b/d	50,000	76,600	
Acc depreciation b/d	–	(24,600)	
	50,000	52,000	102,000
Depn: Property (50,000/20)	(2,500)	–	(2,500)
P&E ((52,000 – 4,000) × 20%)	–	(9,600)	(9,600)
Disposal (8,000 – 4,000)	–	(4,000)	(4,000)
Revaluation (β)	(4,500)	–	(4,500)
	43,000	38,400	81,400

3 *Development expenditure*

	$'000
Cost b/d	20,000
Accumulated amortisation b/d	(6,000)
	14,000
Additional expenditure capitalised (800 × 6)	4,800
Amortisation (20,000 × 20%)	(4,000)
Balance c/d	14,800
Charged to cost of sales:	
Research	1,400
Development when criteria not met (800 × 3)	2,400
Amortisation	4,000
	7,800

4   *Legal claim*

$'000

Damages are not probable, therefore not accrued
– Reverse in admin expenses   400
Legal costs should be provided as results from
past event (claim)   (100)   Provision
                                                                300   Credit to Admin

5   *Preference shares - Financial liability at amortised cost*

                                                                            $'000
Financial liability b/d   20,000
Effective interest ($\times$ 12% $\times$ 6/12)   1,200
Coupon paid (per TB) ($\times$ 8% $\times$ 6/12)   (800)
Financial liability c/d   20,400
Adjustment required:

                                                                            $'000
Dr Finance costs   400
Cr Financial liability   400

The $800k coupon paid in the TB is increased to effective cost of $1,200k.

6   *Taxes*

                                                                            $'000
Current tax:
Dr   Income tax expense (profit or loss)   11,400
Cr   Current tax payable (SOFP)   11,400

Deferred tax:
Dr   Income tax expense (6,000 – 5,800)   200
Cr   Deferred tax liability   200

57 Preparation question: Dexon

(a) $'000 $'000
Draft retained profit   96,700
Dividends paid (W5)   15,500
Draft profit for the year   112,200
Depreciation:
Buildings (165,000 / 15)   11,000
Plant (180,500 $\times$ 20%)   36,100
                                                                            (47,100)
Gain on investment (W2)   1,000
Current year fraud loss   (2,500)
Increase in deferred tax provision (W4)   (800)
Current year tax   (11,400)
                                                                            51,400

(b) DEXON – STATEMENT OF CHANGES IN EQUITY FOR THE YEAR ENDED 31 MARCH 20X8

	Share capital $'000	Share premium $'000	Revaluation surplus $'000	Retained earnings $'000	Total equity $'000
At 1 April 20X7	200,000	30,000	18,000	12,300	260,300
Prior period adjustment (W3)	–	–	–	(1,500)	(1,500)
Restated balance	200,000	30,000	18,000	10,800	258,800
Share issue	50,000	10,000			60,000
Dividends paid				(15,500)	(15,500)
Total comprehensive income for the year	–	–	4,800*	51,400	56,200
At 31 March 20X8	250,000	40,000	22,800	46,700	359,500

*Revaluation surplus:

	$'000
Land and buildings at 31 March 20X7	185,000
Depreciation (165,000 / 15)	(11,000)
	174,000
Valuation at 31 March 20X8	180,000
Surplus	6,000
Deferred tax provision (6,000 × 20%)	(1,200)
Net surplus	4,800

(c) DEXON – STATEMENT OF FINANCIAL POSITION AS AT 31 MARCH 20X8

	$'000	$'000
Non-current assets		
Property (W1)		180,000
Plant (W1)		144,400
Investments (W2)		13,500
		337,900
Current assets		
Inventory	84,000	
Trade receivables (W6)	48,200	
Bank	3,800	
		136,000
Total assets		473,900
Equity and liabilities		
Share capital		250,000
Share premium		40,000
Revaluation surplus		22,800
Retained earnings		46,700
Total equity		359,500
Non-current liabilities		
Deferred tax (19,200 + 2,000 (W4))		21,200
Current liabilities		
As per draft SFP	81,800	
Tax payable	11,400	
		93,200
Total equity and liabilities		473,900

Workings

1   *Property, plant and equipment*

	Land	Buildings	Plant	Total
	$'000	$'000	$'000	$'000
Per question	20,000	165,000	180,500	365,500
Depreciation	–	(11,000)	(36,100)	(47,100)
	20,000	154,000	144,400	318,400
Revaluation	–	6,000	–	6,000
Balance c/d	20,000	160,000	144,400	324,400

2   *Financial assets at FV through profit or loss*

	$'000
FV at year end (12,500 × 1,296 / 1,200)	13,500
Per draft SOFP	(12,500)
Gain – to profit or loss	1,000

3   *Fraud*

	$'000	$'000
DR Retained earnings re prior year	1,500	
DR Current year profit	2,500	
CR Receivables		4,000

4   *Deferred tax*

	$'000	$'000
DR Revaluation surplus (6,000 × 20%)	1,200	
DR Profit or loss (tax charge) (4,000 × 20%)	800	
CR Deferred tax liability (10,000 × 20%)		2,000

5   *Dividends paid*

	$'000
May 20X7 (200m* × $0.04)	8,000
November 20X7 (250m × $0.03)	7,500
	15,500

*250m × 4/5 = 200m

6   *Trade receivables*

	$'000
Per draft SFP	52,200
Adjustment re fraud	(4,000)
	48,200

58 Highwood

Marking scheme

			Marks
(a)	Statement of profit or loss and other comprehensive income		
	Revenue	½	
	Cost of sales	4	
	Distribution costs	½	
	Administrative expenses	1½	
	Finance costs	1½	
	Income tax expense	1½	
	Other comprehensive income	1½	
			11
(b)	Statement of changes in equity		
	Opening balance on retained earnings	1	
	Other component of equity (option)	1	
	Dividend paid	1	
	Comprehensive income	1	
			4
(c)	Statement of financial position		
	Property, plant and equipment	2½	
	Inventory	1	
	Trade receivables	1	
	Deferred tax	1	
	Issue of 8% loan note	1½	
	Liability to Easyfinance	1	
	Bank overdraft	½	
	Trade payables	½	
	Current tax payable	1	
			10
(d)	Basic EPS	2	
	Diluted EPS	3	
			5
			30

(a) STATEMENT OF PROFIT OR LOSS AND OTHER COMPREHENSIVE INCOME FOR THE YEAR ENDED 31 MARCH 20X6

	$'000
Revenue	339,650
Cost of sales (W1)	(216,950)
Gross profit	122,700
Distribution costs	(27,500)
Administrative expenses (W1)	(30,000)
Finance costs (W3)	(2,848)
Profit before tax	62,352
Income tax expense (19,400 + (W4) 400 – 800)	(19,000)
Profit for the year	43,352
Other comprehensive income:	
Revaluation gain on property (W2)	11,250
Total comprehensive income for the year	54,602

(b) STATEMENT OF CHANGES IN EQUITY FOR THE YEAR ENDED 31 MARCH 20X6

	Share capital	Equity option	Retained earnings	Revaluation surplus	Total
	$'000	$'000	$'000	$'000	$'000
Balance 1 April 20X5	56,000	–	7,000	–	63,000
Dividend	–	–	(5,600)	–	(5,600)
Total comprehensive income			43,352	11,250	54,602
Loan note issue (W3)	–	1,524	–	–	1,524
Balance 31 March 20X6	56,000	1,524	44,752	11,250	113,526

(c) STATEMENT OF FINANCIAL POSITION AS AT 31 MARCH 20X6

	$'000	$'000
Non-current assets		
Property, plant and equipment (W2)		117,500
Current assets		
Inventory (W5)	39,300	
Receivables (47,100 + 9,400 (W6))	56,500	
		95,800
Total assets		213,300
Equity		
Share capital	56,000	
Other component of equity (W3)	1,524	
Revaluation surplus (W2)	11,250	
Retained earnings	44,752	
		113,526
Non-current liabilities		
Deferred tax (W4)	6,750	
Convertible loan note (W3)	28,924	
Easyfinance loan (W6)	8,700	
		44,374
Current liabilities		
Trade payables	24,500	
Tax payable	19,400	
Overdraft	11,500	
		55,400
Total equity and liabilities		213,300

(d) Basic EPS:

Profit for the year ($'000) $\quad\underline{43,352}\quad$ = 38.7c
Shares (56 million × 2) $\quad\quad 112,000$

Diluted EPS:

Convertible loan note:

New shares: 30 million/100 × 30 = 9 million shares

Interest saved = $30 million × 8% × 75% = $1.8 million

The effect on EPS is therefore $1.8m / 9 = 20c, which means that the loan notes are dilutive.

Diluted EPS will be:

Profit + interest saved $\quad\underline{43,352 + 1,800}\quad$ = 37.3c
Shares $\quad\quad 112,000 + 9,000$

Workings

1 Expenses

	Cost of sales	Distribution costs	Administrative expenses
	$'000	$'000	$'000
Per question	207,750	27,500	30,700
Depreciation – buildings (W2)	2,500		
– plant (W2)	10,000		
Increase in inventories (W5)	(3,300)		
Reverse factoring charge (W6)			(1,300)
Bad debt (W6)			600
	216,950	27,500	30,000

2 Property, plant and equipment

	Land	Buildings	Plant and equipment	Total
	$'000	$'000	$'000	$'000
Per TB – cost	25,000	50,000	74,500	149,500
Acc'd depreciation 1.4.20X5		(10,000)	(24,500)	(34,500)
Carrying amount 1.4.20X5	25,000	40,000	50,000	115,000
Revaluation surplus	5,000	10,000	–	15,000
Revalued amount 1.4.20X5	30,000	50,000	50,000	130,000
Depn – bldgs (50,000 / 20yrs)		(2,500)		(2,500)
– plant (50,000 × 20%)			(10,000)	(10,000)
	30,000	47,500	40,000	117,500

The deferred tax on the revaluation (15,000 × 25%) will be charged to the revaluation surplus, leaving a balance of 11,250 (15,000 – 3,750).

3 *Loan note*

As this is a convertible loan note, it has to be split between debt and equity:

	$'000
Interest years 1–3 (2,400 × (0.91 + 0.83 + 0.75)	5,976
Repayment year 3 (30,000 × 0.75)	22,500
Liability component	28,476
Equity component	1,524
Cash received	30,000
Liability component	28,476
Interest (28,476 × 10%)	2,848
Less interest paid	(2,400)
Balance at 31.3.20X6	28,924

4   *Deferred tax*

		$'000
Balance required at 31.3.X6 (27m × 25%)		6,750
Current balance		(2,600)
Deferred tax on revaluation (15m × 25%)		(3,750)
Charge to current tax		400

5   *Inventory*

		$'000
Per TB		36,000
Received after year end		(2,700)
Sold after year end (7,800 × 100/130)		6,000
Correct balance		39,300

Adjustment required – deduct 3,300 from cost of sales.

6   *Factoring*

The factoring arrangement is in substance a loan of $8.7m. To reflect this, the $10m receivables are reinstated, less the allowance of 600.

	Dr	Cr
	$'000	$'000
Loan payable		8,700
Receivables	9,400	
Administrative expenses	600	1,300

59 Keystone

Text references. Chapters 14, 16 and 17.

Top tips. There were a number of complications in this question – self-constructed plant, deferred tax on a revaluation, a dividend to calculate back from the yield – and it was important not to get too bogged down in any of them. Make sure you get the proformas down and fill in any straightforward numbers first.

Easy marks. There were enough easy marks here. You could have scored on tax, inventory and receivables. Cost of sales was complex but a lot of marks were allocated to it, so you should have been able to get some of them.

Examiner's comments. This was a traditional accounts preparation question and generally well-answered. Most of the errors involved the calculation of cost of sales. Some candidates had trouble calculating a gross profit margin and some went on to apply the mark-up to the plant manufactured for own use, which had to be deducted and capitalised. This would have implied that the company was selling the plant to itself at a profit. Many candidates failed to include production, labour and factory overheads in cost of sales and some failed to adjust for opening and closing inventory. The property revaluation caused problems in accounting for deferred tax and some students failed to notice that the revaluation had taken place at the beginning, not the end, of the year.

Marking scheme

	Marks
Statement of profit or loss	
Revenue	½
Cost of sales	7
Distribution costs	½
Administrative expenses	1½
Investment income	1
Loss on fair value of investment	1
Finance costs	½
Income tax expense	1½
Other comprehensive income	1
	14½

		Marks
Statement of changes in equity		
Share capital	1½	
Share premium	1½	
Retained earnings	2	
Revaluation surplus	<u>1</u>	
		6
Statement of financial position		
Property, plant and equipment	3	
Equity investments	½	
Inventory	1½	
Trade receivables	1	
Deferred tax	2	
Trade payables	½	
Bank overdraft	½	
Tax payable	<u>½</u>	
		<u>9½</u>
		<u><u>30</u></u>

(a) STATEMENT OF PROFIT OR LOSS AND OTHER COMPREHENSIVE INCOME FOR THE YEAR ENDED 30 SEPTEMBER 20X1

	$'000
Revenue	380,000
Cost of sales (W1)	(259,900)
Gross profit	120,100
Investment income	800
Loss on fair value of investments (18,000 – 17,400)	(600)
Distribution costs	(14,200)
Administrative expenses (46,400 – 24,000 (W1))	(22,400)
Finance costs	(350)
Profit before taxation	83,350
Income tax expense (24,300 + 1,800 (W3))	(26,100)
Profit for the year	57,250
Other comprehensive income:	
Revaluation gain on property	8,000
Less deferred tax (W3)	(2,400)
Total other comprehensive income	5,600
Total comprehensive income for the year	62,850

(b) STATEMENT OF CHANGES IN EQUITY FOR THE YEAR ENDED 30 SEPTEMBER 20X1

	Share capital $'000	Share premium $'000	Retained earnings $'000	Revaluation surplus $'000	Total $'000
Balance at 1 October 20X0	40,000	10,000	33,600	–	83,600
Bonus issue	10,000	(10,000)	–	–	–
Dividend paid (W1)	–	–	(24,000)	–	(24,000)
Total comprehensive income	–	–	57,250	5,600	62,850
Balance at 30 September 20X1	50,000	–	66,850	5,600	122,450

(c) STATEMENT OF FINANCIAL POSITION AS AT 30 SEPTEMBER 20X1

	$'000
ASSETS	
Non-current assets	
Property, plant and equipment (W2)	78,000
Investment in equity assets	17,400
	95,400
Current assets	
Inventories	54,800
Trade receivables	33,550
Total assets	183,750
EQUITY AND LIABILITIES	
Equity	
Share capital	50,000
Retained earnings	66,850
Revaluation surplus (8,000 (W2) – 2,400 (W3))	5,600
	122,450
Non-current liabilities	
Deferred tax (2,700 + 1,800 + 2,400 (W3))	6,900
Current liabilities	
Trade payables	27,800
Tax payable	24,300
Bank overdraft	2,300
Total equity and liabilities	183,750

Workings

1 *Expenses*

	Cost of sales $'000	Distribution costs $'000	Administrative expenses $'000
Per trial balance		14,200	46,400
Opening inventory	46,700		
Material purchases	64,000		
Production labour	124,000		
Factory overheads	80,000		
Capitalised costs (W2)	(10,000)		
Depreciation (3,000 + 7,000 (W2))	10,000		
Closing inventories	(54,800)		
Dividend paid ($2.4 × 4% × 250,000)			(24,000)
	259,900	14,200	22,400

2 *Property, plant and equipment*

	Leased property $'000	Plant and equipment $'000	Total $'000
Per trial balance:			
Cost	50,000	44,500	94,500
Accumulated depreciation b/d	(10,000)	(14,500)	(24,500)
	40,000	30,000	70,000
Revaluation surplus	8,000		8,000
Revalued amount	48,000	30,000	78,000
Own plant manufactured (3,000 + 4,000 + (4,000 × 75%))		10,000	10,000
Depreciation/amortisation			
Leased property (48,000 / (20 – 4 years*)	(3,000)		(3,000)
Plant and equipment ((30,000 × 20%) + (10,000 × 20% × 6/12))	–	(7,000)	(7,000)
	45,000	33,000	78,000

*At 1.10.20X0 leased property was (10 / 50 × 20 =) 4 years old.

3   *Deferred tax*

	$'000	$'000
Taxable difference ((15,000 × 30%) less b/f 2,700)		
Dr Taxation expense (profit or loss)	1,800	
Cr Deferred tax		1,800
Deferred tax on revaluation: (8,000 × 30%)		
Dr Revaluation surplus	2,400	
Cr Deferred tax		2,400

60 Fresco

Text references. Chapters 4 and 16.

Top tips. There was a lot to get through in this question. Get the formats down quickly and then go through the question and transfer any figures that can go straight from the trial balance to the financial statements. You needed to do workings for PPE and for the leased plant but these were not complicated. Leave time for parts (b) and (c).

Easy marks. The statement of changes in equity was all straightforward. If you had remembered the transfer to retained earnings it was possible to score full marks on this. The PPE working made it possible to score marks on both the statement of profit or loss and other comprehensive income and the statement of financial position, so it was worth spending a bit of time on this. The lease working, on the other hand, carried very few marks and the EPS was quite time-consuming for three marks. Part (c) was an easy five marks.

Examiner's comments. Most candidates showed a sound knowledge of preparing financial statements. Most of the errors arose in the adjustments:

Some candidates deducted the loss on the fraud from revenue for the year rather adding it to expenses and treating it as a prior year adjustment, with the other entry being a deduction from receivables.

There were some difficulties with the finance lease, mainly involving the timing of the lease payments and the initial deposit.

Many candidates were confused with the tax, especially failing to realise that the tax for the year was a refund.

The EPS section was very poorly answered and many candidates did not even attempt it.

		Marks
Statement of profit or loss and other comprehensive income:		
Revenue	½	
Cost of sales	3	
Distribution costs	½	
Administrative expenses	1	
Finance costs	1½	
Income tax	2	
Other comprehensive income	½	9
Statement of changes in equity:		
Balances b/f	1	
Prior year adjustment	1	
Rights issue	1	
Total comprehensive income	1	
Transfer to retained earnings	1	5
Statement of financial position:		
Property, plant and equipment	2½	
Inventory	½	
Trade receivables	1	
Current tax	1	
Non-current lease obligation	½	
Deferred tax	1	
Trade payables	½	
Current lease obligation	½	
Bank overdraft	½	8
Basic EPS: Loss for the year	½	
Theoretical ex-rights price	1	
Weighted average number of shares	1½	3
Part (c) – 1 mark per valid point - maximum		5
		30

(a)   (i)   **STATEMENT OF PROFIT OR LOSS AND OTHER COMPREHENSIVE INCOME**
               FOR THE YEAR ENDED 31 MARCH 20X2

	$'000
Revenue	350,000
Cost of sales (W1)	(311,000)
Gross profit	39,000
Distribution costs (W1)	(16,100)
Administrative expenses (W1)	(29,900)
Finance costs (300 + 2,300 (W3))	(2,600)
Loss before tax	(9,600)
Income tax (W5)	1,800
Loss for the year	(7,800)
Other comprehensive income:	
Gain on revaluation of property (W2)	4,000
Total comprehensive loss for the year	(3,800)

(ii) STATEMENT OF CHANGES IN EQUITY FOR THE YEAR ENDED 31 MARCH 20X2

	Share capital $'000	Share premium $'000	Retained earnings $'000	Revaluation surplus $'000	Total $'000
Balance 31.3.X1	45,000	5,000	5,100	–	55,100
Prior year adj (W4)	–	–	(1,000)	–	(1,000)
Balance 1.4.X1	45,000	5,000	4,100	–	54,100
Share issue (W6)	9,000	4,500	–	–	13,500
Total comprehensive income			(7,800)	4,000	(3,800)
Transfer to retained earnings (W2)	–	–	500	(500)	–
Balance 31.3.X2	54,000	9,500	(3,200)	3,500	63,800

(iii) STATEMENT OF FINANCIAL POSITION AS AT 31 MARCH 20X2

	$'000
ASSETS	
Non-current assets	
Property, plant and equipment (W2)	62,700
Current assets	
Inventory	25,200
Receivables (28,500 – 4,000 (W4))	24,500
Tax asset (W5)	2,400
Total assets	114,800
EQUITY AND LIABILITIES	
Equity	
Share capital 50c shares	54,000
Share premium	9,500
Revaluation surplus	3,500
Retained earnings	(3,200)
	63,800
Non-current liabilities	
Deferred tax (W5)	3,000
Lease payable (W3)	15,230
Current liabilities	
Trade payables	27,300
Lease payable (19,300 – 15,230 (W3))	4,070
Bank overdraft	1,400
Total equity and liabilities	114,800

Workings

1 Expenses

	Cost of sales $'000	Distribution costs $'000	Administrative expenses $'000
Per trial balance	298,700	16,100	26,900
Depreciation (W2)	7,800	–	–
Amortisation (W2)	4,500	–	–
Fraud – current year cost (W4)	–	–	3,000
	311,000	16,100	29,900

2 Property, plant and equipment

	Leased property $'000	Plant and equipment $'000	Leased plant $'000	Total $'000
Cost	48,000	47,500		
Acc. amortisation/depreciation	(16,000)	(33,500)		
Balance 1 April 20X1	32,000	14,000	25,000	
Revaluation surplus	4,000			
Revised carrying amount	36,000			
Depreciation / amortisation:				
36,000 / 8	(4,500)			
14,000 × 20%		(2,800)		
25,000 / 5			(5,000)	
	31,500	11,200	20,000	62,700

3 Finance lease

	$'000
Cost	25,000
Deposit	(2,000)
Balance 1.4.X1	23,000
Interest 10%	2,300
Instalment 31.3.X2	(6,000)
Balance 31.3.X2	19,300
Interest 10%	1,930
Instalment 31.3.X3	(6,000)
Balance 31.3.X3	15,230

4 Fraud

	DEBIT $'000	CREDIT $'000
Retained earnings – prior year	1,000	
Current year profit	3,000	
Receivables		4,000

5 Tax credit

	$'000
Underprovided in prior year	800
Tax refund due (asset in SFP)	(2,400)
Reduction in deferred tax provision (3,200 – (12,000 × 25%))	(200)
Current tax (credit to profit or loss)	(1,800)

6 Share issue

Shares issued = 13.5m / 0.75 = 18m

		$'000
Share capital	18m × 50c	9,000
Share premium	18m × 25c	4,500
		13,500

(b) **Earnings per share**

Loss per profit or loss	$7.8m
Weighted average number of shares in issue (W)	99m

EPS = (7.8m) / 99m = Loss per share 7.9 cents

Working

Theoretical ex-rights price:

5 shares @ 1.20	6.00	
1 share @ 0.75	0.75	
	6.75	/ 6 = 1.125

Weighted average number of shares:

Date	Narrative	Shares '000	Time	Bonus fraction	Weighted average '000
1.4.20X1		90,000	9/12	1.20	72,000
				1.25	
1.1.20X2	Rights issue	18,000			
		108,000	3/12		27,000
					99,000

(c) It is quite common for companies to revalue their non-current assets, in particular land and buildings. Most developed countries have seen a long-term increase in property prices, so that the original cost of a property may represent only a small fraction of its current market value. This can lead to a number of distortions. As capital employed is understated, ROCE will be overstated. Similarly, the depreciation charge based on historical cost will be too low to reflect the true cost of using the asset. This will lead to inflated profit and overstated ROCE.

For companies, undervalued assets involve two major issues. They understate equity, increasing the gearing ratio, and they can lead to undervaluation of the company, making it more vulnerable to takeover.

IAS 16 *Property, plant and equipment* allows assets to be carried under a cost model or a revaluation model. If the revaluation model is chosen, it must be applied to all assets in the same class. Entities are not allowed to cherry-pick which assets to revalue.

Under the revaluation model, an asset is restated at its fair value at the date of the revaluation. In the case of properties, valuations are normally carried out by professional valuers. In the case of plant and equipment, fair value can be taken to be market value. The revaluation model is only available if the fair value of the item can be measured reliably.

Following revaluation, depreciation will be based on the fair value of the asset. IAS 16 allows a portion of the revaluation gain to be recognised each year of the asset's remaining useful life by a transfer from the revaluation surplus to retained earnings.

61 Quincy

Text references Chapters 3 and 16.
Top tips. This is quite a time-pressured question so you need to work fast. Get the proformas down for all three statements and then go methodically through the workings, filling in the proformas as you go.
Easy marks. There are some marks available for figures that can be lifted straight from the question and a good, clear PPE working will enable you to fill in several gaps.

Marking scheme

		Marks	
(a)	Statement: of profit or loss and other comprehensive income		
	Revenue	1½	
	Cost of sales	2½	
	Distribution costs	½	
	Administrative expenses	1	
	Investment income	½	
	Loss on investments	1	
	Finance costs	2	
	Income tax	2	
	Gain on revaluation of land and buildings	1	
			12
(b)	Statement of changes in equity		
	Balances b/f	1	
	Total comprehensive income	1	
	Transfer to retained earnings	1	
			3

(c)	Statement of financial position	
	Property, plant and equipment	3
	Investments in equity instruments	1
	Inventory	½
	Trade receivables	½
	Bank	½
	Deferred tax	1
	Deferred revenue	1
	Environmental provision	1½
	6% loan note	1½
	Trade payables	½
	Current tax payable	1
		12
(d)	Increase per statement of financial position	1
	Increase per cash flows	1
	Appropriate comment	1
		3
	Total for question	30

(a) QUINCY – STATEMENT OF PROFIT OR LOSS AND OTHER COMPREHENSIVE INCOME
FOR THE YEAR ENDED 30 SEPTEMBER 20X4

	$'000
Revenue (213,500 – 1,600 (W3))	211,900
Cost of sales (W1)	(146,400)
Gross profit	65,500
Distribution costs	(17,500)
Administrative expenses (W1)	(18,000)
Investment income	400
Loss on fair value of investments (17,000 – 15,700)	(1,300)
Finance costs (1,920 (W4) + 600 (W5))	(2,520)
Profit before tax	26,580
Income tax expense (1,100 – 200 (W6) + 7,400)	(8,300)
Profit for the year	18,280
Other comprehensive income	
Revaluation gain on property (W2)	18,000
Total comprehensive income for the year	36,280

(b) QUINCY – STATEMENT OF CHANGES IN EQUITY FOR THE YEAR ENDED 30 SEPTEMBER 20X4

	Share capital $'000	Retained earnings $'000	Revaluation surplus $'000	Total $'000
B/f 1 October 20X3	60,000	4,300	–	64,300
Total comprehensive income	–	18,280	18,000	36,280
Transfer to retained earnings (W2)	–	1,000	(1,000)	–
Balance at 30 September 20X4	60,000	23,580	17,000	100,580

(c)   QUINCY – STATEMENT OF FINANCIAL POSITION AS AT 30 SEPTEMBER 20X4

	$'000
ASSETS	
Non-current assets	
Property, plant and equipment (W2)	106,400
Equity financial asset investment	15,700
	122,100
Current assets	
Inventory	24,800
Trade receivables	28,500
Cash	2,900
	56,200
Total assets	178,300
EQUITY AND LIABILITIES	
Equity	
Share capital	60,000
Revaluation surplus (Part (b))	17,000
Retained earnings (Part (b))	23,580
	100,580
Non-current liabilities	
Loan note (W4)	24,420
Deferred tax (W6)	1,000
Environmental provision (6,000 + 600 (W5))	6,600
Deferred income (W3)	800
	32,820
Current liabilities	
Trade payables	36,700
Income tax	7,400
Deferred income (W3)	800
	44,900
Total equity and liabilities	178,300

(d)   The increase in the carrying amount of property, plant equipment from 1 October 20X3 to
30 September 20X4 is:

	$'000	$'000
1 October 20X3		
Buildings (50,000 – 8,000)	42,000	
Plant and equipment (83,700 – 33 700)	50,000	
Less processing plant	(10,000)	
		82,000
30 September 20X4		
Property, plant and equipment		106,400
Increase		24,400

If a statement of cash flows were prepared for Quincy, the only cash flow appearing would be the $10
million paid for the processing plant. The other $14.4 million arises from the revaluation and the
capitalisation of the environmental costs, less the depreciation charge for the year. None of these involve the
movement of cash.

Users of the financial statements who are primarily interested in the liquidity position of Quincy, such as
creditors and lenders, will consider the cash flow perspective to be the most relevant and this is also the
most easily understood by the public. Investors and analysts will look at both perspectives.

Workings

1   *Expenses*

	Cost of sales	Distribution costs	Admin expenses
	$'000	$'000	$'000
Per question	136,800	17,500	19,000
Issue costs on loan note (W4)	–	–	(1,000)
Depreciation (W2)	9,600	–	–
	146,400	17,500	18,000

2   *Property, plant and equipment*

	Land	Buildings	Processing plant	Other plant	Total
	$'000	$'000	$'000	$'000	$'000
Cost	10,000	40,000		73,700	123,700
Accumulated depreciation	–	(8,000)		(33,700)	(41,700)
	10,000	32,000		40,000	82,000
Revaluation gain	2,000	16,000		–	18,000
	12,000	48,000		40,000	100,000
Addition (10,000 + 6,000)			16,000		16,000
Depreciation:					
(48,000 / 16)	–	(3,000)*		–	(3,000)
(16,000 / 10)			(1,600)		(1,600)
(40,000 × 12.5%)	–	–	–	(5,000)	(5,000)
	12,000	45,000	14,400	35,000	106,400

* If no revaluation had taken place the depreciation on the building would have been $2m (32/16 yrs)

Therefore the additional depreciation, which represents the realisation of the revaluation surplus, is $1m and this is transferred back to retained earnings.

3   *Deferred income*

	$'000	$'000
Two years' maintenance at 'selling price' ((600 × 100/75) × 2)		
DEBIT Revenue	1,600	
CREDIT Deferred income		1,600

The deferred income will be split between non-current and current liabilities.

4   *Loan note*

	$'000
Proceeds (25,000 – 1,000 (W1))	24,000
Interest at effective interest rate (8%)	1,920
Interest paid at nominal interest rate (6%)	(1,500)
Liability at 30 September 20X4	24,420

5   *Finance costs*

Unwinding of discount on environmental provision ($6m × 10%) $600,000

DR Finance costs / CR Environmental provision

6   *Deferred tax*

	$'000
Balance at 30 September 20X4 (5,000 × 20%)	1,000
Balance at 30 September 20X3	1,200
Reduction in provision – credit to profit or loss	200

62 Xtol

Marking scheme

			Marks
(a)	Statement: of profit or loss		
	Revenue	1	
	Cost of sales	2	
	Distribution costs	½	
	Administrative expenses	½	
	Agency sales	1	
	Finance costs	1½	
	Income tax	1½	
			8
(b)	Statement of changes in equity		
	Balances b/f	2	
	Rights issue	1	
	Equity component	1	
	Dividend paid	1½	
	Profit for the year	½	
			6
(c)	Statement of financial position		
	Property, plant and equipment	1½	
	Inventory	½	
	Trade receivables	½	
	Deferred tax	1	
	Loan note	1½	
	Trade payables	1½	
	Bank overdraft	½	
	Current tax payable	1	
			8
(d)	TERP	1	
	Weighted average number of shares	1½	
	Calculation of EPS	½	
			3
(e)	1 mark per valid point to maximum		5
	Total for question		30

(a) STATEMENT OF PROFIT OR LOSS FOR THE YEAR ENDED 31 MARCH 20X4

	$'000
Revenue (490,000 – 20,000(W3))	470,000
Cost of sales (W1)	(294,600)
Gross profit	175,400
Distribution costs (W1)	(33,500)
Administrative expenses (W1)	(36,800)
Other operating income – agency sales (W3)	2,000
Finance costs (13,380 + 900 + 1,176 (W5) – 10,880 (W6))	(4,576)
Profit before tax	102,524
Income tax expense (28,000 + 3,200 + 3,700 (W7))	(34,900)
Profit for the year	67,624

(b) STATEMENT OF CHANGES IN EQUITY FOR THE YEAR ENDED 31 MARCH 20X4

	Share capital $'000	Share premium $'000	Equity option $'000	Retained earnings $'000	Total equity $'000
Balance at 1 April 20X3	40,000	2,600	–	26,080	68,680
Rights issue (W4)	16,000	22,400			38,400
5% loan note issue (W5)			4,050		4,050
Dividends paid (W6)				(10,880)	(10,880)
Profit for the year				67,624	67,624
Balance at 31 March 20X4	56,000	25,000	4,050	82,824	167,874

(c) STATEMENT OF FINANCIAL POSITION AS AT 31 MARCH 20X4

	$'000	$'000
ASSETS		
Non-current assets		
Property, plant and equipment (W2)		168,000
Current assets		
Inventory	61,000	
Trade receivables	63,000	
		124,000
Total assets		292,000
EQUITY AND LIABILITIES		
Equity		
Equity shares 25c		56,000
Share premium		25,000
Other component of equity – equity option (W5)		4,050
Retained earnings		82,824
		167,874
Non-current liabilities		
Deferred tax (4,600 + 3,700 (W8))	8,300	
5% convertible loan note (50,000 – 4,050 (W5) + 1,176)	47,126	
		55,426
Current liabilities		
Trade payables (32,200 + 3,000 (W3))	35,200	
Bank overdraft	5,500	
Current tax payable	28,000	
		68,700
Total equity and liabilities		292,000

(d) Basic EPS for the year ended 31 March 20X4

Profit for the year (per part (a))	$ 67,624,000
Weighted average number of shares (W8)	209,700,000

EPS = 67,624,000/209,700,000 = 32.2c

Workings

1 Expenses

	Cost of sales $'000	Distribution costs $'000	Administrative expenses $'000
Per question	290,600	33,500	36,800
Agent not principal	(15,000)		
Depreciation – property (W2)	5,000		
Depreciation – plant and equipment (W2)	14,000		
	294,600	33,500	36,800

2 Property, plant and equipment

	Property $'000	Plant and equipment $'000	Total $'000
Cost per TB	100,000	155,500	255,500
Acc depreciation b/d per TB	(25,000)	(43,500)	(68,500)
	75,000	112,000	187,000
Depreciation property (100,000/20 years)	(5,000)		(5,000)
Depreciation P&E (112,000 ×12.5%)		(14,000)	(14,000)
	70,000	98,000	168,000

3 Agency transaction

Should have been:

	$'000
DR Cash	20,000
CR Other income (10%)	2,000
CR Trade payables	18,000
DR Trade payables	15,000
CR Cash	15,000

Did:

	$'000
DR Cash	20,000
CR Revenue	20,000
DR Cost of sales	15,000
CR Cash	15,000

Correction:

	$'000
DR Revenue	20,000
CR Cost of sales	15,000
CR Other income	2,000
CR Trade payables	3,000

4 Rights issue

Already recorded:

	$'000
DR Cash	38,400
CR Share capital (56,000 × $1/0.25 × 2/7 × 25c)	16,000
CR Share premium (56,000 × $1/0.25 × 2/7 × 35c)	22,400

5 Loan notes

		$'000	$'000
PV of principal	(50,000 × 0.79)		39,500
PV interest flows:			
20X4	50,000 × 5% = 2,500 × 0.93 =	2,325	
20X5	50,000 × 5% = 2,500 × 0.86 =	2,150	
20X6	50,000 × 5% = 2,500 × 0.79 =	1,975	
			6,450
Debt component			45,950
Equity component (β)			4,050
Cash received			50,000
Liability component b/d	1.4.20X3	45,950	
Effective interest	(45,950 × 8%)	3,676	
Cash coupon paid		(2,500)	
Liability component c/d	31.3.20X4	47,126	

Adjustment required:

			$'000	$'000
DR Loan notes			4,050	
	CR Other components of equity			4,050
DR Finance costs (3,676 – 2,500)			1,176	
	CR Loan notes			1,176

6 *Dividend paid*

	$'000	$'000
Before rights issue (56,000 × $1/25c × 5/7 = 160m × 4c)		6,400
After rights issue (56,000 × $1/25c × 2c)		4,480
		10,880
DR Retained earnings	10,880	
CR Loan note interest and dividends paid		10,880

7 *Tax*

	$'000	$'000
Current tax: DR Current tax (P/L)	28,000	
CR Current tax payable		28,000
Deferred tax:		
B/d (per TB)		4,600
To P/L		3,700
C/d		8,300

8 *Weighted average number of shares*

Date	Narrative	Shares '000	Time period	Bonus fraction	Weighted average
1.4.20X3	b/d (W4)	160,000	× 4/12	$1.02	60,400
				$ 0.90	
1.8.20X3	Rights issue 2/5	64,000			
		224,000	× 8/12		149,300
					209,700

TERP:	5 × $1.02 =	$5.10		
	2 × $0.60 =	$1.20		
	7	$6.30 / 7 =	$0.90	

(e) An entity may have issued, and have in issue at the end of the period, financial instruments which do not currently have any claim to a share of earnings but which may do so in future. Examples are convertible loan stock or convertible preference shares which give the holder the right at some future date to exchange these financial instruments for ordinary shares of the entity. Another example is share options, often issued to directors, which give the right to purchase shares at a future date for a set price.

These financial instruments give rise to **potential** ordinary shares. Diluted EPS takes into account these potential ordinary shares and shows shareholders what EPS for the current year would be if this dilution had already taken place.

Diluted EPS is calculated by adjusting the number of shares (the denominator) by the number of additional shares resulting from the dilution and adjusting the earnings (the numerator) for any dividends or interest that would otherwise be paid on these instruments. This is intended to indicate to investors the possible effect of a future dilution.

Basic and diluted EPS are closely watched by analysts because of the widespread use of the PE ratio as a yardstick for investment decisions. Because diluted EPS is lower than basic EPS and is adjusted for an element of future risk, it provides useful information to inform the decisions of more conservative investors.

63 Multiple choice answers – reporting financial performance

1   A   A change of depreciation method is treated as a change of accounting estimate. Adoption of the revaluation method is dealt with under IAS 16. Application of a new accounting policy (such as capitalisation of borrowing costs) for transactions that did not previously occur is not a change in accounting policy according to IAS 8.

2   B   It is not necessary for a buyer to have been located for the asset.

3   A   Lower of carrying amount and fair value less costs of disposal. As the assets are to be sold value in use is not relevant and recoverable amount will be fair value less costs of disposal.

4   B   This is a change in presentation which will affect calculation of gross profit and will be retrospectively adjusted when presenting comparatives. A and D are simply adjustments made during preparation of the financial statements, C is a change of accounting estimate.

64 Preparation question: Partway

(a)   (i)   This may be able to be classified as a discontinued operation provided certain criteria are met. The termination was decided on before the financial statements were approved and within two weeks of the year end date. The interested parties were notified at that time and an announcement was made in the press, making the decision irrevocable. Although the company will continue to sell holidays over the internet, the travel agency business represents a separate major line of business. The internet business will have quite different property and staffing requirements and a different customer base. The results of the travel agency business are clearly distinguished.

     (ii)   STATEMENT OF PROFIT OR LOSS FOR THE YEAR ENDED

	31 October 20X6	31 October 20X5
Continuing operations	$'000	$'000
Revenue	25,000	22,000
Cost of sales	(19,500)	(17,000)
Gross profit	5,500	5,000
Operating expenses	(1,100)	(500)
Profit from continuing operations	4,400	4,500
Profit(loss) from discontinued operations	(4,000)	1,500
Profit for the year	400	6,000
Note: discontinued operations		
Revenue	14,000	18,000
Cost of sales	(16,500)	(15,000)
Gross profit (loss)	(2,500)	3,000
Operating expenses	(1,500)	(1,500)
Profit (loss) from discontinued operations	(4,000)	1,500

(b)   (i)   Accounting policies can be described as the principles, conventions, rules and practices applied by an entity that prescribe how transactions and other events are to be reflected in its financial statements. This includes the recognition, presentation and measurement basis to be applied to assets, liabilities, gains, losses and changes to shareholders funds. Once these policies have been adopted, they are not expected to change frequently and comparability requires that ideally they do not change from year to year. However, IAS 8 does envisage situations where a change of accounting policy is required in the interests of fair presentation.

         An entity may have to change an accounting policy in response to changes in a Standard or in applicable legislation. Or it may be an internal decision which can be justified on the basis of presenting a more reliable picture. An accounting policy adopted to deal with transactions or events which did not arise previously is not treated as a change of accounting policy.

Where a change of accounting policy has taken place it must be accounted for by retrospective restatement. This means that the comparative financial statements must be restated in the light of the new accounting policy. This makes it possible to compare results for these years as if the new accounting policy had always been in place. The financial statements must disclose the reason for the change of accounting policy and the effects of the change on the results for the previous year.

(ii)   The directors' proposal here is that revenue recognition can be accelerated based on the imposition of compulsory holiday insurance. This is based on the presumption that the risk of not receiving the balance of the payment has now been covered. However, at the point when the deposit is received, Partway has not yet done anything to earn the revenue. Under IAS 18 *Revenue,* revenue from a service contract should be recognised by reference to the stage of completion of the transaction. Under this method, revenue is recognised in the accounting periods in which the services are rendered. In this case the service is rendered at the time when the holiday is taken. The existing policy is therefore correct and should not be changed.

65 Skeptik

(i)   This would be treated as a change of accounting policy under IAS 8 *Accounting Policies, Changes in Accounting Estimates and Errors.* IAS 8 requires the directors to exercise judgement in determining whether or not a change of accounting policy should be made. It should result in information being more relevant and reliable. The directors should refer to the requirements in other IFRSs dealing with similar and related issues and to the provisions of the *Conceptual Framework.* If the change is appropriate, it should be applied retrospectively, so the financial statements for the year ended 31.320X3 should be restated.

(ii)   Both of these situations are obligating events and should be provided for in accordance with IAS 37 *Provisions, Contingent Liabilities and Contingent Assets.* Regarding the court case, the best estimate of the amount required to settle the obligation is $4 million, so a provision should be made for that amount.

The provision for the product warranty will be based on an expected value calculated as:

	$
200,000 × 20% × $25	1,000,000
200,000 × 10% × $120	2,400,000
	3,400,000

Both of these will result in an expense in the statement of profit or loss on creation of the provision, together with a liability in the statement of financial position for the year ended 31 March 20X4.

(iii)   As Skeptic has no intention of selling the plant before the end of its useful life, it does not need to make a provision for repayment.

The grant should be credited to income over the useful life of the plant, so for the year ended 31.3.20X4 $800,000 ($8,000,000 / 10 years) should be credited to profit or loss and the remaining $7,200,000 should be credited to deferred income. The amount of deferred income to be recognised in income over the following financial year ($800,000) should appear under current liabilities and the balance ($6,400,000) under non-current liabilities.

66 Tunshill

Marking scheme

			Marks
(a)	1 mark per valid point		5
(b)(i)	Recognise as a change in accounting estimate	1	
	Appears an acceptable basis for change	1	
	Correct method is to allocate carrying amount over new remaining life	1	
	Depreciation for current year should be $2million	1	
	Carrying amount at 30 September 20X3 is $10 million	1	
			5
(ii)	Proposed change is probably not for a valid reason	1	
	Change would cause decrease (not increase) in profit	1	
	Changes in policy should be applied retrospectively	1	
	Decrease in year to 30 September 20X3 is $400,000	1	
	Retained earnings restated by $1.6 million	1	
			5
			15

(a)   IAS 8 *Accounting policies, changes in accounting estimates and errors* requires an entity to determine the accounting policy to apply to a transaction or event by reference to any IFRS specifically applying to that transaction or event. Where there is no specific IFRS applicable, management is expected to **use its judgement** in applying an accounting policy which will result in information which is relevant and reliable. In this they should consider the requirements and guidance in IFRSs dealing with similar and related issues and also the *Conceptual Framework* definitions, recognition criteria and measurement concepts for assets, liabilities, income and expenses.

Accounting policies are the specific principles, bases and rules applied in measuring and presenting financial information. **Changes of accounting policy are not very common**. One example would be a change from the FIFO method of valuing inventory to the weighted average method – this is a change in the basis of valuation.

A **change of accounting estimate** is a change in the way in which these principles and bases are applied which leads to an adjustment to any of the elements identified by the *Conceptual Framework* – assets, liabilities, income or expenses. One example would be a change from the straight line method of depreciation to the reducing balance method. In this case the accounting policy is that non-current assets are carried at cost less accumulated depreciation, the accounting estimate is how that depreciation is calculated.

(b) (i) As the plant is wearing well and the production manager now estimates its total life to be eight years, it is **reasonable to adjust its remaining life**. However, the adjustment proposed by the assistant accountant is incorrect. This is a **change in accounting estimate** and is **not applied retrospectively**. At 1 October 20X2 the remaining life of the plant will be six years – the new estimated life of eight year less the two years which have elapsed.

The correct adjustment will be calculated as follows.

	$m
Original cost 1 October 20X0	20
Two years depreciation ((20/5) × 2)	(8)
Carrying amount at 1 October 20X2	12
Depreciation to 30 September 20X3 (12/6)	(2)
Carrying amount at 30 September 20X3	10

There will be no credit to profit or loss for the year and depreciation will continue to be charged, but at a reduced rate.

(ii) It looks here as if this change is being proposed simply in order to increase reported profit, rather than to make the financial information more relevant and reliable. However, if most of Tunshill's competitors are using AVCO this suggests that AVCO is the method generally used in the industry, so it may actually be a more appropriate method.

However the assistant accountant is mistaken to suppose that moving from closing inventory of $20m under FIFO to closing inventory of $18m under AVCO will increase profits by $2m. It will actually **reduce profits** by increasing cost of sales. In any case, this **cannot be done simply as an adjustment to the current year**. This is a change of accounting policy and has to be applied retrospectively.

The effect of the adjustment will be:

	FIFO $m	AVCO $m	Current year profit $m	Retained earnings $m
Year to 30 September 20X2	15	13.4	(1.6)	(1.6)
B/f 1 October 20X2			1.6	1.6
Year to 30 September 20X3	20	18	(2.0)	(2.0)
At 30 September 20X3			(0.4)	(2.0)

The net effect at 30 September 20X3 of this proposal will be to reduce current year profits by $400,000 and to reduce retained earnings by $2m.

67 Manco

Text references. Chapters 7 and 13.

Top tips. This question required you to look at a situation in terms of both a restructuring and a discontinued operation. If you found it a bit off-putting it would be best to pick out the bits you knew how to deal with. For instance you could state that the press announcement made the decision to restructure irrevocable. You probably knew that the provision would cover the redundancy but not the retraining and you could allocate the trading losses to the correct years.

Easy marks. Any easy marks on this question would be the ones above, plus noting the impairment loss on the plant.

Examiner's comments. This was not generally a well-answered question. The information pointed to the closure being irrevocable and most candidates concluded that a provision was needed. What caused problems was knowing which losses to provide for and in which period. It was disappointing that most candidates did not attempt to allocate the loss between the two reporting periods, despite the question specifically asking for this. Most of the marks were for reporting items in the right period.

		Marks
(a)	½ mark per valid point - maximum	5
(b)	Closure is a restructuring event under IAS 37	1
	It is an obligating event in year ended 30 September 20X0	1
	Provide for impairment of plant	1
	Cannot recognise gain on property until sold	1
	Provide for redundancy in year ended 30 September 20X0	1
	Cannot provide for retraining costs in current year	1
	Inclusion of trading losses in correct periods	2
	Consider if and when should be treated as discontinued operation	2
		10
		15

(a) IFRS 5 *Non-current assets held for sale and discontinued operations* defines 'non-current assets held for sale' to be those non-current assets whose carrying amount will be recovered principally through a sale transaction rather than through continuing use'.

A discontinued operation is described in IFRS 5 as 'a component of an entity that either has been disposed of, or is classified as held for sale, and:

(i) Represents a separate major line of business or geographical area of operations;

(ii) Is part of a single co-ordinated plan to dispose of a separate major line of business or geographical area of operations; or

(iii) Is a subsidiary acquired exclusively with a view to resale.'

IFRS 5 states that **a component of an entity** comprises operations and cash flows that can be clearly distinguished, operationally and for financial reporting purposes, from the rest of the entity.

This very precise definition is needed to ensure that only operations which can properly be regarded as discontinued are classified as such. Users of accounts, particularly financial analysts, will be more interested in the results of continuing operations as a guide to the company's future profitability and it is not unacceptable for discontinued operations to show a loss. Companies could therefore be tempted to hide loss-making activities under the umbrella of discontinued operations, hence the requirement for the operations and cash flows of the discontinued operation to be clearly distinguishable from those of continuing operations. It is also conceivable that a company could seek to include the results of a profitable operation which has been sold under continuing operations.

IFRS 5 requires an entity to disclose a single amount on the face of the statement of profit or loss comprising the total of:

(i) The post-tax profit or loss of discontinued operations

(ii) The post-tax gain or loss recognised on the measurement to fair value less costs to sell or on the disposal of the assets constituting the discontinued operation

The separation of the results of continuing and discontinued operations on the face of the statement of profit or loss makes possible more meaningful year on year comparison. The inclusion of prior year information for discontinued operations means that it can be seen exactly how the continuing operations have performed, and it is possible to forecast more accurately how they can be expected to perform in the future.

(b) The actions taken by Manco have resulted in a **constructive obligation** to restructure as set out in IAS 37 *Provisions, contingent liabilities and contingent assets*. It has produced a formal plan and communicated it to those affected (employees and customers), thereby raising a valid expectation that the restructuring will be carried out. It will therefore be correct to make a provision in the financial statements for the year ended 30 September 20X0 for the costs of the restructuring.

As a separate business segment is being closed down, this will be a **discontinued operation**. As they are due to be sold six months from the date of the closure announcement, the factory and plant could be classified as held for sale at 30 September 20X0. If Manco intends to continue using them and does not classify them as held for sale, they will continue to be depreciated up to 31 January 20X1. In this case the closure will not be treated as a discontinued operation at 30 September 20X0, but **will be reported as such in the year to 30 September 20X1 when the assets are sold**.

Year to 30 September 20X0

A **restructuring provision** should be recognised for $750,000, being the cost of redundancies.
The $600,000 trading losses will be included in profit or loss for the year.
The factory will be subject to the normal depreciation charge.
The plant should be written down to its recoverable amount, which will be $500,000.

Year to 30 September 20X1

The redundancies will take place and the costs will be offset against the provision.
The final $1m of trading losses will be treated as the results of a discontinued operation and shown in one figure on the statement of profit or loss combined with final profit/loss on disposal of the assets.
The retraining costs of $200,000 will be accounted for as part of continuing operations.

68 Multiple choice answers – earnings per share

1	A	Earnings on dilution:		$'000
		Basic		1,850
		Add back interest (2,000 × 6% × 70%)		84
				1,934

		Shares on dilution:		'000
		Existing		10,000
		Conversion (2m × 4/5)		1,600
				11,600

Basic EPS = 1,850 / 10,000 = 18.5c

Diluted EPS = 1,934 / 11,600 = 16.7c

2   A   TERP

$$5 \times 1.8 = 9.0$$
$$1 \times 1.5 = 1.5$$
$$10.5 \ / \ 6 = \$1.75$$

Shares	'000
5,000 × 5/12 × 1.8 / 1.75	2,143
6,000 × 7/12	3,500
	5,643

EPS = 7,600 / 5,643 = $1.35

3   D

	Shares '000
B/f (7,500 / 0.5)	15,000
Full market price issue (4,000 × 9/12)	3,000
Bonus issue (18,000 / 3)	6,000
	24,000

EPS = 12 / 24 = 50c

4   D

	Shares '000
B/f	4,000
Bonus issue	1,000
	5,000

EPS = 3.6 / 5 = 72c

EPS 20X7 = 70c × 4,000 / 5,000 = 56c

5   B

	Share capital $'000	Share premium $'000
Balance 30 September X2 (250m shares)	50,000	15,000
Rights issue:		
Share capital (50m × 20c)	(10,000)	
Share premium (50m × 22c)	–	(11,000)
Balance 30 September X1 (200m shares)	40,000	4,000

6   A   Dilution: 2m shares @@$1.20 is equivalent to 800,000 shares at full market price of $3 and the remaining 1.2m issued for no consideration.

Diluted EPS = 1550 / ((2,500 × 2) + 1,200) = 1550 / 6,200 = 25c

69 Preparation question: Fenton

(a)

Date	Narrative	Shares	Time	Bonus fraction	Weighted average
1.1.X1	b/d	5,000,000	$\times \, ^1/_{12}$	$\times \, ^{2.00}/_{1.95} \times \, ^{11}/_{10}$	470,085
31.1.X1	Rights issue	+ 1,250,000			
		6,250,000	$\times \, ^5/_{12}$	$\times \, ^{11}/_{10}$	2,864,583
30.6.X1	FMP	+ 125,000			
		6,375,000	$\times \, ^5/_{12}$	$\times \, ^{11}/_{10}$	2,921,875
30.11.X1	Bonus issue	+ 637,500			
		7,012,500	$\times \, ^1/_{12}$		584,375
					6,840,918

TERP	4 @ 2	=	8.00
	1 @ 1.75	=	1.75
	5		9.75
	$\therefore$ 1.95		

$$\text{EPS for y/e 31.12.X1} = \frac{\$2,900,000}{6,840,918} = 42.4c$$

$$\text{Restated EPS for y/e 31.12.X0} = 46.4c \times \frac{1.95}{2.00} \times \, ^{10}/_{11} = 41.1c$$

(b) **Sinbad**

$$\text{Basic EPS} = \frac{\$644,000}{10,000,000} = 6.44$$

Earnings	
Profit for the year	644,000
Interest saving (1,200,000 @ 5% $\times$ 70%)	42,000
	686,000

Number of shares	
Basic	10,000,000
On conversion	4,800,000
	14,800,000

$$\text{Diluted EPS} = \frac{\$686,000}{14,800,000} = 4.64c$$

(c) **Talbot**

$$\text{Basic EPS} = \frac{540,000}{5,000,000} = 10.8c$$

Diluted EPS:

Consideration on exercise
400,000 $\times$ $1.10 = $440,000

Shares acquired at FV
$440,000/$1.60 = 275,000

$\therefore$ shares issued for no consideration
(400,000 − 275,000) = 125,000

$$\text{EPS} = \frac{540,000}{5,000,000 + 125,000} = 10.5c$$

70 Barstead

Marking scheme

			Marks
(a)	1 mark per valid point		4
(b)	Basic EPS for 20X1	3	
	Restated EPS for 20X0	1	
	Diluted EPS for 20X1	2	
			6
(c)	Basic EPS	1	
	Diluted EPS	4	
			5
			15

(a)   An increase in profit after tax of 80% **will not translate into a comparable increase in EPS** unless the number of shares in issue has remained constant. The disparity between the increase in profit and the increase in EPS shows that Barstead has obtained the resources it needed in order to generate higher profit through share issue(s). This may have been done as part of an acquisition drive, obtaining a controlling interest in other entities through share exchange. In this way, EPS is a more reliable indicator of performance than pure profit because **it matches any additional profit with the resources used to earn it**.

Diluted EPS takes into account the existence **of potential ordinary shares**, arising from financial instruments such as options, warrants and convertible debt. Diluted EPS shows what EPS would be if all of these potential shares came into existence in the current year. In the case of Barstead, the diluted EPS has increased by less than the basic EPS. This shows that some of the profit increase has been financed by the issue of financial instruments carrying future entitlement to ordinary shares. These instruments will carry a lower finance cost than non-convertible debt, which helps to boost current profits. But this means that the finance costs saved when these instruments are converted will probably be insufficient to offset the adverse effect of the additional shares, leading to dilution. This is an advance warning signal to investors.

(b)   Theoretical ex-rights price will be:

4 shares at $3.80 –   15.2
1 share at $2.80 –   2.8
                             18.0 / 5 = $3.60

Weighted average calculation:

Date	Narrative	No. shares (m)	Time period	Bonus fraction	Weighted average (m)
1.10.20X0	b/d	36	× 3/12	× $3.80/$3.60	9.5
1.1.20X1	Rights issue	9			
		45	× 9/12		33.75
					43.25

Basic EPS for the year ended 30 September 20X1 is therefore:

$15m/43.25m = 34.7c

Comparative EPS = 35c × 3.6/3.8 = 33.2c

Diluted EPS:

The additional earnings will be $800,000 ($10m × 8%) less 25% tax = $600,000
The additional shares will be (10m / 100) × 25 = 2.5m
The net effect is therefore $600,000 / 2.5m = 24c. This is below basic EPS and therefore dilutive.

Earnings = $15.6m
Shares = 43.25 + 2.5 = 45.75
Diluted EPS = 34.1c

(c)   Basic EPS = $25.2m / 84m* = 30c

*21m/0.25c

Diluted EPS:

	Shares m	Earnings $m
Existing	84.0	25.2
Loan stock (20m /100 × 50)	10.0	1.2 (W1)
Share options	4.8 (W2)	–
	98.8	26.4

Diluted EPS = 26.4/98.8 = 26.7c

Workings

1   *Loan stock*

	$m
When conversion takes place there will be a saving of:	
Interest (20m × 8%)	1.6
Less tax (1.6 × 25%)	(0.4)
	1.2

2   *Share options*

Shares issued will be 12m @ $1.50 = $18m

At market price of $2.50 the value would be $30m.

The shortfall is $12m, which is equivalent to 4.8m shares at market price.

71 Rebound

Marking scheme

				Marks
(a)		1 mark per valid point/example		6
(b)	(i)	Profit from continuing operations	1	
		Profit from newly acquired operations	2	
				3
	(ii)	EPS for 20X1 and 20X2 at 3 marks each		6
				15

(a) Historically-prepared financial statements of limited companies are used by analysts and stockbrokers to value the company's shares. The valuation placed on a company's shares is an indication of how it is expected to perform in the future. So financial statements are relied upon for their predictive value and this is one reason why it is so important that they faithfully represent financial information.

The difference between historical financial statements and forecasts is that historical financial statements record financial transactions which have already taken place, so they are highly reliable. Forecasts have a much lower degree of reliability because they are based on estimates, which are subjective.

IFRS presentation and disclosure requirements are intended to enhance the quality of information provided to users. For instance, entities are required to present separately the results of discontinued operations and to disclose a breakdown of these results between gains or losses on disposal or reclassification of assets and trading results. They are also required to show separately the details of non-current assets held for sale and to disclose details of the discontinued operation. This give important predictive information to shareholders because they know that this operation will not be running during the next accounting period and that the assets in question are expected to be sold within 12 months.

Another area where financial statements supply predictive information concerns provisions. A provision can be made in the current year for an event expected to arise in a later accounting period. Details of the amount of the provision and why it is being made have to be disclosed, users are aware of the nature and extent of the liability. Entities also disclose contingent liabilities, so users are aware of possible future liabilities of which either the probability or the amount is not certain.

Diluted EPS provides another piece of predictive information. Although it does not represent specific future EPS, it does alert shareholders to the degree of dilution inherent in the entity's financial instruments and users will be able to see from the notes the relevant dates of exercise of options. The notes will also disclose proposed dividends, so shareholders can see how much cash will be paid out and how much they can expect to receive.

(b) (i) Profit after tax for year to 31.3.20X3

	$'000
Existing operations (2,000 × 1.06)	2,120
New operation (450 × 12/8 months × 1.08)	729
	2,849

(ii) Diluted EPS

Earnings	20X2	20X1
	$'000	$'000
Continuing operations	2,450	1,750
Saving on loan stock interest, less tax ($5m × 8% × 70%)	280	280
	2,730	2,030

Shares	20X2	20X1
	'000	'000
Existing ($3m × 4)	12,000	12,000
Loan stock (5m × 40/100)	2,000	2,000
Options ((W) × 6 months)	600	–
	14,600	14,000

Diluted EPS (cents)	20X2	20X1
(2,730,000 / 14,600,000) × 100	18.7	
(2,030,000 / 14,000,000) × 100		14.5

Working

	'000
Shares issued under options	2,000
Shares fully paid (2m/2.5)	(800)
Dilutive shares	1,200

72 Multiple choice answers – analysing and interpreting financial statements

1   D   The low asset turnover suggests a capital-intensive industry. This rules out the estate agency or architectural practice. Supermarkets can also be capital-intensive but tend to operate on low profit margins.

2   A

	$'000
Profit before interest and tax	230 %
Capital employed (3,500 + 1,000)	4,500
	= 5.1%

3   C   This will reduce working capital and means that it will take longer to build up working capital needed for production. The other options will all speed up the operating cycle.

4   D   (Dividends (3.4 + 11.1) / Share price) × 100 = 14.5 / 350 × 100 = 4.1%

5   A   Net profit margin is a component of ROCE, so 16.3% / 4.19 = 3.9%

6   B   EPS = 800 / 4,000 = 20c. P/E ratio = 150 / 20 = 7.5

7   C   A possible three-month difference in year-end date can be significant in a seasonal business and Quartile could be expected to show a proportionately higher ROCE than entities that revalue their properties. Rising costs will have been experienced by all companies and the inventory adjustment will have been corrected to make opening inventory for the current year correct.

8   D

Inventory days (365/6)	61
Payables days (($230,000 / $2m) × 365)	(42)
Receivables days (β)	51
Cash cycle	70

73 Victular

(a)

ROCE	(2,500 − 500 − 10) / (2,800 + 3,200 + 3,000 + 500) %	= 20.9%
Pre-tax ROE	(1,400 / 2,800)%	= 50%
Net asset turnover	20,500 / (14,800 − 5,700)	= 2.3 times
Gross profit margin	(2,500 / 20,500)%	= 12.2%
Operating profit margin	(2,000 / 20,500)%	= 9.8%
Current ratio	7,300 / 5,700	= 1.3 : 1
Closing inventory holding period	(3,600 / 18,000) × 365	= 73 days
Trade receivables collection period	(3,700 / 20,500) × 365	= 66 days
Trade payables payment period	(3,800 / 18,000) × 365	= 77 days
Gearing	(3,200 + 500 + 3,000) / 9,500%	= 71%
Interest cover	2,000 / 600	= 3.3 times
Dividend cover	1,000 / 700	= 1.4 times

(b)   Assessment of relative position and performance of Grappa and Merlot

Profitability

At first sight it appears that Victular would see a much greater return on its investment if it acquired Merlot rather than Grappa. A closer analysis of the figures suggests that this may not be the case.

Merlot has an ROCE over 40% higher than Grappa's and an ROE more than double Grappa's ROE. However, the difference is due more to the lower level of equity in Merlot than to the superiority of its profit. Merlot's equity (2,800) is only half that of Grappa (5,500). This reduces the denominator for ROCE and doubles the ROE. A closer look at the profits of both companies shows that the operating profit margin of Grappa is 10.5% and that of Merlot is 9.75%.

The net asset turnover of Merlot (2.3 times) suggests that it is running the more efficient operation. Merlot has certainly achieved a much greater turnover than Grappa and with a lower level of net assets. The problem is that, on a much higher level of turnover, its net profit is not much higher than Grappa's.

Further analysis of net assets shows that Grappa owns its factory, while Merlot's factory must be rented, partly accounting for the higher level of operating expenses. Grappa's factory is carried at current value, as shown by the property revaluation reserve, which increases the negative impact on Grappa's ROCE.

Gearing

Merlot has double the gearing of Grappa, due to its finance lease obligations. At 7.5% Merlot is paying less on the finance lease than on its loan notes, but this still amounts to a doubling of its interest payments. Its interest cover is 3.4 times compared to six times for Grappa, making its level of risk higher. In a bad year Merlot could have trouble servicing its debts and have nothing left to pay to shareholders. However, the fact that Merlot has chosen to operate with a higher level of gearing rather than raise funds from a share issue also increases the potential return to shareholders.

Liquidity

Grappa and Merlot have broadly similar current ratios, but showing a slightly higher level of risk in the case of Merlot. Merlot is also running an overdraft while Grappa has $1.2m in the bank. Grappa is pursuing its receivables slightly less aggressively than Merlot, but taking significantly longer to pay its suppliers. As this does not appear to be due to shortage of cash, it must be due to Grappa being able to negotiate more favourable terms than Merlot.

Summary

Merlot has a higher turnover than Grappa and a policy of paying out most of its earnings to shareholders. This makes it an attractive proposition from a shareholder viewpoint. However, if its turnover were to fall, there would be little left to distribute. This is the risk and return of a highly geared company. Merlot is already running an overdraft and so has no cash to invest in any more plant and equipment. In the light of this, its dividend policy is not particularly wise. Grappa has a lower turnover and a much more conservative dividend policy but may be a better long-term investment. Victular's decision will probably depend upon its attitude to risk and the relative purchase prices of Grappa and Merlot

(c)   While ratio analysis is a useful tool, it has a number of limitations, particularly when comparing ratios for different companies.

Some ratios can be calculated in different ways. For instance, gearing can be expressed using debt as a proportion of debt and equity or simply debt as a proportion of equity. Ratios can be distorted by inflation, especially where non-current assets are carried at original cost.

Ratios are based upon financial statements which may not be comparable due to the adoption of different accounting policies and different estimation techniques. For instance, whether non-current assets are carried at original cost or current value will affect ROCE, as will the use of different depreciation rates. In addition, financial statements are often prepared with the key ratios in mind, so may have been subject to creative accounting. The year-end values also may not be representative of values during the year, due to seasonal trading.

Victular will find further information useful in making a decision regarding this acquisition. Victular should look at the composition of the Board of each company and the expertise it may be acquiring. It will also want to see the audited final statements and any available management information, such as management accounts, budgets and cash flow forecasts.

74 Bengal

Marking scheme

	Marks
1 mark per valid point (including up to 5 points for ratios)	15

It is correct that revenue has increased by 48% while profit for the year has only increased by 20%. However, on closer inspection, we can see that this is to a large degree attributable to the tax charge for the year. The tax charge was 28.6% of the profit before tax in the year ended 31.3.20X0 and 42.8% of the profit before tax in the year ended 31.3.20X1. We do not have a breakdown of the tax charge but it could include underpayments in previous years, which distorts the trading results.

A better comparison between the two years is the profit before tax % and the gross profit %. Both of these are higher in 20X1 than in 20X0. The shareholders will also be interested in the ROCE. There has been a significant increase in capital employed during the year ended 31.3. 20X1. Bengal has acquired nearly $13m in tangible and intangible assets, financed from cash reserves and a new issue of 8% loan notes. An additional $2m of non-current assets have been reclassified as held for sale. This suggests that Bengal has taken over the trade of another business and is disposing of the surplus assets. This is a long-term project which may take time to show a return and the ROCE does show a significant drop in 20X1. However, if we disregard the loan capital and look at the ROE we can see a considerable increase in 20X1.

The increase in loan capital does have significance for shareholders. The interest charge has increased from $100,000 to $650,000, which reduces the amount available for dividend. Gearing has increased significantly. The rate that Bengal has to offer to loan note holders has already increased from 5% to 8%. If it required further borrowing, with this high gearing, it would have to pay substantially more. Shares in Bengal have become a riskier investment. One indicator of this is the interest cover, which has fallen from 36 times to 9 times. The acquisition could presumably have been financed from a share issue or share exchange, rather than loan capital. However, this would have diluted the return available to shareholders.

The area in which there is most cause for concern is liquidity. As we can see from the statement of cash flows, cash and cash equivalents have fallen by $4.2m and the company is now running an overdraft. It has tax to pay of $2.2m and this will incur penalties if it is not paid on time. The current ratio has declined from 2.1:1 to 1.5:1 and this is including the non-current assets held for sale as part of non-current assets. The quick ratio, excluding inventory and non-current assets held for sale, indicates the immediate cash situation and this shows a fall from 1.6:1 to 0.46:1. Bengal needs to remedy this by disposing of the non-current assets held for sale as soon as possible and selling off surplus inventory, which may have been acquired as part of the acquisition.

Overall, the shareholder should be reassured that Bengal is profitable and expanding. The company has perhaps overstretched itself and significantly raised its gearing, but it is to be hoped that the investment will bring in future returns. This is no doubt the picture the company wants to give to shareholders, which is why it has paid a dividend in spite of having very little cash with which to do so.

Appendix: Ratios

		20X1	20X0
Net profit %	(3,000 / 25,500) / (2,500 / 17,250)	11.8%	14.5%
Net profit % (pre-tax)	(5,250 / 25,500) / (3,500 / 17,250)	20.6%	20.3%
Gross profit %	(10,700 / 25,500) / (6,900 / 17,250)	42%	40%
ROCE	(5,900 / 18,500) / (3,600 / 9,250)	31.9%	38.9%
ROE	(5,250 / 9,500) / (3,500 / 7,250)	55.3%	48.3%
Gearing	(9,000 / 9,500) / (2,000 / 7,250)	94.7%	27.6%
Interest cover	(5,900 / 650) / (3,600 / 100)	9 times	36 times
Current ratio	(8,000 / 5,200) / (7,200 / 3,350)	1.5:1	2.1:1
Quick ratio	(2,400 / 5,200) / (5,400 / 3,350)	0.5:1	1.6:1

75 Tangier (specimen paper)

Text reference. Chapter 19.

Top tips. There are 15 marks for this question but only five are for ratios. Most of the marks are for your analysis, so read the information carefully and make sure you are answering the question.

Easy marks. Only five marks were available for ratios, so it was important to decide which were the important ratios. The question helped by ruling out working capital ratios.

Marking scheme

	Marks
1 mark per valid point (up to 5 for ratios)	15

It is not difficult to see why the non-executive director of Tangier is disappointed at the results for the year to 31 March 20X4. Revenue has increased by $880m but has only generated an additional $82m gross profit and an increase in expenses has left profit before tax at less than half of the 20X3 profit. Profit appears to have been sacrificed to revenue and, if the executive directors are being paid bonuses on the basis of revenue, this is something that the non-executive directors will want to investigate.

The first thing we notice is that the gross profit % has fallen from 40% to 30%. This is because the increase in revenue has been accompanied by an increase of $798m in cost of sales. As the bidding process for the contract was very competitive, Tangier has probably gone in at a very low price in order to secure the contract and is now making a loss on it.

In order to fulfil the contract Tangier has had to pay at least $100m ($300m - $200m), possibly more taking into account that the 20X3 amount of $200m would have been amortised, for a manufacturing licence and invest $230m in shares of Raremetal. This was in order to secure material supplies, but the low profit margin on this contract implies that the investment did not result in any agreement to deliver materials at a competitive price. Perhaps, as its name suggests, Raremetal has no competitors. The shareholding in Raremetal has also performed very poorly as an investment, yielding neither dividend nor capital growth.

ROCE for the year ended 31 March 20X4 has fallen from 61.7% to 19.5%. This reflects both the fall in net profit % from 21.86% to 8.7% and the fall in asset turnover from 2.82 to 2.24. Capital employed has increased from $645m to $1,205m, reflecting the debt and equity issued to fund the increase in non-current assets, but this has not generated additional profits.

The debt issued has increased finance costs by $35m and, despite the share issue, gearing has more than doubled, from 15.5% to 33% – an increase from 18.3% to 49.7% if we measure it as debt/equity. Tangier's new loan is at twice the interest rate of the existing loan and is secured, presumably on its property. This suggests that the markets are worried about the company's level of debt. Tangier is now running an overdraft of $110m.

It would be useful to know when production actually commenced on the Jetside contract and what the duration of the contract is. It could be that productivity and profit on the contract will improve over the next financial year. It would also be useful to have a breakdown of distribution and administrative expenses, which also seem to have been adversely affected by this contract. There could be one-off expenses included, perhaps relating to the negotiation of the contract, which will not recur.

Ratios

		20X4	20X3
Gross profit %	810 / 2,700 % / 738 / 1,820 %	30%	40%
ROCE	235/1,205 % / 398 / 645 %	19.5%	61.7%
Net profit (PBIT)%	235 / 2,700 % / 398 / 1,820 %	8.7%	21.86%
Asset turnover	2,700 / 1,205 / 1,820 / 645	2.24	2.82
Gearing (debt/debt + equity)	400 / 1,205 % / 100 / 645%	33%	15.5%
Debt/equity %	400 / 805 % / 100 / 545 %	49.7%`	18.3%

76 Woodbank (6/14 amended)

Text reference. Chapter 19.

Top tips. The question makes it very clear where your analysis should be heading – the effect of the purchase of Shaw – so concentrate on this and review the information from this angle.

Easy marks. The ratios were easy marks and a thorough reading of the question would have given you some obvious points to make.

Examiner's comments. Many candidates paid too little attention to the incremental effect of the acquisition of Shaw and few commented on the fact that profit or loss only included the results of Shaw for three months. This led a lot of candidates to conclude that the acquisition was not advantageous, which is not the conclusion borne out by taking into account the expected profits of Shaw over 12 months.

Marking scheme

	Marks
1 mark per valid point (including 4 for ratios)	<u>15</u>

(a) **Equivalent ratios for Woodbank without Shaw.**

ROCE	((18 - 5)/(150 - 50))	13%
Net asset turnover	((150 – 30)/100)	1.2 times
Gross profit margin	((33-9)/(150 – 30))	20%
Profit before interest and tax %	((18 – 5)/(150 – 30))	10.8%

(b) **Analysis of performance and position**

The acquisition of Shaw has materially affected the results of Woodbank for the year ended 31 March 20X4. In order to meaningfully compare the performance of Woodbank during the year to 31 March 20X4 with its performance during the year to 31 March 20X3 it is therefore necessary to isolate the effects of the acquisition and consider how Woodbank's performance would have looked without Shaw.

Profitability

Shaw has contributed significantly to profitability with its gross profit margin of 30% and PBIT% of 16.6%. However the $50 million of loan notes which financed the acquisition have increased capital employed and so exerted a downward pull on ROCE. With Shaw ROCE is 12%. Without Shaw it would have been 13%. If we check the ROCE for Shaw alone we can see that it is only 10% (5,000/50,000). But this is based on the total net assets of Shaw and only three months profits. If twelve months profits were used, we could expect the return to be correspondingly higher.

During the three months to 31 March 20X4 Shaw had a gross profit margin of 30%. Combined with Woodbank, it raises Woodbank gross profit margin from 20% to 22%. Woodbank's individual gross profit has therefore declined by 2% since 20X3. While revenue has risen by 9%, cost of sales has increased by 11%. However, Woodbank has done well at keeping down expenses and its PBIT margin without Shaw (10.8%) would have been up on 20X3 (9.1%). It is important to remember that Shaw was only owned for the final three months of the financial year, not much time for the additional assets to show a return. It is likely that the acquisition will enhance profitability to a greater extent over the next twelve months.

Liquidity

The current ratio of Woodbank has fallen from 1.7:1 to 1.08:1. This is a steep drop. We can see immediately that cash reserves have declined by $4.5 million and trade payables have increased by $8 million. This suggests that Woodbank is having trouble paying its suppliers on time. Payables days have increased from 55 to 66. The retained earnings balance shows that Woodbank paid a dividend of $5.5 million during 20X4. This was perhaps unwise when working capital was needed to finance expansion and pay the additional loan interest. Had the dividend not been paid the current ratio for 20X4 would be 1.3:1 – still a fall from 20X3, but less alarming.

Gearing

Gearing has risen from 5.3% to 36.7%, attributable to an additional $50 million loan notes issued to finance the acquisition of Shaw. The interest payments each year will be $5.5 million – the amount of the dividend paid in 20X4. Shareholders may expect to receive less in future years as the servicing of the debt will take priority, but had the acquisition been funded by a share issue their returns would have been diluted. Gearing of 36.7% is still within acceptable limits and future good returns from the acquisition will build up retained earnings and keep gearing in check.

Conclusion

Woodbank's performance would have been broadly comparable to the previous year had no acquisition taken place. The acquisition of Shaw has had a detrimental effect on liquidity and gearing for 20X4 but appears from three months results to have the capacity to significantly increase profits for Woodbank. It seems likely that over a longer period this will also improve liquidity and gearing, giving an overall positive result for shareholders.

77 Multiple choice answers – limitations of financial statements and interpretation techniques

1   D   Capital employed (assets) would decrease, increasing ROCE. The impairment loss will reduce equity (revaluation surplus) and so increase gearing.

2   A   The value of the inventory will be added to both current assets and current liabilities. It will add proportionately more to liabilities and so reduce the current ratio. The effect on the quick ratio will be even greater as inventory is excluded from assets.

3   B   The new product will have an operating profit of 120 / 1,600 = 7.5%, so will reduce the current margin. It will have an ROCE of 120 / 500 = 24%, higher than the current 20%.

4   C   Obsolete goods can lead to a build-up of unsold inventory, thereby increasing the holding period. A reduction in selling price or an increase in demand could increase sales leading to a fall in the holding period. Seasonal fluctuations will change the holding period throughout the year, but should not affect the year-on-year picture.

5   B   The use of historical cost accounting during a period of inflation can lead to overstatement of profits. Non-current assets carried at historical cost may be presented at a value well below their fair value, leading to understated depreciation and consequently overstated profits. This can be compounded by the use of FIFO, if inventory is held at an original cost which is significantly below replacement cost. The charge to cost of sales will be understated and profit overstated.

   The use of historical cost accounting will lead to understatement rather than overstatement of non-current asset values and will not affect interest costs. It is likely to lead to overstatement rather than understatement of ROCE.

6   A   Renegotiating to secure a lower interest rate may save interest costs but will have no effect on gearing. The other options are methods that could be resorted to in order to reduce or avoid any increase in gearing.

7   A   A sale and operating leaseback would be an unlikely transaction as it would remove the asset from the statement of financial position.

   The deferral method of accounting for government grants leaves the carrying amount of the asset intact, rather than deducting the amount of the grant from the asset amount.

   Revaluing assets is the obvious way of increasing the carrying amount of assets.

   Under the reducing balance method, more depreciation is charged in the earlier years of the life of an asset, so a change to 10% straight line would reduce the depreciation charge for the first few years. Of course this effect is only temporary as the charge will catch up after a few years.

8   D   A receivable factored with recourse will still be included in trade receivables at the year end. Option A will create particular distortion if the busiest period is just before the year end. Cash sales will need to be removed from the calculation and an adjustment will have to be made for sales tax.

78 Waxwork

Text reference. Chapter 20.

Top tips. Note that part (a) carries five marks. This means that the examiner is expecting more than two sentences. If you really think about this and answer it properly it will help you with part (b).

Easy marks. This was quite an easy question as long as you were clear about the period dealt with by IAS 10 and the distinction between adjusting and non-adjusting events. You may have been uncertain whether or not the commission earned should have been deducted to arrive at NRV in (b)(ii), but this would only have lost you a mark.

Marking scheme

			Marks
(a)	Definition	1	
	Discussion of adjusting events	2	
	Reference to going concern	1	
	Discussion of non-adjusting events	1	
			5
(b)	(i) to (iii) 1 mark per valid point as indicated		10
			15

(a) IAS 10 *Events after the reporting period* relates to events taking place between the last day of the reporting period (the year end date) and the date on which the financial statements are approved and signed by the directors. This period is usually several months.

Adjusting events are events taking place after the reporting period which provide further evidence of conditions existing at the end of the reporting period or which call into question the going concern status of the entity. For this reason, adjusting events require adjustment to be made to the financial statements. If going concern is no longer applicable, the financial statements must be prepared on a break-up basis.

Non-adjusting events provide evidence of conditions arising **after** the end of the reporting period. If material, these should be disclosed by note, but they do not require that the financial statements be adjusted.

(b) (i) This is a non-adjusting event as it does not affect the valuation of property or inventory at the year end. However, it would be treated as adjusting if the scale of losses were judged to threaten the going concern status of Waxwork. It will certainly need to be disclosed in the notes to the financial statements, disclosing separately the $16m loss and the expected insurance recovery of $9m.

(ii) The sale in April 20X9 gives further evidence regarding the realisable value of inventory at the year end and so an adjustment will be required. If 70% of the inventory was sold for $280,000 less commission of $42,000, it had a net realisable value of $238,000. On this basis, the total cost of $460,000 should be restated at NRV of $340,000. So inventory at the end of the reporting period should be written down by $120,000.

(iii) This change has occurred outside the period specified by IAS 10, so it is not treated as an event after the reporting period. Had it occurred prior to 6 May 20X9, it would have been treated as a non-adjusting event requiring disclosure in the notes. The increase in the deferred tax liability will be accounted for in the 20Y0 financial statements.

79 Quartile

Text references. Chapters 19 and 20

Top tips. A bit of planning is useful for a question like this and the categories of profitability, liquidity and gearing give you a structure around which to base your analysis. Note that this is a retail business, so this will affect the ratios.

Easy marks. Analysis of the ratios is straightforward and some useful points on the limitations on usefulness of a sector average comparison could have earned four marks.

		Marks
(a)	1 mark per valid comment	11
(b)	1 mark per issue	$\frac{4}{15}$
Total for question		

(a) **Analysis of financial and operating performance of Quartile compared to sector average**

Profitability

Quartile has a ROCE **significantly lower** at 12.1% than the sector average of 16.8%. This is mainly due to the lower than average gross profit margin and consequent **low operating profit margin**. The operating expenses are actually lower (17.5%) as a percentage of revenue than the sector average of 23% (35% – 12%) so the problem lies between revenue and cost of sales. Inventory turnover is quite brisk (4.5 times compared to a sector average of three times) but Quartile's mark-up of 33.3% ((25 / 75) × 100) is significantly below the sector average of 54% (35 / 65) × 100). Quartile is maintaining turnover **by keeping prices down**.

The other component of ROCE, net asset turnover, is slightly higher than the sector average. This is due to the buoyant turnover, as the ratio will have been depressed by the property revaluation and the capitalisation of the development expenditure, which have increased the asset base. It is to be hoped that the development expenditure will generate the expected revenue. If it had been necessary to expense it for the year ended 30 September 20X2 Quartile would have reported a loss before tax of $1.6m.

Liquidity

Quartile has a current ratio of 1.55:1 compared to the sector average of 1.25:1. Both appear low, but satisfactory for the retail sector as the cash cycle is fairly rapid. Inventory can be turned into immediate cash and this is particularly true for Quartile with its high inventory turnover level. The lower than average payables days (45 compared to 64) and the absence of an overdraft suggest that **Quartile is not suffering liquidity problems**.

Gearing

Quartile's debt to equity ratio is 30%, well below the sector average of 38% and the interest rate on the loan notes is below the ROCE of 12.1%, meaning that the **borrowings are earning a good return** for the business. The interest cover of 5.25 times (4,200 / 800) is satisfactory. Quartile is not having any problems servicing its loan and is unlikely to give lenders any particular concern,

Conclusion

There are no going concern worries for Quartile but it does have an issue with **low profitability**. It appears to be positioned at the bottom end of the jewellery market selling high volume cheap items rather than more valuable pieces on which there would be significantly higher profit margins. This may or may not be the most advantageous strategy in a period of recession.

(b) The following factors may limit the usefulness of comparisons based on business sector averages.

(i) The companies included in the average may have used different accounting policies. Some may be applying the revaluation basis to their assets and some may not. This will affect asset turnover and ROCE.

(ii) Some companies in the average may have used some form of creative accounting, such as sale and leaseback transactions, which will have boosted both profit for the year and ROCE.

(iii) The average may include a wide variety of entities with different trading methods and risk profiles. Very high-end jewellers may even operate on an invoice rather than a cash basis and will have receivables included in their current assets. Very large chains will probably have more access to cheap borrowing.

(iv) Some ratios, in particular ROCE and gearing, can be calculated in different ways. It is up to the organisation carrying out the comparison to ensure that a standard definition is used, and they may or may not do this.

80 Multiple choice answers – statement of cash flows

1   A

	$m
B/f (500 + 100)	600
Cash received (β)	500
C/f (750 + 350)	1,100

2   D

	$m
B/f	410
Depreciation	(115)
Revaluation	80
Purchases (β)	305
C/f	680

3   B

	$'000
Balance b/f	1,860
Revaluation	100
Disposal	(240)
Depreciation	(280)
	1,440
Additions (β)	1,440
Balance c/f	2,880

4   C

	$'000
B/f (2,000 + 800)	2,800
Additions (6,500 – 2,500 + 1,800)	5,800
Payments made (β)	(2,100)
C/f (4,800 + 1,700)	6,500

81 Preparation question: Dickson

(a) DICKSON – STATEMENT OF CASH FLOWS FOR YEAR ENDED 31 MARCH 20X8

	$'000	$'000
Cash flows from operating activities		
Profit before taxation	342	
Adjustments for:		
Depreciation	57	
Amortisation (W1)	60	
Interest expense	15	
Profit on disposal of assets (110 – 103)	(7)	
	467	
Increase in inventories (W4)	(133)	
Decrease in trade receivables (W4)	50	
Decrease in trade payables (W4)	(78)	
Cash generated from operations	306	
Interest paid (W3)	(10)	
Income taxes paid (W3)	(256)	
Net cash from operating activities		40
Cash flows from investing activities		
Development expenditure	(190)	
Purchase of property, plant & equipment (W1)	(192)	
Proceeds from sale of property, plant & equipment	110	
Net cash used in investing activities		(272)
Cash flows from financing activities		
Proceeds from issue of shares (W2)	300	
Proceeds from issue of debentures	50	
Payment of finance lease liabilities (W3)	(31)	
Dividends paid (W2)	(156)	
Net cash from financing activities		163
Net decrease in cash and cash equivalents		(69)
Cash and cash equivalents at beginning of period		109
Cash and cash equivalents at end of period		40

Workings

1   Assets

	Property, plant and equipment	Development expenditure
	$'000	$'000
B/d	737	160
Disposals	(103)	
P/L	(57)	
OCI	100	
Purchase under F/L	56	
Additions (β)		190
Amortisation		(60)
Cash additions (β)	192	–
C/d	925	290

2   Equity

	Share capital and premium $'000	Revaluation surplus $'000	Retained earnings $'000
B/d	500	60	255
P/L			180
OCI		100	
Bonus issue	50		(50)
Rights issue (β)	300		
Dividend paid (β)	–	–	(156)
C/d	850	160	229

3   Liabilities

	Debentures $'000	Finance leases $'000	Taxation $'000	Interest $'000
B/d	100	92*	198**	–
SPLOCI			162	15
New lease		56		
Cash received (paid) (β)	50	(31)	(256)	(10)
C/d	150	117	104	5

*Non-current + current

**Deferred + current

4   Working capital

	Inventories $'000	Receivables $'000	Payables $'000
B/d	227	324	352
Movement (β)	133	(50)	(78)
C/d	360	274	274

(b)   CASH FLOWS FROM OPERATING ACTIVITIES (direct method)

	$'000
Cash received from customers (W2)	1,526
Cash paid to suppliers and employees (W1)	(1,220)
Cash generated from operations	306
Interest paid	(10)
Income taxes paid	(256)
Net cash from operating activities	40

Workings

1   Payables

	$'000
Payables balance b/d	352
Purchases (W3)	1,095
Other expenses (W4)	47
Payments (β)	1,220
Payables balance c/d	274

2   Receivables

	$'000
Receivables balance b/d	324
Sales revenue	1,476
Cash received (β)	(1,526)
	274

3   *Purchases*

	$'000
Inventory balance b/d	227
Transfer to cost of sales	(962)
Purchases (β)	1,095
Inventory balance c/d	360

4   *Other expenses*

	$'000
Balance per statement of profit or loss	157
Depreciation	(57)
Amortisation	(60)
Profit on disposal	7
	47

82 Mocha

Text references. Chapter 4, 13, 14, 21.

Top tips. Statements of cash flow are popular questions with students. This one has a few complications, but is basically straightforward. As always, get the proforma down and do the standard workings.

Easy marks. There are plenty of easy marks available for dealing with the usual adjustments – working capital, tax, finance lease and share capital and 1½ marks just for showing that interest charged is the same as interest paid.

Examiner's comments. The statement of cash flows was very well answered, with many candidates scoring full marks. The main errors involved the profit on disposal, the warranty provision, the tax calculation, the finance lease and the share issue. The bonus issue is not a cash flow. Many candidates seemed to misinterpret the requirement for (c), which was to explain the discrepancy between reported profit and cash flow. This involved discussing working capital adjustments, product warranties and other non-cash items. Some candidates ignored this and just calculated ratios.

Marking scheme

			Marks
(a)	Profit before tax	½	
	Depreciation	1	
	Profit on disposal of property	1	
	Investment income deducted	½	
	Interest expense added back	½	
	Working capital items	1½	
	Decrease in product warranty	1½	
	Interest paid	1	
	Income tax paid	2	
	Purchase of PPE	1	
	Disposal of PPE	1	
	Disposal of investment	1	
	Dividends received	1	
	Share issue	2½	
	Payments under finance lease	2	
	Cash b/f / c/f	1	
			19
(b)	½ mark per valid point		5
(c)	(i) and (ii) 3 marks each		6
			30

(a)   STATEMENT OF CASH FLOWS FOR THE YEAR ENDED 30 SEPTEMBER 20X1

	$'000	$'000
Cash flows from operating activities		
Profit before tax	3,900	
Adjustments for:		
Depreciation	2,500	
Profit on sale of property	(4,100)	
Investment income	(1,100)	
Interest expense	500	
	1,700	
Increase in inventories (W4)	(3,000)	
Decrease in receivables (W4)	200	
Decrease in payables (W4)	(1,400)	
Decrease in warranty provision (4,000 – 1,600)	(2,400)	
Cash used in operations	(4,900)	
Interest paid	(500)	
Income tax paid (W3)	(800)	
Net cash used in operating activities		(6,200)
Cash flows from investing activities		
Sale of property	8,100	
Purchase of plant	(8,300)	
Sale of investment	3,400	
Dividends received	200	
Net cash from investing activities		3,400
Cash flows from financing activities		
Issue of share capital (W2)	2,400	
Payments under finance leases (W3)	(3,900)	
Net cash from financing activities		(1,500)
Decrease in cash and cash equivalents		(4,300)
Cash and cash equivalents b/f		1,400
Cash and cash equivalents c/f		(2,900)

Workings

1   *Assets*

	PPE $'000	Financial asset $'000
B/d	24,100	7,000
New F/L additions	6,700	
Purchase of new plant	8,300	
Disposal	(4,000)	(3,000)
Depreciation	(2,500)	
Increase in fair value		500
	32,600	4,500

2   *Equity*

	Share capital $'000	Share premium $'000	Revaluation surplus $'000	Retained earnings $'000
B/d	8,000	2,000	3,600	10,100
Bonus issue:	3,600	(2,000)	(1,600)	
SPLOCI				2,900
Issued for cash (β)	2,400	–		–
C/d	14,000	–	2,000	13,000

3   Liabilities

	Finance leases $'000	Income tax $'000
B/d	9,000*	2,100**
Additions	6,700	
SPLOCI		1,000
Paid (β)	(3,900)	(800)
	11,800*	2,300**

*Non-current + current
**Deferred + current

4   Working capital

	Inventories $'000	Receivables $'000	Payables $'000
B/d	7,200	3,700	4,600
Movement	3,000	(200)	(1,400)
C/d	10,200	3,500	3,200

(b)   During the year Mocha's cash balances declined by $4.3 million, despite a profit for the year of $2.9 million. The first point to note is that a 43% increase in revenue from $41 million to $58.5 million has been accompanied by a 55% increase in cost of sales and a 93% increase in operating expenses. This leads to a profit for the year which is 42% down on 20X0.

Cost of sales has increased by $16.5 million over the year. Some of this increase will be due to increased depreciation following investment in plant and equipment, but total depreciation for the year was only $2.5 million, so this does not account for any substantial part of the difference. Cost of sales has been kept down by the reduction in the product warranty provision – without this the increase would have been $18.9 million. The reduction in the product warranty provision suggests that Mocha has switched to new, more expensive and more reliable materials. This would explain the increase in cost of sales. The increase in revenue has not kept pace because Mocha has not yet been able to pass on the full amount of the increase to its customers. This has eroded gross profit. In this context, the increase in inventory holding of (only) 41% could mean that Mocha has actually **reduced** its volume holding of inventory in order to avoid tying up too much cash.

The almost doubling of operating expenses has compounded this situation. Some of these costs are probably to do with the new machinery, perhaps use of consultants, retraining of the workforce or maybe redundancy payments following mechanisation of some functions. There is no restructuring provision in place, so this is not part of a long-term plan, but more likely a reaction to a sudden change in the business environment. On a more positive note, Mocha is meeting its interest and lease payments and has reduced its payables days (perhaps stricter terms from a new supplier). If some of these additional costs are one-off and it succeeds in raising its prices, profits could turn around next year.

The management of Mocha has dealt as best it can with the financial situation. It has sold property for $8.1 million, sold investments for $3.4 million, issued shares for $2.4 million and negotiated an overdraft currently standing at $2.9 million. These measures have raised cash without the effect on gearing that would have arisen from a loan stock issue. It has not paid a dividend this year and the fact that the share issue was at par suggests that the business is not seen as a desirable investment at the moment.

(c)   (i)   The statement of profit or loss of Mocha shows profit for the year of $3.9 million. However this figure includes amounts based on estimates, such as the reduction in product warranties and gains which have not translated into cash, such as the increase in fair value of investments. $4.1 million of the profit for the year related to sale of a property – if this was removed there would be a trading loss of $0.2 million.

Net cash from operating activities records only those transactions which have resulted in movement of cash, so items which rely on judgement or are unrealised are automatically excluded. It is to this degree a more verifiable amount than profit before tax and many users would consider it more useful.

(ii)   Accrual-based financial information spreads the lives of property, plant and equipment over the periods expected to benefit from their use and this can be affected by revaluations, impairment and changes in expected life, which are all issues based on judgement. Also, entities can choose whether or not to transfer back excess depreciation to retained earnings following a revaluation. So there is a lot of subjectivity involved in asset values. In the case of Mocha the carrying amount of property, plant and equipment has increased by $8.5 million over the year, but the statement of financial position needs to be properly examined in order to see that $6.7 million of the increased plant was obtained under finance leases and therefore carries a corresponding liability.

Net cash from investing activities deals simply in amounts paid to acquire property, plant and equipment and in any proceeds of selling property, plant and equipment. This is valuable and verifiable additional information which is not shown by the statement of financial position.

83 Multiple choice answers – accounting for inflation

1   C   Historical cost accounting does not avoid the overstatement of profit which arises during periods of inflation, which is why alternative models have been proposed.

2   A   The concept of 'physical capital maintenance' is applied in current cost accounting.

3   B   Current purchasing power accounting adjusts for general price inflation.

4   B   Under CCA goods sold are charged to profit or loss at replacement cost.

5   C   A,B and D are all likely consequences of overstatement of profits. In the case of C, what tends to happen when profits are overstated is that **too much** cash is paid out in dividends to shareholders, depleting funds needed for investment.

6   B   Historical cost accounts can always be verified as asset values are based on transaction costs of which there should be a record. Many values will be out of date and this understatement of asset values will lead to an understatement of equity and overstatement of gearing.

84 Preparation question: Changing prices

(a)   CURRENT COST OPERATING PROFIT FOR 20X6

	$m	$m
Historical cost profit		15
Current cost adjustments:		
Depreciation adjustment	3	
Cost of sales adjustment	5	
		(8)
Current cost profit		7

SUMMARISED CURRENT COST STATEMENT OF FINANCIAL POSITION
AS AT 31 DECEMBER 20X6

	$m	$m
Property, plant & equipment		85
Current assets		
Inventories	21	
Receivables	30	
Bank	2	
		53
		138
Equity		88
Non-current liability		20
Current liabilities		30
		138

(b)   (i)   *Interest cover*

HC accounts: 15 / 3 = 5 times
CC accounts: 7 / 3 = 2.3 times

(ii)   *Return on shareholders' equity*

HC accounts: 12 / 62 = 19.4%
CC accounts: 4 / 88 = 4.5%

(iii)   *Debt/equity ratio*

HC accounts: 20 / 62 = 32.3%
CC accounts: 20 / 88 = 22.7%

(c)   (i)   *Interest cover*

Companies must maintain their capital base if they wish to stay in business. The significance of the interest cover calculation is that it indicates the extent to which profits after tax are being eaten into by payments to finance external capital. The figures calculated above indicate that only one-fifth of historical cost profit is being absorbed in this way, while four-fifths are being retained to finance future growth. On the face of it, this might seem satisfactory; however, the current cost interest cover is only 2.3 times indicating that, after allowing for the impact of rising prices, interest payments absorb nearly half of profits after tax.

(ii)   *Return on shareholders' equity*

This is the ratio of profits earned for shareholders (ie profits after interest) to shareholders' equity. Once again, the position disclosed by the historical cost accounts is more favourable than appears from the current cost ratio. The historical cost profit is higher than the current cost profit because no allowance is made for the adverse impact of rising prices, and, at the same time, the denominator in the historical cost fraction is lower because, shareholders' capital is stated at historical values rather than their higher current values.

The significance of the ratio is that it enables shareholders to assess the rate of return on their investment and to compare it with alternative investments that might be available to them.

(iii)   *Debt/equity ratio*

The significance of this ratio is as a measure of the extent to which the company's net assets are financed by external borrowing and shareholders' funds respectively.

In times of rising prices it can be beneficial to finance assets from loan capital. While the assets appreciate in value over time (and the gain accrues to shareholders), the liability is fixed in monetary amount. The effect of this is that current cost accounts tend to give a more favourable picture of the debt/equity ratio than historical cost accounts. In the ratios calculated above, the amount of debt is $20m in both statements of financial position. This represents nearly one-third of the historical cost value of shareholders' funds, but only one-fifth of the equity calculated on a current cost basis.

85 Update

			Marks
(a)	1 mark per valid point to maximum		7
(b)	Historical cost	2	
	CPP	3	
	CCA	3	
			8
			15

(a)   *Problems with historical cost*

Although retail price inflation has eased throughout the developed world, it is still a big issue for many businesses.

The carrying values of property and other assets with long useful lives soon become unrealistic if based on historical cost, leading to the following problems.

- Even with modest inflation, the depreciation charge on these assets will be too low in comparison with the revenues that the assets are generating, inflating operating profits.
- The return on capital employed is doubly distorted; not only are operating profits overstated, but the related net assets will be understated, resulting in a flattering and unrealistic return. This makes it difficult to compare two companies with similar assets if those assets were bought at different times.
- Low asset values reduce the net assets of a business. This exaggerates the gearing ratio, which might dissuade banks from advancing loans to the business. It might also cause the stock market to undervalue a business.

The traditional solution to these problems is to revalue certain items. However, this creates a hybrid set of financial statements, with some assets at historical cost others at valuation.

(b) *Alternative methods*

	Historical cost $		CPP $		Current cost $
Cost/Valuation	250,000	(a)	300,000	(b)	280,000
Carrying value based on 2 years depreciation (c)	160,000		192,000		179,200
Carrying value based on 3 years depreciation (d)	128,000		153,600		143,360
Depreciation charge for this year (c – d = e)	32,000		38,400		35,840

(1) The original cost of $250,000 will be indexed up for the change in the retail price index between the date of purchase and the end of the reporting period.

$250,000 × 216 / 180 = $300,000

(2) The current cost will be reduced to reflect the lower productivity of the old asset.

$320,000 × 420 / 480 = $280,000

(3) The carrying value after two years depreciation at 20% reducing balance will be 64% of the gross amount (0.8 × 0.8).

(4) The carrying value after three years depreciation at 20% reducing balance will be 51.2% of the gross amount (0.8 × 0.8 × 0.8).

(5) This years charge will be the difference between (c) and (d).

86 Multiple choice answers – specialised, not-for-profit and public sector entities

1   C   Charities do not usually have shareholders, in the commercial sense of the term.

2   B   Public sector accounting needs to move from cash-based accounting to application of the accruals concept.

3   A   A local council would not pay dividends and would be unlikely to measure ROCE, which deals with return to investors.

4   D   Charities have to consider a very wide group of shareholders, which can include donors, beneficiaries, volunteers, local organisations, government bodies and the public at large.

5   B   Public sector bodies have a major advantage not generally enjoyed by charities – government funding.

6   C   Not-for-profit entities do not have share capital so EPS is not relevant. The other requirements could be relevant to a not-for-profit entity.

87 Preparation question: Appraisal

(a)   A **not-for-profit organisation** needs funds to operate, just as a profit-making organisation does. It is also required to make good and sensible use of its assets and spend within its budget. To this degree, calculation of certain financial ratios and their comparison to the previous year is valid and would yield information about how well the organisation is run, and how well it manages its funds.

However, there are a number of differences between a profit-making and a not-for-profit organisation. A not-for-profit organisation does not have the basic purpose of increasing the wealth of its shareholders or of achieving a return on capital. Its success or failure is judged by the degree to which it achieves its objectives. These are laid down in a whole different set of parameters. A hospital has many different targets to meet – some of them apparently not that useful. One of its major targets will be to cut the length of its waiting lists for operations. Local government bodies may be judged on the basis of whether they have secured VFM (value for money) in spending local taxes. Schools are judged on their examination passes and their budgets may be affected by issues such as how many of their children are considered to have 'special needs'.

A charity will judge its success by the amount of work it has achieved in line with its mission statement, and by the level of funding and donations it has secured – without which nothing can be achieved.

It is worth pointing out that, just as a profit-making organisation may seek to enhance the picture given by its financial statements, not-for-profit organisations may also be driven in the same direction. It has been found in the UK that some hospitals have brought forward minor operations and delayed major ones in order to secure maximum impact on the waiting list and meet government targets. Some schools have a policy of only entering pupils for exams which they have a good chance of passing. This keeps up their pass rate and their position in the school league tables.

(b)   Although the sports club is a not-for-profit organisation, any potential loan provider will have to apply the same criteria to its loan request as it would use in assessing a request from a profit-making entity.

The first ratio to look at would be gearing. There will be no share capital, so this would be calculated as the ratio of long-term borrowing to net assets. If the club is already carrying a large amount of borrowing, then a further loan may carry too much risk.

The income and expenditure statement will show whether any interest is currently being paid and interest cover can be calculated by dividing the surplus of income over expenditure by the interest payments. This should then also be done taking into account the projected interest payments from the loan that has been requested.

It will be a good idea to look at the current ratio. As there is presumably very little inventory involved, this will probably be the same as the quick ratio and will give some idea of solvency and of how well the cash is being managed.

These ratios should be calculated for all four years to see any underlying trends, and it will also be useful to look at the sources of income, such as memberships and whether they are increasing or decreasing over the period. If an extension is needed, there should be an increasing number of members.

The accounts will also show what assets the club owns, which could be used as security, and whether there are any prior charges against these assets. It is also possible that the trustees may be able to provide additional security.

Mock Exams

ACCA

Fundamentals Level

Paper F7

Financial Reporting

Mock Examination 1

Question Paper	
Time allowed	
Reading and Planning Writing	15 minutes 3 hours
Answer all FIVE questions	

**DO NOT OPEN THIS PAPER UNTIL YOU ARE READY TO START UNDER
EXAMINATION CONDITIONS**

Section A – ALL 20 questions are compulsory and MUST be attempted

1   Monty had profit before tax of $3 million for the year ended 31 March 20X3, after charging loan interest of $150,000 and interest on a finance lease of $250,000. Extracts from the equity and liabilities section of the statement of financial position of Monty at 31 March 20X3 are as follows.

	$'000	$'000
Total equity		12,550
Non-current liabilities		
8% loan notes	1,400	
Deferred tax	1,500	
Finance lease obligation	1,200	
		4,100
Current liabilities		
Finance lease obligation	750	
Trade payables	2,650	
Current tax	1,250	
		4,650

What is the return on year-end capital employed?

A   16.3%
B   21.4%
C   18.6%
D   24.3%   **(2 marks)**

2   How can ROCE be further analysed into its component ratios?

A   Gross profit margin / net asset turnover
B   Gross profit margin × net asset turnover
C   Net profit margin / net asset turnover
D   Net profit margin × net asset turnover   **(2 marks)**

3   At 1 April 20X2 Atlas had in issue 80 million 50c equity shares. On 1 July 20X2 Atlas made and recorded a fully subscribed rights issue of 1 for 4 at $1.20 each. Immediately before this issue the stock market value of Atlas's shares was $2 each, giving a theoretical ex-rights price of $1.84. Earnings for the year amounted to $31.2 million.

What is the basic earnings per share of Atlas for the year ended 31 March 20X3?

A   32.8c
B   31.2c
C   32.3c
D   33.4c   **(2 marks)**

4   At 31 March 20X2 Monty had equity of $9.75 million, loan notes of $3.125 million and finance lease obligations totalling $1.5 million.

During the year to 31 March 20X3 equity increased by $2.8 million, $1.725 million of the loan notes were repaid and finance lease obligations increased by $450,000.

What was gearing (debt / debt + equity) at 31 March 20X3?

A   10%
B   35%
C   28%
D   21%   **(2 marks)**

5   On 1 October 20X2 Atlas sold $10 million of maturing inventory to Xpede. The cost of the goods at the date of sale was $7 million and Atlas has the option to repurchase these goods at any time within three years of the sale at a price of $10 million plus accrued interest from the date of sale at 10% per annum. At 31 March 20X3 the option had not been exercised but it is highly likely that it will be before the date it lapses.

What should be the net effect on profit or loss of this transaction for the year ended 31 March 20X3?

A   Credit $3,000,000
B   Charge $500,000
C   Credit $2,500,000
D   Credit $2,000,000   (2 marks)

6   Radar's sole activity is the operation of hotels all over the world. After a period of declining profitability, Radar's management took the following steps during the year ended 31 March 20X3:

(i)   It entered into negotiations with a buyer to sell all of its hotels in country A
(ii)   It disposed of two loss-making hotels in country B

Which of these decisions meet the criteria for being classified as discontinued operations in the financial statements for the year ended 31 March 20X3?

A   (i)
B   (ii)
C   Both of them
D   Neither of them   (2 marks)

7   Which of the following is **not** an advantage which could be expected to follow from global harmonisation of accounting standards?

A   Elimination of exchange differences
B   Easier transfer of accounting staff across national borders
C   Ability to comply with the requirements of overseas stock exchanges
D   Better access to foreign investor funds   (2 marks)

8   Ravenscroft is closing one of its production facilities and satisfies the requirements for a restructuring provision. The facility has 250 employees. 50 will be retrained and deployed to other subsidiaries; the remainder will accept redundancy and be paid an average of $5,000 each. Plant has a carrying amount of $2.2 million but is only expected to sell for $500,000, incurring $50,000 of selling costs. The facility itself is expected to sell for a profit of $1.2 million.

What amount should be provided for restructuring?

A $2,750,000
B $2,875,000
C $2,650,000
D $2,775,000   (2 marks)

9   Which of the following would **not** give rise to a valid provision in accordance with IAS 37 *Provisions, Contingent Liabilities and Contingent Assets*?

A   A company's operations have caused environmental damage. It is not legally obliged to rectify this but always does so in order to maintain its eco-credentials.

B   A company is vacating a factory building that it was occupying under an operating lease. It is moving to a new building on 1 July but the lease on the existing building runs up to 1 September and cannot be cancelled.

C   A company has decided to change one of its current raw materials for a substitute which is more environmentally friendly. This material is more expensive and it is estimated that this will lead to a $2 million reduction in profit in the coming year.

D   A company sells a product with a six-month guarantee which provides customers with free repairs or replacement for any defect which arises within that period.   (2 marks)

10   Speculate owned an office building with a depreciated historical cost of $2 million and a remaining useful life of 20 years at 1 April 20X2. On 1 October 20X2 Speculate ceased to occupy the building and let it out to a third party. The property was reclassified as an investment property, applying the fair value model in accordance with IAS 40 *Investment Property*. The value of the property was independently assessed at $2.3 million at 1 October 20X2 and had risen to $2.34 million by 31 March 20X3.

What amount will be charged/credited to profit or loss in respect of this property for the year ended 31 March 20X3?

   A   Credit $40,000
   B   Charge $50,000
   C   Charge $10,000
   D   No charge or credit   (2 marks)

11   At what amount does IAS 41 *Agriculture* generally require biological assets to be measured upon initial recognition?

   A   Cost
   B   Fair value
   C   Market value
   D   Fair value less costs to sell   (2 marks)

12   What are the two fundamental qualitative characteristics of financial information according to the *Conceptual Framework*?

   A   Relevance and faithful representation
   B   Accruals and going concern
   C   Going concern and faithful representation
   D   Relevance and accruals   (2 marks)

13   The *Conceptual Framework* describes a number of different measurement bases. One of them is described as follows.

'Assets are carried at the amount of cash or cash equivalents that would have to be paid if the same or an equivalent asset was acquired currently. Liabilities are carried at the undiscounted amount of cash or cash equivalents that would be required to settle the obligation currently.'

Which measurement basis is being described?

   A   Historical cost
   B   Current cost
   C   Realisable (settlement) value
   D   Present value   (2 marks)

14   Pisces has an asset carried at $6.5 million in its statement of financial position at 31 December 20X2. The present value of the cash flows which the asset will generate for the rest of its useful life is $5.8 million. The current cost of an identical asset of the same age is $6.1 million. Pisces has received an offer of $6.2 million for the asset. The cost of dismantling the asset and transporting it to the customer would be $200,000.

At what amount should the asset be recognised in the statement of financial position at 31 December 20X2?

   A $6 million
   B $6.5 million
   C $6.1 million
   D $5.8 million   (2 marks)

15   Which one of the following would require adjustment to the financial statements according to IAS 10 *Events After the Reporting Period* if they took place between the end of the reporting period and the date the financial statements were authorised for issue?

    A   A decision to discontinue an operation
    B   A collapse in property prices, affecting the company's portfolio
    C   Sale of inventory in its year-end condition at a price below its year end carrying amount
    D   Legal action commenced by a supplier   **(2 marks)**

16   IFRS 10 *Consolidated Financial Statements* provides a definition of control and identifies three separate elements of control. Which one of the following is **not** one of these elements of control?

    A   Power over the investee
    B   The power to participate in the financial and operating policies of the investee
    C   Exposure to, or rights to, variable returns from its involvement with the investee
    D   The ability to use its power over the investee to affect the amount of the investor's returns   **(2 marks)**

17   Springthorpe entered into a three-year contract on 1 January 20X2 to build a factory. This is a contract where performance obligations are satisfied over time. The percentage of performance obligations satisfied is measured according to certificates issued by a surveyor. The contract price was $12 million. At 31 December 20X2 details of the contract were as follows.

	$m
Costs to date	6
Estimated costs to complete	9
Amounts invoiced	4
Certified complete	40%

What amount should appear in the statement of financial position of Springthorpe as at 31 December 20X2 as contract assets/liabilities in respect of this contract?

    A $1 million contract liability
    B $2 million contract liability
    C $1 million contract asset
    D $2 million contract asset   **(2 marks)**

18   How does IFRS 9 *Financial Instruments* require investments in equity instruments to be measured and accounted for (in the absence of any election at initial recognition)?

    A   Fair value with changes going through profit or loss
    B   Fair value with changes going through other comprehensive income
    C   Amortised cost with changes going through profit or loss
    D   Amortised cost with changes going through other comprehensive income   **(2 marks)**

19   On 1 January 20X1 Penfold purchased a debt instrument for its fair value of $500,000. It had a principal amount of $550,000 and was due to mature in five years. The debt instrument carries fixed interest of 6% paid annually in arrears and has an effective interest rate of 8%. It is held at amortised cost.

    At what amount will the debt instrument be shown in the statement of financial position of Penfold as at 31 December 20X2?

    A $514,560
    B $566,000
    C $564,560
    D $520,800   **(2 marks)**

20   A sale and leaseback transaction involves the sale of an asset and the leasing back of the same asset. If the lease arrangement results in a finance lease, how should any 'profit' on the sale be treated?

    A   Recognise immediately in profit or loss
    B   Defer and amortise over the lease term
    C   Any excess above fair value to be deferred and amortised, rest to be recognised in profit or loss
    D   No profit should be recognised   **(2 marks)**

Section B – ALL 3 questions are compulsory and MUST be attempted

1 Atlas

The following trial balance relates to Atlas at 31 March 20X3.

	$'000	$'000
Equity shares of 50 cents each		50,000
Share premium		20,000
Retained earnings at 1 April 20X2		11,200
Land and buildings – at cost (land $10 million) (Note (i))	60,000	
Plant and equipment – at cost (Note (i))	94,500	
Accumulated depreciation at 1 April 20X2: – buildings		20,000
– plant and equipment		24,500
Inventory at 31 March 20X3	43,700	
Trade receivables	42,200	
Bank		6,800
Deferred tax (Note (ii))		6,200
Trade payables		35,100
Revenue		550,000
Cost of sales	411,500	
Distribution costs	21,500	
Administrative expenses	30,900	
Dividends paid	20,000	
Bank interest	700	
Current tax (Note (ii))		1,200
	725,000	725,000

The following notes are relevant.

(i)   Non-current assets:

On 1 April 20X2, the directors of Atlas decided that the financial statements would show an improved position if the land and buildings were revalued to market value. At that date, an independent valuer valued the land at $12 million and the buildings at $35 million and these valuations were accepted by the directors. The remaining life of the buildings at that date was 14 years. Atlas does not make a transfer to retained earnings for excess depreciation. Ignore deferred tax on the revaluation surplus.

Plant and equipment is depreciated at 20% per annum using the reducing balance method and time apportioned as appropriate. All depreciation is charged to cost of sales, but none has yet been charged on any non-current asset for the year ended 31 March 20X3.

(ii)   Atlas estimates that an income tax provision of $27.2 million is required for the year ended 31 March 20X3 and at that date the liability to deferred tax is $9.4 million. The movement on deferred tax should be taken to profit or loss. The balance on current tax in the trial balance represents the under/over provision of the tax liability for the year ended 31 March 20X2.

Required

(a)   Prepare the statement of profit or loss and other comprehensive income for Atlas for the year ended 31 March 20X3.   **(7 marks)**

(b)   Prepare the statement of financial position of Atlas as at 31 March 20X3.   **(8 marks)**

(15 marks)

2 Monty

Monty is a publicly listed company. Its financial statements for the year ended 31 March 20X3 including comparatives are shown below.

STATEMENTS OF PROFIT OR LOSS AND OTHER COMPREHENSIVE INCOME FOR THE YEAR ENDED 31 MARCH

	20X3 $'000	20X2 $'000
Revenue	31,000	25,000
Cost of sales	(21,800)	(18,600)
Gross profit	9,200	6,400
Distribution costs	(3,600)	(2,400)
Administrative expenses	(2,200)	(1,600)
Finance costs – loan interest	(150)	(250)
– lease interest	(250)	(150)
Profit before tax	3,000	2,050
Income tax expense	(1,000)	(750)
Profit for the year	2,000	1,300
Other comprehensive income (Note (i))	1,350	–
Total comprehensive income	3,350	1,300

STATEMENTS OF FINANCIAL POSITION AS AT 31 MARCH

	20X3 $'000	20X2 $'000
ASSETS		
Non-current assets		
Property, plant and equipment	14,000	10,700
Deferred development expenditure	1,000	–
	15,000	10,700
Current assets		
Inventory	3,300	3,800
Trade receivables	2,950	2,200
Bank	50	1,300
	6,300	7,300
Total assets	21,300	18,000
EQUITY AND LIABILITIES		
Equity shares of $1 each	8,000	8,000
Revaluation surplus	1,350	–
Retained earnings	3,200	1,750
	12,550	9,750
Non-current liabilities		
8% loan notes	1,400	3,125
Deferred tax	1,500	800
Finance lease obligation	1,200	900
	4,100	4,825
Current liabilities		
Finance lease obligation	750	600
Trade payables	2,650	2,100
Current tax payable	1,250	725
	4,650	3,425
Total equity and liabilities	21,300	18,000

The following information is relevant.

(i)   On 1 July 20X2, Monty acquired additional plant under a finance lease that had a fair value of $1.5 million. On this date it also revalued its property upwards by $2 million and transferred $650,000 of the resulting revaluation reserve this created to deferred tax. There were no disposals of non-current assets during the period.

(ii)   Depreciation of property, plant and equipment was $900,000 and amortisation of the deferred development expenditure was $200,000 for the year ended 31 March 20X3.

Required

Prepare a statement of cash flows for Monty for the year ended 31 March 20X3, in accordance with IAS 7 *Statement of Cash Flows*, using the indirect method.   **(15 marks)**

3 Paradigm

(a)   On 1 October 20X2, Paradigm acquired 75% of Strata's equity shares by means of a share exchange of two new shares in Paradigm for every five acquired shares in Strata. In addition, Paradigm issued to the shareholders of Strata a $100 10% loan note for every 1,000 shares it acquired in Strata. Paradigm has not recorded any of the purchase consideration, although it does have other 10% loan notes already in issue.

The market value of Paradigm's shares at 1 October 20X2 was $2 each.

The summarised statements of financial position of the two companies at 31 March 20X3 are:

	Paradigm $'000	Strata $'000
ASSETS		
Non-current assets		
Property, plant and equipment	47,400	25,500
Financial asset: equity investments (Notes (i) and (iv))	10,500	3,200
	57,900	28,700
Current assets		
Inventory (Note (ii))	17,400	8,400
Trade receivables (Note (iii))	14,800	9,000
Bank	2,100	–
Total assets	92,200	46,100
EQUITY AND LIABILITIES		
Equity		
Equity shares of $1 each	40,000	20,000
Retained earnings/(losses) – at 1 April 20X2	19,200	(4,000)
– for year ended 31 March 20X3	7,400	8,000
	66,600	24,000
Non-current liabilities		
10% loan notes	8,000	–
Current liabilities		
Trade payables (Note (iii))	17,600	13,000
Bank overdraft	–	9,100
Total equity and liabilities	92,200	46,100

The following information is relevant.

(i)   At the date of acquisition, Strata produced a draft statement of profit or loss which showed it had made a net loss after tax of $2 million at that date. Paradigm accepted this figure as the basis for calculating the pre- and post-acquisition split of Strata's profit for the year ended 31 March 20X3.

Also at the date of acquisition, Paradigm conducted a fair value exercise on Strata's net assets which were equal to their carrying amounts (including Strata's financial asset equity investments) with the exception of an item of plant which had a fair value of $3 million below its carrying amount. The plant had a remaining economic life of three years at 1 October 20X2.

Paradigm's policy is to value the non-controlling interest at fair value at the date of acquisition. For this purpose, a share price for Strata of $1.20 each is representative of the fair value of the shares held by the non-controlling interest.

(ii)   Each month since acquisition, Paradigm's sales to Strata were consistently $4.6 million. Paradigm had marked these up by 15% on cost. Strata had one month's supply ($4.6 million) of these goods in inventory at 31 March 20X3. Paradigm's normal mark-up (to third party customers) is 40%.

(iii)   Strata's current account balance with Paradigm at 31 March 20X3 was $2.8 million, which did not agree with Paradigm's equivalent receivable due to a payment of $900,000 made by Strata on 28 March 20X3, which was not received by Paradigm until 3 April 20X3.

(iv)   On 1 January 20X3 Paradigm acquired 35% of the equity shares in Rainbow. This holding enabled it to exercise significant influence. Rainbow had retained earnings of $7.5 million at 31 March 20X2 and $13.5 million at 31 March 20X3. Its profits accrue evenly over the year.

(v)   The financial asset equity investments of Paradigm include $3 million paid for the shares in Rainbow. The other financial asset equity investments of Paradigm and Strata are carried at their fair values as at 1 April 20X2. As at 31 March 20X3, these had fair values of $7.1 million and $3.9 million respectively.

(vi)   There were no impairment losses within the group during the year ended 31 March 20X3

Required

Prepare the consolidated statement of financial position for Paradigm as at 31 March 20X3.

(25 marks)

(b)   Paradigm has a strategy of buying struggling businesses, reversing their decline and then selling them on at a profit within a short period of time. Paradigm is hoping to do this with Strata.

Required

As an advisor to a prospective purchaser of Strata, explain any concerns you would raise about basing an investment decision on the information available in Paradigm's consolidated financial statements and Strata's entity financial statements.

(5 marks)

(30 marks)

Answers

DO NOT TURN THIS PAGE UNTIL YOU HAVE
COMPLETED THE MOCK EXAM

A plan of attack

If this were the real Financial Reporting exam and you had been told to turn over and begin, what would be going through your mind?

Perhaps you're having a panic. You've spent most of your study time on groups and interpretation of accounts (because that's what your tutor/BPP study Text told you to do), plus a selection of other topics, and you're really not sure that you know enough. So calm down. Spend the first few moments or so **looking at the paper,** and develop a **plan of attack.**

Looking through the paper:

The first section is 20 MCQs. These will cover all sections of the syllabus. Some you may find easy and some more difficult. Don't spend a lot of time on anything you really don't know. You are not penalised for wrong answers, so you should answer all of them. If all else fails – guess!

In **Section B** you have **three questions:**

- Question 1 is a single company financial statements preparation question. The first requirement is to get the formats down correctly – this will really help you to organise the information.

- Question 2 is a statement of cash flows including a finance lease.

- Question 3 a consolidated statement of financial position and comment on the consolidated financial statements from a user perspective. Make sure you leave time for this short written part.

All of these questions are compulsory.

This means that you do not have to waste time wondering which questions to answer.

Allocating your time

BPP's advice is always allocate your time **according to the marks for the question** in total and for the parts of the question. But **use common sense**. If you're confronted by an MCQ on a topic of which you know nothing, pick an answer and move on. Use the time to pick up marks elsewhere.

After the exam...Forget about it!

And don't worry if you found the paper difficult. More than likely other candidates will too. If this were the real thing you would need to **forget** the exam the minute you left the exam hall and **think about the next one**. Or, if it's the last one, **celebrate**!

SECTION A

1   B

		$'000
Return	(3,000 + 150 + 250)	3,400%
Capital employed	(12,550 + 1,400 + 1,200 + 750)	15,900
		= 21.4%

2   D   Net profit margin × net asset turnover

3   C

	Shares '000
80million × 2 / 1.84 × 3/12	21,739
100million × 9/12	75,000
	96,739

EPS = 31,200 / 96,739 = 32.3c

4   D

Equity	(9.75 + 2.8)	12.55
Debt	(3.125 + 1.5 – 1.725 + .45)	3.35
Gearing:	(3.35 / (3.35 + 12.55)) × 100 =	21%

10% ignores the finance leases
35% adds the loan note repayment instead of deducting it
28% incorporates both of these errors

5   B   The only amount to be included is loan interest of $500,000 ($10 million × 10% × 6/12). The transaction is a financing arrangement, not a sale, so there is no profit to be credited.

6   A   (i) does represent withdrawal from a separate geographical area, so qualifies to be classified as a discontinued operation. (ii) does not represent withdrawal from either a geographical area or a major line of business (as it has other hotels in Country B) so would not be treated as a discontinued operation.

7   A   Global harmonisation of accounting standards does not affect currencies, so exchange differences would still arise. The other options have all been identified as possible advantages.

8   A

	$'000
Redundancy (200 × 5)	1,000
Plant impairment (2,200 – (500 – 50))	1,750
	2,750

Retraining costs are not included in a restructuring provision. The profit on sale of the facility cannot be recognised until realised.

9   C   Provisions cannot be made for future operating losses. The other options would all give rise to valid provisions.

10   C

	$'000
Depreciation to 1.10.20X2 (($2m / 20) × 6/12)	(50)
Revaluation gain ($2.34m – $2.3m)	40
Charge to profit or loss	(10)

Note that the surplus from $2m to $2.3m will go to other comprehensive income, not profit or loss.

11   D   Fair value less costs to sell

12   A   Relevance and faithful representation

13   B   Current cost. Historical cost is the original amount of the asset or liability. Realisable value is the amount that would be received to transfer the asset or the amount that would have to be paid to settle the liability. Present value is the discounted amount of the future cash flows that can be obtained from continuing to use an asset.

14	A	Fair value less costs of disposal ($6.2m – $0.2m)	$6 million
		Value in use	$5.8 million
		Recoverable amount (higher)	$6 million

15 C This calls into question the inventory valuation at the year end. The other options describe events that have arisen after the year end and do not call into question conditions at the year end.

16 B This is the definition of **significant influence**, not control.

17 A

	$m
Contract price	12
Total costs (6 + 9)	(15)
Foreseeable loss	(3)
Costs to date	6
Foreseeable loss	(3)
Amounts invoiced	(4)
Contract liability	(1)

18 A Fair value with changes going through profit or loss. Fair value through OCI would be correct if an election had been made to recognise changes in value through other comprehensive income. Amortised cost is used for debt instruments, not equity instruments.

19 A

	$
1 January 20X1	500,000
Interest 8%	40,000
Interest received (550,000 × 6%)	(33,000)
31 December 20X1	507,000
Interest 8%	40,560
Interest received	(33,000)
31 December 20X2	514,560

20 B The profit should be deferred and amortised over the lease term. Immediate recognition in profit or loss would apply if there was no leaseback. Deferral of the excess over FV would apply if the leaseback involved an operating lease.

SECTION B

1 Atlas

Text references. Chapters 3, 4, 15, 17.

Top tips. This is a standard question – preparation of financial statements from a trial balance.

Easy marks. While there were a few difficult bits, some marks were available for items which just needed to be brought across from the trial balance and dealing correctly with PPE and tax would have brought in five marks.

Marking scheme

			Marks
(a)	Statement of profit or loss and OCI		
	Revenue	1	
	Cost of sales	2	
	Distribution costs	½	
	Administrative expenses	½	
	Finance costs	½	
	Income tax	1½	
	Other comprehensive income	1	
			7
(b)	Statement of financial position		
	Property, plant and equipment	3	
	Inventory	½	
	Trade receivables	½	
	Retained earnings	1½	
	Deferred tax	1	
	Trade payables	½	
	Current tax	½	
	Bank overdraft	½	
			8
			15

(a) STATEMENT OF PROFIT OR LOSS AND OTHER COMPREHENSIVE INCOME FOR THE YEAR ENDED 31 MARCH 20X3

	$'000
Revenue	550,000
Cost of sales (W1)	(428,000)
Gross profit	122,000
Distribution costs	(21,500)
Administrative expenses	(30,900)
Finance costs	(700)
Profit before tax	68,900
Income tax expense ((27,200 – 1,200) + (9,400 – 6,200))	(29,200)
Profit for the year	39,700
Other comprehensive income:	
Gain on revaluation of property (W3)	7,000
Total comprehensive income for the year	46,700

(b) STATEMENT OF FINANCIAL POSITION AS AT 31 MARCH 20X3

	$'000	$'000
ASSETS		
Non-current assets		
Property, plant and equipment (W2)		100,500
Current assets		
Inventory	43,700	
Trade receivables	42,200	
		85,900
Total assets		186,400
EQUITY AND LIABILITIES		
Equity		
Share capital		50,000
Share premium		20,000
Revaluation surplus		7,000
Retained earnings (11,200 + 39,700 – dividend 20,000)		30,900
		107,900
Non-current liabilities		
Deferred tax		9,400
Current liabilities		
Trade payables	35,100	
Tax payable	27,200	
Overdraft	6,800	
		69,100
		186,400

Workings

1   Expenses

	Cost of sales $'000	Distribution costs $'000	Administrative expenses $'000
Per TB	411,500	21,500	30,900
Depreciation (W2)	16,500	–	–
	428,000	21,500	30,900

2   Property, plant and equipment

	Land $'000	Buildings $'000	Plant $'000	Total $'000
Cost	10,000	50,000	94,500	
Accumulated depreciation	–	(20,000)	(24,500)	
Balance 1 April 20X3	10,000	30,000	70,000	110,000
Revaluation surplus	2,000	5,000		7,000
Revalued amount	12,000	35,000		
Depreciation (35/14) (70 × 20%)	–	(2,500)	(14,000)	(16,500)
	12,000	32,500	56,000	100,500

2 Monty

Marking scheme

	Marks
Profit before tax	½
Depreciation/amortisation	1
Finance costs added back	½
Working capital items (½ mark each)	1½
Finance cost paid (outflow)	½
Income tax paid	2½
Purchase of property, plant and equipment	2½
Deferred development expenditure	1
Repayment of 8% loan notes	1
Repayment of finance lease obligations	2
Equity dividend paid	1
Cash b/f	½
Cash c/f	½
	15

STATEMENT OF CASH FLOWS FOR THE YEAR ENDED 31 MARCH 20X3

	$'000	$'000
Cash flows from operating activities		
Profit before tax	3,000	
Depreciation	900	
Amortisation	200	
Interest payable	400	
Decrease in inventory (W4)	500	
Increase in trade receivables (W4)	(750)	
Increase in trade payables (W4)	550	
Cash generated from operations	4,800	
Interest paid	(400)	
Income tax paid (W3)	(425)	
Net cash from operating activities		3,975
Cash flows from investing activities		
Purchase of property, plant and equipment (W1)	(700)	
Development expenditure (W1)	(1,200)	
Net cash used in investing activities		(1,900)

	$'000	$'000
Cash flows from financing activities		
Redemption of loan notes (W3)	(1,725)	
Payments under finance leases (W3)	(1,050)	
Dividend paid (W2)	(550)	
Net cash used in financing activities		(3,325)
Net decrease in cash and cash equivalents		(1,250)
Cash and cash equivalents at beginning of period		1,300
Cash and cash equivalents at end of period		50

Workings

1 Assets

	PPE $'000	Development expenditure $'000
B/d	10,700	–
Revaluation	2,000	
Depreciation/amortisation	(900)	(200)
Non-cash addition (i)	1,500	
Cash paid (β)	700	1,200
C/d	14,000	1,000

2 Equity

	Share capital / premium $'000	Retained earnings $'000
B/d	8,000	1,750
SPLOCI		2,000
Cash paid (dividend)	–	(550)
C/d	8,000	3,200

3 Liabilities

	Loan notes $'000	Tax $'000	Finance leases $'000	Interest $'000
B/d	3,125	1,525*	1,500**	–
SPLOCI		1,000		400
Deferred tax on reval		650		
Additions			1,500	
Cash paid (β)	(1,725)	(425)	(1,050)	(400)
C/d	1,400	2,750	1,950	–

*Deferred and current
**Non-current and current

4 Working capital

	Inventories $'000	Receivables $'000	Payables $'000
B/d	3,800	2,200	2,100
Movement	(500)	750	550
C/d	3,300	2,950	2,650

3 Paradigm

Marking scheme

		Marks
(a)	Statement of financial position	
	Property, plant and equipment	1½
	Goodwill	5
	Equity investments	1½
	Investment in associate	3½
	Inventory	1
	Trade receivables	1½
	Bank	1
	Equity shares	1½
	Share premium	½
	Retained earnings	4
	Non-controlling interest	1½
	10% loan notes	1
	Trade payables	1
	Bank overdraft	½
		25
(b)	1 mark per valid point	5
		30

(a)   CONSOLIDATED STATEMENT OF FINANCIAL POSITION AS AT 31 MARCH 20X3

	$'000	$'000
ASSETS		
Non-current assets		
Property, plant and equipment (47,400 + 25,500 – 2,500 (W6))		70,400
Goodwill (W1)		8,500
Financial asset: equity investments (7,100 + 3,900)		11,000
Investment in associate (W7)		3,525
		93,425
Current assets		
Inventory (17,400 + 8,400 – 600 (W2))	25,200	
Receivables (14,800 + 9,000 – 900 (W3) – 2,800 interco)	20,100	
Cash (2,100 + 900 (W3))	3,000	
		48,300
Total assets		141,725
EQUITY AND LIABILITIES		
Equity attributable to owners of Paradigm		
Share capital (40,000 + 6,000 (W1))		46,000
Share premium (W1)		6,000
Retained earnings (W4)		34,525
		86,525
Non-controlling interest (W5)		8,800
		95,325
Non-current liabilities		
10% loan notes (8,000 + 1,500 (W1))		9,500
Current liabilities		
Trade payables (17,600 + 13,000 – 2,800 intercompany)	27,800	
Overdraft	9,100	
		36,900
Total equity and liabilities		141,725

Workings

1   *Goodwill*

	$'000	$'000
Consideration transferred:		
Shares (20m × 2/5 × 75% × $2)		12,000
Loan notes (15m × 100 / 1,000)		1,500
		13,500
Non-controlling interest (5m × $1.2)		6,000
		19,500
Net assets at acquisition;		
Share capital	20,000	
Retained earnings ((4,000) + (2,000))	(6,000)	
Fair value adjustment (W5)	(3,000)	
		(11,000)
Goodwill		8,500

2   *PURP*

Intercompany sales in inventory $4.6m
PURP = $4.6m x 15 / 115 = $600,000

3   *Intercompany cash in transit*

	$'000	$'000
Dr Cash	900	
Cr Receivables		900

4   *Retained earnings*

	Paradigm $'000	Strata $'000
Per draft	26,600	4,000
Add back pre-acquisition loss		6,000
		10,000
PURP (W2)	(600)	
Gain (loss) on equity investments*	(400)	700
Movement on fair value adjustment (W6)		500
		11,200
Group share of Strata – 75% × 11,200	8,400	
Group share of Rainbow (W7)	525	
Group retained earnings	34,525	

*Loss on equity investments in Paradigm: ((10,500 – 3,000) – 7,100)

5   *Non-controlling interest*

	$'000
Fair value at acquisition (W1)	6,000
Share of post –acquisition retained earnings (11,200 (W4) × 25%)	2,800
	8,800

6   *Movement on fair value adjustment*

	At acquisition $'000	Movement $'000	At year end $'000
FVA on plant (W1)	(3,000)	500	(2,500)

7   *Investment in Rainbow*

	$'000
Cost of investment	3,000
Share of post-acquisition earnings (13.5m – 7.5m) × 3/12 × 35%	525
	3,525

(b)   The consolidated financial statements of Paradigm would not give much useful information regarding the individual performance and financial position of Strata. The individual financial statements of Strata are also likely to be subject to certain shortcomings.

As Paradigm is hoping to sell Strata in the near future, it wants to present Strata's results as favourably as possible. One way in which the appearance of results can be improved is through transfer pricing. We know that intercompany trading has taken place and that Paradigm has been selling to Strata at below its normal trading price, effectively transferring profit from the parent to the subsidiary. The goods bought from Paradigm, marked up by 15% on cost, have cost Strata $4.6m per month. At the normal mark-up of 40% on cost, Strata would have been paying $5.6m per month. In this way, Paradigm has transferred $6m profits to Strata. Without this intervention, Strata's retained earnings for the year ended 31 March 20X3 would have been down to $2m and the overdraft consequently increased.

There is also the matter of the £3m fair value loss on Strata's plant. This means that assets in Strata's individual statement of financial position are overvalued by £3m and the adjustment to deal with this is lost in the consolidated financial statements.

An investor looking over the financial statements of Strata for the year ended 31 March 20X3 may be tempted to see an impressive turnaround in profitability attributable to the expertise of Paradigm's management. They should dig a bit deeper, beginning with the financial statements for the prior year, before the acquisition by Paradigm.

ACCA

Fundamentals Level

Paper F7

Financial Reporting

Mock Examination 2

Question Paper	
Time allowed	
Reading and Planning Writing	**15 minutes** **3 hours**
Answer all FIVE questions	

DO NOT OPEN THIS PAPER UNTIL YOU ARE READY TO START UNDER EXAMINATION CONDITIONS

Section A – ALL 20 questions are compulsory and MUST be attempted

1   Which of the following are possible effects of rising prices upon financial statements?

   (i)   Understatement of operating costs
   (ii)   Understatement of capital employed
   (iii)   Overstatement of capital employed
   (iv)   Overstatement of profits
   (v)   Understatement of profits

   A   (i), (ii) and (iv)
   B   (ii), (iii) and (v)
   C   (i), (iii) and (iv)
   D   (ii), (iv) and (v)   **(2 marks)**

2   On 1 September 20X3 Laidlaw factored (sold) $2 million of trade receivables to Finease for an immediate payment of $1.8 million and further amounts depending on how quickly Finease collects the receivables. Finease will charge a monthly administration fee and interest on the outstanding balance and any receivables not collected after four months would be sold back to Laidlaw.

   How should Laidlaw account for this factoring arrangement in its financial statements for the year ended 30 September 20X3?

   A   Derecognise the receivables and recognise a loss on disposal of $200,000
   B   Continue to recognise the receivables and treat the $1.8 million received as a loan
   C   Continue to recognise the receivables and treat the $1.8 million as deferred income
   D   Derecognise the receivables and make a provision for the loss of $200,000   **(2 marks)**

3   Which pair of ratios would provide the most useful information to a bank providing a long-term loan to a business?

   A   Asset turnover and ratio of expenses to sales
   B   Gearing and interest cover
   C   ROCE and gross profit margin
   D   Return on equity and EPS   **(2 marks)**

4   Penfold holds several properties under operating leases. If these were treated as finance leases how would that affect these ratios?

	ROCE	Gearing
A	Decrease	Decrease
B	Decrease	Increase
C	Increase	Decrease
D	Increase	Increase

   (2 marks)

5   Raycroft operates a nuclear power station. The power station is due to be decommissioned on 31 December 20X8 but will be fully operational up to that date. It has been estimated that the cost of decommissioning the power station and cleaning up any environmental damage, as required by legislation, will be $60 million. Raycroft recognised a provision for the present value of this expenditure at 31 December 20X0. A suitable discount rate for evaluating costs of this nature is 12%, equivalent to a present value factor after eight years of 0.404. The decommissioning cost will be depreciated over eight years.

What is the total charge to profit or loss in respect of this provision for the year ended 31 December 20X1?

A $2,880,800
B $3,030,000
C $5,938,800
D $7,500,000   (2 marks)

6   On 1 December 20X4 Scaffold acquired 80% of the 3,000,000 issued ordinary shares of Plank. The consideration for each share acquired comprised a cash payment of $1.20 and two ordinary shares in Scaffold. The market value of a $1 ordinary share in Scaffold on 1 December 20X4 was $1.50, rising to $1.60 by the entity's year end on 31 December 20X4. Professional fees paid to Scaffold's external accountants and legal advisors in respect of the acquisition were $400,000.

At what amount would the investment in Plank be recorded in the entity financial statements of Scaffold for the year ended 31 December 20X4?

A $10,480,000
B $10,080,000
C $10,560,000
D $10,960,000   (2 marks)

7   Where the purchase price of an acquisition is less than the aggregate amount of the non-controlling interest plus fair value of net assets acquired, IFRS 3 requires that the value of the assets acquired and liabilities assumed be reassessed. If no change is made as a result of this reassessment, how should the difference be treated?

A   Deduct from goodwill in the consolidated statement of financial position
B   Recognise immediately as a gain in other comprehensive income
C   Recognise in profit or loss over its useful life
D   Recognise immediately as a gain in profit or loss   (2 marks)

8   At a year-end board meeting on 31 March 20X2, Pulsar's directors made the decision to close down one of its factories at the end of the following year, on 31 March 20X3. The factory and its related plant would then be sold. A formal plan was formulated and the factory's employees were given three months' notice of redundancy on 1 January 20X3. Customers and suppliers were also informed of the closure at this date.

How should the closure be accounted for?

A   Discontinued operation as at 31 March 20X2
B   Discontinued operation during the year to 31 March 20X3
C   No discontinued operation, but restructuring provision at 31 March 20X3
D   No discontinued operation or restructuring provision   (2 marks)

9   Which of the following items would qualify for treatment as a change in accounting estimate according to IAS 8 *Accounting Policies, Changes in Accounting Estimates and Errors*?

(i)   Provision for obsolescence of inventory
(ii)   Correction necessitated by a material error
(iii)   A change of inventory valuation from FIFO to weighted average
(iv)   A change in the useful life of a non-current asset

A   All four items
B   (ii) and (iii) only
C   (i) and (iii) only
D   (i) and (iv) only   **(2 marks)**

10   A company purchased a machine for $50,000 on 1 January 20X1. It was judged to have a five-year life with a residual value of $5,000. On 1 January 20X3 $15,000 was spent on an upgrade to the machine. his extended its remaining useful life to 5 years with the same residual value. During 20X3 the market for the product declined and the machine was sold on 1 January 20X4 for $7,000.

What was the loss on disposal?

A $30,600
B $40,000
C $31,600
D $29,000   **(2 marks)**

11   The components of the cost of a major item of equipment are given below:

	$
Purchase price	780,000
Import duties	117,000
VAT (refundable)	78,000
Site preparation	30,000
Installation	28,000
Testing	10,000
Initial losses before asset reaches planned performance	50,000
Discounted cost of dismantling and removal at end of useful life	40,000
	1,133,000

What amount should be recognised as the cost of the asset in accordance with IAS 16 *Property, Plant and Equipment* ?

A $896,000
B $1,045,000
C $1,005,000
D $1,133,000   **(2 marks)**

12   Which one of the following would be included in the cost of inventories of goods for resale in accordance with IAS 2 *Inventories*?

A   Storage costs
B   Administrative overheads
C   Import duties
D   Selling costs   **(2 marks)**

13   The following information relates to the position at 31 March 20X9 of a contract where performance
     obligations are satisfied over time.

	$
Contract price	900,000
At 31 March:	
Costs to date	720,000
Estimated costs to complete	480,000
Progress payments invoiced	400,000
Percentage complete	60%

What amount should appear as 'contract asset/liability' in respect of this contract in the statement of
financial position as at 31 March 20X9?

A $220,000 contract liability
B $20,000 contract asset
C $180,000 contract liability
D $100,000 contract asset   (2 marks)

---

14   On 1 January 20X3 Wincarnis purchased 30,000 $1 shares in a listed entity for $5 per share.   Transaction
     costs were $2,000 and Wincarnis elected to recognise the shares at fair value through other comprehensive
     income. At the year end of 31 December 20X3 the shares were trading at $6.50.

     At what amount will the shares be recognised in the statement of financial position of Wincarnis at 31
     December 20X3?

A $197,000
B $195,000
C $193,000
D $152,000   (2 marks)

---

15   A company's statement of profit or loss showed a profit before tax of $1.8 million. After the end of
     the reporting period and before the financial statements were authorised for issue, the following
     events took place.

(i)   The value of an investment held at the year end fell by $85,000.

(ii)   A customer who owed $116,000 at the year end went bankrupt owing a total of $138,000.

(iii) Inventory valued at $161,000 in the statement of financial position was sold in year-end condition for
       $141,000.

(iv)   Assets with a carrying amount at the year end of $240,000 were unexpectedly expropriated by the
       government.

What is the company's profit before tax after making the necessary adjustments for these events?

A $1,399,000
B $1,579,000
C $1,664,000
D $1,800,000   (2 marks)

16 Which of the following statements are correct in accordance with IAS 37 *Provisions, Contingent Liabilities and Contingent Assets*?

(i) Provisions should be made for both constructive and legal obligations.

(ii) Discounting may be used when estimating the amount of a provision.

(iii) A restructuring provision must include the estimated costs of retraining or relocating continuing staff.

(iv) A restructuring provision may only be made when a company has a detailed plan for the restructuring and has communicated to interested parties a firm intention to carry it out.

A All four statements are correct
B (i), (ii) and (iv) only
C (i), (iii) and (iv) only
D (ii) and (iii) only   **(2 marks)**

---

17 On 25 June 20X9 Cambridge received an order from a new customer, Circus, for products with a sales value of $900,000. Circus enclosed a deposit with the order of $90,000.

On 30 June Cambridge had not completed credit checks on Circus and had not despatched any goods. Cambridge is considering the following possible entries for this transaction in its financial statements for the year ended 30 June 20X9.

(i) Include $900,000 in revenue for the year
(ii) Include $90,000 in revenue for the year
(iii) Do not include anything in revenue for the year
(iv) Create a trade receivable for $810,000
(v) Show $90,000 as a current liability

According to IFRS 15 *Revenue from contracts with customers*, how should Cambridge record this transaction in its financial statements for the year ended 30 June 20X9?

A (i) and (iv)
B (ii) and (v)
C (ii) and (iv)
D (iii) and (v)   **(2 marks)**

---

18 Phantom acquired 70% of the $100,000 equity share capital of Ghost, its only subsidiary, for $200,000 on 1 January 20X9 when the retained earnings of Ghost were $156,000.

At 31 December 20X9 retained earnings are as follows.

	$
Phantom	275,000
Ghost	177,000

Phantom considers that goodwill on acquisition is impaired by 50%. Non-controlling interest is measured at fair value, estimated at $82,800.

What are group retained earnings at 31 December 20X9?

A $276,300
B $289,700
C $280,320
D $269,200   **(2 marks)**

19   Ruby owns 30% of Emerald and exercises significant influence over it. Emerald sold goods to Ruby for $160,000. Emerald applies a one third mark up on cost. Ruby still had 25% of these goods in inventory at the year end.

What amount should be deducted from consolidated retained earnings in respect of this transaction?

A $40,000
B $3,000
C $10,000
D $4,000   (2 marks)

---

20   The following information relates to an entity.

(i)   At 1 January 20X8 the carrying amount of non-current assets exceeded their tax written down value by $850,000.

(ii)   For the year to 31 December 20X8 the entity claimed depreciation for tax purposes of $500,000 and charged depreciation of $450,000 in the financial statements.

(iii)   During the year ended 31 December 20X8 the entity revalued a property. The revaluation surplus was $250,000. There are no current plans to sell the property.

(iv)   The tax rate was 30% throughout the year.

What is the provision for deferred tax required by IAS 12 *Income Taxes* at 31 December 20X8?

A $240,000
B $270,000
C $315,000
D $345,000   (2 marks)

SECTION B – ALL 3 questions are compulsory and MUST be attempted

1 Polestar

On 1 April 20X3, Polestar acquired 75% of the 12 million 50 cent equity shares of Southstar. Southstar had been experiencing difficult trading conditions and making significant losses. Its retained earnings at the acquisition date were $14.3 million. In allowing for Southstar's difficulties, Polestar made an immediate cash payment of only £1.50 per share. In addition, Polestar will pay a further amount in cash on 30 September 20X4 if Southstar returns to profitability by that date. The value of this contingent consideration at the date of acquisition was estimated to be $1.8 million, but at 30 September 20X3 in the light of continuing losses, its value was estimated at only $1.5 million. The contingent consideration has not been recorded by Polestar. Overall, the directors of Polestar expect the acquisition to be a bargain purchase leading to negative goodwill.

At the date of acquisition shares in Southstar had a listed market price of $1.20 each.

The statements of profit or loss of both companies are as follows.

STATEMENTS OF PROFIT OR LOSS FOR THE YEAR ENDED 30 SEPTEMBER 20X3

	Polestar	Southstar
	$'000	$'000
Revenue	110,000	66,000
Cost of sales	(88,000)	(67,200)
Gross profit (loss)	22,000	(1,200)
Distribution costs	(3,000)	(2,000)
Administrative expenses	(5,250)	(2,400)
Finance costs	(250)	–
Profit (loss) before tax	13,500	(5,600)
Income tax (expense)/relief	(3,500)	1,000
Profit (loss) for the year	10,000	(4,600)

The following information is relevant:

(i)   At the date of acquisition, the fair values of Southstar's assets were equal to their carrying amounts with the exception of a leased property. This had a fair value of $2 million above its carrying amount and a remaining lease term of ten years at that date. All depreciation is included in cost of sales.

(ii)   Polestar transferred raw materials at their cost of $4 million to Southstar in June 20X3. Southstar processed all of these materials incurring additional direct costs of $1.4 million and sold them back to Polestar in August 20X3 for $9 million. At 30 September 20X3 Polestar had $1.5 million of these goods still in inventory. There were no other intragroup sales.

(iii)   Polestar has recorded its investment in Southstar at the cost of the immediate cash payment; other equity investments are carried at fair value through profit or loss as at 1 October 20X2. The other equity investments have fallen in value by $200,000 during the year ended 30 September 20X3.

(iv)   Polestar's policy is to value the non-controlling interest at fair value at the date of acquisition. For this purpose, Southstar's share price at that date can be deemed to be representative of the fair value of the shares held by the non-controlling interest.

(v)   All items in the above statements of profit or loss are deemed to accrue evenly over the year unless otherwise indicated.

Required

(a)   Calculate the goodwill on acquisition of Southstar.   **(4 marks)**

(b)   Prepare the consolidated statement of profit or loss for Polestar for the year ended 30 September 20X3.   **(11 marks)**

                                                                                                            (15 marks)

2 Harbin

Shown below are the recently issued (summarised) financial statements of Harbin, a listed company, for the year ended 30 September 20X7, together with comparatives for 20X6 and extracts from the Chief Executive's report that accompanied their issue.

STATEMENT OF PROFIT OR LOSS

	20X7	20X6
	$'000	$'000
Revenue	250,000	180,000
Cost of sales	(200,000)	(150,000)
Gross profit	50,000	30,000
Operating expenses	(26,000)	(22,000)
Finance costs	(8,000)	(nil)
Profit before tax	16,000	8,000
Income tax expense (at 25%)	(4,000)	(2,000)
Profit for the year	12,000	6,000

STATEMENT OF FINANCIAL POSITION

	20X7	20X6
	$'000	$'000
Non-current assets		
Property, plant and equipment	210,000	90,000
Goodwill	10,000	nil
	220,000	90,000
Current assets		
Inventory	25,000	15,000
Trade receivables	13,000	8,000
Bank	nil	14,000
	38,000	37,000
Total assets	258,000	127,000
Equity and liabilities		
Equity shares of $1 each	100,000	100,000
Retained earnings	14,000	12,000
	114,000	112,000
Non-current liabilities		
8% loan notes	100,000	nil
Current liabilities		
Bank overdraft	17,000	nil
Trade payables	23,000	13,000
Current tax payable	4,000	2,000
	44,000	15,000
Total equity and liabilities	258,000	127,000

Extracts from the Chief Executive's report:

'Highlights of Harbin's performance for the year ended 30 September 20X7:

An increase in sales revenue of 39%

Gross profit margin up from 16.7% to 20%

A doubling of the profit for the period

In response to the improved position the Board paid a dividend of 10 cents per share in September 20X7 an increase of 25% on the previous year.'

You have also been provided with the following further information.

On 1 October 20X6 Harbin purchased the whole of the net assets of Fatima (previously a privately owned entity) for $100 million, financed by the issue of $100,000 8% loan notes. The contribution of the purchase to Harbin's results for the year ended 30 September 20X7 was:

	$'000
Revenue	70,000
Cost of sales	(40,000)
Gross profit	30,000
Operating expenses	(8,000)
Profit before tax	22,000

There were no disposals of non-current assets during the year.

The following ratios have been calculated for Harbin for the year ended 30 September.

	20X6	20X7
Return on year-end capital employed	7.1%	11.2%
(profit before interest and tax over total assets less current liabilities)		
Net asset (equal to capital employed) turnover	1.6	1.17
Net profit (before tax) margin	4.4%	6.4%
Current ratio	2.5	0.86:1
Closing inventory holding period (in days)	37	46
Trade receivables' collection period (in days)	16	19
Trade payables' payment period (based on cost of sales) (in days)	32	42
Gearing (debt over debt plus equity)	nil	46.7%

Required

Assess the financial performance and position of Harbin for the year ended 30 September 20X7 compared to the previous year. Your answer should refer to the information in the Chief Executive's report and the impact of the purchase of the net assets of Fatima. Up to three marks are available for additional ratios. **(15 marks)**

3 Moby

The following trial balance relates to Moby as at 30 September 20X3.

	$'000	$'000
Revenue		227,800
Cost of sales	164,500	
Long-term contract (note (i))	4,000	
Distribution costs	13,500	
Administrative expenses	16,500	
Bank interest	900	
Dividend	2,000	
Lease rental paid on 30 September 20X3 (note (ii))	9,200	
Land ($12 million) and building ($48 million) at cost (note (ii))	60,000	
Owned plant and equipment at cost (note (ii))	65,700	
Leased plant at initial carrying amount (note (ii))	35,000	
Accumulated depreciation at 1 October 20X2:		
Building		10,000
Owned plant and equipment		17,700
Leased plant		7,000
Inventory at 30 September 20X3	26,600	
Trade receivables	38,500	
Bank		5,300
Insurance provision (note (iii))		150
Deferred tax (note (iv))		8,000
Finance lease obligation at 1 October 20X2 (note (ii))		29,300
Trade payables		21,300
Current tax (note (iv))		1,050
Equity shares of 20 cents each		45,800
Share premium		3,200
Loan note (note (v))		40,000
Retained earnings at 1 October 20X2	–	19,800
	436,400	436,400

The following notes are relevant.

(i) The balance on the long-term contract is made up of the following items.

Cost incurred to date	$14 million
Value of invoices issued (work certified)	$10 million

The contract commenced on 1 October 20X2 and is for a fixed price of $25 million. Performance obligations are satisfied over time. The costs to complete the contract at 30 September 20X3 are estimated at $6 million. Moby's policy is to recognise satisfaction of performance obligations (and therefore accrue profits) on such contracts based on a stage of completion given by the work certified as a percentage of the contract price.

(ii) Non-current assets:

Moby decided to revalue its land and buildings for the first time on 1 October 20X2. A qualified valuer determined the relevant revalued amounts to be $16 million for the land and $38.4 million for the building. The building's remaining life at the date of the revaluation was 16 years. This revaluation has not yet been reflected in the trial balance figures. Moby does not make a transfer from the revaluation surplus to retained earnings in respect of the realisation of the revaluation surplus. Deferred tax is applicable to the revaluation surplus at 25%.

The leased plant was acquired on 1 October 20X1 under a five-year finance lease which has an implicit interest rate of 10% per annum. The rentals are $9.2 million per annum payable on 30 September each year.

Owned plant and equipment is depreciated at 12.5% per annum using the reducing balance method.

No depreciation has yet been charged on any non-current asset for the year ended 30 September 20X3. All depreciation is charged to cost of sales.

(iii) On 1 October 20X2 Moby received renewal quote of $400,000 from the company's property insurer. The directors were surprised at how much it had increased and believed it would be less expensive for the company to 'self-insure'. Accordingly, they charged $400,000 to administrative expenses and credited the same amount to the insurance provision. During the year, the company incurred $250,000 of expenses relating to previously insured property damage which it has debited to the provision.

(iv) A provision for income tax for the year ended 30 September 20X3 of $3.4 million is required. The balance on current tax represents the under/over provision of the tax liability for the year ended 30 September 20X2. At 30 September 20X3 the tax base of Moby's net assets was $24 million less than their carrying amounts. This does not include the effect of the revaluation in Note 2 above. The income tax rate of Moby is 25%.

(v) The $40 million loan note was issued at par on 1 October 20X2. No interest will be paid on the loan; however it will be redeemed on 30 September 20X5 for $53,240,000, which gives an effective finance cost of 10% per annum.

(vi) A share issue was made on 31 December 20X2 of 4 million shares for $1 per share. It was correctly accounted for.

Required

(a) Prepare the statement of profit or loss and other comprehensive income for Moby for the year ended 30 September 20X3. **(12 marks)**

(b) Prepare the statement of changes in equity for Moby for the year ended 30 September 20X3.

(6 marks)

(c) Prepare the statement of financial position for Moby as at 30 September 20X3. **(12 marks)**

(30 marks)

Answers

DO NOT TURN THIS PAGE UNTIL YOU HAVE
COMPLETED THE MOCK EXAM

A plan of attack

Managing your nerves

As you turn the pages to start this mock exam a number of thoughts are likely to cross your mind. At best, examinations cause anxiety so it is important to stay focused on your task for the next three hours! Developing an awareness of what is going on emotionally within you may help you manage your nerves. Remember, you are unlikely to banish the flow of adrenaline, but the key is to harness it to help you work steadily and quickly through your answers.

Working through this mock exam will help you develop the exam stamina you will need to keep going for three hours.

Managing your time

Planning and time management are two of the key skills which complement the technical knowledge you need to succeed. To keep yourself on time, do not be afraid to jot down your target completion times for each question, perhaps next to the title of the question on the paper. As all the questions are **compulsory**, you do not have to spend time wondering which question to answer!

Doing the exam

Actually doing the exam is a personal experience. There is not a single **right way**. As long as you submit complete answers to all questions after the three hours are up, then your approach obviously works.

Looking through the paper

Section A has 20 MCQs. This is the section of the paper where the examiner can test knowledge across the breadth of the syllabus. Make sure you read these questions carefully. The distractors are designed to present plausible, but incorrect, answers. Don't let them mislead you. If you really have no idea – guess. You may even be right.

Section has three longer questions:

- Question 1 is on **group accounts**. This time it requires calculation of goodwill and a consolidated statement of profit or loss. You have to deal with contingent consideration and unrealised profit.
- Question 2 is an **interpretation of financial statements** question. You have been given the ratios. The marks are all for your analysis.
- Question 3 is a single entity statement of profit or loss and other comprehensive income, statement of changes in equity and statement of financial position. This includes a construction contract, a finance lease, deferred tax and a financial instrument.

Allocating your time

BPP's advice is to always allocate your time **according to the marks for the question**. However, **use common sense**. If you're doing a question but haven't a clue how to do part (b), you might be better off re-allocating your time and getting more marks on another question, where you can add something you didn't have time for earlier on. Make sure you leave time to recheck the MCQs and make sure you have answered them all.

SECTION A

1   A   When prices are rising, the historical cost of inventory will be less than the cost of replacing it, giving rise to an understatement of operating costs and overstatement of profits. Where non-current assets are held at cost, they may have fallen significantly below replacement cost, leading to an understatement of the value of capital employed.

2   B   The receivables have been factored 'with recourse', so Laidlaw still bears the risks and rewards. A and D assume the receivables have been factored 'without recourse'. C is not correct because the substance of the transaction is a secured loan.

3   B   Gearing and interest cover will give the bank the most information regarding whether this client will be able to make repayments on a loan. A and C will be monitored by management, D will be of interest to shareholders.

4   B   Capital employed (assets) would increase, causing ROCE to decrease and debt (amounts due under finance leases) would increase, thereby increasing gearing.

5   C

	$
Unwinding of discount (24,240,000* × 12%)	2,908,800
Depreciation (24,240,000/8)	3,030,000
	5,938,800

* 60 million × 0.404 = 24,240,000

6   B

	$'000
Cash (80% × 3 million × $1.20)	2,880
Shares (80% × 3 million × 2 × $1.50)	7,200
	10,080

7   D   This is treated as negative goodwill arising from a bargain purchase and recognised as a gain in profit or loss.

8   C   This does not qualify as a discontinued operation, so A and B are incorrect, but a restructuring provision should be made. It is not a discontinued operation because it does not represent withdrawal from either a major line of business or a geographical area of operations.

9   D   The provision for inventory obsolescence and a change in useful life are both arrived at using estimates. Correction of a material error and a change in inventory valuation will both be accounted for retrospectively.

10   C

	$
Balance 1 January 20X1	50,000
Depreciation (45,000 × 2/5)	(18,000)
Balance 1 January 20X3	32,000
Upgrade	15,000
	47,000
Depreciation (42,000 / 5)	(8,400)
Balance 1 January 20X4	38,600
Proceeds	(7,000)
Loss on disposal	31,600

11   C

	$
Purchase price	780
Import duty	117
Site preparation	30
Installation	28
Testing	10
Dismantling	40
	1,005

| 12 | C | Import duties are included in the cost of inventory. The other expenses are included in distribution or administrative costs. |

13	B		$
		Costs to date	720
		Less loss (900 − (720 + 480))	(300)
			420
		Less billings	(400)
		Due from customer	20

14	A		$'000
		30,000 × $6.50	195,000
		Transaction costs	2,000
			197,000

Note that because the shares are held at fair value through other comprehensive income the transaction costs are added to fair value in the statement of financial position.

15	C		$'000
		Unadjusted profit	1,800
		Irrecoverable debt	(116)
		Loss on sale of inventory	(20)
			1,664

| 16 | B | A restructuring provision must **not** include the costs of retraining or relocating staff. |

| 17 | D | No sale has taken place as control of the goods has not been transferred, but Cambridge must show that it is holding $90,000 which belongs to Circus. |

18	C		$	$
		Consideration		200,000
		NCI		82,800
		Net assets:		
		Shares	100,000	
		Retained earnings	156,000	256,000
		Goodwill		26,800
		Phantom		275,000
		Ghost:		
		(177 − 156) × 70%		14,700
		Goodwill impairment (26,800 / 2) × 70%		(9,380)
		Group retained earnings		280,320

| 19 | B | ($160,000 / 4) × 25% × 30% = $3,000 |

20	D		$'000
		Difference b/f	850
		Additional difference (500 − 450)	50
		Revaluation surplus	250
			1,150
		× 30%	345

SECTION B

1 Polestar

Top tips. As always, pay close attention to dates. In this case Southstar is a mid-year acquisition, so profit or loss will need to be apportioned.

Easy marks. There were not any major technical difficulties in this question. The negative goodwill was flagged in the question, so it was only necessary to know how to deal with it. There were plenty of marks available for the goodwill calculation.

(a) Goodwill on acquisition

	$'000	$'000
Consideration transferred:		
Cash		13,500
Contingent consideration		1,800
		15,300
Non-controlling interest at fair value		3,600
		18,900
Fair value of net assets:		
Share capital	6,000	
Retained earnings at 30.9.X3	12,000	
Add back post-acquisition losses (4,600 × 6/12)	2,300	
Fair value adjustment on property	2,000	
		(22,300)
Negative goodwill		(3,400)

(b) CONSOLIDATED STATEMENT OF PROFIT OR LOSS FOR THE YEAR ENDED 30 SEPTEMBER 20X3

	$'000
Revenue (110,000 + (66,000 × 6/12) – 13,000(W2))	130,000
Cost of sales (W1)	(109,300)
Gross profit	20,700
Distribution costs (W1)	(4,000)
Administrative expenses (W1)	(2,950)
Finance costs	(250)
Profit before tax	13,500
Income tax (3,500,- 500)	(3,000)
Profit for the year	13,500
Profit attributable to:	
Owners of Polestar (β)	14,250
Non-controlling interest (W3)	(750)
	13,500

Workings

1   *Expenses*

	Cost of sales $'000	Distribution costs $'000	Administrative expenses $'000
Polestar	88,000	3,000	5,250
Southstar × 6/12	33,600	1,000	1,200
Intragroup (W2)	(13,000)		
PURP (W2)	600		
Depreciation on FVA (20,00 / 10 × 6/12)	100		
Adj contingent consideration (1.8 – 1.5)			(300)
Negative goodwill (W2)			(3,400)
Loss on investments			200
	109,300	4,000	2,950

2   *Intragroup trading*

	$'000	$'000
Polestar sales to Southstar		4,000
Southstar sales to Polestar		9,000
		13,000
DR Revenue	13,000	
CR Cost of sales		13,000

Unrealised profit = 9,000 – 5,400 = 3,600
Still in inventory = 3,600 × 1.5 / 9 = 600

	$'000	$'000
DR Cost of sales (Southstar)	600	
CR Group inventory		600

3   *Non-controlling interest*

	$'000
Post-acquisition loss ((4,600) × 6/12)	(2,300)
Depreciation on FVA (W1)	(100)
PURP (W2)	(600)
	(3,000)
× 25%	(750)

2 Harbin

Marking scheme

	Marks
Ratios	3
Consideration of Chief Executive's report	3
Impact of purchase	6
Remaining issues -½ mark per valid point	3
	15

It is clear that the acquisition of Fatima has had a very positive impact on Harbin's results for the year ended 30 September 20X7. For this reason it is instructive to look at the 20X7 ratios which have been affected by the acquisition and see what they would have been without the addition of Fatima's results. The additional ratios are at the end of this report.

Profitability

It is immediately apparent that without the purchase of Fatima the Chief Executive's report would have looked very different. The increase in sales revenue of 39% would have disappeared. The sales revenue of Harbin is static. The increase in gross profit margin from 16.7% to 20% would have been a fall to 11.1%. The profit for the period would not have doubled. It would have gone from an $8m profit before tax in 20X6 to a $2m profit before tax in 20X7, assuming that the loan note interest would not have arisen. This would have given an ROCE of 2.05% for 20X7 rather than the 11.2% when Fatima is included. If we break ROCE down into net profit% and asset turnover, we can see that Fatima's results have increased the net profit% by almost six times, while having an adverse effect on the asset turnover due to the $100m funding through loan notes. There is some distortion in the 20X7 figures arising from interest charges which are not deducted in calculating ROCE but have been deducted in arriving at net profit.

Liquidity

While it has greatly enhanced Harbin's profitability, the purchase of Fatima has done little for liquidity, an aspect not touched on in the extract from the Chief Executive's report. Harbin borrowed $100m to pay for Fatima, so the purchase was not funded from working capital. However, it has paid $8m loan note interest, increased its inventory holding by $10m, invested in additional property, plant and equipment and paid a $10m dividend. In this way it has, despite the increased profit, converted a positive cash balance of $14m to an overdraft of $17m. The ratios show this very clearly. Harbin's current ratio has declined from 2.5:1 to 0.86:1 and its quick ratio (not shown above) has declined from 1.47:1 to 0.30:1, casting some doubt upon whether it will be able to continue to meet its commitments as they fall due.

The increase in the inventory holding period is worrying, as it suggests that Harbin may have inventory which is slow-moving, and the increase in the payables period by ten days suggests problems paying suppliers. Harbin has a $4m tax bill outstanding. If this is not paid on time it will incur interest, which will further weaken the cash position.

Gearing

The cost of acquiring Fatima is directly reflected in the gearing ratio, which has gone from nil in 20X6 to 46.7% in 20X7, with the issue of the loan notes. This will reduce profits available for distribution to shareholders in the future and if Harbin's cash position does not improve it may be forced to seek further loans. In the light of this, the increase of 25% in the dividend is hard to justify.

Appendix – ratios adjusted for purchase of Fatima

	With Fatima 20X7	Without Fatima 20X7
Return on year-end capital employed	11.2%	
24,000* – 22,000/ 114,000 – (22,000 – 5.500**)		2.05%
(profit before interest and tax over total assets less current liabilities)		
Net asset (equal to capital employed) turnover	1.17	
250,000 – 70,000 / 114,000 – (22,000 – 5,500)		1.85
Net profit (before tax) margin	6.4%	
24,000 – 22,000 / 250,000 – 70,000		1.1%

* Without the acquisition of Fatima the finance costs of $8,000 would not be incurred.

** $5,500 = 25% tax

3 Moby

> **Top tips.** The issues to deal with here were the contract with performance obligations satisfied over time, the revaluation and the deferred tax. None of these were complicated, but make sure you know how to calculate contract assets/liabilities and how to deal with deferred tax on a revaluation.
>
> **Easy marks.** There were quite a few marks for items which only had to be lifted from the trial balance, so it was important to get the proformas down and collect those marks. The lease and the loan note were both simple and worth several marks.

Marking scheme

			Marks
(a)	Statement of profit or loss and other comprehensive income		
	Revenue	1½	
	Cost of sales	3	
	Distribution costs	½	
	Administrative expenses	1	
	Finance costs	2	
	Income tax expense	2	
	Gain on revaluation	1	
	Deferred tax on gain	1	
			12
(b)	Statement of changes in equity		
	Opening balances	1	
	Share issue	2	
	Dividend	1	
	Total comprehensive income	1	
	Closing balances	1	
			6
(c)	Statement of financial position		
	Property, plant and equipment	2½	
	Inventory	½	
	Contract asset	1½	
	Trade receivables	½	
	Revaluation surplus	1	
	Retained earnings	½	
	Non-current lease obligation	1	
	Deferred tax	1	
	Loan note	1	
	Current lease obligation	½	
	Bank overdraft	½	
	Trade payables	½	
	Current tax payable	1	
			12
			30

(a) STATEMENT OF PROFIT OR LOSS AND OTHER COMPREHENSIVE INCOME FOR THE YEAR ENDED 30 SEPTEMBER 20X3

	$'000
Revenue (227,800 + 10,000 (W3))	237,800
Cost of sales (164,500 + 8,000 (W1) + 15,400 (W1))	(187,900)
Gross profit	49,900
Distribution costs	(13,500)
Administrative expenses (16,500 – 150)	(16,350)
Finance costs (900 + 4,000 (W5) + 2,930 (W6))	(7,830)
Profit before tax	12,220
Income tax expense (W4)	(350)
Profit for the year	11,870
Other comprehensive income:	
Gain on revaluation of land and buildings (W2)	4,400
Deferred tax on gain (W4)	(1,100)
Total other comprehensive income	3,300
Total comprehensive income for the year	15,170

(b) STATEMENT OF CHANGES IN EQUITY FOR THE YEAR ENDED 30 SEPTEMBER 20X3

	Share capital $'000	Share premium $'000	Retained earnings $'000	Revaluation surplus $'000	Total $'000
Balance at 1 October 20X2	45,000	–	19,800	–	64,800
Share issue	800	3,200			4,000
Dividend paid			(2,000)		(2,000)
Total comprehensive income	–	–	11,870	3,300	15,170
Balance at 30 September 20X3	45,800	3,200	29,670	3,300	81,970

(c) STATEMENT OF FINANCIAL POSITION AS AT 30 SEPTEMBER 20X3

	$'000	$'000
ASSETS		
Non-current assets		
Property, plant and equipment (W2)		115,000
Current assets		
Inventory	26,600	
Receivables	38,500	
Contract asset (W3)	6,000	
		71,100
		186,100

EQUITY AND LIABILITIES			$'000
Equity			
Share capital			45,800
Share premium			3,200
Revaluation surplus (OCI)			3,300
Retained earnings			29,670
			81,970
Non-current liabilities			
Loan note (W5)		44,000	
Deferred tax (W4)		7,100	
Amount due under finance lease (W6)		16,133	
			67,233
Current liabilities			
Trade payables		21,300	
Income tax payable		3,400	
Amount due under finance lease (W6)		6,897	
Overdraft		5,300	
			36,897
			186,100

Workings

1   *Expenses*

	Cost of sales	Distribution costs	Administrative expenses
	$'000	$'000	$'000
Per question	164,500	13,500	16,500
Contract (W3)	8,000		
Depreciation (W2) – building	2,400		
– owned plant	6,000		
– leased plant	7,000		
Insurance provision reversal			(150)
	187,900	13,500	16,350

2   *Property, plant and equipment*

	Land	Building	Plant	Leased plant	Total
	$'000	$'000	$'000	$'000	$'000
Cost 1.10.X2	12,000	48,000	65,700	35,000	160,700
Depreciation b/f		(10,000)	(17,700)	(7,000)	(34,700)
	12,000	38,000	48,000	28,000	126,000
Revaluation	4,000	400			4,400
	16,000	38,400	48,000	28,000	130,400
Depreciation:					
Building		(2,400)			(2,400)
Plant (48,000 × 12.5%)			(6,000)		(6,000)
Leased (35,000 / 5)				(7,000)	(7,000)
Balance 30.9.X3	16,000	36,000	42,000	19,000	113,000

3   *Contract with performance obligations satisfied over time*

	$'000
Revenue (work certified (10 / 25 = 40%)	10,000
Cost of sales ((14 + 6) × 40%)	(8,000)
Profit to date	2,000
Contract asset:	
Costs to date	14,000
Profit to date	2,000
Less invoiced to date	(10,000)
	6,000

4   *Income tax*

	$'000
Deferred tax balance:	
On taxable temporary difference (24m × 25%)	6,000
On revaluation (4,400 × 25%)	1,100
Liability at 30 September 20X3	7,100
Balance b/f at 1 October 20X2	8,000
Reduce balance by	900
Income tax charge:	
Provision for year	3,400
Prior year over-provision	(1,050)
Reduction in deferred tax balance	(900)
Deferred tax on revaluation debited to revaluation surplus	(1,100)
Charge for year	350

5   *Loan note*

	$'000
Proceeds	40,000
Interest 10%	4,000
Balance	44,000

6   *Leased plant*

	$'000
Cost 1.10.X1	35,000
Interest 10%	3,500
Instalment paid	(9,200)
Balance 30.9.X2	29,300
Interest 10%	2,930
Instalment paid	(9,200)
Balance 30.9.X3	23,030
Interest to 30.9.X4	2,303
Instalment payable	(9,200)
Balance 30.9.X4	16,133
Non-current balance	16,133
Current balance	6,897
	23,030

ACCA

Fundamentals Level

Paper F7

Financial Reporting

Mock Examination 3

Question Paper	
Time allowed	
Reading and Planning Writing	**15 minutes** **3 hours**
Answer all FIVE questions	

DO NOT OPEN THIS PAPER UNTIL YOU ARE READY TO START UNDER EXAMINATION CONDITIONS

Section A – ALL 20 question are compulsory and MUST be attempted

1   Which of the following items is a change of accounting policy under IAS 8 *Accounting policies, Changes in Accounting Estimates and Errors*?

    A   Classifying commission earned as revenue in the statement of profit or loss, having previously classified it as other operating income

    B   Switching to purchasing plant using finance leases from a previous policy of purchasing plant for cash

    C   Changing the value of a subsidiary's inventory in line with the group policy for inventory valuation when preparing the consolidated financial statements

    D   Revising the remaining useful life of a depreciable asset   **(2 marks)**

2   Aqua has correctly calculated its basic earnings per share (EPS) for the current year.

    Which of the following items need to be additionally considered when calculating the diluted EPS of Aqua for the year?

    (i)   A 1 for 5 rights issue of equity shares during the year at $1.20 when the market price of the equity shares was $2.00

    (ii)   The issue during the year of a convertible (to equity shares) loan note

    (iii)   The granting during the year of directors' share options exercisable in three years' time

    (iv)   Equity shares issued during the year as the purchase consideration for the acquisition of a new subsidiary company

    A   All four
    B   (i) and (ii) only
    C   (ii) and (iii) only
    D   (iii) and (iv) only   **(2 marks)**

3   Although most items in financial statements are shown at their historical cost, increasingly the IASB is requiring or allowing current cost can be used in many areas of financial reporting.

    Drexler acquired an item of plant on 1 October 20X2 at a cost of $500,000. It has an expected life of five years (straight line depreciation) and an estimated residual value of 10% of its historical cost or current cost as appropriate. As at 30 September 20X4, the manufacturer of the plant still makes the same item of plant and its current price is $600,000.

    What is the correct carrying amount to be shown in the statement of financial position of Drexler as at 30 September 20X4 under historical cost and current cost?

	Historical cost	Current cost
	$	$
A	320,000	600,000
B	320,000	384,000
C	300,000	600,000
D	300,000	384,000

    (2 marks)

4   Repro, a company which sells photocopying equipment, has prepared its draft financial statements for the year ended 30 September 20X4. It has included the following transactions in revenue at the stated amounts below.

Which of these has been correctly included in revenue according to IFRS 15 *Revenue from contracts with customers*?

A   Agency sales of $250,000 on which Repro is entitled to a commission

B   Sale proceeds of $20,000 for motor vehicles which were no longer required by Repro

C   Sales of $150,000 on 30 September 20X4. The amount invoiced to and received from the customer was $180,000, which included $30,000 for ongoing servicing work to be done by Repro over the next two years

D   Sales of $200,000 on 1 October 20X3 to an established customer which, (with the agreement of Repro), will be paid in full on 30 September 20X5. Repro has a cost of capital of 10%.

(2 marks)

5   Tynan's year end is 30 September 20X4 and the following potential liabilities have been identified:

(i)   The signing of a non-cancellable contract in September 20X4 to supply goods in the following year on which, due to a pricing error, a loss will be made

(ii)   The cost of a reorganisation which was approved by the board in August 20X4 but has not yet been implemented, communicated to interested parties or announced publicly

(iii)   An amount of deferred tax relating to the gain on the revaluation of a property during the current year. Tynan has no intention of selling the property in the foreseeable future.

(iv)   The balance on the warranty provision which related to products for which there are no outstanding claims and whose warranties had expired by 30 September 20X4

Which of the above should Tynan recognise as liabilities as at 30 September 20X4?

A   All four
B   (i) and (ii) only
C   (i) and (iii) only
D   (iii) and (iv) only

(2 marks)

6   Yling entered into a contract in respect of which performance obligations are satisfied over time on 1 January 20X4. The contract is expected to last 24 months. The price which has been agreed for the contract is $5 million. At 30 September 20X4 the costs incurred on the contract were $1.6 million and the estimated remaining costs to complete were $2.4 million. On 20 September 20X4 Yling received a payment from the customer of $1.8 million which was equal to the total of the amounts invoiced. Yling calculates the stage of completion of its performance obligations on contracts on the basis of amounts invoiced to the contract price.

What amount would be reported in Yling's statement of financial position as at 30 September 20X4 as the contract asset arising from the above contract?

A   Nil
B $160,000
C $800,000
D $200,000

(2 marks)

7   Recognition is the process of including within the financial statements items which meet the definition of an element according to the IASB's *Conceptual Framework for Financial Reporting*.

Which of the following items should be recognised as an asset in the statement of financial position of a company?

A   A skilled and efficient workforce which has been very expensive to train. Some of these staff are still in the employment of the company.

B   A highly lucrative contract signed during the year which is due to commence shortly after the year end

C   A government grant relating to the purchase of an item of plant several years ago, which has a remaining life of four years

D   A receivable from a customer which has been sold (factored) to a finance company. The finance company has full recourse to the company for any losses.   **(2 marks)**

8   On 30 September 20X4 Razor's closing inventory was counted and valued at its cost of $1 million. Some items of inventory which had cost $210,000 had been damaged in a flood (on 15 September 20X4) and are not expected to achieve their normal selling price which is calculated to achieve a gross profit margin of 30%. The sale of these goods will be handled by an agent who sells them at 80% of the normal selling price and charges Razor a commission of 25%.

At what value will the closing inventory of Razor be reported in its statement of financial position as at 30 September 20X4?

A $1 million
B $790,000
C $180,000
D $970,000   **(2 marks)**

9   The following information is available for the property, plant and equipment of Fry as at 30 September:

	20X4	20X3
	$'000	$'000
Carrying amounts	23,400	14,400

The following items were recorded during the year ended 30 September 20X4:

(i)   Depreciation charge of $2.5 million

(ii) An item of plant with a carrying amount of $3 million was sold for $1.8 million

(iii) A property was revalued upwards by $2 million

(iv) Environmental provisions of $4 million relating to property, plant and equipment were capitalised during the year

What amount would be shown in Fry's statement of cash flows for purchase of property, plant and equipment for the year ended 30 September 20X4?

A $8.5 million
B $12.5 million
C $7.3 million
D $10.5 million   **(2 marks)**

10 Petre owns 100% of the share capital of the following companies. The directors are unsure of whether the investments should be consolidated.

In which of the following circumstances would the investment NOT be consolidated?

A Petre has decided to sell its investment in Alpha as it is loss-making; the directors believe its exclusion from consolidation would assist users in predicting the group's future profits

B Beta is a bank and its activity is so different from the engineering activities of the rest of the group that it would be meaningless to consolidate it

C Delta is located in a country where local accounting standards are compulsory and these are not compatible with IFRS used by the rest of the group

D Gamma is located in a country where a military coup has taken place and Petre has lost control of the investment for the foreseeable future

(2 marks)

---

11 On 1 October 20X3 Bertrand issued $10 million convertible loan notes which carry a nominal interest (coupon) rate of 5% per annum. The loan notes are redeemable on 30 September 20X6 at par for cash or can be exchanged for equity shares. A similar loan note without the conversion option would have required Bertrand to pay an interest rate of 8%.

The present value of $1 receivable at the end of each year based on discount rates of 5% and 8% can be taken as:

		5%	8%
End of year	1	0.95	0.93
	2	0.91	0.86
	3	0.86	0.79

How would the convertible loan note appear in Bertrand's statement of financial position on initial recognition   (1 October 20X3)?

	Equity	Non-current liability
	$'000	$'000
A	810	9,190
B	Nil	10,000
C	10,000	Nil
D	40	9,960

(2 marks)

---

12 The net assets of Fyngle, a cash generating unit (CGU) are:

	$
Property, plant and equipment	200,000
Allocated goodwill	50,000
Product patent	20,000
Net current assets (at net realisable value)	30,000
	300,000

As a result of adverse publicity, Fyngle has a recoverable amount of only $200,000.

What would be the value of Fyngle's property, plant and equipment after the allocation of the impairment loss?

A $154,545
B $170,000
C $160,000
D $133,333

(2 marks)

13. Many commentators believe that the trend of earnings per share (EPS) is a more reliable indicator of underlying performance than the trend of net profit for the year.

Which of the following statements supports this view?

A   Net profit can be manipulated by the choice of accounting policies but EPS cannot be manipulated in this way

B   EPS takes into account the additional resources made available to earn profit when new shares are issued for cash, whereas net profit does not

C   The disclosure of a diluted EPS figure is a forecast of the future trend of profit

D   The comparative EPS is restated where a change of accounting policy affects the previous year's profits

(2 marks)

14. As at 30 September 20X3 Dune's property in its statement of financial position was:

Property at cost (useful life 15 years)	$45 million
Accumulated depreciation	$6 million

On 1 April 20X4 Dune decided to sell the property. The property is being marketed by a property agent at a price of $42 million, which was considered a reasonably achievable price at that date. The expected costs to sell have been agreed at $1 million. Recent market transactions suggest that actual selling prices achieved for this type of property in the current market conditions are 10% less than the price at which they are marketed.

At 30 September 20X4 the property has not been sold.

At what amount should the property be reported in Dune's statement of financial position as at 30 September 20X4?

A $36 million
B $37.5 million
C $36.8 million
D $42 million

(2 marks)

15. Which of the following statements about a not-for-profit entity is valid?

A   There is no requirement to calculate an earnings per share figure as it is not likely to have shareholders who need to assess its earnings performance.

B   The current value of its property, plant and equipment is not relevant as it is not a commercial entity.

C   Interpretation of its financial performance using ratio analysis is meaningless.

D   Its financial statements will not be closely scrutinised as it does not have any investors.   **(2 marks)**

16. Tazer, a parent company, acquired Lowdown, an unincorporated entity, for $2.8 million. A fair value exercise performed on Lowdown's net assets at the date of purchase showed:

	$'000
Property, plant and equipment	3,000
Identifiable intangible asset	500
Inventory	300
Trade receivables less payables	200
	4,000

How should the purchase of Lowdown be reflected in Tazer's consolidated statement of financial position?

A   Record the net assets at their values shown above and credit profit or loss with $1.2 million

B   Record the net assets at their values shown above and credit Tazer's consolidated goodwill with $1.2 million

C   Write off the intangible asset ($500,000), record the remaining net assets at their values shown above and credit profit or loss with $700,000

D   Record the purchase as a financial asset investment at $2.8 million   **(2 marks)**

17 On 1 October 20X3 Xplorer commenced drilling for oil from an undersea oilfield. The extraction of oil causes damage to the seabed which has a restorative cost (ignore discounting) of $10,000 per million barrels of oil extracted. Xplorer extracted 250 million barrels in the year ended 30 September 20X4.

Xplorer is also required to dismantle the drilling equipment at the end of its five year licence. This has an estimated cost of $30 million on 30 September 20X8. Xplorer's cost of capital is 8% per annum and $1 has a present value of 68 cents in five years' time.

What is the total provision (extraction plus dismantling) which Xplorer would report in its statement of financial position as at 30 September 20X4 in respect of its oil operations?

A $34,900,000
B $24,532,000
C $22,900,000
D $4,132,000 (2 marks)

18 Which of the following is NOT an indicator of impairment under IAS 36 *Impairment of Assets*?

A Advances in the technological environment in which an asset is employed have an adverse impact on its future use

B An increase in interest rates which increases the discount rate an entity uses

C The carrying amount of an entity's net assets is lower than the entity's number of shares in issue multiplied by its share price

D The estimated net realisable value of inventory has been reduced due to fire damage although this value is greater than its carrying amount (2 marks)

19 During the year ended 30 September 20X4 Hyper entered into two lease transactions:

On 1 October 20X3 a payment of $90,000, being the first of five equal annual payments of a finance lease for an item of plant. The lease has an implicit interest rate of 10% and the fair value (cost to purchase) of the leased equipment on 1 October 20X3 was $340,000

On 1 January 20X4 a payment of $18,000 for a one-year lease of an item of excavation equipment.

What amount in total would be charged to Hyper's statement of profit or loss for the year ended 30 September 20X4 in respect of the above transactions?

A $108,000
B $111,000
C $106,500
D $115,500 (2 marks)

20 Comparability is identified as an enhancing qualitative characteristic in the IASB's *Conceptual Framework for Financial Reporting*.

Which of the following does NOT improve comparability?

A Restating the financial statements of previous years when there has been a change of accounting policy

B Prohibiting changes of accounting policy unless required by an IFRS or to give more relevant and reliable information

C Disclosing discontinued operations in financial statements

D Applying an entity's current accounting policy to a transaction which an entity has not engaged in before (2 marks)

(40 marks)

Section B – ALL 3 questions are compulsory and MUST be attempted

1   Xpand is a publicly listed company which has experienced rapid growth in recent years through the acquisition and integration of other companies. Xpand is interested in acquiring Hydan, a retailing company, which is one of several companies owned and managed by the same family.

The summarised financial statements of Hydan for the year ended 30 September 20X4 are:

STATEMENT OF PROFIT OR LOSS

	$'000
Revenue	70,000
Cost of sales	(45,000)
Gross profit	25,000
Operating costs	(7,000)
Directors' salaries	(1,000)
Profit before taxation	17,000
Income tax expense	(3,000)
Profit for the year	14,000

STATEMENT OF FINANCIAL POSITION

	$'000	$'000
ASSETS		
Non-current assets		
Property, plant and equipment		32,400
Current assets		
Inventory	7,500	
Bank	100	
		7,600
Total assets		40,000
EQUITY AND LIABILITIES		
Equity		
Equity shares of $1 each		1,000
Retained earnings		18,700
		19,700
Non-current liabilities		
Directors' loan accounts (interest free)		10,000
Current liabilities		
Trade payables	7,500	
Current tax payable	2,800	
		10,300
Total equity and liabilities		40,000

From the above financial statements Xpand has calculated for Hydan the ratios below for the year ended 30 September 20X4. It has also obtained the equivalent ratios for the retail sector average which can be taken to represent Hydan's sector.

	Hydan	Sector average
Return on equity (ROE) (including directors' loan accounts)	47.1%	22.0%
Net asset turnover	2.36 times	1.67 times
Gross profit margin	35.7%	30.0%
Net profit margin	20.0%	12.0%

From enquiries made, Xpand has learned the following information:

(i) Hydan buys all of its trading inventory from another of the family companies at a price which is 10% less than the market price for such goods.

(ii) After the acquisition, Xpand would replace the existing board of directors and need to pay remuneration of $2·5 million per annum.

(iii) The directors' loan accounts would be repaid by obtaining a loan of the same amount with interest at 10% per annum.

(iv) Xpand expects the purchase price of Hydan to be $30 million.

Required

(a) Recalculate the ratios for Hydan after making appropriate adjustments to the financial statements for notes (i) to (iv) above. For this purpose, the expected purchase price of $30 million should be taken as Hydan's equity and net assets are equal to this equity plus the loan.

(b) In relation to the ratios calculated in (a) above, and the ratios for Hydan given in the question, comment on the performance of Hydan compared to its retail sector average. **15 marks)**

2   After preparing a draft statement of profit or loss for the year ended 30 September 20X4 and adding the
     year's profit (before any adjustments required by notes (i) to (iii) below) to retained earnings, the
     summarised trial balance of Kandy as at 30 September 20X4 is:

	$'000	$'000
Equity shares of $1 each		40,000
Retained earnings as at 30 September 20X4		17,500
Proceeds of 6% loan (note (i))		30,000
Land ($5 million) and buildings – at cost (note (ii))	55,000	
Plant and equipment – at cost (note (ii))	58,500	
Accumulated depreciation at 1 October 20X3: buildings		20,000
plant and equipment		34,500
Current assets	68,700	
Current liabilities		38,400
Deferred tax (note (iii))		2,500
Interest payment (note (i))	1,800	
Current tax (note (iii))		1,100
	184,000	184,000

The following notes are relevant:

(i)   The loan note was issued on 1 October 20X3 and incurred issue costs of $1 million which were
       charged to profit or loss. Interest of $1·8 million ($30 million at 6%) was paid on 30 September
       20X4. The loan is redeemable on 30 September 20X8 at a substantial premium which gives an
       effective interest rate of 9% per annum. No other repayments are due until 30 September 20X8.

(ii)   Non-current assets:

       The price of property has increased significantly in recent years and on 1 October 20X3, the directors
       decided to revalue the land and buildings. The directors accepted the report of an independent
       surveyor who valued the land at $8 million and the buildings at $39 million on that date. The
       remaining life of the buildings at 1 October 20X3 was 15 years. Kandy does not make an annual
       transfer to retained profits to reflect the realisation of the revaluation gain; however, the revaluation
       will give rise to a deferred tax liability. The income tax rate of Kandy is 20%.

       Plant and equipment is depreciated at 12½% per annum using the reducing balance method.

       No depreciation has yet been charged on any non-current asset for the year ended 30 September
       20X4.

(iii) A provision of $2·4 million is required for current income tax on the profit of the year to 30
       September 20X4.

       The balance on current tax in the trial balance is the under/over provision of tax for the previous year.
       In addition to the temporary differences relating to the information in note (ii), Kandy has further
       taxable temporary differences of $10 million as at 30 September 20X4.

Required

(a)   Prepare a schedule of adjustments required to the retained earnings of Kandy as at 30 September
       20X4 as a result of the information in notes (i) to (iii) above.   **(6 marks)**

(b)   Prepare the statement of financial position of Kandy as at 30 September 20X4.   **(9 marks)**

       The notes to the statement of financial position are not required.

                                                                                                          (15 marks)

3   On 1 January 20X4, Plastik acquired 80% of the equity share capital of Subtrak. The consideration was
     satisfied by a share exchange of two shares in Plastik for every three acquired shares in Subtrak. At the date
     of acquisition, shares in Plastik and Subtrak had a market value of $3 and $2·50 each respectively. Plastik
     will also pay cash consideration of 27·5 cents on 1 January 20X5 for each acquired share in Subtrak. Plastik
     has a cost of capital of 10% per annum. None of the consideration has been recorded by Plastik.

     Below are the summarised draft financial statements of both companies.

STATEMENTS OF PROFIT OR LOSS AND OTHER COMPREHENSIVE INCOME FOR THE YEAR ENDED 30
SEPTEMBER 20X4

	Plastik $'000	Subtrak $'000
Revenue	62,600	30,000
Cost of sales	(45,800)	(24,000)
Gross profit	16,800	6,000
Distribution costs	(2,000)	(1,200)
Administrative expenses	(3,500)	(1,800)
Finance costs	(200)	–
Profit before tax	11,100	3,000
Income tax expense	(3,100)	(1,000)
Profit for the year	8,000	2,000
Other comprehensive income:		
Gain on revaluation of property	1,500	–
Total comprehensive income	9,500	2,000

STATEMENTS OF FINANCIAL POSITION AS AT 30 SEPTEMBER 20X4

	Plastik $'000	Subtrak $'000
ASSETS		
Non-current assets		
Property, plant and equipment	18,700	13,900
Investments: 10% loan note from Subtrak (note(ii))	1,000	-
	19,700	13,900
Current assets		
Inventory (note(iii))	4,300	1,200
Trade receivables (note(iv))	4,700	2,500
Bank	-	300
	9,000	4,000
Total assets	28,700	28,700
EQUITY AND LIABILITIES		
Equity		
Equity shares of $1 each	10,000	9,000
Revaluation surplus (note(i))	2,000	-
Retained earnings	6,300	3,500
	18,300	12,500
Non-current liabilities		
10% loan notes (note(ii))	2,500	1,000
Current liabilities		
Trade payables (note(iv))	3,400	3,600
Bank	1,700	-
Current tax payable	2,800	800
	7,900	4,400
Total equity and liabilities	28,700	28,700

The following information is relevant:

(i) At the date of acquisition, the fair values of Subtrak's assets and liabilities were equal to their carrying amounts with the exception of Subtrak's property which had a fair value of $4 million above its carrying amount. For consolidation purposes, this led to an increase in depreciation charges (in cost of sales) of $100,000 in the post-acquisition period to 30 September 20X4. Subtrak has not incorporated the fair value property increase into its entity financial statements.

The policy of the Plastik group is to revalue all properties to fair value at each year end. On 30 September 20X4, the increase in Plastik's property has already been recorded, however, a further increase of $600,000 in the value of Subtrak's property since its value at acquisition and 30 September 2014 has not been recorded.

(ii) On 30 September 20X4, Plastik accepted a $1 million 10% loan note from Subtrak.

(iii) Sales from Plastik to Subtrak throughout the year ended 30 September 20X4 had consistently been $300,000 per month. Plastik made a mark-up on cost of 25% on all these sales. $600,000 (at cost to Subtrak) of Subtrak's inventory at 30 September 20X4 had been supplied by Plastik in the post-acquisition period.

(iv) Plastik had a trade receivable balance owing from Subtrak of $1·2 million as at 30 September 20X4. This differed to the equivalent trade payable of Subtrak due to a payment by Subtrak of $400,000 made in September 20X4 which did not clear Plastik's bank account until 4 October 20X4. Plastik's policy for cash timing differences is to adjust the parent's financial statements.

(v) Plastik's policy is to value the non-controlling interest at fair value at the date of acquisition. For this purpose Subtrak's share price at that date can be deemed to be representative of the fair value of the shares held by the non-controlling interest.

(vi) Due to recent adverse publicity concerning one of Subtrak's major product lines, the goodwill which arose on the acquisition of Subtrak has been impaired by $500,000 as at 30 September 20X4. Goodwill impairment should be treated as an administrative expense.

(vii) Assume, except where indicated otherwise, that all items of income and expenditure accrue evenly throughout the year.

Required

(a) Prepare the consolidated statement of profit or loss and other comprehensive income for Plastik for the year ended 30 September 20X4. **(10 marks)**

(b) Prepare the consolidated statement of financial position for Plastik as at 30 September 20X4.
(17 marks)

(c) Plastik is in the process of recording the acquisition of another subsidiary, Dilemma, and has identified two items when reviewing the fair values of Dilemma's assets.

The first item relates to $1 million spent on a new research project. This amount has been correctly charged to profit or loss by Dilemma, but the directors of Plastik have reliably assessed the fair value of this research to be $1·2million.

The second item relates to the customers of Dilemma. The directors of Plastik believe Dilemma has a particularly strong list of reputable customers which could be 'sold' to other companies and have assessed the fair value of the customer list at $3 million.

Required

State whether (and if so, at what value) the two items should be recognised in the consolidated statement of financial position of Plastik on the acquisition of Dilemma. **(3 marks)**

(30 marks)

Answers

DO NOT TURN THIS PAGE UNTIL YOU HAVE
COMPLETED THE MOCK EXAM

A plan of attack

What's the worst thing you could be doing right now if this was the actual exam paper? Sharpening your pencil? Wondering how to celebrate the end of the exam in about three-hours' time? Panicking, flapping and generally getting in a right old state?

Well, they're all pretty bad, so turn back to the paper and let's sort out a **plan of attack**!

First things first

You have fifteen minutes of reading time. This paper is the examiners specimen paper, so it is the best indication of what you will see in your exam. Read it carefully.

The F7 paper has 20 MCQs and three compulsory questions. Therefore, you do not have to spend your 15 minutes reading time working out which questions to answer. So you can use it to read the paper and get some idea of what you need to do. At this stage you can make notes on the question paper but not in the answer book. So scribble down anything you feel you might otherwise forget.

It's a good idea to just start with the MCQs. Once you have them done, you will feel more relaxed. Leave any that you are unsure of and come back to them later but don't leave any unanswered.

In Section B:

Question 1 is an interpretation of accounts question. Here you are given the ratios and asked to adjust them. Remember you do not get marks for simply saying that a ratio went up or down. It is your job to look at why this happened.

Question 2 requires you to adjust retained earnings and prepare a statement of financial position. There is nothing difficult here but you need to work methodically.

Question 3 is a consolidated financial statements preparation question. The adjustments you have to deal with are unrealised profit, a property revaluation and intragroup balances. Set the formats out and then tackle the workings. Make it very clear to the marker which workings belong to which statement and cross-reference them.

You've got spare time at the end of the exam.....?

If you have allocated your time properly then you **shouldn't have time on your hands** at the end of the exam and you should start by checking the MCQs to make sure you have left none unanswered. But if you find yourself with five or ten minutes to spare, check over your work to make sure that there are no silly arithmetical errors.

Forget about it!

And don't worry if you found the paper difficult. More than likely other candidates will too. If this were the real thing you would need to **forget** the exam the minute you leave the exam hall and **think about the next one**. Or, if it's the last one, **celebrate**!

SECTION A

1   A   This is a change in presentation so qualifies as a change in accounting policy.

2   C   The convertible loan note and the share options should be taken into account when calculating diluted EPS.

3   B

	Historical cost $'000	Current cost $'000
Cost/valuation	500	600
Depreciation ((500,000 × 90%) /5) × 2	(180)	
Depreciation ((600,000 × 90%) /5) × 2		(216)
Carrying amount	320	384

4   C   The amount to recognise in revenue is $150,000 as the servicing amount of $30,000 has not yet been earned. This would be recognised as deferred income.

5   C   (i) and (iii) only. The reorganisation does not meet the criteria for a provision and a provision is no longer needed for the warranties.

6   B   Expected profit = ($5m – ($2.4m + $1.6m) = $1m
Profit to date = ($1m × (1.8m/5)) = $0.36m
Contract asset:

	$'000
Costs to date	1,600
Profit to date	360
Less amounts invoiced	(1,800)
	160

7   D   The receivable has been factored with recourse so should continue to be recognised as an asset. The other options do not meet the criteria to be recognised as an asset.

8   D   Normal selling price = (210k × 100/70) = 300k

The fall in value will be:

	$'000
Original cost	210
Actual selling price (300 × 80% × 75%)	(180)
	30

Therefore, closing inventory will be valued at $970,000 (1m – 30,000).

9   A

	$'000
Carrying amount 20X3	14,400
Depreciation	(2,500)
Sale of plant	(3,000)
Revaluation	2,000
Environmental provision	4,000
	14,900
Purchases (β)	8,500
	23,400

10 D   Consolidation is not appropriate in this case as the parent has lost control.

11 A

	$'000
Interest years 1-3 (10m × 5% × 2.58)	1,290
Redemption (10m × 0.79)	7,900
Non-current liability	9,190
Equity (β)	810
	10,000

12 A

	Net assets prior to impairment	Impairment	Impaired net assets
	$	$	$
PPE	200,000	(45,455)	154,545
Goodwill	50,000	(50,000)	-
Patent	20,000	(4,545)	15,455
Net current assets	30,000	–	30,000
	300,000	(100,000)	200,000

Goodwill is written off in full and the balance of the loss is pro-rated between PPE and the patent.

13 B EPS takes into account the additional resources made available to earn profit when new shares are issued for cash, whereas net profit does not.

14 C Selling price × 90% minus selling costs.

15 A The objectives of a not-for-profit entity do not include making a profit so it would not calculate earnings per share or report to shareholders.

16 A This combination results in negative goodwill of $1.2 million which should be credited to profit or loss.

17 B

	$'000
Restoration of seabed (10,000 × 250)	2,500
Dismantling of equipment (30m × 0.68)	20,400
Unwinding of discount (20,400 × 8%)	1,632
	24,532

18 D If the NRV of inventory is greater than its carrying amount, no impairment has arisen.

19 C

	$
Finance lease interest ((340,000 -90,000) × 10%)	25,000
Plant depreciation (340,000 / 5)	68,000
Operating lease (18,000 × 9/12)	13,500
Total charge to profit or loss	106,500

20 D As the transaction has not been engaged in before, comparability is not an issue.

SECTION B

1 Xpand

Marking scheme

		Marks
(a)	Recalculation of ratios - 1½ marks each	6
(b)	1 mark per valid point	9
		15

Adjusted statement of profit or loss:

	$'000
Revenue	70,000
Cost of sales (45,000/0.9 (i))	(50,000)
Gross profit	20,000
Operating costs	(7,000)
Directors salaries (ii)	(2,500)
Loan interest (10% x 10,000 (iii))	(1,000)
Profit before tax	9,500
Income tax expense	(3,000)
Profit for the year	6,500

The adjusted ratios, based on the statement of profit or loss as above, the equity of $30 million and the replacement of the directors' loan accounts by a commercial loan are as follows:

Return on equity	((6,500/30,000) × 100)	21.7%
Net asset turnover	(70,000/(30,000 + 10,000))	1.75 times
Gross profit margin	((20,000/70,000) × 100)	28.6%
Net profit margin	((6,500/70,000) × 100)	9.3%

The ratios based on the original summarised financial statements of Hydan show a very healthy picture, well above the sector average. Hydan has high gross and net profit margins and an impressive net asset turnover, giving a return on equity of more than twice the sector average. On the face of it, Hydan is trading very profitably and efficiently, keeping costs well under control.

However, when the financial statements are adjusted to show the likely picture post-acquisition, it becomes clear that Hydan has been to quite a large degree cushioned by the family and by the other family-owned companies. Removing the 10% discount Hydan enjoys on its purchases reduces the gross profit margin from 35.7% to 28.6%, slightly under the sector average.

If Xpand purchases Hydan, it will need to appoint a new board of directors and replace the directors' loan accounts with a commercial loan. Both of these expenses have up to now been subsidised by the family.

Adjusting further for the increased directors' remuneration and interest on the loan takes the net profit margin down from 20% to 9.3%, significantly below the sector average of 12%. The value of equity would not change

significantly as a result of the acquisition, as the increase to $30m is compensated for by the reclassification of the loan as debt. The fall in the return on equity from 47.1% to 21.7% is therefore driven by the fall in net profit. However it is worth noting that 21.7% return on equity is not much below the sector average of 22%.

Xpand should take the view that if it acquires Hydan it will be acquiring a business that is performing slightly below the average for its sector. The impressive profitability pictured in the summarised financial statements is obviously not going to survive the acquisition. But Hydan will still be trading quite profitably and it could be that there are cost savings which were not considered necessary by the previous management but which could now be made, which will bring its performance into line with the average for its sector.

2 Kandy

Text references. Chapters 9 and 11.

Top tips. This question required calculation of adjusted retained earnings and preparation of the statement of financial position. Read the question carefully and follow through each step.

Easy marks. The only complex bits in this question were the deferred tax and the loan note. Other than that, there were plenty of easy marks.

Examiner's answer. The examiner's answer to this question is at the end of this Kit.

Marking scheme

			Marks
(a)	Schedule of retained earnings		
	Retained earnings per trial balance	½	
	Issue costs	1	
	Loan finance costs	1	
	Depreciation charges	2	
	Income tax expense	1½	
			6
	Statement of financial position		
	Property, plant and equipment	2	
	Current assets	½	
	Equity shares	½	
	Revaluation surplus	2	
	Deferred tax	1	
	6% loan note	1½	
	Current liabilities (per trial balance)	½	
	Current tax payable	1	
			9
			15

(a) **Schedule of adjustments**

	$'000
Retained earnings per trial balance	17,500
Loan issue costs (W1)	1,000
Loan interest (W1)	(2,610)
Depreciation (W2)	(5,600)
Income tax (W3)	(800)
Adjusted retained earnings	9,490

(b)   STATEMENT OF FINANCIAL POSITION AS AT 30 SEPTEMBER 20X4

	$'000	$'000
ASSETS		
Non-current assets		
Property, plant and equipment (W2)		65,400
Current assets		68,700
		134,100
EQUITY AND LIABILITIES		
Equity		
Equity shares of $1 each	40,000	
Revaluation surplus (W2)	9,600	
Retained earnings (per part (a))	9,490	
		59,090
Non-current liabilities		
Deferred tax (W4)	4,400	
6% loan note (W1)	29,810	
		34,210
Current liabilities		
Per trial balance	38,400	
Current tax payable	2,400	
		40,800
		134,100

Workings

1   *Loan note*

	$'000
Loan note – face value	30,000
Issue costs	(1,000)
	29,000
Interest (29,000 × 9%)	2,610
Less interest paid	(1,800)
Carrying amount	29,810

2   *Property, plant and equipment*

	Land and buildings $'000	Plant and equipment $'000	Total $'000
Cost	55,000	58,500	
Accumulated depreciation	(20,000)	(34,500)	
	35,000	24,000	
Revaluation	12,000		
Revalued amount	47,000		
Depreciation (39,000/15)	(2,600)		
Depreciation (24,000 × 12.5%)		(3,000)	
	44,400	21,000	65,400

3   *Income tax*

	$'000
Current year charge	2,400
Less prior year over-provision	(1,100)
Deferred tax adjustment (W4)	(500)
	800

4   *Deferred tax*

	$'000
Provision required (12,000 + 10,000) × 20%	4,400
Existing provision	(2,500)
Increase in provision	1,900
Chargeable to revaluation surplus (12,000 × 20%)	2,400
Credit to profit or loss	(500)
	1,900

3 Plastik

Text references Chapters 3, 4 and 14.

Top tips. This is quite a time-pressured question so you need to work fast. Get the proformas down for both statements and then go methodically through the workings, filling in the proformas as you go.

Easy marks. There are some marks available for figures that can be lifted straight from the question and good, clear goodwill and retained earnings workings will help you to fill in several gaps.

Examiner's answer. The examiner's answer to this question is at the end of this kit.

			Marks
(a)	Consolidated statement of profit or loss and other comprehensive income		
	Revenue	1½	
	Cost of sales	2½	
	Distribution costs	½	
	Administrative expenses (including goodwill impairment)	1	
	Finance costs	1	
	Income tax expense	½	
	Gain on revaluation of properties	1	
	Non-controlling interest - profit for the year	1	
	- total comprehensive income	1	
			10
(b)	Consolidated statement of financial position		
	Property, plant and equipment	2	
	Goodwill	2½	
	Inventory	1	
	Trade receivables	1	
	Bank	½	
	Share capital	1	
	Share premium	1	
	Revaluation surplus	1	
	Retained earnings	1½	
	Non-controlling interest	1	
	10% loan notes	1	
	Trade payables	1	
	Current tax payable	½	
	Deferred consideration	1	
	Overdraft	1	
			17
(c)	Research	2	
	Customer list	1	
			3
	Total for question		30

(a) CONSOLIDATED STATEMENT OF PROFIT OR LOSS AND OTHER COMPREHENSIVE INCOME FOR THE YEAR
     ENDED 30 SEPTEMBER 20X4

	$'000
Revenue (62,600 + (30,000 × 9/12) − 2,700 (W8))	82,400
Cost of sales (45,800 + (24,000 × 9/12) − 2,580 (W8) + 100 (W7))	61,320
Gross profit	21,080
Distribution costs (2,000 + (1,200 × 9/12))	(2,900)
Administrative expenses (3,500 + (1,800 × 9/12) + 500 (W3))	(5,350)
Finance costs (200 + 135 (W4))	(335)
Profit before tax	12,495
Income tax (3,100 + (1,000 × 9/12))	(3,850)
	8,645
Other comprehensive income	
Gain on revaluation of property (1,500 + 600)	2,100
Total comprehensive income	10,745
Profit for the year attributable to:	
Owners of the parent (β)	8,465
Non-controlling interest (W2)	180
	8,645
Total comprehensive income attributable to:	
Owners of the parent (β)	10,445
Non-controlling interest (W2)	300
	10,745

(b) CONSOLIDATED STATEMENT OF FINANCIAL POSITION AS AT 30 SEPTEMBER 20X4

	$'000	$'000
ASSETS		
Non-current assets		
Property, plant and equipment		
(18,700 + 13,900 + 3,900 (W7) + 600)		37,100
Goodwill (W3)		5,200
		42,300
Current assets		
Inventory (4,300 + 1,200 − 120 (W8))	5,380	
Trade receivables (4,700 + 2,500 − 1,200 (W8))	6,000	
Bank	300	
		11,680
Total assets		53,980
EQUITY AND LIABILITIES		
Equity		
Equity attributable to owners of the parent		
Equity shares of $1 each (W6)		14,800
Share premium (W6)		9,600
Revaluation surplus (2,000 + (600 × 80%))		2,480
Retained earnings (W4)		6,765
		33,645
Non-controlling interest (W5)		4,800
		38,445
Non-current liabilities		
10% loan note		2,500

	$'000	$'000
Current liabilities		
Trade payables (3,400 + 3,600 – 800 (W8))	6,200	
Tax payable (2,800 + 800)	3,600	
Deferred consideration (1,800 + 135 (W4))	1,935	
Overdraft (1,700 – 400 (W8))	1,300	
		13,035
		53,980

Workings

1 *Group structure*

Plastik

1.1.20X4

(9m before year end)

↓

Subtrak

80%

2 *Non-controlling interests (SPLOCI)*

	Profit for year	Total comprehensive income
	$'000	$'000
Per question (2,000 × 9/12)	1,500	1,500
Fair value depreciation	(100)	(100)
Goodwill impairment	(500)	(500)
Gain on property revaluation		600
	900	1,500
NCI 20%	180	300

3 *Goodwill*

	$'000	$'000
Consideration transferred - 4.8m shares @ $3		14,400
Deferred consideration (7.2m × $0.275 × 1/1.1)		1,800
		16,200
Fair value of NCI (1.8m shares @ $2.50)		4,500
		20,700
Fair value of net assets:		
Shares	9,000	
Retained earnings (3,500 – 1,500)	2,000	
Fair value adjustment - property	4,000	
		(15,000)
Goodwill at acquisition		5,700
Impairment		(500)
Carrying amount 30 September 20X4		5,200

4 *Retained earnings*

	Plastik	Subtrak
	$'000	$'000
Per question	6,300	3,500
Less pre-acquisition (1,500 + (2,000 × 3/12))		(2,000)
Goodwill impairment		(500)
Unwinding of discount on deferred consideration (1,800 (W3) × 10% × 9/12)	(135)	
Depreciation on FVA		(100)
PURP (600,000 × 25/125)	(120)	
	6,045	900
Share of Subtrak (900 × 80%)	720	
	6,765	

5   Non-controlling interest (SOFP)

	$'000
NCI at acquisition (W3)	4,500
Share of post-acquisition retained earnings (900 (W4) × 20%)	180
Share of property revaluation gain (600 × 20%)	120
	4,800

6   Purchase of Subtrak

	Share capital $'000	Share premium $'000
Per question	10,000	-
Shares issued (9m × 80% × 2/3 × $3)	4,800	9,600
	14,800	9,600

7   Fair value adjustment

	Acquisition $'000	Movement $'000	Year end $'000
Property	4,000	(100)	3,900

8   Intragroup trading

		$'000	$'000
(1)	Cancel intragroup sales/purchases		
	DEBIT Group revenue (300,000 × 9)	2,700	
	CREDIT Group cost of sales		2,700
(2)	Eliminate unrealised profit		
	DEBIT Cost of sales (600,000 × 25/125)	120	
	CREDIT Group inventories		120
(3)	Cancel intragroup balances		
	DEBIT Trade payables	800	
	DEBIT Cash (cash in transit)	400	
	CREDIT Trade receivables		1,200

(c)   In accordance with IAS 38 *Intangible Assets* neither the research costs not the customer list can be recognised as assets in the individual entity financial statements of Dilemma. However, when a business combination takes place IAS 38 states that an acquirer recognises at the acquisition date, separately from goodwill, an intangible asset of the acquiree, irrespective of whether the asset had been recognised by the acquiree before the business combination. The intangible asset should be recognised at its fair value.

In this case, both of these assets can be identified separately from goodwill, so both should be recognised, the research costs at $1.2 million and the customer list at $3 million.In this case, both of these assets can be identified separately from goodwill, so both should be recognised, the research costs at $1.2 million and the customer list at $3 million.

ACCA's exam answers:
June and December 2014

Note. The ACCA's exam answers are correct at the time of going to press but may be subject to some amendments before the final versions are published.

1 (a) Penketh – Consolidated goodwill as at 1 October 2013

	$'000	$'000
Controlling interest		
Share exchange (90,000 x 1/3 x $4)		120,000
Deferred consideration (90,000 x $1·54/1·1)		126,000
Non-controlling interest (60,000 x $2·50)		150,000
		396,000
Equity shares	150,000	
Pre-acquisition retained profits:		
– at 1 April 2013	120,000	
– 1 April to 30 September 2013 (80,000 x 6/12) (excluding OCI)	40,000	
Fair value adjustments: land	2,000	
plant	6,000	
customer relationships	5,000	(323,000)
Goodwill arising on acquisition		73,000

(b) Penketh – Consolidated statement of profit or loss and other comprehensive income for the year ended 31 March 2014

	$'000
Revenue (620,000 + (310,000 x 6/12) – 20,000 intra-group sales)	755,000
Cost of sales (w (i))	(458,200)
Gross profit	296,800
Distribution costs (40,000 + (20,000 x 6/12))	(50,000)
Administrative expenses (36,000 + (25,000 x 6/12) + (5,000/5 years x 6/12))	(49,000)
Investment income: Share of profit from associate (10,000 x 30% x 6/12)	1,500
Other ((5,000 – 1,800 dividend from associate) + (1,600 x 6/12))	4,000
Finance costs (2,000 + (5,600 x 6/12) + (126,000 x 10% x 6/12 re deferred consideration))	(11,100)
Profit before tax	192,200
Income tax expense (45,000 + (31,000 x 6/12))	(60,500)
Profit for the year	131,700
Other comprehensive income	
Loss on revaluation of land (2,200 – (3,000 – 2,000) gain for Sphere)	(1,200)
Total comprehensive income for the year	130,500
Profit attributable to:	
Owners of the parent	116,500
Non-controlling interest (w (ii))	15,200
	131,700
Total comprehensive income attributable to:	
Owners of the parent	114,900
Non-controlling interest (w (ii))	15,600
	130,500

Workings (figures in brackets in $'000)

(i)   Cost of sales

	$'000
Penketh	400,000
Sphere (150,000 x 6/12)	75,000
Intra-group purchases	(20,000)
Additional depreciation of plant (6,000/2 years x 6/12)	1,500
Unrealised profit in inventory:	
Sales to Sphere (20,000 x 1/5 x 25/125)	800
Sales to Ventor (15,000 x 30% x 25/125)	900
	458,200

(ii) Non-controlling interest in profit for the year:

	$'000
Sphere's post-acquisition profit (80,000 x 6/12)	40,000
Less: Additional depreciation of plant (w (i)) (1,500)	
Additional amortisation of intangible (5,000/5 years x 6/12) (500)	(2,000)
	38,000
	x 40% =
	15,200

Non-controlling interest in total comprehensive income:	
Non-controlling interest in statement of profit or loss (above)	15,200
Other comprehensive income ((3,000 – 2,000) x 40%)	400
	15,600

2 (a) Xtol – Statement of profit or loss for the year ended 31 March 2014

	$'000
Revenue (490,000 – 20,000 agency sales (w (i)))	470,000
Cost of sales (w (i))	(294,600)
Gross profit	175,400
Distribution costs	(33,500)
Administrative expenses	(36,800)
Other operating income – agency sales	2,000
Finance costs (900 overdraft + 3,676 (w (ii)))	(4,576)
Profit before tax	102,524
Income tax expense (28,000 + 3,200 + 3,700 (w (iii)))	(34,900)
Profit for the year	67,624

(b) Xtol – Statement of changes in equity for the year ended 31 March 2014

	Share capital $'000	Share premium $'000	Equity option $'000	Retained earnings $'000	Total equity $'000
Balance at 1 April 2013	40,000	2,600	nil	26,080	68,680
Rights issue (see below)	16,000	22,400			38,400
5% loan note issue (w (ii))			4,050		4,050
Dividends paid (w (iv))				(10,880)	(10,880)
Profit for the year				67,624	67,624
Balance at 31 March 2014	56,000	25,000	4,050	82,824	167,874

The number of shares prior to the 2 for 5 rights issue was 160 million (56,000 x 4 (i.e. 25 cents shares) x 5/7). Therefore the rights issue was 64 million shares at 60 cents each, giving additional share capital of $16 million (64 million x 25 cents) and share premium of $22·4 million (64 million x (60 cents – 25 cents)).

(c) Xtol – Statement of financial position as at 31 March 2014

	$'000	$'000
Assets		
Non-current assets		
Property, plant and equipment ((100,000 – 30,000) + (155,500 – 57,500))		168,000
Current assets		
Inventory	61,000	
Trade receivables	63,000	124,000
Total assets		292,000
Equity and liabilities		
Equity (see (b) above)		
Equity shares of 25 cents each		56,000
Share premium		25,000
Other component of equity – equity option		4,050
Retained earnings		82,824
		167,874
Non-current liabilities		
Deferred tax	8,300	
5% convertible loan note (w (ii))	47,126	55,426
Current liabilities		
Trade payables (32,200 + 3,000 re Francais (w (i)))	35,200	
Bank overdraft	5,500	
Current tax payable	28,000	68,700
Total equity and liabilities		292,000

(d) Xtol – Basic earnings per share for the year ended 31 March 2014

Profit per statement of profit or loss	$67·624 million
Weighted average number of shares (w (v))	209·7 million
Earnings per share ($67·624m/209·7m)	32·2 cents

Workings (figures in brackets in $'000)

(i) Cost of sales (including the effect of agency sales on cost of sales and trade payables)

	$'000
Cost of sales per question	290,600
Remove agency costs	(15,000)
Amortisation of leased property (100,000/20 years)	5,000
Depreciation of plant and equipment ((155,500 – 43,500) x 12½%)	14,000
	294,600

The agency sales should be removed from revenue (debit $20 million) and their 'cost' from cost of sales (credit $15 million). Instead, Xtol should report the commission earned of $2 million (credit) as other operating income (or as revenue would be acceptable). This leaves a net amount of $3 million ((20,000 – 15,000) – 2,000) owing to Francais as a trade payable.

(ii) 5% convertible loan note

The convertible loan note is a compound financial instrument having a debt and an equity component which must be accounted for separately:

Year ended 31 March	outflow $'000	8%	present value $'000
2014	2,500	0·93	2,325
2015	2,500	0·86	2,150
2016	52,500	0·79	41,475
Debt component			45,950
Equity component (= balance)			4,050
Proceeds of issue			50,000

The finance cost for the year will be $3,676,000 (45,950 x 8%) and the carrying amount of the loan as at 31 March 2014 will be $47,126,000 (45,950 + (3,676 – 2,500)).

(iii) Deferred tax

	$'000
Provision at 31 March 2014	8,300
Balance at 1 April 2013	(4,600)
Charge to statement of profit or loss	3,700

(iv) Dividends

The dividend paid on 30 May 2013 was $6·4 million (4 cents on 160 million shares ($40 million x 4, i.e. 25 cents shares)) and the dividend paid on 30 November 2013 (after the rights issue) was $4·48 million (2 cents on 224 million shares (56 million x 4)). Total dividends paid in the year were $10·88 million.

(v) Number of shares outstanding (including the effect of the rights issue)

Theoretical ex-rights fair value:

	Shares	$	$
Holding (say)	100	1·02	102
Rights issue (2 for 5)	40	0·60	24
	140		126

| Theoretical ex-rights fair value | | 0·90 ($126/140) | |

Weighted average number of shares:

1 April 2013 to 31 July 2013	160 million x $1·02/$0·90 x 4/12 =	60·4 million
1 August 2013 to 31 March 2014	224 million x 8/12 =	149·3 million
Weighted average for year		209·7 million

3 (a) Note: Figures in the calculations of the ratios are in $million

	(i) 2014 As reported		(ii) 2014 Excluding Shaw		2013 From question
Return on (year-end) capital employed	12·0%	18/(175 – 25)	13·0%	(18 – 5)/(150 – 50)	10·5%
Net asset turnover	1·0 times	150/150	1·2 times	(150 – 30)/100	1·16 times
Gross profit margin	22·0%	33/150	20·0%	(33 – 9)/(150 – 30)	22·0%
Profit before loan interest and tax margin	12·0%	18/150	10·8%	(18 – 5)/(150 – 30)	9·1%
Current ratio	1·08:1	27/25			1·67:1
Gearing	36·7%	55/(95 + 55)			5·3%

(b) Analysis of the comparative financial performance and position of Woodbank for the year ended 31 March 2014

Note: References to 2014 and 2013 should be taken as the years ended 31 March 2014 and 2013 respectively.

Introduction

When comparing a company's current performance and position with the previous year (or years), using trend analysis, it is necessary to take into account the effect of any circumstances which may create an inconsistency in the comparison. In the case of Woodbank, the purchase of Shaw is an example of such an inconsistency. 2014's figures include, for a three-month period, the operating results of Shaw, and Woodbank's statement of financial position includes all of Shaw's net assets (including goodwill) together with the additional 10% loan notes used to finance the purchase of Shaw. None of these items were included in the 2013 financial statements. The net assets of Shaw when purchased were $50 million, which represents one third of Woodbank's net assets (capital employed) as at 31 March 2014; thus it represents a major investment for Woodbank and any analysis necessitates careful consideration of its impact.

Profitability

ROCE is considered by many analysts to be the most important profitability ratio. A ROCE of 12·0% in 2014, compared to 10·5% in 2013, represents a creditable 14·3% (12·0 – 10·5)/10·5) improvement in profitability. When ROCE is calculated excluding the contribution from Shaw, at 13·0%, it shows an even more favourable performance. Although this comparison (13·0% from 10·5%) is valid, it would seem to imply that the purchase of Shaw has had a detrimental effect on Woodbank's ROCE. However, caution is needed when interpreting this information as ROCE compares the return (profit for a period) to the capital employed (equivalent to net assets at a single point in time). In the case of Woodbank, the statement of profit or loss only includes three months' results from Shaw whereas the statement of financial position includes all of Shaw's net assets; this is a form of inconsistency. It would be fair to speculate that in future years, when a full year's results from Shaw are reported, the ROCE effect of Shaw will be favourable. Indeed, assuming a continuation of Shaw's current level of performance, profit in a full year could be $20 million. On an investment of $50 million, this represents a ROCE of 40% (based on the initial capital employed) which is much higher than Woodbank's pre-existing business.

The cause of the improvement in ROCE is revealed by consideration of the secondary profitability ratios: asset turnover and profit margins. For Woodbank this reveals a complicated picture. Woodbank's results, as reported, show that it is the increase in the profit before interest and tax margin (12·0% from 9·1%) which is responsible for the improvement in ROCE, as the asset turnover has actually decreased (1·0 times from 1·16 times) and gross profit is exactly the same in both years (at 22·0%). When the effect of the purchase of Shaw is excluded the position changes; the overall improvement in ROCE (13·0% from 10·5%) is caused by both an increase in profit margin (at the before interest and tax level, at 10·8% from 9·1%), despite a fall in gross profit (20·0% from 22·0%) and a very slight improvement in asset turnover (1·2 times from 1·16 times). Summarising, this means that the purchase of Shaw has improved Woodbank's overall profit margins, but caused a fall in asset turnover. Again, as with the ROCE, this is misleading because the calculation of asset turnover only includes three months' revenue from Shaw, but all of its net assets; when a full year of Shaw's results are reported, asset turnover will be much improved (assuming its three-months performance is continued).

Liquidity

The company's liquidity position, as measured by the current ratio, has fallen considerably in 2014 and is a cause for concern. At 1·67:1 in 2013, it was within the acceptable range (normally between 1·5:1 and 2·0:1); however, the 2014 ratio of 1·08:1 is very low, indeed it is more like what would be expected for the quick ratio (acid test). Without needing to calculate the component ratios of the current ratio (for inventory, receivables and payables), it can be seen from the statements of financial position that the main causes of the deterioration in the liquidity position are the reduction in the cash (bank) position and the dramatic increase in trade payables. The bank balance has fallen by $4·5 million (5,000 – 500) and the trade payables have increased by $8 million.

An analysis of the movement in the retained earnings shows that Woodbank paid a dividend of $5·5 million (10,000 + 10,500 – 15,000) or 6·88 cents per share. It could be argued that during a period of expansion, with demands on cash flow, dividends could be suspended or heavily curtailed. Had no dividend been paid, the 2014 bank balance would be $6·0 million and the current ratio would have been 1·3:1 ((27,000 + 5,500):25,000). This would be still on the low side, but much more reassuring to credit suppliers than the reported ratio of 1·08:1.

Gearing

The company has gone from a position of very modest gearing at 5·3% in 2013 to 36·7% in 2014. This has largely been caused by the issue of the additional 10% loan notes to finance the purchase of Shaw. Arguably, it might have been better if some of the finance had been raised from a share issue, but the level of gearing is still acceptable and the financing cost of 10% should be more than covered by the prospect of future high returns from Shaw, thus benefiting shareholders overall.

Conclusion

The overall operating performance of Woodbank has improved during the period (although the gross profit margin on sales other than those made by Shaw has fallen) and this should be even more marked next year when a full year's results from Shaw will be reported (assuming that Shaw can maintain its current performance). The changes in the financial position, particularly liquidity, are less favourable and call into question the current dividend policy. Gearing has increased substantially, due to the financing of the purchase of Shaw; however, it is still acceptable and has benefited shareholders. It is interesting to note that of the $50 million purchase price, $30 million of this is represented by goodwill. Although this may seem high, Shaw is certainly delivering in terms of generating revenue with good profit margins.

4 (a) The requirements of IAS 16 *Property, Plant and Equipment* may, in part, offer a solution to the director's concerns. IAS 16 allows (but does not require) entities to revalue their property, plant and equipment to fair value; however, it imposes conditions where an entity chooses to do this. First, where an item of property, plant and equipment is revalued under the revaluation model of IAS 16, the whole class of assets to which it belongs must also be revalued. This is to prevent what is known as 'cherry picking' where an entity might only wish to revalue items which have increased in value and leave other items at their (depreciated) cost. Second, where an item of property, plant and equipment has been revalued, its valuation (fair value) must be kept up-to-date. In practice, this means that, where the carrying amount of the asset differs significantly from its fair value, a (new) revaluation should be carried out. Even if there are no significant changes, assets should still be subject to a revaluation every three to five years.

A revaluation surplus (gain) should be credited to a revaluation surplus (reserve), via other comprehensive income, whereas a revaluation deficit (loss) should be expensed immediately (assuming, in both cases, no previous revaluation of the asset has taken place). A surplus on one asset cannot be used to offset a deficit on a different asset (even in the same class of asset).

Subsequent to a revaluation, the asset should be depreciated based on its revalued amount (less any estimated residual value) over its estimated remaining useful life, which should be reviewed annually irrespective of whether it has been revalued.

An entity may choose to transfer annually an amount of the revaluation surplus relating to a revalued asset to retained earnings corresponding to the 'excess' depreciation caused by an upwards revaluation. Alternatively, it may transfer all of the relevant surplus at the time of the asset's disposal.

The effect of this, on Enca's financial statements, is that its statement of financial position will be strengthened by reflecting the fair value of its property, plant and equipment. However, the downside (from the director's perspective) is that the depreciation charge will actually increase (as it will be based on the higher fair value) and profits will be lower than using the cost model. Although the director may not be happy with the higher depreciation, it is conceptually correct. The director has misunderstood the purpose of depreciation; it is not meant to reflect the change (increase in this case) in the value of an asset, but rather the cost of using up part of the asset's remaining life.

(b) (i) Delta – Extracts from statement of profit or loss (see workings):

	$'000
Year ended 31 March 2013	
Plant impairment loss	20,000
Plant depreciation (32,000 + 22,400)	54,400
Year ended 31 March 2014	
Loss on sale	8,000
Plant depreciation (32,000 + 26,000)	58,000

(ii) Delta – Extracts from statement of financial position (see workings):

	$'000
As at 31 March 2013	
Property, plant and equipment (128,000 + 89,600)	217,600
Revaluation surplus	
Revaluation of item B (1 April 2012)	32,000
Transfer to retained earnings (32,000/5 years)	(6,400)
Balance at 31 March 2013	25,600
As at 31 March 2014	
Property, plant and equipment (item A only)	96,000
Revaluation surplus	
Balance at 1 April 2013	25,600
Transfer to retained earnings (asset now sold)	(25,600)
Balance at 31 March 2014	nil

Workings (figures in brackets in $'000)

	Item A $'000	Item B $'000	
Carrying amounts at 31 March 2012	180,000	80,000	
Balance = loss to statement of profit or loss	(20,000)		
Balance = gain to revaluation surplus		32,000	
Revaluation on 1 April 2012	160,000	112,000	
Depreciation year ended 31 March 2013 (160,000/5 years)	(32,000)	(22,400)	(112,000/5 years)
Carrying amount at 31 March 2013	128,000	89,600	
Subsequent expenditure capitalised on 1 April 2013	nil	14,400	
		104,000	
Depreciation year ended 31 March 2014 (unchanged)	(32,000)	(26,000)	(104,000/4 years)
		78,000	
Sale proceeds on 31 March 2014		(70,000)	
Loss on sale		(8,000)	
Carrying amount at 31 March 2014	96,000	nil	

5 (i) Changing the classification of an item of expense is an example of a change in accounting policy, in accordance with IAS 8 *Accounting Policies, Changes in Accounting Estimates and Errors*. Such a change should only be made where it is required by an IFRS or where it would lead to the information in the financial statements being more reliable and relevant. It may be that this change does represent an example of the latter, although it is arguable that amortised development costs should continue to be included in cost of sales as amortisation only occurs when the benefits from the related project(s) come on-stream. If it is accepted that this change does constitute a change of accounting policy, then the proposed treatment by the directors is acceptable; however, the comparative results for the year ended 31 March 2013 must be restated as if the new policy had always been applied (known as retrospective application).

(ii) The two provisions must be calculated on different bases because IAS 37 *Provisions, Contingent Liabilities and Contingent Assets* distinguishes between a single obligation (the court case) and a large population of items (the product warranty claims).

For the court case the most probable single likely outcome is normally considered to be the best estimate of the liability, i.e. $4 million. This is particularly the case as the possible outcomes are either side of this amount. The $4 million will be an expense for the year ended 31 March 2014 and recognised as a provision.

The provision for the product warranty claims should be calculated on an expected value basis at $3·4 million (((75% x nil) + (20% x $25) + (10% x $120)) x 200,000 units). This will also be an expense for the year ended 31 March 2014 and recognised as a current liability (it is a one-year warranty scheme) in the statement of financial position as at 31 March 2014.

(iii) Government grants related to non-current assets should be credited to the statement of profit or loss over the life of the asset to which they relate, not in accordance with the schedule of any potential repayment. The directors' proposed treatment is implying that the government grant is a liability which decreases over four years. This is not correct as there would only be a liability if the directors intended to sell the related plant, which they do not. Thus in the year ended 31 March 2014, $800,000 (8 million/10 years) should be credited to the statement of profit or loss and $7·2 million should be shown as deferred income ($800,000 current and $6·4 million non-current) in the statement of financial position.

This marking scheme is given as a guide in the context of the suggested answers. Scope is given to markers to award marks for alternative approaches to a question, including relevant comment, and where well-reasoned conclusions are provided. This is particularly the case for written answers where there may be more than one acceptable solution.

			Marks
1	**(a)**	consolidated goodwill	6
	(b)	Consolidated statement of profit or loss and other comprehensive income	
		revenue	2
		cost of sales	4
		distribution costs	½
		administrative expenses	1½
		investment income: associate	2
		other	2
		finance costs	1½
		income tax expense	1
		other comprehensive income	1½
		non-controlling interest in profit for year	2
		non-controlling interest in other comprehensive income	1
			19
		Total for question	**25**

2	**(a)**	Statement of profit or loss	
		revenue	1
		cost of sales	2
		distribution costs	½
		administrative expenses	½
		operating income agency sales	1
		finance costs	1½
		income tax expense	1½
			8
	(b)	Statement of changes in equity	
		balances b/f	2
		rights issue	1
		5% loan note: equity component	1
		dividends paid	1½
		profit for the year	½
			6
	(c)	Statement of financial position	
		property, plant and equipment	1½
		inventory	½
		trade receivables	½
		deferred tax	1
		5% loan note	1½
		trade payables	1½
		bank overdraft	½
		current tax	1
			8
	(d)	Basic earnings per share	
		theoretical ex-rights fair value	1
		calculation of weighted average number of shares	1½
		calculation of EPS using profit per statement of profit or loss	½
			3
		Total for question	**25**

					Marks
3	**(a)**	**(i)** and **(ii)**	1 mark per ratio		10
	(b)		1 mark per relevant point to maximum		15
				Total for question	**25**
4	**(a)**		1 mark per valid point	maximum	5
	(b)	**(i)**	Statement of profit or loss extracts		
			year ended 31 March 2013		3
			year ended 31 March 2014		2
					5
		(ii)	Statement of financial position extracts		
			as at 31 March 2013		3
			as at 31 March 2014		2
					5
				Total for question	**15**
5	**(i)**		changing expense classification is an example of a change in accounting policy		1
			must be required by IFRS or improve reliability/relevance		1
			discuss and conclude that the proposed treatment may be permitted		1
			if change must restate previous year's financial statements		1
				maximum	3
	(ii)		provision for damages at $4 million		2
			provision for product warranty claim at $3·4 million		2
					4
	(iii)		government grant is not a liability (do not use repayment schedule)		1
			government grant credited over life of the asset at $800,000 per annum		1
			$7·2 million deferred income in statement of financial position		1
					3
				Total for question	**10**

Section A

1   A

A change of classification in presentation in financial statements is a change of accounting policy (CAP) under IAS 8.

2   C

3   B

Historical cost annual depreciation = $90,000 ((500,000 x 90%)/5 years).
After two years carrying amount would be $320,000 (500,000 – (2 x 90,000)).
Current cost annual depreciation = $108,000 ((600,000 x 90%)/5 years).
After two years carrying amount would be $384,000 (600,000 – (2 x 108,000)).

4   C

Although the invoiced amount is $180,000, $30,000 of this has not yet been earned and must be deferred until the servicing work has been completed.

5   C

(i) is an onerous contract and (iii) the provision is still required if there is no intention to sell

6   B

The total profit on the contract is expected to be $1 million (5,000 – (1,600 + 2,400)).
At 30 September 2014 the profit recognised would be $360,000 (1,000 x 1,800/5,000).

Therefore the amount due from the customer would be:

	$'000
Cost to date	1,600
Profit recognised	360
Progress billings	(1,800)
Amount due from the customer	160

7   D

As the receivable is 'sold' with recourse it must remain as an asset on the statement of financial position; it is not derecognised.

8   D

The normal selling price of damaged inventory is $300,000 (210/70%).

This will now sell for $240,000 (300,000 x 80%), and have a NRV of $180,000 (240 – (240 x 25%)). The expected loss on the inventory is $30,000 (210 cost – 180 NRV) and therefore the inventory should be valued at $970,000 (1,000 – 30).

9   A

Cash flow is (in $ million):
23·4 – 14·4 b/f + 2·5 dep + 3 disposal – 2 revaluation – 4 non-cash acquisition = 8·5

10   D

The investment no longer meets the definition of a subsidiary (ability to control) and therefore would not be consolidated.

11 A

Year ended 30 September	Cash flow	Discount rate	Discounted cash flows
	$'000	at 8%	$'000
2014	500	0·93	465
2015	500	0·86	430
2016	10,500	0·79	8,295
Value of debt component			9,190
Difference – value of equity option component			810
Proceeds			10,000

12 A

Goodwill should be written off in full and the remaining loss is allocated pro rata to property plant and equipment and the product patent.

	B/f	Loss	Post loss
	$	$	$
Property, plant and equipment	200,000	(45,455)	154,545
Goodwill	50,000	(50,000)	nil
Product patent	20,000	(4,545)	15,455
Net current assets (at NRV)	30,000	nil	30,000
	300,000	(100,000)	200,000

13 B

Correct for the reason given in the question.

14 C

At 30 September 2014:
Carrying amount = $37·5 million (45,000 – 6,000 b/f – 1,500 for 6 months; no further depreciation when classified as held for sale).
Recoverable amount = $36·8 million ((42,000 x 90%) – 1,000).
Therefore included at $36·8 million (lower of carrying amount and fair value less cost to sell).

15 A

A not-for-profit entity is not likely to have shareholders or 'earnings'.

16 A

Is the correct treatment for a bargain purchase (negative goodwill).

17 B

Extraction provision at 30 September 2014 is $2·5 million (250 x 10).
Dismantling provision at 1 October 2013 is $20·4 million (30,000 x 0·68).
This will increase by an 8% finance cost by 30 September 2014 = $22,032,000.
Total provision is $24,532,000.

18 D

Although the estimated NRV is lower than it was (due to fire damage), the entity will still make a profit on the inventory and thus it is not an indicator of impairment.

19 C

> Rental of excavation equipment $13,500 (18 x 9/12)
> Depreciation of finance leased plant $68,000 (340/5 years)
> Finance cost $25,000 ((340 – 90) x 10%)
> Total $106,500

20 D

> As it is a new type of transaction, comparability with existing treatments is not relevant.

Section B

1 (a) For comparison

	Hydan adjusted	Hydan as reported	Sector average
Return on equity (ROE)	21·7%	47·1%	22·0%
Net asset turnover	1·75 times	2·36 times	1·67 times
Gross profit margin	28·6%	35·7%	30·0%
Net profit margin	9·3%	20·0%	12·0%

Hydan's adjusted ratios:

On the assumption that after the purchase of Hydan, the favourable effects of the transactions with other companies owned by the family would not occur, the following adjustments to the statement of profit or loss should be made:

	$'000
Cost of sales (45,000/0·9)	50,000
Directors' remuneration	2,500
Loan interest (10% x 10,000)	1,000

These adjustments would give a revised statement of profit or loss:

Revenue	70,000
Cost of sales	(50,000)
Gross profit	20,000
Operating costs	(7,000)
Directors' remuneration	(2,500)
Loan interest	(1,000)
Profit before tax	9,500
Income tax expense	(3,000)
Profit for the year	6,500

In the statement of financial position:

Equity would be the purchase price of Hydan (per question)	30,000
The commercial loan (replacing the directors' loan) would now be debt	10,000

From these figures the adjusted ratios above are calculated as:

Return on equity	((6,500 /30,000) x 100)	21·7%
Net asset turnover	(70,000/(30,000 + 10,000))	1·75 times
Gross profit margin	((20,000)/70,000) x 100)	28·6%
Net profit margin	((6,500/70,000) x 100)	9·30%

(b) An analysis of Hydan's ratios based on the financial statements provided reveals a strong position, particularly in relation to profitability when compared to other businesses in this retail sector. Hydan has a very high ROE which is a product of higher-than-average profit margins (at both the gross and net profit level) and a significantly higher net asset turnover. Thus, on the face of it, Hydan is managing to achieve higher prices (or reduced cost of sales), has better control of overheads and is using its net assets more efficiently in terms of generating revenue.

However, when adjustments are made for the effects of its favourable transactions with other companies owned by the family, the position changes somewhat. The effect of purchasing its inventory from another family owned supplier at favourable market prices means that its reported gross profit percentage of 35·7% is flattered; had these purchases been made at market prices, it would fall to 28·6% which is below the sector average of 30·0%. The effects of the favourable inventory purchases carry through to net profit. Based on Xpand's estimate of future directors' remuneration, it would seem the existing directors of Hydan are not charging commercial rates for their remuneration. When Xpand replaces the board of Hydan, it will have to increase directors' remuneration by $1·5 million. Additionally, when the interest free directors' loans are replaced with a commercial loan, with interest at 10% per annum, this would reduce net profit by a further $1 million. The accumulation of these adjustments means that the ROE which Xpand should expect would be 21·7% (rather than the reported 47·1%) which is almost exactly in line with the sector average of 22·0%.

In a similar vein, when the asset turnover is calculated based on the equity purchase price and the commercial loan (equating to net assets), it falls from 2·36 times to 1·75 times which is above, but much closer to, the sector average of 1·67 times.

In summary, Hydan's adjusted results would still be slightly ahead of the sector averages in most areas and may well justify the anticipated purchase price of $30 million; however, Hydan will be nowhere near the excellently performing company suggested by the reported figures and Xpand needs to exercise a degree of caution in its negotiations.

2 **(a)** Kandy – Schedule of retained earnings of Kandy as at 30 September 2014

	$'000
Retained earnings per trial balance	17,500
Adjustments re:	
Note (i)	
Add back issue costs of loan note (w (i))	1,000
Loan finance costs (29,000 x 9% (w (i)))	(2,610)
Note (ii)	
Depreciation of buildings (w (ii))	(2,600)
Depreciation of plant and equipment (w (ii))	(3,000)
Note (iii)	
Income tax expense (w (iii))	(800)
Adjusted retained earnings	9,490

(b) Kandy – Statement of financial position as at 30 September 2014

Assets	$'000	$'000
Non-current assets		
Property, plant and equipment (44,400 + 21,000 (w (ii)))		65,400
Current assets (per trial balance)		68,700
Total assets		134,100
Equity and liabilities		
Equity		
Equity shares of $1 each		40,000
Revaluation surplus (12,000 – 2,400 (w (ii) and (iii)))	9,600	
Retained earnings (from (a))	9,490	19,090
		59,090
Non-current liabilities		
Deferred tax (w (iii))	4,400	
6% loan note (w (i))	29,810	34,210
Current liabilities		
Per trial balance	38,400	
Current tax payable	2,400	40,800
Total equity and liabilities		134,100

Workings (monetary figures in brackets in $'000)

(i) Loan note

The issue costs should be deducted from the proceeds of the loan note and not charged as an expense. The finance cost of the loan note, at the effective rate of 9% applied to the carrying amount of the loan note of $29 million (30,000 – 1,000), is $2,610,000. The interest actually paid is $1·8 million. The difference between these amounts of $810,000 (2,610 – 1,800) is added to the carrying amount of the loan note to give $29,810,000 (29,000 + 810) for inclusion as a non-current liability in the statement of financial position.

(ii) Non-current assets

Land and buildings

The gain on revaluation and carrying amount of the land and buildings will be:

	$'000
Carrying amount at 1 October 2013 (55,000 – 20,000)	35,000
Revaluation at that date (8,000 + 39,000)	47,000
Gain on revaluation	12,000
Buildings depreciation for the year ended 30 September 2014 (39,000/15 years)	(2,600)
Carrying amount at 30 September 2014 (47,000 – 2,600)	44,400

	$'000
Plant and equipment	
Carrying amount at 1 October 2013 (58,500 – 34,500)	24,000
Depreciation for year ended 30 September 2014 (12½% reducing balance)	(3,000)
Carrying amount at 30 September 2014	21,000

(iii) **Taxation**

	$'000
Income tax expense	
Provision for year ended 30 September 2014	2,400
Less over-provision in previous year	(1,100)
Deferred tax (see below)	(500)
	800

	$'000
Deferred tax	
Provision required at 30 September 2014 ((10,000 + 12,000) x 20%)	4,400
Provision at 1 October 2013	(2,500)
Movement in provision	1,900
Charge to revaluation of land and buildings (12,000 x 20%)	(2,400)
Balance – credit to profit or loss	(500)

3 (a) **Plastik**

Consolidated statement of profit or loss and other comprehensive income for the year ended 30 September 2014

	$'000
Revenue (62,600 + (30,000 x 9/12) – (300 x 9 months intra-group sales))	82,400
Cost of sales (w (i))	(61,320)
Gross profit	21,080
Distribution costs (2,000 + (1,200 x 9/12))	(2,900)
Administrative expenses (3,500 + (1,800 x 9/12) + 500 goodwill impairment)	(5,350)
Finance costs (200 + 135 (w (v)))	(335)
Profit before tax	12,495
Income tax expense (3,100 + (1,000 x 9/12))	(3,850)
Profit for the year	8,645
Other comprehensive income	
Gain on revaluation of property (1,500 + 600)	2,100
Total comprehensive income	10,745
Profit for year attributable to:	
Equity holders of the parent (balance)	8,465
Non-controlling interest (w (ii))	180
	8,645
Total comprehensive income attributable to:	
Equity holders of the parent (balance)	10,445
Non-controlling interest (180 above + (600 x 20%))	300
	10,745

(b) Plastik – Consolidated statement of financial position as at 30 September 2014

	$'000
Assets	
Non-current assets	
Property, plant and equipment (w (iii))	37,100
Intangible asset: goodwill (w (iv))	5,200
	42,300
Current assets	
Inventory (4,300 + 1,200 – 120 URP (w (i)))	5,380
Trade receivables (4,700 + 2,500 – 1,200 intra-group)	6,000
Bank	300
	11,680
Total assets	53,980
Equity and liabilities	
Equity attributable to owners of the parent	
Equity shares of $1 each ((10, 000 + 4,800) w (iv))	14,800
Other component of equity (share premium) (w (iv))	9,600
Revaluation surplus (2,000 + (600 x 80%))	2,480
Retained earnings (w (v))	6,765
	33,645
Non-controlling interest (w (vi))	4,800
Total equity	38,445
Non-current liabilities	
10% loan notes (2,500 + 1,000 – 1,000 intra-group)	2,500
Current liabilities	
Trade payables (3,400 + 3,600 – 800 intra-group)	6,200
Current tax payable (2,800 + 800)	3,600
Deferred consideration (1,800 + 135 w (v))	1,935
Bank (1,700 – 400 cash in transit)	1,300
	13,035
Total equity and liabilities	53,980

(c) IFRS 3 *Business Combinations* addresses the recognition of separable intangibles assets. Both of the items which the directors of Plastik have identified in the acquisition of Dilemma should be recognised as separate intangible assets on the acquisition of Dilemma. Both IFRS 3 *Business Combinations* and IAS 38 *Intangible Assets* require in-process research in a business combination to be separately recognised at its fair value provided this can be reliably measured ($1·2 million in this case). The recognition of customer list as an intangible asset is a specific illustrative example given in IFRS 3 (IE 24) and should also be recognised at its fair value of $3 million.

Workings (note figure in brackets are in $'000)

	$'000	$'000
(i) Cost of sales		
Plastik		45,800
Subtrak (24,000 x 9/12)		18,000
Intra-group purchases (300 x 9 months)		(2,700)
URP in inventory (600 x 25/125)		120
Additional depreciation on property		100
		61,320
(ii) Non-controlling interests in Subtrak's profit or loss		
Subtrak's profit as reported		2,000
9/12 post-acquisition =		1,500
Deduct: Additional depreciation on property		(100)
Goodwill impairment		(500)
Adjusted post-acquisition profit		900
x 20% non-controlling interest		180

	$'000	$'000
(iii) **Non-current assets**		
Plastik		18,700
Subtrak		13,900
Fair value increase at acquisition		4,000
Additional depreciation on property		(100)
Fair value increase since acquisition		600
		37,100

	$'000	$'000
(iv) **Goodwill in Subtrak**		
Investment at cost		
Shares (9,000 x 80% x 2/3 x $3)		14,400
Deferred consideration (9,000 x 80% x 27·5 cents x 1/1·1)		1,800
Non-controlling interest (9,000 x 20% x $2·50)		4,500
		20,700
Net assets (equity) of Subtrak at 30 September 2014	(12,500)	
Less post-acquisition profits (2,000 x 9/12)	1,500	
Fair value adjustment: property	(4,000)	
Net assets at date of acquisition		(15,000)
Goodwill on consolidation		5,700
Impairment as at 30 September 2014		(500)
		5,200

Note: *The 4·8 million (9,000 x 80% x 2/3) shares issued by Plastik at $3 each would be recorded as share capital of $4·8 million (4,800 x $1) and share premium of $9·6 million (4,800 x $2).*

	$'000
(v) **Retained earnings**	
Plastik	6,300
Subtrak's post-acquisition adjusted profit (900 (w (ii)) x 80%)	720
Finance costs on deferred consideration (1,800 x 10% x 9/12)	(135)
Unrealised profit in inventory (w (i))	(120)
	6,765
Alternative calculation	
Plastik's retained earnings at 30 September 2014	6,300
Less Plastik's profit for the year	(8,000)
Consolidated profit for the year from part (a)	8,465
	6,765

	$'000
(vi) **Non-controlling interest in statement of financial position**	
At date of acquisition (w (iv))	4,500
Post-acquisition from statement of profit or loss and other comprehensive income	300
	4,800

This marking scheme is given as a guide in the context of the suggested answers. Scope is given to markers to award marks for alternative approaches to a question, including relevant comment, and where well-reasoned conclusions are provided. This is particularly the case for written answers where there may be more than one acceptable solution.

				Marks
Section A				
2 marks per question				**40**
Section B				
1	**(a)**	1½ marks per ratio		6
	(b)	1 mark per valid point. A good answer must emphasise the different		
		interpretation when using adjusted figures		9
			Total for question	15
2	**(a)**	Schedule of retained earnings as at 30 September 2014		
		retained earnings per trial balance		½
		issue costs		1
		loan finance costs		1
		depreciation charges		2
		income tax expense		1½
				6
	(b)	Statement of financial position		
		property, plant and equipment		2
		current assets		½
		equity shares		½
		revaluation surplus		2
		deferred tax		1
		6% loan note		1½
		current liabilities (per trial balance)		½
		current tax payable		1
				9
			Total for question	15

			Marks
3	**(a)**	Consolidated statement of profit or loss and other comprehensive income:	
		revenue	1½
		cost of sales	2½
		distribution costs	½
		administrative expenses (including goodwill impairment)	1
		finance costs	1
		income tax expense	½
		gain on revaluation of properties	1
		non-controlling interest: profit for the year	1
		total comprehensive income	1
			10
	(b)	Consolidated statement of financial position:	
		property, plant and equipment	2
		goodwill	2½
		inventory	1
		trade receivables	1
		bank	½
		equity shares	1
		other component of equity (share premium)	1
		revaluation surplus	1
		retained earnings	1½
		non-controlling interest	1
		10% loan notes	1
		trade payables	1
		taxation	½
		deferred consideration	1
		bank overdraft	1
			17
	(c)	Recognition of: research	2
		customer list	1
			3
		Total for question	30

Review Form – Paper F7 Financial Reporting (04/15)

Name: _____   Address: _____
                                                _____
                                                _____

How have you used this Kit?
(Tick one box only)

☐ On its own (book only)
☐ On a BPP in-centre course_____
☐ On a BPP online course
☐ On a course with another college
☐ Other _____

Why did you decide to purchase this Kit?
(Tick one box only)

☐ Have used the complimentary Study Text
☐ Have used other BPP products in the past
☐ Recommendation by friend/colleague
☐ Recommendation by a lecturer at college
☐ Saw advertising
☐ Other _____

During the past six months do you recall seeing/receiving any of the following?
(Tick as many boxes as are relevant)

☐ Our advertisement in *Student Accountant*
☐ Our advertisement in *Pass*
☐ Our advertisement in *PQ*
☐ Our brochure with a letter through the post
☐ Our website www.bpp.com

Which (if any) aspects of our advertising do you find useful?
(Tick as many boxes as are relevant)

☐ Prices and publication dates of new editions
☐ Information on product content
☐ Facility to order books
☐ None of the above

Which BPP products have you used?

Study Text	☐	Passcards	☐	Other	☐
Kit	☑	i-Pass	☐		

Your ratings, comments and suggestions would be appreciated on the following areas.

	Very useful	Useful	Not useful
Passing F7			
Questions			
Top Tips etc in answers			
Content and structure of answers			
Mock exam answers			

Overall opinion of this Kit	Excellent ☐	Good ☐	Adequate ☐	Poor ☐

Do you intend to continue using BPP products?	Yes ☐	No ☐

The BPP author of this edition can be emailed at: accaqueries@bpp.com

Please return this form to: Head of ACCA & FIA Programmes, BPP Learning Media Ltd, FREEPOST, London, W12 8AA

Review Form (continued)

TELL US WHAT YOU THINK

Please note any further comments and suggestions/errors below.